Laura Tucci

RECLAIMING
OUR SCHOOLS

RECLAIMING OUR SCHOOLS

The Struggle for Chicago School Reform

by Maribeth Vander Weele

Foreword by John Callaway

A Campion Book

Loyola University Press

Chicago

Loyola University Press
3441 North Ashland Avenue
Chicago, Illinois 60657

Cover and interior design by Nancy Gruenke.
Cover: Von Steuben High School interior, Chicago.
Cover photograph by Brett Kramer.
Title page photo by John H. White.

Library of Congress Cataloging-in-Publication Data
Vander Weele, Maribeth.
    Reclaiming our schools : the struggle for Chicago school reform/Maribeth
Vander Weele.
        p. cm.
    Includes bibliographical references and index.
    ISBN 0-8294-0773-1
    1. Public schools–Illinois–Chicago. 2. School management and organi-
zation–Illinois–Chicago. 3. Educational change–Illinois–Chicago. I. Title.
LA269.C4V36 1994
371'.01'0977311–dc20   93-38445
                                                                                              CIP

The excerpt on pp. 101–2 is from *Escalante: The Best Teacher in America* by
Jay Mathews. Copyright © 1988 by Jay Mathews. Reprinted by permission of
Henry Holt and Company, Inc.

*To those in Chicago public schools
who refuse to let hope die.*

*To my loving parents,
Harold and Elizabeth Vander Weele.*

To Frank Tenorio, love of my life and my best friend.

*And, most importantly, to my Heavenly Father,
whose love sustains all.*

Contents

Foreword
  by John Callaway   *ix*

Preface   *xiii*

Introduction   *xix*

1. *The Stakes, the Obstacles*   *3*

2. *A Whirlwind Start*   *15*

3. *Chaos on Pershing Road*   *29*

4. *Governance Affects Kids*   *45*

5. *Caretakers of Our Children*   *61*

6. *Everybody Passes*   *87*

7. *Discipline Makes a Difference*   *107*

8. *Schoolhouses in Disrepair*   *129*

9. *Revolving Leadership*   *155*

10. *Union Might*   *177*

11. *No Accountability, No Controls*   *207*

12. *A Legislative Will*   *231*

13. *Heroes on the Front Lines*   *253*

14. *Conclusion: Chaos and Hope*   *269*

Appendix   *287*

Resources   *293*

Notes   *303*

Bibliography   *351*

Index   *357*

Foreword

Maribeth Vander Weele's book about the tragedy and promise of the Chicago public school system is a brilliant study of what I call the *new colonialism*. Unlike the traditional colonialism that, however brutal and exploitative, built nations and civilizations on the backs of the poor and disenfranchised, the new colonialism isolates its victims in inner-city ghettos. The result is the building of little more than jails and prisons that are filled with thousands of young, mostly minority men, who become discards from the dysfunctional plantation called the Chicago public school system.

The overseers of this new colonial plantation are the men and women of the Illinois General Assembly who bear the responsibility to create, fund, and maintain a Chicago public school system that functions in at least a modestly successful fashion. The vast majority of these men and women do not have children in the Chicago public schools—and this includes those who form the leadership from the city of Chicago, not just those legislators who live in the safely removed, mostly affluent, and mostly white suburbs.

In other words, unlike the original slave masters and colonial overseers, most of these new colonial leaders do not even live anywhere near the plantations they are charged with running. And, bitter irony, the plantations of today are not as well run as many of the original estates. The impoverished kids who live there are mostly out of sight and out of mind of their modern masters. They are visible only when they are killed and become the subject of front-page Chicago newspaper stories. Even then the frequency of youth homicide is so great that many otherwise caring readers tune out after awhile to these relentless accounts of child killings in Chicago.

The new colonial masters are also the black politicians who fight Chicago Housing Authority chairman Vincent Lane's attempts to clean up the lethal environment of the "projects." They are the mostly white suburban and downstate legislators who sustain a tax system that permits a wealthy suburb to invest $10,000 or more a year in the public education of kids who come from the most advantaged homes while investing half that amount in the Chicago public school system where 80 percent or more of the students come from homes with incomes under the poverty level. The new colonial masters are the legislators in the city who, for obvious political reasons, support those who have an investment in resisting changes in union work rules that add millions of dollars in school spending—dollars that otherwise could be used on all the services and materials a deprived plantation school system so urgently needs. They are the legislators who, when finally but reluctantly agreeing to support changes in work rules, do so only while borrowing money to pay for school operating expenses; thus, once again, burdening the Chicago public school system with a debt that inevitably will create a worse financial crisis in the future.

These new plantation managers think they can get away with their crimes. What they do not spend on education for inner-city schools, they try to compensate for by building prisons for the human effluent of these schools. Inner-city kids could receive a year's education at Harvard for the same amount of money that is spent on keeping them in prison. Instead, the absentee leaders will tell you that they will not spend another dollar on the Chicago public school system until it is cleansed of corruption and bureaucratic waste.

But these same off-plantation managers support national leaders who think nothing of maintaining a huge, wasteful military-industrial complex, a modern intelligence empire that consumes $29 billion per year, an agricultural subsidy scheme for the richest farmers, and a middle-class welfare provision in the tax code—otherwise known as mortgage and real estate tax deductions. This may sound like a diatribe against the Republican national leadership, but it is not. The Democrats have and continue to do more than their share in perpetuating the new colonial subsidy for the great middle class. We all are on the take, and the kids in the inner cities be damned.

Maribeth Vander Weele blows the whistle on all of us. No one escapes her urgent, passionate, meticulous reporting. Her exposé of the colossal hypocrisy of the Illinois General Assembly's approach to school reform is both hilarious, in a Menckian way, and heartbreaking. Unlike the state of Kentucky, the Illinois legislators did not accompany their school reform legislation package with the necessary funding to ensure a shot at success. And unlike their Kentucky counterparts, they did not establish an auditing and inspections system that would confront the very bureaucratic corruption of which they never cease to complain. In other words, they established school reform in such a way as to work for its eventual failure. And believe me, many of these legislators want school reform in Chicago to fail so that they can confirm their worst prejudices, of which race is prominent.

As one who has been reporting on and discussing Chicago public school issues since 1957, I can admit to my own prejudices. I admit that when I finished reading *Reclaiming Our Schools* I was overwhelmed by the multiplicity and complexity of issues that need to be addressed and that frequently are not being addressed. I admit that I am sometimes reluctantly skeptical about even the best efforts of the various corporations, foundations, and other civic volunteer groups that have poured millions of dollars and thousands of hours into trying to help pull the Chicago public schools out of their quagmire. My skepticism is based on the notion that all of the hard work, good faith, and monetary efforts of these fine people only let those who really should be doing the work and the financing—that is, our legislators and we the people, the taxpayers ourselves—off the hook.

But skepticism aside, *Reclaiming Our Schools* tells us the enthralling story of the revolutionary idea—from a political point of view, at least—of giving power to people in hundreds of local schools so that they might begin to take destiny into their own hands, improve their schools, and, ultimately, save their children. This story gives great meaning to the contention that all politics is local. But, at the same time, the story of Chicago school reform is also a truly global one. Anyone in Russia or Eastern Europe wondering how the roots of democracy are nourished should read this book. Those roots, as Vander Weele makes abundantly clear, are fragile, as fragile as trying to teach committed but barely literate parents how to use *Roberts' Rules of Order* in a local school council meeting.

I write this not long after returning from a trip to South Africa. Just as decades of state-sponsored apartheid is coming to an end in that country, the new government will be handed a generation of unschooled, unemployed black youth. South Africa's major cities are surrounded by townships filled with these gun-toting, angry young men. Ask yourself how you would like finally to win the right to democratic elections and then be handed that time bomb as a reward.

Maribeth Vander Weele, in heartbreaking detail, shows us the time bomb we are building in our own public schools. Her account, in my view, is entirely fair and balanced even while, I am sure, it is fueled by an anger that no sensitive front-line reporter could deny. The concrete suggestions that she asks our leaders to implement in order to ensure the success of the valiant efforts at Chicago school reform must be followed or failure is surely guaranteed. As the world watches the drama of Chicago school reform unfold, this book should be used as a primary source of information on who the players are and as a straightforward accounting of the tale's complex educational, political, racial, financial, and historical ingredients. For all of those who need an investigative and analytical tool with which to press the case for school reform, *Reclaiming Our Schools* is essential reading.

John Callaway
Broadcaster and host of *Chicago Tonight*
Chicago

Preface

This book is not a primer on teaching Antwan or Crystal how to read and write. It is not an analysis of phonics versus whole language, or of testing rote memorization. Rather, it leaves the crucial subject of school curriculum to educators who know it best.

Instead, *Reclaiming Our Schools* is about factors even more fundamental to education, such as getting teachers in front of Antwan and Crystal in the first place, putting updated textbooks in their hands, and sending them to schools that are warm in winter and ventilated in summer, free from threat of collapsing ceilings or the ugliness of discolored walls left unpainted for decades.

Reclaiming Our Schools is about providing educators with the tools and oversight they need to make Chicago school reform—that most radical of experiments in decentralization—work in the great hope that eventually Antwan and Crystal will flourish in reading, writing, math, and the sciences. In short, this book is about the basics *before* the basics. It is about the Chicago public school system—its failings and commonsense cures.

Another book could be written solely on the early successes of school reform. With the creation of programs and the influx of volunteers, some schools are being revolutionized. If you ask those responsible, they will tell you their accomplishments were made not because of the system, but in spite of it. This book is the collection of those and other voices whose words I have heard and whose stories I have chronicled as education writer for the *Chicago Sun-Times*.

Regular readers will recognize most of it, but even those well-versed in the system may find that impediments to reform, disheartening when considered individually, are overwhelming when assembled together.

It is no wonder half the children in the system drop out.

There is cause for hope, however, in the heroism of those fighting to create a system that functions. Already countless people have poured untold effort into reform. The political action that created this unprecedented movement must continue.

As in any book, this one could not have been written without the help of many people. More than two dozen veterans of the system—including principals, teachers, central office administrators, reform activists, parents, attorneys, and union members—pored over its pages to ensure accuracy. Except for those who chose to lend their history and expertise anonymously, their voices are reflected in these pages. I thank them heartily for contributing without remuneration.

I gratefully appreciate the use of photos taken by the capable staff of the *Chicago Sun-Times*. They include Amanda Alcock, Rich Chapman, Tom Cruze, Robert A. Davis, Richard Derk, Ellen Domke, Rich Hein, Jack Lenahan, Bob Ringham, and Phil Velasquez. Pulitzer-prize winning photographer John H. White, also from the *Sun-Times,* contributed several photos taken specifically for this book. Attorney Gilbert Jimenez, a professor of media law at Columbia College and a *Chicago Sun-Times* editor, provided legal counsel.

In addition, I appreciate the help of *Sun-Times* librarian Terri Golembiewski, who provided guidance in my research, as well as that of education editor Nancy Moffett and of computer whiz Elizabeth S. Novickas for their invaluable input on projects when originally published. I am further indebted to Maureen O'Donnell, my colleague in producing the *Chicago Sun-Times* series "Schools in Ruins," which makes up much of chapter 8. Thanks, too, should be given to Sarah Karp, the onetime editor of the citywide student newspaper *New Expressions,* for pushing the concept of chapter 5.

I would also like to thank Wheaton College associate professor of English Paul Fromer for teaching me more about writing than anyone, and Wheaton anthropology professor

Dean E. Arnold for giving me the idea to write this book. We met for the first time at my ten-year reunion at Wheaton College, where his curiosity prompted my discourse on Chicago schools. He recounted the problems back to me—in chapters. And he proofread my proposal. After one rejection, it lay dormant for months. In April 1993, after watching the system head toward a September shutdown, I felt compelled to resurrect it. At Loyola University Press, Father Joseph F. Downey, editorial director, and Father George A. Lane, director, took a chance on the idea. The project was ably overseen by associate editor June S. Sawyers.

Additional thanks to Connie Goddard, *Publishers Weekly* Midwestern correspondent, for her marketing advice.

I am obliged also to the editors of the *Chicago Sun-Times* for their support, including the use of photographs and charts. When he hired me on October 1, 1990, editor Dennis A. Britton gave me the opportunity of a lifetime. For that I remain truly grateful.

Maribeth Vander Weele
Chicago

Morning break.

Photo by John H. White.

Introduction

The Chicago public schools are a terrible human tragedy. The lives, dreams, and potential of young children are being discarded by an anachronistic, self-indulgent educational bureaucracy that has sapped the vitality of the system in a game of politics and power.

> William J. Bennett, former U.S.
> secretary of education [1]

For good or for evil, decisions of public leaders leave their imprints on generations. Consider the example of Massachusetts educator William Harvey Wells. When he became superintendent of Chicago public schools in 1856, he was responsible for a collection of dreary and drafty buildings filled with poor children whose wealthier peers attended private schools. Class sizes numbered as high as two hundred students and averaged eighty-one. The system had no high school, no uniform curriculum. Its makeshift buildings were so crowded that the smaller children sat two to a seat. Without classrooms to accommodate them, three thousand youngsters were turned away.[2]

Wells immediately went to work. In his first year, he opened a long-planned high school, introduced a two-year course to train its teachers, and enrolled students based on written examinations identifying them by number, not name, so no parents could pull political strings to win their child's admittance. Within five years, Wells created a complete graded curriculum for 14,200 children, set regular schedules for reading, spelling, and arithmetic, and produced a curriculum guide that outlined what every child should know and at what grade. Five-year-olds, for example, were expected to learn colors, shapes, and the letters of the alphabet; six-year-olds, how to tell time, count to one hundred, read simple words, and add. The curriculum guide became standard throughout America.

Wells also set up blackboards and, concerned about children's health, introduced gymnastics. He opened five night schools, for both 3,800 immigrant students learning English and for students who worked during the day. Under his administration, more children were provided a public education than at any other time in Chicago's young life.[3]

In eight years' time, Wells set a course for Chicago schools that continued long after he departed. In the words of Chicago teacher and noted historian Mary J. Herrick, "He had turned the tide of public opinion toward some concern, rather than scorn, for the public schools . . . . In spite of his lack of authority, and in spite of the political exploitation of jobs and contracts—increasing as the number of projects and the amount of school expenditures rose—he had made a school system. He lamented the danger of the 'fetid tide of official corruption,' which threatened the future of the country, but he was more successful in facing it than many of those who succeeded him."[4] Wells proved that a committed person can leave an indelible mark on children's lives even amidst politics that can so terribly sabotage education.

Today, more than a century later, Chicago cries out for leadership to turn around a troubled system, a system that, as long as anyone can remember, served primarily as a hiring hall for patronage workers and a fountain of lucrative contracts and then, almost as an afterthought, as a place to educate children.

In 1922, during the height of a political scandal, the Chicago Board of Education attorney Ernest Withal went to jail but remained on the payroll nonetheless. In 1927, attorney Joseph Savage ran for a county judge seat with open support from legendary gangster Al Capone. When Savage lost, Mayor William Hale Thompson appointed him to the school board as recompense. Aldermen routinely used civil service examinations to control school jobs. One, in particular, "stated blandly to a University of Chicago student interviewer just how many janitresses from his ward would be passed on the next examination," reported Herrick in *The Chicago Schools: A Social and Political History*.[5] During the Great Depression, school patronage jobs were at a premium and dedication to the Democratic party that controlled them became more important that ever. In 1936, at least three fourths of the Democratic precinct captains in Cook County, which encompasses Chicago, held public jobs. School janitors covered half the precincts in the city, which meant none were in their buildings on election day.[6]

The close relationship between school jobs and the Democratic political machine continued through the years. "The main problem with the Chicago public school system is it has never been about education. It's been more about employment than education. It's been a place that people made money, got contracts, and landed jobs," declared Kenneth McNeil, who worked on education issues for the Chicago Urban League before becoming staff attorney for Illinois Lieutenant Governor Robert Kustra. Mismanagement dogged Chicago public schools from their inception, draining public support for funding education of Chicago's children and creating ongoing moral battles between the William Harvey Wells of the world and those who used the system as their own private cookie jar.

When did the system go bad? More important, why did it go bad? Pose those questions to school veterans, and you'll hear the generalization that the system is not bad—especially not for middle-class and wealthy children who attend magnet schools. But for most of the poor, it has always been inadequate. The situation worsened as the school population became increasingly poor and as Chicago's middle class either fled to the suburbs or sent its children to private schools. Not coincidentally, the Archdiocese of Chicago runs the largest private school system in the nation.

Despite the long troubled history of the public schools, many see the 1960s as a turning point in the system's decline. That tumultuous decade followed the migration of hundreds of thousands of blacks from the South, fueling shortages of textbooks, supplies, and classroom space that hit African-American communities the hardest. An ensuing teacher shortage brought many unqualified teachers into the system, long-time educators insist, and their work bore sour fruit for generations.

The Chicago Teachers Union gained bargaining rights during the 1960s and became closely entwined with the Democratic machine. In 1968, the late Mayor Richard J. Daley began a practice that outsiders said jeopardized the system's financial stability for years to come. He intervened during labor strikes and forged settlements favorable to the unions by using financial gimmicks, such as borrowing from future years' receipts. Even so, the Chicago Teachers Union argued that the contracts were no more favorable than contracts negotiated for unions in other school districts across the country. The system suffered a financial collapse in 1979 when bondholders realized that the money they lent was used to pay back previous loans and that the board was financing day-to-day operations by borrowing from special accounts earmarked to repay long-term loans.

Instability became the norm following the 1979 debacle. Seven superintendents managed the system. Five union strikes closed down classes. Three quarters of the schools' principals left the system between 1989 and 1994. And fifty-five people sat on the Chicago Board of Education in the fourteen years since the demise. As a result, educators and their students were continually victimized by senseless decisions made by a revolving door of often well-intentioned board members whose terms were set and reset time and time again by the state legislature.

Meanwhile, state support for education declined. Gains made one year in Chicago schools—such as lower class sizes, new reading programs, building renovations, additional counselors—were eventually scrapped as basic programs were stripped to the bone, and school buildings fell into disrepair.

Contributing to the lack of public and state support was a system structured primarily for employees, not for children. It began at 1819 West Pershing Road, school board headquarters, where tales of lavish spending, cronyism, and bureaucratic snafus were legendary. But it extended to the schools as well. The 280-page teachers' contract signed in 1990 continued many practices negatively affecting school operations. In a backlash against hirings and firings for political purposes, for example, workers gained unprecedented job protection. Firing an incompetent or even criminal employee could take one to two years of due process hearings at a cost as high as $50,000 or more in legal fees. Meanwhile, state mandates grew with no funding to back them, and teachers throughout Illinois faced the prospect of more paperwork. Teachers also faced growing social problems among their young charges. Children failed by the system in earlier years were now parents themselves, and a vicious cycle began. Drugs, violence, poverty, and the breakdown of the family took a deep toll on education. Although many societal forces contributed, one catalyst to the breakdown was the welfare system, which offered a seemingly glistening promise for the poor, providing, as it did, free monthly checks with nothing required in return. Decades later, the promise—like a drug dealer's free samples that convert a vulnerable person into an addict and a criminal—turned bitter. "Welfare has been the most destructive force for my people since slavery," said long-time school activist Coretta McFerren, a key player in forging the school reform movement launched in 1989.[7]

Consider the message government policies send to children growing up in public housing. Virtually none of the adults they know goes to work in the morning, therefore making deadlines and punctuality foreign notions. The only successful person they see is the neighborhood drug dealer, a job to which they may aspire some day. In many areas, children attend schools that presume their failure and place few expectations on them. They find little success there and, if they are clever, learn that after failing a grade once, they will be promoted to high school at age fifteen, even if they never finish another assignment. Meanwhile on the streets, gang members recognize their natural talents and recruit them into surrogate families that feed on hate. No one cares enough to stop them. In fact, their fathers may be members of the same gang—or even, in one of the strange twists of life, of a rival gang. If they have difficulty learning, they get no help in school. To hide their academic weaknesses and to get the attention they desperately crave, they adopt a tough exterior and disrupt classrooms. If they carry a gun to school and repeatedly get into fights, they are called disabled because of a "behavior disorder." With this label comes strict limits on the school's ability to discipline them. When these children are young, drug dealers circumvent the law by persuading them to transport drugs and weapons. The justice system and the schools fail to work with them the first time they get into trouble. They release them with a slap on the wrist. No one has taught them that actions have consequences. It is a missing lesson of life that eventually turns deadly.

Society is breaking apart, and government and public institutions each play their own distinctive roles. As in the days of William Harvey Wells, a great struggle is underway to reverse that trend. In Chicago, nowhere is that more evident than in the immense quest to reform its public schools.

Teach your children.

Photo by John H. White.

1

The Stakes, the Obstacles

Hello. My name is Charlie Williams. As you might know, I live in a slum some people call it a hell on earth and so do I. My neighborhood is not a nice place. We have rats, roches [sic], spiders, and killers, some not with guns but with drugs. I love my family. I spend most of my time at home in the house. I don't want to be one lesser black male dead. I plan to be a doctor after 8 years in collage [sic] if I don't get caught up in gangs or girls.

Twelve-year-old Charlie Williams in My Neighborhood, *a collection of works by inner-city Chicago children[1]*

Half of the 411,000 children in Chicago public schools never graduate. Tens of thousands more receive diplomas but can barely read, write, or compute.

On the ACT college entrance exam, nearly two thirds of city high schools average in the bottom 1 percent of the nation—and only two of sixty-four high schools surpass the national average.[2] Except for the magnet schools that select the children they educate, Chicago public schools rank as arguably the nation's worst.

Such a controversial conclusion was first advanced by William J. Bennett, then the U.S. Secretary of Education when he visited Chicago in 1987 and told the city, "You've got close to educational meltdown here."[3]

Bennett's label of "worst in America," coupled with public outrage over a nineteen-day teacher strike that year, fueled an unprecedented reform movement in the nation's heartland.

Years of neglect. Edwin Green, chairman of the Calumet High School local school council, assesses the damaged ceiling and floor in the school gymnasium.

Courtesy *Chicago Sun-Times*. Photo by Rich Chapman.

More than five thousand people became part of the grand experiment in October 1989 when they took their seats on 542 newly created local school councils that were comprised primarily of parents who, presumably, cared more about their children than a distant bureaucracy.

Under reform, thousands of unsung—and unpaid—heroes were born. Calumet High School council chairman Edwin Green contacted the media and exposed unbelievable dilapidation in his school. The roof had leaked for two decades, showing slivers of daylight and dropping one water-soaked tile at a time. His persistence resulted in a multimillion-dollar renovation of an inner-city high school long forgotten by authorities.

Kathryn and John Kuranda, high school dropouts themselves, became leaders in the reform movement through common sense and uncommon determination. They battled to get gangbangers off school turf, fought administrative red tape, and maneuvered through the halls of the state capitol as parent lobbyists on critical school legislation.

Carlos Malave, owner of a North Side gas station, made his first-ever public speech in 1989 at a candidates' night for the Kilmer School council. Nervous—he forgot portions of his speech—he nonetheless won the election. Thus was baptized another tireless school advocate who has since led crusades to relieve overcrowding, change principals, and provide teachers more opportunity for training.

The philosophy of decentralization—transferring power and money to schools—was sweeping the nation when Chicago embraced the idea. It was among a number of reform measures that followed a landmark report in 1983 issued by the National Commission on Excellence in Education. Entitled *Nation at Risk: The Imperative for Educational Reform,* it reported steady declines in student achievement, alarming illiteracy, and the untold social costs of America's failing schools. School systems in New York City, Los Angeles, Detroit, and Dade County as well as Edmonton in the Canadian province of Alberta were among thousands to experiment with what became known as *site-based management.* But while other systems phased in the concept or tinkered with it, none attempted to decentralize so completely and in so little time as Chicago.

"This is the biggest change in American school control since the 1900s," said Stanford University professor Michael Kirst in a *New York Times* report. "It is the most drastic change in any school system I can think of. It is absolutely precedent breaking."[4]

Chicagoans greeted the experiment with gusto. Aided by foundations, businesses, and community organizations, 17,256 people ran for the first council elections, which posted a more than 15 percent voter turnout. "It probably was the most democratic election ever held in the United States," said Chicago superintendent Ted D. Kimbrough, reflecting on the election a year later. "When you get over three hundred thousand people to go to the polls to vote on an issue, that's truly commendable."[5]

Chicagoans, after all, had little time to waste. Generations were—and continue to be—at stake. Imagine the horror of honor students arriving in college only to find they need remedial math and reading courses. "They were given A's and B's in high school, and then they come in and find they can't pass a basic competency test in reading or writing or math," said Jan Barshis, head of a remedial education program at Harold Washington College in Chicago. "And they are really devastated."[6] Imagine the confusion of an illiterate teenager struggling to fill out a job application. Or the defiance of an ingenious youth bored by school but skilled enough to convert a door hinge into a zip gun that shoots bullets thirty feet.

Imagine, too, the anguish of someone watching it all happen. "Sometimes when I get depressed or when I get tired of fighting the bureaucrats or I feel like quitting, I go to a school and wait in the hallway and watch the kids," Carlos Malave said. "In kindergarten, first grade, and second grade, I see that fire in their eyes." But his relief is tempered by reality. "When I look at seventh and eighth graders, it's extinguished. They kind of know they're not ready. I look at the seventh and eighth graders—beautiful kids, multicultural kids—you know that no matter who they are, one of two kids will not make it out of high school.

"That hurts," he said.

Chicago schools ranked highest in four-year dropout rates and lowest in achievement test scores among the nation's largest public school systems, according to a 1992 report by the Council of the Great City Schools. Of forty-three systems, Chicago schools had the largest percentage of children scoring in the bottom quarter of the nation on reading and math achievement tests.[7]

Although Chicago's woes run deep, they are not unique. Across America, city homicides have hit their highest rate in decades, governments scramble to build more jails, homelessness increases, and employers and colleges spend hundreds of millions of dollars on basic skills programs to make up for what high school graduates lack. Even those comfortably removed from urban ills pay the price of a society that fails to educate its children.

Undoubtedly social problems—fostered for several generations by failing school systems—are formidable. Of the urban districts studied by the council, Chicago public schools had the fifth poorest population of students.[8] Low-income children make up 79 percent of the student population. Chicago schools are also subject to constant student turnover. One third leave or arrive at their schools after the school year begins—creating unimaginable challenges for teachers, who must devote extra time to help latecomers catch up on lessons.[9] In addition, Chicago is the gateway to the second largest immigration wave to hit the United States since early this century. Illinois schools contain the nation's fifth largest population of students who speak limited English.[10] Foreign-speaking children made up nearly 14 percent of Chicago students in 1993—50 percent higher than five years before.[11] Chicago students speak more than one hundred languages, reflecting the beauty of the school system as well as one of its greatest challenges. Rapid increases in the numbers of students who speak limited English severely affect education throughout the United States. "Every region finds itself catapulted, sometimes literally overnight, into transforming its educational services expeditiously to meet the demands of student bodies increasingly diverse in culture and language," noted a 1992 report by the U.S. Department of Education.[12]

For Amundsen High School teacher George Schmidt, diversity meant teaching English class to Chicago students who speak twenty-five different languages, including Arabic, Assyrian, Bulgarian, Korean, Mandarin, Polish, Rumanian, Russian, Spanish, and Vietnamese. To teach English writing, Schmidt had to learn which languages use verb tenses, prepositions, and articles differently—if at all. "It's a wonderful thing, but it takes a lot of work," said Schmidt, a local school council member and writer for a scrappy antiestablishment teachers' newspaper. "You don't have time to individualize because of the number of kids."

Like a family tragedy, violence wears both on communities and schools. "Before coming to Hefferan, I had never seen a person shot," said Patricia A. Harvey, principal of the West Side school. "I had to keep 670 children in the building one day because there was a young man lying outside with a bullet in his forehead."

Drug dealers abound in the neighborhood, and children sometimes bring drug samples to school. As Harvey describes it, "When my children write, they write about parents being incarcerated. When they write what they want for Christmas, they don't ask for new bicycles—they want their mother to come home—not their father, their *mother*."

Family and community problems refuse to stop at the schoolhouse door. "In almost every class, there are three to five children who are chronically violent or disruptive," said Maria Fonseca, a third-grade teacher at Hamilton School on the North Side.[13]

At one near Northwest Side school, there is Edward. "Edward's mother brought him in the first day of kindergarten and said, 'Here's my son—he's bad,'" explained the school's assistant principal. "Edward, at first, was totally off-the-wall. He couldn't sit still. He twitched. He was very physical. You couldn't get him to do a task or a game. He couldn't focus on what he was supposed to be doing for more than twenty seconds. He's getting a lot of extra attention now."

The mother of another student told teachers that when her son was four-years-old, he stood on a window ledge one day and threatened to commit suicide. Another time, he set fire to his mother's bed. At school, the boy throws chairs and threatens classmates. Says the assistant principal, "He puts the collar of his coat up over his mouth and pulls his hat down almost over his eyes, so there's this little slit of the world. Then he tries to run out of the school—poor baby. He's violent. He hurts people. He steals."

Providing children in need with extra attention requires extra staff, if teachers are to avoid neglecting other students. Helping foreign-born high schoolers write English takes time and should be done, ideally, with small class sizes. And sending troubled students to around-the-clock private facilities cost money that the school system insists it does not have. In the Council of the Great City Schools study, Chicago ranked twenty-seven in per-pupil revenues in 1991. New York City schools received $7,539 per student, compared to Chicago's $5,249 at that time.[14] And neither, experts say, is enough.

Although it has slightly fewer than a quarter of the state's public school children, Chicago has nearly 60 percent of its low-income students. It has nearly a quarter of the state's students with disabilities—an expensive proposition considering the cost of teacher aides, nurses, and psychologists, not to mention the average $43,000-a-year salary of teachers hired to supervise classes with as few as one or two children in attendance. Despite the need, Illinois lags the nation in state funding of schools, ranking forty-fifth in the amount paid per capita for education, according to the National Education Association.[15] "It's a miracle to me that Chicago public schools are doing even as well as they're doing," said Michael Casserly, director of the Council of the Great City Schools. "It's no mystery to me that some of the indicators don't look as well for Chicago with that kind of investment from the state."[16]

State legislators have long blamed their resistance to funding Chicago schools adequately on the system's very real waste and inefficiencies, which were pegged in a 1992 study at a whopping $78 million to $107 million a year. But even if those problems were eliminated, the system still faces a half-billion-dollar annual budget shortfall by 1996, concluded two Chicago consulting firms.[17] The shortfall lay in its basic $1.5 billion fund for day-to-day operations, from which $250 million in state poverty funds was gradually being shifted to schools for supplementary programs. Before the reform law mandated the transfer, the central administration used the funds for general purposes. Authors of the 1988 law correctly projected large increases in property tax revenue and, as a result, no new state funds were provided to make up the loss to the basic budget. But healthy pay raises awarded in union contracts sapped the additional revenues, creating a mounting crisis. The result is a massive internal contradiction: for the first time, schools have discretion over large sums of money earmarked only for supplementary programs while basic programs have been cut to the core.

For years, Chicago public school leaders have blamed a chronic lack of funds and massive social problems for the dismal performance of the schools.

But there's more to the story.

Behind the scenes of reform are many unnecessary but crippling roadblocks. They are born of poorly written legislation and union contracts, political self-preservation, apathy, ignorance, incompetence, and misplaced priorities within the system. They are shocking real-life policy decisions such as the one to eliminate high school programmers and remedial reading programs three days before school began one year. Or allowing thousands of classrooms to go without teachers the first month of school each year. Or keeping convicts on the payroll, letting $300 million borrowed for desperately needed school repairs sit unused, and promoting generations of children unable to read or write.

Chicago schools have long been led by a bureaucracy, and in some cases, by school boards focused not on children but on jobs, politics, and contracts. In the 1980s, the school system's bureaucracy grew steadily, according to the Chicago Panel on Public School Policy and Finance. Between 1981 and 1988, the number of central office administrators rose by 29 percent while the number of staff members in the schools rose 2 percent.[18] In the view of G. Alfred Hess, Jr., executive director of the panel, it became obvious that reform would occur only if it were imposed from outside.[19] Streamlining the bureaucracy became a key goal of the reform movement.

Chicago's bureaucratic buildup—and subsequent efforts to curtail it—were part of nationwide trends in both education and business, according to Xerox Corporation chairman David T. Kearns, who later became U.S. deputy secretary for education. "In an extraordinary parallel, schools are doing just what American business did in the late 60s and early 70s—instead of genuine restructuring, new labels were applied and top management grew rapidly. No wonder that one of the first signs of genuine restructuring is eliminating bureaucracy and vesting responsibility and confidence in front-line workers," Kearns wrote in the foreword of *Taking Charge: State Action on School Reform in the 1980s*.[20]

The cornerstone of Chicago school reform is transferring power to educators and parents who best know their schools' needs. The 1988 law created local school councils each made of a principal, six parents, two teachers, and two nonparental community representatives. The legislation authorized LSCs, as the school councils were called, to each select a principal, write a long-range improvement plan, and oversee spending of poverty funds. In high schools, each council has a student member as well.

Many council members took on the unpaid posts with great expectation. "I thought by having the local school council, you'd have the community involved, then the community would be able to demand. And power, we know, concedes to nothing but demand," said Smith Wiiams, who became a local school council member in 1991. "I thought I would be able to contribute. I thought I would be able to make a difference—and I have."

But it soon became clear that the battle was not only against inadequate school funding and social evils. The battle was against the system, wracked by a cataclysmic power struggle between different interests: unions v. councils, central office v. schools, principals v. staff, Democrats v. Republicans, city v. suburbs, supporters of Mayor Richard M. Daley v. the communities that so badly wanted to topple him. In the midst of it all were the children. "This is a gargantuan bureaucracy with vested interests in different areas, with different agendas," said Sylvia Ortiz-Revollo, principal of Cardenas Elementary School on the Southwest Side. "The agenda with the least priority is children."[21]

Under reform, school councils discovered that the system is sabotaged by a series of restrictions that leave good schools hamstrung, with no accountability for those that fail or misuse money. This, in turn, fuels the reluctance to fund the schools.

"I feel rewarded by this experience, but I'm very frustrated," said Wiiams, two years after being seated on the councils at Wirth Elementary and DuSable High schools. Despite the publicity surrounding decentralization, schools are still required to follow central office regulations as specific as those stipulating the color of paint and thickness of drop cloths that could be used by members of volunteer painting parties—parties that are organized, after all, to make up for years of neglect by the central office.

In the early years of reform, achievement test scores fell, prompting outside pronouncements that reform had failed, a conclusion vigorously contested by those who understood the system. "Reform in Chicago hasn't had a fair trial," said Barbara Holt, executive director of the Chicago School Finance Authority, the system's financial oversight panel. "It hasn't been tried in the way it was designed. It's been a battle, a constant struggle by people at the local level."[22]

Despite the difficulties, test scores reported their first wholesale gains in 1993. Prior to that much needed tangible sign of progress, however, reform provided another more elusive element that test scores had been slow to measure up to then: hope. "There was a time I would drive up, and my stomach would turn over because I didn't want to be here," said Dulles Elementary School principal Donna L. Clayton. "Now it's a pleasure to be here." With $150,000 in discretionary funds available during the first year of reform, the school hired a reading and writing resource teacher and instituted a Principal's Scholar Club, honor roll, classes for gifted students, an after-school homework center, and Book-It, a program that awards pizza to students who complete their reading assignments. Reform also brought in an entourage of parent volunteers.[23] In fact, survey after survey reflected optimism for the failing system, possibly because the solutions were obvious to anyone with common sense and the courage to implement them. "This system can be corrected," said Edwin Green, from Calumet High School. "There is an answer, but it's going to require a person who can take the flak—and I mean flak like we've never seen before."[24]

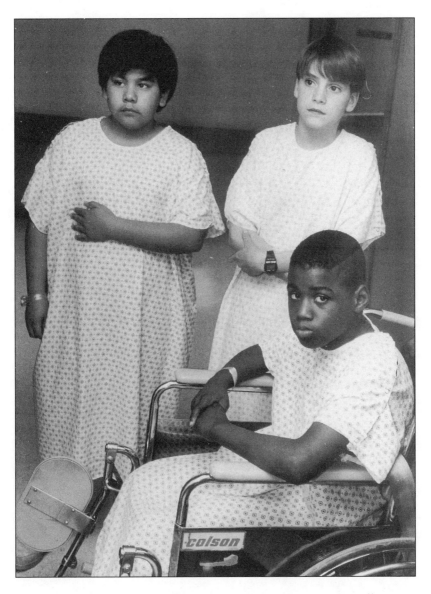

Students injured in a confrontation with police at Morrill Elementary School recuperate at St. Anthony Hospital.

Courtesy *Chicago Sun-Times*. Photo by Jack Lenahan.

2

A Whirlwind Start

I was going in the building, and one police officer swung at me with a club. I ducked, and it hit a friend.

> Thirteen-year-old Morrill School student Shonteal Norwood, who was injured after a clash with police over the selection of a principal[1]

When three quarters of Chicago principals left during the first four years of reform, some welcomed the change as a healthy infusion of new blood. Many principals retired, but a few exited in a mad roar of conflict, marked by picketing, boycotts, and—in about a dozen cases—lawsuits. Veteran principals complained they were victimized by reform's rookie councils and unfairly dumped.

In a few cases, some students agreed.

At Burns Elementary School on the West Side, more than five hundred students boycotted classes in April 1990 after the council voted not to rehire Donald Kriz, the school's principal of ten years. The situation became so heated that council member Roberto Diaz feared for his own safety. "We need some protection," he said. "We feel threatened."[2] A day later, police and protesters clashed after about 150 students walked out of Morrill Elementary School on the South Side to protest the firing of interim principal Eduardo Cadavid. More than a dozen children were treated for bruises and sprains as a result.[3]

At Morgan Park High School, the ouster of principal Walter E. Pilditch prompted a student walkout, racially-charged riots,

Two students embrace after violence erupts at Morgan Park
High School.

Courtesy *Chicago Sun-Times*. Photo by Tom Cruze.

and clashes with police in which twelve people were injured
at the far South Side school.[4] Pilditch sued, alleging he was
fired because he is white. A federal jury agreed with
Pilditch—who later became principal at Curie High School—
and awarded him nearly $155,000 in benefits and compen-

satory damages while ordering four council members to pay $1,000 to $3,000 each in punitive damages.[5] Although the award was overturned by a federal appeals court four years after the council's decision, it sent a chilling message to volunteer council members and underscored the seriousness of their work.[6]

Such conflict, however heated, was limited to a few schools, according to Designs for Change, a reform advocacy group. In 264 of 276 schools that selected principals in the first year of reform, the process went smoothly, the Chicago group said. Schools that sought a new principal typically had thirty-five applicants; some had more than one hundred.[7]

Those who question why achievement test scores dropped in the early years of Chicago school reform should consider the colossal change that convulsed the system. In more than half of city schools in 1992, from one-tenth to one-third of the teaching staffs were new, according to a survey by the Consortium on Chicago School Research.[8] Those numbers did not include the exodus created by an early retirement program the following year, when another 9 percent of teachers and a fifth of principals left the system.[9] In any workplace it takes time for new staff to get acclimated.

In the first three years of reform, Boone Elementary School on the North Side suffered through a host of traumas. Its math and reading scores dropped for all three grades tested. Having four principals in five years contributed, as principal Paul E. Zavitkovsky explains: "There's no question that here and at every other school, it's important to have leadership stability. A lack of continuity translates into a problem with student achievement." In addition, enrollment soared in 1991—two hundred more students than Boone could handle. By the following year, however, the school found a measure of stability. For one thing, Zavitkovsky promised to stay. For another, bilingual programs caught up with the increase in non-English-speaking students, who made up more than a third of the school's student population. Despite the decline, Boone test scores still ranked near national averages.[10]

Educational research makes resoundingly clear that the key to a good school is a good principal. But reform has placed more pressure—and new responsibilities—on principals than ever before.

`Among the greatest pressures placed on principals are last-minute budget cuts. In what Chicago School Finance Authority member, Maxwell Griffin, Jr., called a "game of chicken," the school board waits until the end of August to make cuts. Some believe it is an attempt by the board to prove to the state it cannot squeeze more money out of its $2.7 billion dollar budget and, by doing so, to persuade the state to provide more funding. Many observers think it may also be intended to convince the finance authority to grant the district permission to spend future revenues early, which the district cannot do without the approval of the oversight panel. Whatever the motivation, the result is that funding for everything from truant officers, clerks, custodians, and library workers to reading programs, supplies, and—until private foundations and businesses contributed—sports and other extracurricular programs underwent the knife days before school began in 1991 and 1992.

Despite decentralization, schools have no say where cuts are made. What's more, the fifteen-member volunteer school board, not to mention the public, often has no idea what cuts have been made until their grim effects surface weeks, and sometimes months later. The board relies on the administration, an administration that repeatedly—for whatever the reason—supplies wrong information. For example, in a budget-cutting blitz days before school began in 1991, the Chicago Board of Education cut supplies by 90 percent in the schools but only by 25 percent in the central administration. One administrator said that the supplies in question were not essential. In reality, they were quite critical. As a result, some schools rationed toilet paper, square by square. Others made appeals to parents to have their youngsters each bring a roll or a box of tissues. Some schools even lobbied businesses for donations.

In another last-minute action, the board cut eighty-one high school assistant principals who did not hold teaching positions. Some board members apparently did not know that many were actually programmers who scheduled students into classes. Others held the important roles of disciplinarians.

Perhaps the greatest chaos caused by last-minute decisions came during the financial crisis of 1993. In September of that year, the school board authorized the administration to lengthen each forty-minute high school period by ten minutes after the Chicago Teachers Union—engaged for months in bitter negotiations with the board—tentatively agreed to the measure, a measure that increased teaching time for its high school members. The idea in itself was not necessarily bad. For some schools, it made sense because it eliminated study halls that for years were used to simply fill time. But the timing and the fact that the school board assumed that the measure would work well in all schools—even for those schools that used free periods for electives such as drafting or orchestra—caused major headaches.

Less than a week before the school year began, high schools received the bad news: the months workers had spent programming students were for naught; within five days all students were to be rescheduled to fifty-minute periods. High schools were also ordered to eliminate double periods of eighty minutes each, thereby cutting teaching jobs since teachers would now be teaching classes for more students. The move eliminated 496 teaching jobs for a projected $37 million savings over the life of the two-year union contract, but it also eliminated laboratory classes in advanced physics, biology, and chemistry as well as vocational shops and remedial writing classes that gave students and teachers extra time to spend on various projects. The last-minute move cut chemistry classes by 37 percent, according to Pierre LeBreton, professor of chemistry at the University of Illinois at Chicago. "To think that you can learn chemistry without having adequate access to a chemistry laboratory is like thinking that you can learn to play baseball without having access to a practice field," he wrote.[11]

At Dunbar Vocational High School on the South Side, one of every three vocational shop programs were cut the week before school began, according to Dunbar principal Floyd M. Banks.[12] At Lane Technical High School, which calls itself the flagship of the Chicago public school system partly because of its consistently high test scores, thirty-five of two hundred teaching positions were cut. A fifth of the science department, more than a quarter of the shop teachers, and 40 percent of the commercial art staff were eliminated. "This is the worst September I can remember in thirty years," said principal David Schlichting.[13]

In the ensuing weeks, teacher and student protests erupted at high schools throughout the city, but system leaders appeared to be unaware of the devastation caused by the last-minute cuts.

In a public meeting ten days after the order, board president D. Sharon Grant posed a surprising question to new superintendent Argie K. Johnson: "I've had many students call me saying they had double periods of science at eighty minutes, and now they're being cut back to fifty. Or they had a science class, and they're not able to get a lab. Would you take me through the rationale?" That such a question came from the president of the board after the media had covered the results was startling enough. But the response from the school superintendent was even more so: "You can have a school day for students that can run from period one through period nine. That means the students would be available to take classes for eight of those periods, one period being used for lunch. So I really don't understand how scheduling can be such a problem."[14]

In reality, the superintendent was describing the old schedule. Johnson, a newcomer fresh from New York City, was mistaken. The conversation illustrated a long-running problem in the massive system: namely, the lack of understanding by system leaders on how their decisions affect the day-to-day routine of education. To the newly appointed superintendent's credit, she launched a principals' task force shortly thereafter to study the effects of the fifty-minute periods on the schools. It was tragic that such a move had not been initiated before the order was given.

While Chicago school reform was billed nationwide as turning over money and power to schools, principals and councils quickly learned the limits imposed not only by budget cuts but also by other system practices. Herbert Elementary School principal William Rankin tried for four years to transfer money for an extra custodian, which his school did not need, to pay for extra supplies, such as bleach and diapers, which were sorely needed because some of the school's autistic youngsters had hepatitis. But Rankin had been unable to win central office approval of the transfer due to a long-standing administration agreement with the union that assigned custodians based on the size of the building. At one point, the central office approved Rankin's transfer but revoked it one week later, taking away both the supply and the position money.

At Muñoz Marin Primary Center, it took one year to win central office permission to hold a community painting party at the West Side school. "Supposedly, the paperwork was lost," principal David Espinoza said. Volunteers used donated paint, but it was not the color approved by central office. "They're giving us dull colors that are not brightening up our building," Espinoza complained. "They come in and say, 'That's not the appropriate color.'"

In addition, although reform gave principals the authority to select new teachers, they still had to rely on Pershing Road for technical authorization that was provided in the form of budget position numbers. The week before school began in September 1992, McCutcheon School principal Edward A. Ploog waited to hear whether two teachers on sick leave had clearance to return. By union contract, teachers need provide only two days' notice if they wish to return during the first ten months of sick leave, although they must provide the central office with doctors' certificates. Ploog had replacements waiting, but he could not confirm whether the teachers on leave were approved to return to the North Side school. Instead, when he contacted the central office headquarters he was greeted by a recorded message: "The person you are calling is presently unavailable. We are sorry. We are unable to accept any messages at this time. Goodbye." [15] Principals throughout the city complained. The administration's response was to blame deep cuts in central office staff and the public pressure that conceived them.

If site-based management is to succeed, middle managers—such as principals—must be given dramatic new authority, and their roles must be drastically redefined, concluded Paul T. Hill and Josephine Bonan, researchers from the Rand Corporation's Institute for Education and Training. "As businesses in the United States and abroad have found, holding middle managers responsible for events they cannot control—an inherently inequitable arrangement—cannot be productive. By design, middle managers are caught between central office productivity demands and worker desires for the freedom to take the initiative. Site-based management of schools cannot succeed if it treats principals unfairly."[16] Chicago leaders have overlooked that obvious tenet of good management.

The pressures on principals also take a personal toll. While teachers' pay increased because of their powerful union, principals were not so fortunate. They were lumped by the central office with its own administrators and consequently bypassed on $3.7 million in raises because of public pressure to freeze administrative salaries. Unlike teachers, principals did not receive a 3 percent annual raise in 1991, a 7 percent raise in 1992, and seniority increases. Indeed, some teachers still make more than their bosses despite the 7 percent raise that principals finally did receive in 1993. When overtime pay is included, some head custodians and tradespeople also make more than principals. And because pensions are calculated based on salary, principals who were about to retire faced the loss of thousands of dollars in pension pay they otherwise would have had during their retirement years. Attempts by principals to bargain collectively as a union in the early 1980s were dismissed in the courts.

Also damaging to principal morale was the loss of job tenure, which was replaced by four-year contracts granted by councils. Reform groups saw the law as a triumphant end to an old boy's network, but the Chicago Principals Association objected that its members were singled out by the same legislation that virtually guaranteed teachers their jobs for life.[17] In addition, while other urban school districts instituted principal academies, Chicago principals were provided little training or support when they undertook their new roles. Although the job under reform includes keeping track of large sums of money, for example, neither principals nor their clerks are trained in accounting. Further, the central office does not allow schools to help themselves; that is, it prohibits them from recruiting clerks with financial expertise by paying them more, even if the schools use their so-called discretionary funds to do so. Nor is more than one school allowed to pool resources to hire an accountant, which would free principals for educational duties, principals complain. In 1992, the board of education cut 139 clerks from the system, throwing financial recordkeeping into disarray and triggering clerk transfers across the city since their jobs are preserved by systemwide seniority. Despite the disruptions, principals are held responsible for missing money.

Clerks also do not work the critical week or two before the school year begins. Thus in most schools the only person available to answer the telephone during that busy period is the principal. Inundated with opening week worries, some principals do not answer the phone at all. Principals, especially in poorer neighborhoods, find themselves driving council members to meetings with no reimbursement for gas or refreshments. Like many school staff members, ranging from teachers to engineers, many principals dig into their own pockets to answer school needs. Meanwhile, meetings held by central office administrators are well supplied. In the first two years of reform, donuts, coffee, and other refreshments from the central office cafeteria alone topped $85,000 in public funds for staff meetings and conferences, not including refreshments ordered from outside the building.[18]

Furthermore, principals' new bosses—the local school councils—were not trained by the school board to handle the tremendous responsibilities they were given. There was no period for planning. With barely an introduction to one another, council members elected officers. One month after the first council elections in October 1989 came the first deadline: councils were required to write a plan for spending state Chapter One funds. By the following February, half of the councils were expected to notify principals whether or not they would open a search for principal jobs for which incumbents were eligible to apply. By April 15, councils were to select their principals, and by May they were to approve long-range improvement plans.[19]

Council members were poorly equipped to handle so quickly such critical tasks that so greatly affected principals. "Huge numbers of council members were thrown into waters in which they could not swim," said Lu Palmer, a school council member and chair of Chicago Black United Communities.[20] Melvin Johnson, a council member at Coles Elementary School on the South Side, would have welcomed training in areas such as board policies and school law. "I was surprised at how much responsibility was given to a school council member, just by virtue of being a member. It's an awful lot of responsibility with no training. You have the full weight to change something in a school with which you could have no association other than you live in the neighborhood."

In spring 1990, the interim board, a temporary seven-member panel that presided during the first seventeen months of reform, attempted to address widespread complaints about lack of council training. It hosted a more than $275,000 mega-conference for two-and-a-half days at the University of Illinois at Chicago. In typical fashion, the board flew in experts from around the nation and put them up at fancy hotels to train the city's more than five thousand council members. But the conference did not provide training in budgeting, central administration policies, and school law that the council members had requested. Out-of-town experts understandably did not know the intricacies of the Chicago system. "In the workshops I went to, the facilitators turned it all over to the participants," said Patricia A. Daley, who became a board member later that year. "They'd play games. They'd have icebreakers. They'd write little things on paper. I spent an hour at this workshop, and I didn't know anything more after it than when I went in. I didn't even go back the second day. The first day was such a waste of time."

Julie Woestehoff, associate director of the school reform group Parents United for Responsible Education (PURE), had the same reaction: "Most local school council members would agree that the board training events were not necessary and not effective." In fact, the board had hoped to obtain outside funding for the conference but ended up paying for most of it from regular education funds. Interim board president James W. Compton defended its exorbitant cost. "You would get as many opinions as you have people that attended that conference," Compton said. "It was the intention that there were people there with expertise and know-how to impart the appropriate information. One is not going to learn everything that needs to be learned in one conference. Certainly one wouldn't look upon that as some kind of luxury and extravagant expense."[21]

The administration in 1989 also ordered $37,500 worth of souvenir marble paperweights for the inauguration of council members. As councils begged for training materials, the central office once again demonstrated an amazing lack of understanding of schools' needs. For one thing, many council members did not even have desks on which to place the decorative paperweights. Second, the money came out of already scarce training funds.[22] Lack of training undermined reform, and the central administration proved to be enormously ill-equipped to provide it.

Besides floundering without training, councils occasionally put undue pressure on principals, whose jobs now lay primarily in the hands of parents. Some principals complained that they were forced to politick to keep their positions, which, at times, created incentives to act unethically. In the 1992 principals' survey, for example, 5 percent said they felt pressured to spend money inappropriately.[23]

Henderson Elementary School principal Milton Hall used student fees and concession money for a $300 dinner at which council members signed his four-year contract, an internal audit charged. An unspecified number of Henderson council members used student monies to buy themselves and family members $2,110 trips to a Wisconsin resort, auditors also reported. The checks later bounced. Hall, who said money was commingled in the accounts before he arrived at the school, was later fired by the board. Further, the school ordered a memorial plaque for the church of a council member who served as pastor there, auditors alleged. When auditors discovered the expenditure, they forced the pastor to retrieve it. The cost of the 16-by-20-inch plaque? $270.[24]

Funston Elementary School assistant principal Pat Tamburrino
with preschoolers.

Courtesy *Chicago Sun-Times.* Photo by Rich Chapman.

3

Chaos on Pershing Road

Our yearbook man is gone. Our newspaper teacher is gone. The man teaching advanced computers is gone. Our French teacher is teaching Spanish. So many program changes have taken place since we walked in the first day. Every day is different. I feel that every student is being cheated out of their education.

Seventeen-year-old Chastity Martin, a student at Fenger High [1]

It was late October 1990, and schools across Chicago still waited for workbooks, computers, and thousands of other items authorized by local school councils. The authorizations all lacked the same thing: a signature from the system's central office. The administration had assigned only three people to review proposals that filled a row of filing cabinets. The proposals were to be used for spending state Chapter One poverty funds, a key component of decentralization because they are the primary funds that schools control.

After reform, it was not long before schools discovered that despite the hype of decentralization, "control" depended on the mood, staffing, and competence of the central office. Schubert Elementary School on the Northwest Side waited six months for central office approval of teachers, school aides, a clerk, and workbooks—at a cost of $179,000 that was budgeted and sitting in school board coffers, according to principal Cynthia M. Wnek. At Armstrong Elementary School on the West Side, teachers could not copy homework assignments because a new copier fell victim to the snafus. Barry

Elementary School lost a talented teaching candidate to a suburban school because Barry lacked the necessary signature to
make a firm offer. For weeks the classroom was led by a substitute while the Northwest Side school scurried to find a re-
placement. "The system was supposed to be eradicated and
changed, but it doesn't seem that way," said council chairperson Steven Ziemblicki.[2]

"Pershing Road," the moniker for the system's central office
located on that South Side Chicago thoroughfare, had once
again become the saboteur of schools.

Throughout the nation, decentralization bumped heads
with entrenched education establishments that were apparently unwilling to relinquish control to a movement intent on
reversing the buildup of school bureaucracies that occurred
during the 1970s. In Chicago, a showdown between the two
forces was inevitable. Ted D. Kimbrough, school superintendent from 1990 to 1993, blamed the havoc on the speed in
which reform was put into place. There was no phase-in for
decentralizing the nation's third largest school system. "It's
never been done before," he said. "There really is no guide
how to do it."

Kimbrough also placed the blame on administrative cuts,
spawned by widespread pressure from school councils and
educators working to reclaim their schools. "If you downsize
the central office, you can't give them more administrators,"
he said. "You can't have it both ways."[3] He also blamed
schools, many under new and untrained leadership themselves, for not filling out forms correctly to conform with state
law and system regulations.

Under reform, those three explanations—lack of funds,
public pressure to cut central office staff, and an obligation to
ensure that schools followed regulations—made up the system's chief defense for the central office chaos that continually disrupted school plans.

Outsiders, in turn, accused the administration of balking at
dismantling its powers. "Maybe our problem is we're asking a
centralized body to decentralize itself—but that is what the
reform law asks," said Maxwell Griffin, Jr., a member of the
Chicago School Finance Authority.[4] "Bureaucracy's main goal,
it appears to me, would be to perpetuate itself. What the leg-

islature has asked it to do is dismantle itself voluntarily. I have reached the conclusion it will not be done in that manner."[5]

Nationwide, most school systems that experimented with site-based management failed to completely revamp their central headquarters in the process—leading to conflict between schools that gained new authority and bureaucracies that lost it, concluded researchers for the Rand Corporation in Santa Monica, California. Their advice? Central offices should assist schools, not control them, and give schools freedom from bureaucratic constraints.[6] That was the precise plea of Chicago reformers and educators who conceded deep administrative cuts caused havoc but, at the same time, accused the leadership of sabotaging reform by cutting places most critical to education while allowing pet projects to flourish.

The way the system handled the crisis of 1993—the worst in more than a decade—was a prime example of an unsupportive central office.

Because of a law emanating from the 1979 financial collapse, the system cannot operate without a balanced budget. By the start of the 1993–94 fiscal year on September 1, the school board was still $300 million short of that goal. A teachers' contract had yet to be signed and the state legislature had yet to approve the borrowing of enough money to close the budget gap. Schools opened one week late and the system shut down twice, but only for four days, thanks to five temporary federal court orders and one temporary legislative waiver of the balanced budget requirement.[7] Although schools were open, many barely functioned. During that time the administration decided not to enter the budget information into the mainframe computer, reasoning that it would be too difficult to make adjustments later. The decision meant that schools did not have access to money for the new school year, even federal and state grants, such as Chapter One funds, that were unaffected by the budget battles. Consequently, principals could not order textbooks, supplies, and equipment or arrange for services.

Further, the administration froze spending of all state Chapter One monies, bringing back memories of fall 1990, except this time every school plan for the poverty funds was at a standstill through October. Like the cuts of 1993, the decision had a devastating effect on education. At Julian High School on the South Side, many students in freshman English classes were still without textbooks six weeks into the year.[8] Dunbar Vocational High School could not buy equipment for its auto shop classes, paint for its decorating class, or lumber for its carpentry classes. The television production program remained closed because the school could not buy equipment or renovate the studio. Similarly, Brighton Park Elementary School on the Southwest Side could not buy the math and science materials, dictionaries, encyclopedias, and computers it planned to purchase through poverty funds. Nor could it open its recreational reading program, conduct staff training, or run its afternoon preschool.[9] Schurz High School on the Northwest Side lacked mathematics and bilingual textbooks; at Morgan Park High School on the South Side, it was freshman biology books. Then there was the desk shortage—some Morgan Park students stood during homeroom period because of the larger class sizes that were created by schedule changes.[10] Kelly High School on the Southwest Side could not order magazines and newspapers for its library.

At Anderson Community Academy on the South Side, classes of children with severe emotional and behavioral problems were short of teachers well into November, according to assistant principal Katherine A. Konopasek. Although three teaching positions were approved, the school could not fill them because budget information was not entered. Once the budget was approved in late October, it took weeks for an understaffed budget department to put position numbers—that is, job identification numbers—in individual school budgets. Consequently, children with mental disabilities—some of whom spoke only Arabic or Spanish—were placed in the same classroom with classmates who had severe behavior problems, a euphemism often describing troubled and violent youths. Class sizes for such children are supposed to range from five to fifteen students each, depending on the category. The classes at Anderson, however, exceeded twenty for the entire first quarter of the school year, Konopasek said.

Board officials responded to media questions by insisting that the computer system was not flexible enough to selectively load programs for which money was available. Such an explanation did not hold true, however, when it came to paying its own consultants and some central office vendors. Then exceptions were made. The school board passed a special budget authorization to pay administrators who retired but returned to the central office to help alleviate the crunch caused by the sudden exodus of staff under an August early retirement program. Those consultants—while probably necessary—were entitled to both a full pension at typically 75 percent of their former salaries plus daily stipends. Meanwhile, teachers at Funston Elementary School went for weeks without pay because of a computer snafu. Some, troubled that at-risk preschoolers were missing classes, volunteered to operate the after-school program in hopes they would eventually get paid for their efforts.[11]

Budget cuts during reform did not only affect the schools. They also affected central office, specifically in areas that were designed to directly support education. In 1991, the Chicago Board of Education eliminated its $500,000-a-year professional library, a valued resource for teachers that was used, too, by librarians to inspect materials before buying them.[12] The school board also cut rank-and-file workers in key departments such as personnel and budgeting. "You can't blame the people stuck there for doing a horrendous job. You can't expect them to call back in a day, or three days," one principal said. "They have people making $100,000 who don't even touch kids. Those people always stay, and the worker bees who deal with us principals are cut to the bare bone."

At the same time, the central office cafeteria was subsidized by about $500,000 a year in education funds that could have been used for other purposes, such as hiring more people to comb through Chapter One plans. In 1992, central office spending on computers quietly skyrocketed by millions. Meanwhile, the so-called central support services that year exceeded its budget by about $1 million, apparently because of special education services.[13] And, according to reports in 1993, the school system could have saved $7 million in one year by instituting commonsense procedures governing building repairs by outside contractors who were known to regularly overcharge the board, an audit alleged. In addition, the board spent more than $1 million annually on useless publications and relied on outside vendors for printing work it could have done itself, a 1990 audit showed.[14] The board concluded that 30 to 50 percent of $3.4 million worth of publications were unnecessary and unhelpful. Travel and convention costs in both central office and schools, meanwhile, soared to more than $4 million during the first eighteen months of reform.[15] Certainly some of that money could have been used to staff central office departments most critical to schools.

The list of inefficiencies goes on. In 1992, inspectors from the United States Department of Agriculture discovered that the system kept nearly $1 million worth of food stockpiled for years after the recommended shelf life expired. According to auditors, the system also failed to test food frequently enough to ensure it met federal guidelines. Indeed, the government may have reimbursed Chicago schools as much as $26.8 million for nearly eighteen million prepackaged meals supplied by food vendors who, although paid by the system, nevertheless failed to meet federal requirements. The school system's own audits in 1992 reported that more than half the milk tested for vitamin A content fell short of the required levels.[16] The investigation explained why even the poorest and hungriest of children complained about the inferior quality of some Chicago school lunches despite $89 million a year in federal food subsidies.

In yet another example of inefficiency, the system in 1986 inexplicably dropped out of a U.S. government program that donated surplus property. The program run by the General Services Administration offered filing cabinets, computers, audiovisual equipment, musical instruments, tools, and even trucks—just the type of equipment schools so desperately need. In 1988, the GSA attempted to persuade the school system to rejoin the program. A school superior nixed the idea, recalled Jack Colen, GSA property utilization officer for Illinois.

"We met with a couple of gentlemen from the school board, and they were very encouraged," said Faustino Gonzalez, a GSA administrator in the Chicago office. "We checked back later, and the enthusiasm seemed to be gone." The decision was not publicized until 1991, when federal officials saw a *Chicago Sun-Times* photograph of a study hall filled with broken, graffiti-scarred desks at Schurz High School on the Northwest Side. "We were appalled," said Gonzalez. "Literally, we have to sell desks better than that to the public for three to five cents on the dollar." Chicago school officials responded that they were not aware the program existed. In the wake of publicity, however, they reenlisted.[17]

Perhaps the most astonishing example of apparent Pershing Road waste came to light in 1992, two years after the interim school board signed a $484 million no-bid health-care contract that—it announced with great fanfare—was supposed to save millions of dollars. But the courts disagreed and in response to a slighted vendor's lawsuit, Illinois Appellate Court justice Mary Ann G. McMorrow arrived at a startling conclusion: the school board could have saved 15 to 20 percent on the three-year contract had it shopped competitively from the start.[18] If those estimates were correct—they originated with an expert witness—the system could have saved as much as $96.8 million in one contract alone. Board officials strenuously disputed the number, saying that they were not allowed to offer evidence in court to disprove it. But even if savings were half what McMorrow estimated, it would have been enough to pay for one year's worth of remedial reading programs, the continuation of the professional library, the salaries of truant officers and library aides, the cost of running alternative schools, and a host of other programs that directly affect education. Despite the ruling, the Chicago Board of Education that succeeded the interim panel in August 1993 extended the contract twice.

Public pressure to cut central office expenditures was steeped in a legacy of incompetence, lavish spending, cronyism with vendors, and apathy at the Pershing Road headquarters.

Funston School assistant principal Patricia R. Tamburrino related how her school clerk spent two afternoons in the three-building complex at 1819 West Pershing Road, where there are no room numbers—only a maze of offices sectioned off by white partitions. The clerk tried to obtain necessary signatures for certain documents. "She was rebuffed and thwarted in nearly every department. In many cases, the proper person was unavailable. In other cases, it was fairly obvious that no one knew what was required," she said. It often takes six or more phone calls to get the proper answers. Such a practice is often called the "39th Street Shuffle," said Tamburrino, referring to the other name for Pershing Road, a sprawling converted Army headquarters. "There has long been a policy among us old-timers that, in order to get an answer, one should call the same department at least three times. If you're lucky, you'll get the same answer two out of three times."

Contributing to the problems of staff was the enormous number of turnovers. Under reform, as central office cuts set in, dozens of administrators left.[19] The director of accounting and control as well as supervisors in computer operations, curriculum, dropout prevention, personnel, purchasing, real estate, school operations, security, special education, treasury, and union negotiations were among those who retired or left for other jobs. Most had been with the system for years and carried its history, practices, and regulations with them. "Chicago has a strong oral tradition," observed special education chief Thomas Hehir, who assembled a maze of special education rules into one large book during his two-year tenure that ended in 1992. "Previously they were orally passed down from one administrator to another. In a city of six hundred schools, that doesn't make sense."[20] Just before union negotiations began in 1993, a key budget official suffered a stroke, taking with him critical knowledge about how to retrieve spending information. Fortunately for the school system, he recovered in time to share his expertise. An outside consultant warned in 1992 that too few people knew how to operate the district's aging computer system—leaving the potential for a major failure in the computers that undergirded the system. "What they're saying is, if we're not careful, we could have a complete collapse of the management information system," chief financial officer Charley Gillispie said. "It's very serious. You would not like to be a stockholder in a public company that received this kind of report."[21]

The problem was aggravated by the legislature's last-minute decision to impose an early retirement plan in August 1993. More than fifty central office administrators accepted the option. In the bureau of salary administration, for example, the top three administrators resigned. Because the board would not hire replacements until the three administrators' jobs were vacant, no one was trained for the position, according to Thomas M. Finnegan, chief of the Bureau of Salary Administration that calculates teacher salary adjustments for added schooling and for new teachers from out of state. He later stayed on as a consultant.[22]

Lack of staff was not always the problem, however. A vivid example is the 1989 directory of schools published by the central office. Its authors programmed the computer with only four digits in school addresses and, therefore, far South Side schools with addresses such as "10015 S. Leavitt" appeared instead as "1001 S. Leavitt." In a city that runs on a grid system, such a grievous error placed first-time visitors and mail miles from their destinations. Meanwhile in 1993, interim school superintendent Richard E. Stephenson called a meeting with principals during his first week on the job. An electronic computer message notified principals of special parking arrangements, but the otherwise helpful advice arrived the day after the event. In yet another case, a teacher was notified by mail in October 1993 to report to a different school. The letter arrived four days after the transfer was to take effect.

There are other examples. When certain schools were placed on a proposed closing list, principals were shocked to discover that the school board would base such critical decisions affecting so many children on inaccurate information that summarized their enrollments and school capacities. One school was listed at the wrong location, and another school's name was misspelled. Kimbrough himself encountered the system shuffle when he became superintendent in January 1990. "My own quests for information are often met with shrugs, denials, and delays," he told *Chicago Sun-Times* columnist Raymond R. Coffey. "For one important project, I received four different and conflicting responses in answer to a single request. Today this administration is plagued by red tape. A simple phone call becomes a chain reaction of misinformation and delays."[23]

Gleaming exceptions exist, of course. Some Pershing Road employees work feverishly under enormous stress. In the Department of Human Resources, for example, it is not unusual for employees to answer the telephone as early as 6 a.m. and work seven days a week during the first critical weeks of the school year. According to a 1992 poll, half of Chicago principals graded as "very helpful" administration work in interpreting government regulations, handling sensitive personnel and human relations issues, budgeting, teacher evaluations, staff selection, and lunch programs. On the other hand, the poll also illustrated how widespread the problems were. While principals apparently supported the idea of maintaining some central office functions, one fifth said they have no regard for Pershing Road services at all. "If 20 percent of your customers routinely said your services are not helpful at all, I don't know how many businesses would stay in business with that level of customer dissatisfaction," said Anthony Bryk, chairman of the steering committee of the consortium that conducted the poll.[24]

Although chaos continued to characterize certain aspects of the central office, by the fourth year of reform there were indications that management was beginning to improve in some areas, such as in the transportation, special education, and purchasing departments. Even so, Charley Gillispie, a former partner in an accounting firm who was named finance chief in 1992, acknowledged what critics had long maintained: the central office was cut haphazardly because no one took the time to determine how its role should change under reform. "So offices have attempted to perform the same roles with fewer people. The result has been predictable: delays in services, reductions in the quality of services, and rising dissatisfaction among schools," he wrote in a 1993 proposed restructuring plan.[25] Meanwhile, the Civic Federation, a financial watchdog group, studied ways to revamp the budget, which Gillispie conceded was eminently unreadable.

But there were some success stories. In 1991 a shortage of one hundred buses left children stranded at bus stops or after school for hours at a time. One year later, the matter was virtually resolved when transportation chief Robert Johnson instituted a computerized routing system and staggered school hours, among other measures. Efficiency in transportation was improved. In special education, department chief Thomas Hehir revolutionized the system of evaluating and placing students. By 1992, the backlog of evaluations had dropped from more than 3,000 to half that number and the backlog of placements from 2,400 to virtually zero. In response to reform group complaints, the Pershing Road cafeteria was privatized.

Schools were finally given greater leeway to buy equipment and supplies directly from vendors. Instead of requiring three quotes for every item over $500 or ordering from a board catalog so vague that principals did not know what they were requesting, schools could simply submit purchase orders for instructional materials, equipment, and supplies under $10,000. For the first time, the board granted principals the right to adjust purchase orders from their schools and talk directly to vendors about something as simple as the inadvertent failure to calculate shipping costs. William Haran, principal of Brennemann Elementary School on the North Side, was among those who welcomed the improvements. "It gives us so much more freedom. It's been such a cumbersome thing in the past, trying to deal with the red tape at the board. Not only did we have to wait, but you could never pin down where the foul-ups were, so you couldn't correct them if you wanted to," he said.[26] In the words of Schubert School principal Cynthia A. Wnek: "Somehow it's becoming a system where it's getting a little easier. But the bigness of the organization still defeats efficiency."

Of 157 principals who answered a 1993 school board survey, 87 percent reported improvements in central office purchasing; 85 percent saw improvements in warehouse deliveries. Previously, delivery of goods from the central office warehouse to schools took as long as six weeks, but a reorganization of the department shortened the delivery time to just two days, the central office claimed. In addition, 68 percent of principals who responded reported improvements in the time it took for vendors to be paid.[27]

Administrators began to rewrite bid specifications, a move expected to save $5 million or more a year. A four-month study by the consulting firm of Booz-Allen & Hamilton reported that the system used specifications so old that, in one example, they required a 100-watt soldering iron when the standard was 80 watts, boosting the cost considerably.[28] Administrators launched an effort to remove thirty thousand inactive vendors from computer records. They also made plans to pay vendors monthly, instead of through individual invoices. Such a move was expected to save $1 million per year. It also expected to save $3 to $4 million per year by tightening procedures for nonbid emergency repair contracts and by arranging for contractors to bid before emergency repairs were actually needed. The improvements were made possible through the assistance of the Financial Research and Advisory Committee, a business-sponsored group that worked for more than a year to streamline operations at Pershing Road, according to Gillispie. The anticipated success of these and other changes only confirmed complaints that the school board could have avoided some cuts had restructuring begun at the onset of reform.

Despite the improvements, principals complained that central office practices still worked against the schools in some areas. One of the principals' biggest complaints—that last-minute centralized budget cuts dramatically undercut education—actually worsened during 1993. In addition, schools complained that central office still did not pay some bills on time. Consequently, many vendors refused to do business with the system. "I'm tired of salesmen coming a year later and saying, 'I haven't been paid,'" said Patricia R. Tamburrino. Many principals still believe the board did not go far enough in purchasing changes. They sought complete control of key funds with some ground rules and regular, thorough, auditing to ferret out the unscrupulous. "I'm willing to sign a paper that I'll go to jail if something is missing. I won't let anybody steal. I would rather have it in the bank and be completely 100 percent accountable and be audited," said Wnek, arguing that money for equipment, workshops, and materials should be channeled to schools, while payroll should be kept centralized. "You don't have the staff? Put it in our hands," said Fred Kravarik, principal of Marquette Elementary School on the Southwest Side. "Let me go out and purchase the things I need for my school."

Central office balked at turning over money and control to schools, partly for fear they would misuse such power. Indeed, internal audits reveal that thousands of dollars in student monies disappear every year at the hands of principals, teachers, and clerks. But in a worst case scenario, schools would do no better than central office. At least that was the argument of Michael M. Woods, principal at Westcott Elementary School on the South Side: "I don't think I can misuse any more money than has already been misused. Reform cannot be reform until our monies are in the schools. We must look at the system through totally different lenses."

Examining the way the system spent money or distributed services to schools was repeatedly labeled a waste of time by the leadership during the first three years of reform. As test scores dropped overall, Kimbrough blamed the schools and the energy spent on battling over control of funds and authority. "We educators, business leaders, parents, teachers, and editors are embroiled in prolonged disputes over who controls what funds and who has what power," he wrote in an opinion piece in 1992. "Meanwhile, far too many of our children are intellectually crippled."[29] In March of that year, Kimbrough made an impassioned speech to the Chicago School Finance Authority, as the oversight panel once again rejected the system's long-range plan for failing to address a key element of reform: decentralization. Kimbrough told panel members that the focus and the call for accountability should be turned from the central office to the schools. "Frankly, the lack of results of what's happening in the classroom is frightening," he said, pointing to 1991 achievement test scores that showed only 7 percent of Chicago's elementary schools averaged above national norms in reading. He singled out a school in which 83 percent of eighth graders scored in the bottom half of the nation in reading, but where the principal was acclaimed for innovation. "We put garlands and wreaths around the principal," he said. "That's a lot of baloney."[30]

Kimbrough was right, of course, about focusing on achievement. But for those in the schools, governance had a direct connection to learning.

For one thing, the system's reputation for waste and inefficiency was the chief reason given by state leadership for not properly funding Chicago schools, which meant that children continued to be warehoused in dilapidated buildings, some of them overcrowded, with inadequate supplies and not enough teachers, truant officers, or science labs. Its reputation also deflated morale and gave the Chicago Teachers Union little incentive to cooperate with the self-serving administration—thus leading to threatened work stoppages and making children the ultimate victims. The system's terrible management problem meant too that money was siphoned away from children and that schools could not obtain the tools they needed in order to educate—tools as basic as desks, books, and computer programs.

Eight months after it ordered chairs with state Chapter One funds through the central office, Wirth School had not received them, forcing students to take classes in shifts. "Anyone knows that if kids can't sit, they can't study," council member Smith Wiiams said. "And if they can't study, they don't learn."[31]

Students wait for teacher assignments in a packed Amundsen
High School library.

Courtesy *Chicago Sun-Times*. Photo by Rich Hein.

4

Governance Affects Kids

It makes them feel "Maybe no one cares I'm missing class time for twenty-one days. Maybe no one cares about my education."

Chicago Board of Education student member Kevin Davenport
about thousands of teacherless classrooms each September[1]

Perhaps no starker example of how governance affects learning lies in the way that the Chicago public school system assigns teachers.

Each year, thousands of students are stranded without teachers for the first four to six weeks of school, contributing to rock-bottom achievement and one of the nation's worst dropout rates. In schools where enrollment soars during September, students who should be learning attend study halls by the hundreds, skip classes, or sit through a string of teachers volunteering to fill in on their free time. Students sometimes are assigned homework that is never collected.

At Lake View High School, students in five English and eight biology classes were among those without teachers through September 1991. The North Side school was short a math and science teacher the following year. Because teaching positions—and therefore position numbers—do not exist in such cases, principals cannot hire substitutes. Sometimes classes were covered by teachers with a free period, but on other days there were no classroom monitors at all. What happened then? Fifteen-year-old biology student Kirby Casey explained: "On those days, the classroom was a total madhouse. We didn't do much there but throw erasers."[2] The effect of missing a month of biology or English on students is obvious to Lake View principal Donna J. Macey: "It cheats them. It diminishes the amount of material you can present. It breathes in a certain amount of insecurity and certainly sends a subtle message that their education is not valuable."

At Amundsen High School, forty-five classes had no teachers during the first month of the 1992 school year. Hundreds of students packed into study halls while the North Side school waited for clearance to hire seven additional teachers in such critical subjects as science, math, English, and business. Students normally would have attended study hall in the auditorium, but a mix-up with asbestos abatement contractors left a summer construction project unfinished, forcing students to waste time in the library—the sheer numbers of people made it difficult to study. Science teacher James Doyiakos, who volunteered to cover some classes, recalled the effects from the previous year when he was hired weeks after school opened. The students had to play catch-up, only skimming important material. "I had no choice," he lamented.[3]

At Boone Elementary School, nearly one hundred Russian-speaking students arrived in the fall of 1992, but principal Paul E. Zavitkovsky could not hire two Russian teachers until weeks into the school year. This increased class sizes and made it impossible to immediately expand the Russian bilingual program, which, in turn, put much of the primary program on hold until the beginning of November. "To wait for the entire first quarter to get staff in place requires some really heroic efforts on the part of parents and teachers—efforts they should not have to make," said Zavitkovsky. "Even the best of our teachers are being stretched farther than they can be stretched."[4]

What led to such insanity? The answer lies with a computerized assignment system that staffs teachers according to actual—not projected—enrollment. Such a system means that until new students materialize in fall, the teachers who should be there to serve them are not assigned. The system was introduced under school reform by chief operating officer Robert A. Sampieri to end what administrators say is a long-standing practice of schools to overspend—sometimes by assigning students too many classes and sometimes by inflating enrollments in order to get more staff from the cash-strapped system. In 1992, some seven thousand student

names were on enrollment lists with no proof they represented actual students attending classes, according to Margaret
M. Harrigan, associate superintendent of human resources for
the school system. Staffing for that number would require
some 260 teachers—a $13-million-a-year proposition that
would also inflate principal salaries since principals are paid
partly according to the number of staff they supervise. At Orr
Community Academy on the West Side, inflated reports of
enrollment and attendance resulted in overstaffing of 8.5 to
14.5 teaching positions at an estimated cost of $399,500 to
$676,800 a year, according to an internal audit conducted in
the fall of 1992. Auditors concluded there was a conscious
effort on the part of staff to misrepresent student membership
and attendance. School leaders denied the charges, insisting
they were nothing more than paperwork errors.[5]

High student mobility was another rationale given for using
the computerized method of assigning teachers, a method
that, perhaps not coincidentally, saves untold millions in
salaries during the first few weeks of the school year. Partly
because poor families tend to be apartment dwellers who
move more frequently than wealthier homeowners, enrollment in Chicago schools fluctuates wildly after the school year
begins. In some schools, such as those serving children of
migrant workers and children from shelters, the entire student
body turns over twice after classes begin. Chicago officials say
a chronic shortfall of funds combined with the demographics
of the student body forces them to base staff assignments on
actual enrollment.

Other big-city school systems, however, hire based on projected enrollment. In New York City, subdistricts receive personnel allocations as early as July. Problems arise only when
enrollment soars above projections, spokesperson James
Vlasto said. "If one high school has two hundred or three
hundred students more than they expected, they have to
recruit the teachers. But 90 percent of the teachers are in
place when the bell rings," he said, maintaining that those
who are not are quickly assigned. "It involves a very short
period of time." Of course, New York City schools receive
about $2,300 more per student than Chicago schools.[6]

The New York City school system, the nation's largest, also
keeps its district offices open twelve months a year in order to

handle new enrollments. But Chicago contributes to its own high mobility rate by not allowing new students to enroll or transfer until after school begins. The chief reason is that the system does not pay clerks to work during summer breaks. School officials concede that hiring clerks for at least two weeks during summer would make for a much smoother opening, but it would be costly. What's more, they argue, Chicago parents are accustomed to waiting until the school year begins before enrolling students. Encouraging families to begin earlier would require an all-out campaign.

One cannot help but wonder, however, how students can be encouraged to attend at all during the system's chaotic opening weeks. In September 1991, the system opened nearly two thousand teaching jobs after school began, but it cut another twenty eight hundred in schools where enrollment dropped. The following year, it opened twelve hundred positions.[7] Imagine the numbers of students affected by those statistics. Students in one classroom, for example, reported being assigned a history paper over a weekend in November 1993. When they returned the next Monday, the teacher was gone.

When asked about the teacher assignment procedures, superintendent Ted D. Kimbrough was blunt: "It doesn't matter whether it's disruptive. You cannot spend dollars that you don't have," he said. "The high schools are notorious for spending money they don't have. It's as simple as that. I would not be fiduciarily responsible if I did not call that to the attention of the public. They overspend," he concluded.[8]

In the view of Austin Community Academy principal DeCalvin Hughes, it would be a dream for every principal to have an overstaffed school. Still, he had expected his enrollment to justify four new teaching jobs in 1992, but the students, he conceded, never materialized. Kimbrough said the system cannot afford such miscalculations. Hughes countered that schools such as Austin, where 80 percent of freshmen need remedial courses in reading, deserve the extra staff. In 1992, the school had a *graduation* rate of 17.6 percent.[9]

Principals contend that the central office should give them the teachers they think they need but should remove them if their estimated enrollments do not prove true, either in the same year or in future years. An alternative would be to penalize offending principals in some other way. At the very least, the central office should provide substitutes for otherwise teacherless classes. "I resent it," said John J. Garvey, principal of Foreman High School on the Northwest Side. "It's saying we don't know what's going on in our schools, and somebody else knows better. I've never opened a position I didn't need."[10]

While 1991 and 1992 were marked by rocky openings in some schools, the fall of 1993 appeared to set all records for disruptions of staffing systemwide. It began with a legislative decision to adopt an early retirement program for Chicago public schools. The Chicago Teachers Union aggressively lobbied for the program, which made great sense since it was projected to save at least $10.2 million a year through the difference of salaries between older retiring employees and new replacements. It also was a way to recruit a fresh infusion of younger, and presumably, enthusiastic teachers, which the system badly needed.

The problems were derived from the ground rules.

While the legislature allowed suburban schools at least four months to plan for vacancies caused by a similar early retirement program, it gave Chicago schools fewer than four weeks. And while it phased in suburban and downstate retirements over two and three years, it told teachers early retirement would be a one-time offer in Chicago schools, setting August 15 as the deadline. Although educators had little time to make up their minds, nearly 2,500 employees finally decided to take the offer—three weeks before school began. Systemwide, 53 central office staffers, 101 principals, and 2,310 teachers (including assistant principals) retired. The effect was immediate and quite disruptive. Classes, for example, opened at Burke Elementary School on the South Side without a permanent principal, assistant principal, and one of two clerks, not to mention some teachers.[11] Two days before his own retirement on August 23, Wells Community Academy High School principal David T. Peterson was scrambling to fill 22 teaching positions left vacant on his staff of 110.

Meanwhile, during rocky negotiations with the teachers union, the school board imposed a hiring freeze gambling on the theory that the union would concede nearly one thousand high school jobs. There was no guarantee, of course, that the board would receive the concessions. In fact, months later the union surrendered only half that number. In the meantime, schools were under the hiring freeze, wondering what to do about vacant positions that, at Wells at least, included three English teaching positions, four social studies positions, and one physics and one chemistry position. In the end, many schools rehired retirees as substitutes—a measure that was allowed for one hundred days—enough time to get schools through the first semester.[12]

Following the citywide disruptions caused by early retirement came the change from forty-minute to fifty-minute periods, which eliminated more than 496 high school teaching jobs days before school began. One day after programmers were told to reschedule to accommodate the original order came yet another command: add two students to every high school class and one student at the elementary level. This latest action eliminated another five hundred jobs.[13] Then came regular cuts in teaching staff due to declining enrollment in individual schools to which, it must be added, the financial crisis of 1993 contributed. For weeks parents wondered how long schools would stay open; some took their children to other school systems or chose home schooling. Julian High School on the South Side lost twenty-four positions, roughly a quarter of the teaching staff. In addition, a $1 million television-radio studio, a successful cosmetology program, and a pilot engineering program were brought to a halt when the teachers of those programs were cut.[14] Walt Disney Magnet School on the North Side lost sixteen teachers. Principal Raphael Guajardo recounted how he received the news several weeks into the school year—without direct contact: "I dialed up the computer screen on Monday morning, just as I do every day. And I looked at the numbers, and some of the numbers were lower than they were before. So I called the district office, and they got back to me the next day. They said, yes, it was true. I was losing eleven more teachers, as of October. They said the decision had been made in August."[15]

Other principals received no notice whatsoever. During one weekend in October, hundreds of teachers were called at home and told to transfer to other schools. The transfers came at a time when the department of human resources was itself hit hard by early retirement cuts, including that of its director, Margaret M. Harrigan. The result was, once again, chaos. Some teachers reportedly discovered three messages waiting for them on their home answering machines. Each message came from different central office staff telling them to report to different schools the following week. Principals were shocked to learn of the transfers by word-of-mouth.

The school system's budget office was also surprised how the dismissals were handled by the principals themselves. Lutaf Dhanidina, director of the budget development and analysis department, said he expected that principals who were told to cut a specific number of jobs would do so in a logical order: positions vacated by early retirement should have been the first to go, followed by other vacant positions, then jobs filled by full-time substitute teachers, and lastly, the jobs of permanent teachers still on staff. Instead, principals used the opportunity to close positions of long-time teachers they did not want in their schools while filling positions vacated by early retirement with their own appointments. "The order was reversed—that really blindsided us," Dhanidina said. "My sense is that if you were to look at teachers who were displaced and then look at who the most vocal leaders are among the teachers, you'd find a pretty high correlation." The teacher's paper *Substance* complained of the same phenomenon.

Such an enormous movement of staff after the school year begins exacts an incalculable toll on education and was expected to lead to lower test scores. The question remains whether the public will understand the reason: moving a teacher after school begins typically disrupts five classrooms. Moreover, each disruption cheats students of the stable and carefully planned instruction that is taken for granted in many suburban and private schools. "Students think, 'Why am I going to schools if school isn't even caring about me?'" asked student Rima Vesely, a 1992 city editor of *New Expressions,* a citywide student newspaper.[16]

When Julian High School teachers were cut, freshman Katharyn Savary sat before a string of substitutes who each taught the same first lesson—Africa in history class and short stories in English. "I can tell you everything about Africa and short stories," said Savary, who, five weeks into the school year, had still not advanced to Lesson 2 in either subject. And because budgetary information was not entered into the computer system, textbooks were in short supply. Indeed, only a fraction of freshman English students at Julian had books; Savary was not among them, which left her with little of academic substance—her only other courses were two learning disabled classes and gym—during her introductory year in high school.[17] Similarly, Schurz High School on the Northwest Side lacked teachers in geography, physics, and art as well as Polish and Spanish bilingual math for almost the entire first quarter of 1993, sending students to study halls en masse, according to principal Sharon Rae Bender.[18] At Lake View High School, parents could not meet their children's teachers at a school open house in late September 1992 because teachers had yet to be assigned.

There are other damaging effects of teacher shortages. In the case of those caused by enrollment changes, city schools often lose prime teaching candidates to suburban and private schools when jobs are sensibly offered *before* the school year begins. It also adds to the already intense pressure of overcrowding. Those schools with skyrocketing enrollments are hit hardest by staff shortages.

Opening schools without a full complement of teachers is one limitation on Chicago school principals' much-publicized right to choose teaching staff for the first time under reform. It is a welcomed right and admittedly far better than when they had only limited power of selection. But complications remain, caused by both a 1988 state law and union rules that guaranteed jobs to the majority of teachers whose positions were eliminated due to declining enrollment or closed programs. Essentially this meant that all teachers whose jobs were cut at individual schools were guaranteed positions elsewhere in the system. Displaced teachers who could not find a principal to hire them were called *supernumeraries,* later renamed *reserve teachers.* Given the massive job transfers, some could not find work for as simple a reason as that their positions were cut after the school year began or that their subjects had become obsolete. The lifetime job guarantees made the system reluctant to allow principals to hire new teachers, especially when it had no authority to remove them if enrollment did not justify their positions, noted Margaret M. Harrigan, associate superintendent for human resources. But assigning teachers and removing them weeks later would also be unfair, reflecting a transitory mind-set of "put someone in and if we don't need them we'll get rid of them."

"Who would ever want to work in this system?" asked Chicago Teachers Union spokesperson Jackie Gallagher. "That would put teachers in a position that is untenable."[19]

Steve Brown, spokesperson for Illinois Speaker of the House Michael J. Madigan—who protected the lifetime guarantee— noted that the central office finds jobs for most supernumeraries eventually, leaving only a handful without assignments.

Job cuts, combined with the job guarantees, created a dilemma for the system's department of human resources. When the Chicago Board of Education closed schools and eliminated more than five hundred teaching jobs in budget cuts in late August 1991, it triggered a chain reaction that displaced hundreds of other teachers, some of whom became supernumeraries. The central office's answer was to bump teachers whose jobs were not guaranteed because they were not fully assigned by a principal, either by choice of the principal or because they lacked full certification. Typically such positions belonged to younger teachers a course or two shy of their state teaching certificates or to those waiting for a certificate, which the state normally took a year to approve.

Theoretically, the situation made sense. In reality, it disrupted programs citywide and conflicted with the system's long-time goal of attracting new teachers. It also forced principals to accept teachers they did not choose in order to lay off or demote those they did, thus violating one tenet of school reform: the principals' right to choose staff. Consequently, some of the supernumerary teachers were forced into jobs for which they had no training. "This isn't a welcome situation for either the principals or the teachers, but they're accepting it professionally," Harrigan said.

At DuSable High School, principal Charles E. Mingo recruited a former medical doctor from New Jersey who had switched fields to enter teaching. Jacquelin McCord took summer classes to prepare for a special assignment in the heart of the South Side public housing developments teaching students lagging far behind their peers. But about one week before school began, the state notified McCord that she lacked a gym course for the Illinois certificate for which she had applied a year-and-a-half earlier. Central office then notified her fewer than twenty-four hours before classes began that a supernumerary was to fill her position. She was reclassified as a "floating substitute," a job that carried substantially lower pay and fewer benefits. "It's a nightmare," she said. "I'm still in shock."[20] Through some maneuvering and publicity, Mc-Cord was able to teach the course after all, but other teachers remained affected.

At Sayre Language Academy, a fourth-grade teacher was replaced by an eighth-grade science teacher who had never taught intermediate classes. The bumped teacher was a single mother who, with no notice, lost medical benefits for her family after the school year began. In another case, Calumet High School hurriedly closed its print shop program after graphic arts teacher Percy Brown was replaced by an art teacher with no experience in the field. Brown held a master's degree but had not been "fully assigned" by a new principal still getting to know her staff. Consequently, Brown lost a third of his pay. Another individual, a high school business teacher, was transferred and assigned to teach math, then music, and then math again. With expertise in accounting, business law, and bookkeeping, he had no special training in either subject and concluded, "It's not really fair to anybody. It's unsettling to the students. They don't know who their teacher is from day to day." Such teachers, who are thrown into situations for which they are given no time to prepare, can hardly be expected to improve student achievement.

"It's a gigantic problem," admitted chief operating officer Robert A. Sampieri. "We have to keep them by law, but we don't have an appropriate place for them. That has got to be a major economic detriment to the solvency of this district."[21]

Chicago Teachers Union attorney Lawrence A. Poltrock defended the supernumerary law by insisting that the job guarantee is designed to be a compromise between the seniority rights held by suburban and downstate teachers—who do not face surprise September job losses—while giving the Chicago system flexibility in assigning teachers. In Illinois schools outside Chicago, teachers are laid off according to seniority status and given at least sixty days' notice before dismissal. Because of the size of the Chicago district, however, laying off teachers in order of district-wide seniority would create a chain reaction of disruptions, Poltrock insisted. Chicago teachers, therefore, are justifiably the only teachers in the state guaranteed their jobs. "None of these individuals are poor teachers," said David M. Peterson, the union's assistant to the president for legislation. "You're talking about qualified personnel who have, in many instances, worked for our system twenty or twenty-five years."[22]

Teachers were placed in areas covered by their state certificates, Sampieri said, although not necessarily in their areas of expertise. At King High School on the South Side, for example, a home economics teacher was assigned to teach science courses. "That's why you're a professional," Sampieri offered. "You're supposed to be able to handle that difference."

The last-minute changes gave teachers little time to look for new jobs or revise their personal budgets, much less prepare academically. "If I knew about it over this summer," said the business teacher who was assigned to teach math, "I would have taken a class or two."

Ultimately, principals were given the right to replace the appointments hurriedly made to their schools, but only with teachers holding full state certificates. Such an exception locked out young and promising teaching candidates still shy a few state courses, in the opinion of DuSable's Mingo, who planned to have the owner of a video-production company use video cameras to teach public speaking. The teacher, however, lacked the appropriate certificate. "You need balance on the staff. You don't always need old folks like me," he said. "At some point, you need young folks who can talk to kids and get them excited."[23]

A compromise on the heated issue was reached between the school board and the teachers union in 1993. The job guarantees were shortened to two years, with the stipulation that the teachers either find a position during that time frame or immediately begin retraining in subjects in critical need of teachers, such as special and bilingual education.

Once again, Chicago was the site of a showdown between reform and a cherished educational tradition: tenure rights for teachers.

In the view of Rand Corporation researchers Hill and Bonan, teachers must be more flexible regarding tenure rights if America's schools are going to improve under site-based management. "As site-managed schools develop their own distinctive missions and approaches, each will require staff members whose teaching skills and style work compatibly with those of the existing program. If teachers continue to be assigned on the basis of seniority or other general criteria, staff assignment could become a serious barrier to the continuation of healthy site-managed schools," they wrote.

The logical answer would be to allow schools and teachers to choose each other: "A labor market would ultimately eliminate teachers' rights of tenure in a particular school. Such teachers would have to find schools to work in, but neither the union nor the central office could guarantee employment to teachers who could not find a school that wanted to hire them."[24]

Such a solution, however, presumes a management focused on children and anxious to hire teachers based on ability, not one that seeks to further political power plays by promoting friends and transferring critics—a frequent complaint that arose in the system. Therefore, any proposed change in the status quo met with fierce opposition from teachers. Schurz High School teacher Arnold Drobny was among the opponents: "No union worth its salt can ever give away seniority rights. Otherwise, there's no need for a union. If a board thinks any teacher will cross that picket line to give up seniority rights, they're living in La La Land. It's even more important than wages."[25]

Other practices under reform minimized principals' control over selecting staff. The contract negotiated by the interim board, for example, created career service examinations for 136 job titles. This, in turn, posed an inconvenience on Courtenay School when it found a Spanish-speaking teacher's aide for its large population of Latino students. It soon discovered, however, that the selection of aides was left to a central office seniority list based on civil service examinations resurrected for the first time in years—decades, in some categories—when reform went into place. The next aide on the hiring list spoke Urdu, not Spanish, according to council member Warren Mueller. Ultimately, Courtenay School managed to hire its

Spanish-speaking aide, but only after a battle that lasted almost one year, he said.

Herbert School principal William Rankin called the eligibility lists "a virus" planted in the reform legislation. "What criteria certify janitors, bus attendants, truck drivers, cafeteria workers, aides? It is all a secret," he wrote in a *Chicago Sun-Times* opinion piece. "The tests are devised and graded by bureaucrats. The local school has the ability to select teachers and a principal, but not an engineer or janitor. Does that make sense? Gone are the days when a principal could appoint an aide or bus attendant from the parent volunteers who have served the school well."[26]

Technically, the eligibility lists were not graded by "bureaucrats." Rather they were determined by a firm that received a $435,000 no-bid contract to administer the tests.[27]

Rankin's assessment was confirmed by Margaret M. Harrigan. Harrigan did not negotiate the 1990 union contract but her personnel department was left to deal with its aftermath. "There is nothing more antithetical to reform than this: A principal can hire a teacher, but not a teacher aide. A principal can hire an assistant principal but not a clerk. We need to be consistent," she maintained. "If we're talking about local school empowerment, if we're talking about principals in charge, then principals ought to be able to select staff." Harrigan suggested a compromise of establishing eligibility lists without a rank order.

There were other limits placed on principals' selection of staff. In staffing summer school, principals could choose only teachers who had not worked more than two summers in succession, which meant schools that had already used their own staff were required to bring in outside teachers unless the union and school board agreed to exceptions. Principals also had no control over who left when enrollment dropped, since the rules required that the least senior staff member in a specific category be automatically eliminated. At Herbert School, according to Rankin, no student in a particular teacher's class advanced a grade level on achievement tests during one year. On the other hand, more than half the students in another teacher's class in the same school advanced a year—quite an accomplishment in the ravaged West Side of Chicago. But when enrollment declined, Rankin was forced to transfer the good teacher because the other one had seniority.

"It means that we put the interests of the adults ahead of the interests of children," Rankin declared.

Mobile units—once called "Willis wagons"—at Hammond Elementary School.

Courtesy *Chicago Sun-Times*. Photo by Phil Velasquez.

5

Caretakers of Our Children

Good teachers should get a raise or bonus or something . . . while the other teachers should get fired or get sent back to school.

Goodlow Upper Grade Center student Leniene Sherman[1]

At one Chicago school, a teacher locked a special education kindergartner for hours in a closet for defecating in his pants. Another teacher repeatedly used emergencies as excuses for being late, arriving minutes before 10 a.m.—the magic hour before which, under union contract, she could not be marked absent and docked pay.

The principal who alleged the infractions used a common method of getting rid of the pair: he won their transfers to other schools.[2]

Some Chicago classrooms go through a revolving door of teachers that can amount to as many as two thousand transfers annually after the school year begins.[3] In 1992, Chicago parent Mildred Ray hired a tutor for her daughter, after the second grader had a succession of four teachers in a year. "Last year, she scored six months below grade level," Ray remarked. "She was an honor student before. Now I have her in tutoring classes to bring her up to par, which is costing me $85 a week."

In the case of incompetent teachers, the alternative to transfers is dismissal hearings that can take one year or more to complete, soaking up critically needed time for the principal and tens of thousands of dollars in legal fees for the system.

Even then, success is not guaranteed. In the words of DuSable High School principal Charles E. Mingo, "You never want to be involved in two dismissal hearings at once."

School officials throughout the nation complain about a shared problem: the extensive time and procedures required to fire inadequate teachers. "You have to provide documentation on top of documentation on top of documentation," said Erica Zurer, vice president of New York City's Community School Board 13, which oversees one of thirty-two subdistricts in the nation's largest school system. Although good teachers are the single most essential ingredient in improving education, union power and legislatures have all but completely protected the usually small percentages of those who fail. The catch is that even small numbers of ineffective teachers harm thousands of children for life. "Even if only 5 percent of the teachers in public elementary and secondary schools are incompetent, the number of students being taught by these teachers exceeds the combined public-school enrollments of the 14 smallest states," Stanford University professor Edwin M. Bridges wrote in *Education Week*.[4]

In Illinois, the legislature set up an unwieldly process that in 1992 resulted in dismissals of seven tenured Chicago public school teachers—just over three hundreds of 1 percent of the teaching work force—and that included teachers who later successfully appealed unfavorable decisions made by hearing officers provided by the state.[5] Far more should be fired, according to a 1992 survey by the Consortium on Chicago School Research of Chicago public elementary school principals. An astounding number of principals—more than two thirds—said they would fire 6 to 20 percent of their teachers if they could bypass due process hearings, and another 9 percent would fire more than a fifth of their teaching staffs, if given that luxury. The teachers union responded that many principals simply do not understand good teaching. In the words of union official John Kotsakis, many principals are either uninterested in quality instruction or do not recognize it. "There's a big difference between whether somebody can keep a classroom quiet, as opposed to someone who can really teach kids. One person is providing basic service. The other is providing inspiration. I don't think most principals can differentiate between the two," said Kotsakis, assistant to the union president for education issues.[6]

In Illinois case law, Chicago teachers cannot be dismissed unless they have failed to improve after a remediation period of forty-five days or unless they are deemed "irremediable." In such a situation, the board has to prove both that there was damage done to students, faculty, or the school and the conduct could not have been prevented had the teachers been forewarned.[7]

Perhaps the most difficult cases to prove are those that involve poor teaching. Of the seven tenured city teachers fired in 1992, three were dismissed precisely for that reason. In 1990, Ray Elementary School principal Cydney B. Fields issued an unsatisfactory notice to teacher Marcia Smith for poor teaching. (An unsatisfactory rating automatically triggers the dismissal process.) A central office administrator in Smith's area of instruction—teaching of the hearing impaired—confirmed Smith's "serious difficulties," according to testimony at her dismissal hearing. And a consulting teacher, appointed to help Smith, reported no progress after meeting with her on fourteen occasions, testimony showed. But Fields' bid to fire Smith was unsuccessful. Why? Because Fields failed to provide forty-five days of in-class remediation, which is intended to give the teacher a chance to improve as required by law. Instead, the time period spanned forty-four classroom days and one teacher institute day, which violated Smith's rights to a full remediation period, hearing officer Ellen J. Alexander ruled in 1992.

Such behavior alone would not have been reason enough to reinstate the teacher after the school board fired her though, Alexander ruled. What weakened the case considerably was the principal's ineffective written evaluation. Fields alleged the teacher's flaws—which in addition to poor teaching skills included tardiness, berating students publicly, and raising her voice to parents—in a detailed written remediation plan and in classroom visitation checklists, according to the hearing officer's decision. While Alexander acknowledged that Fields verbally explained to Smith her weaknesses following the forty-five days, Fields confined her final written criticism to only one paragraph and failed to use the proper teacher evaluation form required in board rules. Such an oversight, Alexander ruled, was inexcusable. In addition, Fields failed to observe Smith on the final two days of the remediation period. Fifteen months after Fields first notified Smith of her alleged deficiencies and nine months after the teacher was fired by the school board, the hearing officer ordered that she be reinstated and given back pay.[8] Smith—who denied having teacher skill problems—then requested and received a transfer from the Southeast Side school.

A number of cases throughout the years have involved accusations of sexual misconduct by staff.

In one incident, a substitute teacher was assigned to a second-grade classroom at Tilton Elementary School when students became rowdy, allegedly because they had been promised a party that never took place, according to state records. Teacher Alvin Packer, first employed in 1969 as a provisional teacher and then a full-time substitute, allegedly hit students with a ruler and put his hands down girls' blouses. Accused of touching second graders in other inappropriate places, Packer was fired four months after the alleged incident. Hearing officer Harvey A. Nathan called the conduct outrageous, violating "the most basic of moral standards expected from any adult, let alone a professional school teacher."[9] Although Packer admitted hitting children's hands with a ruler, he denied the allegations of touching. He also denied that he was drinking the day of the alleged incident. Attorneys for Packer argued unsuccessfully that the teacher should have received a warning that the alleged action could jeopardize his job. In addition, they insisted that the alleged physical conduct was not overtly sexual and did not damage students, if it indeed happened at all.[10]

In yet another case, it took five months to fire Orr High School wrestling coach Leroy F. Blackful, Jr., a forty-six-year-old teacher who allegedly took a sixteen-year-old to a hotel and to his van where she consented to have sexual relations with him and be photographed nude, according to state records of the dismissal hearing. The student, a troubled ward of the state who later recanted her testimony, initially made the allegations during counseling sessions with a state social worker in November 1986. Blackful admitted befriending the student and going on an overnight trip with her and several other students during a wrestling meet, but he denied that he had sexual relations with her. Charges by the board were filed against Blackful in April 1987 and, more than two years after the alleged incidents, hearing officer Allen D. Schwartz found enough evidence to uphold his dismissal.[11]

Perhaps the most famous sex abuse case in Chicago public schools concerns James G. Moffat, one of the most powerful men in the system at the time. Moffat was deputy superintendent of school management services, the second highest job in the system, until he was demoted during a changeover in administrations in 1980. He then became principal of Kelvyn Park High School on the Northwest Side. There, Chicago social worker Marsha Niazmand was counseling a student one day when the teenager alleged that Moffat propositioned her, according to published reports. Weeks later, the girl divulged more. Moffat had allegedly kissed her and removed her bra. Niazmand lodged a complaint, but the administration apparently did nothing, assuming the charges could not be proven.

Niazmand persisted, however, even after Moffat transferred her from Kelvyn Park in January 1985. With the assistance of attorney Michael Radzilowsky, she tracked down other victims and collected affidavits that eventually led to Moffat's conviction years later. A courageous teacher, Maxine Lowe, also testified against him. George Schmidt, a writer for the antiestablishment newspaper *Substance,* aggressively pursued the allegations as well.[12] Finally, the board instituted dismissal hearings—which also apply to principals—but was unsuccessful when state hearing officer John W. Schelthoff overruled the decision. "The hearing officer does not feel that a thirty-year distinguished career devoted to the education of the community's young should be destroyed on the basis of uncorroborated statements of self-acknowledged sexual miscreants, drug abusers, or a few disaffected teachers with obvious personal motives."[13]

In 1987, Moffat was sentenced to fifteen years in prison for pressuring five male and female students into having sex with him in his office at Kelvyn Park.

At Truth Elementary School on the Near West Side, principal Pernecie Pugh and school board lawyers worked unsuccessfully for more than than two years to dismiss Sheila Golub, a twenty-one-year teaching veteran whose alleged abuse of a third grader in September 1990 sent the youngster to seek medical attention for a head injury, state records show. Although Golub claimed she was trying to prevent the child from spinning out of control, the Illinois Department of Children and Family Services investigated the incident and ruled the complaint legitimate, according to state records. Meanwhile, parents petitioned to remove the teacher, who, they charged, hit students and came to class with urine and feces stains on her clothing. Principal Pugh testified she confronted Golub about menstruation stains as well and accused the teacher of excessive absenteeism, tardiness, and smoking in school. The school board issued a formal warning in December 1990 that if Golub did not correct her behavior, she would be dismissed. Five months after the first incident, however, Golub was accused of pushing, grabbing, and hitting five more children and slamming a sixth child's hand in a book. The school board dismissed her the following March. In her dismissal hearing before the state, Golub denied the abuse allegations made by seven children, two parents, and the principal. She also denied that Pugh warned her against using corporal punishment. In January 1992, hearing officer Julius Menacker upheld the board action.[14]

But it did not end there. The teacher appealed to the Cook County Circuit Court and, in April 1993, was reinstated with two years' back pay. Judge Mary Jane Theis ruled her actions were not "irremediable" because the second set of injuries were not severe enough. In fact, there were no physical marks on the third graders. Theis wrote: "The incidents in the third grade classroom of Miss Golub could not be termed severe or premeditated. The principal observed no injuries to any of the children and no medical treatment was sought." In addition, previous principals had rated the teacher as satisfactory or excellent, a conclusion that ultimately worked against Pugh. Besides, the judge sympathized with the teacher: "The children's testimony before the hearing officer reveals a classroom totally out of control. Maintaining discipline in that setting would have been difficult for the most able teacher."[15]

The community was so enraged that the principal feared for the teacher's safety and successfully won her a nonteaching transfer in late spring 1993 to a subdistrict office. District officials at the time were trying to find her a teaching job in another school. During the hearing, Pugh said, the union accused her of trying to fire the teacher because of a personal vendetta. In self-defense, Pugh testified she would not have sought the dismissal had it not been for the alleged abuse. Pugh was indignant: "It is hard to get rid of a teacher—even when they are hurting children. It is *hard.*"

In yet another case, Laura Ward Elementary School teacher Eli Johnson, who was fired in 1986 for allegedly pushing a fourth grader into a wall and throwing him on the floor, was reinstated with back pay in 1988. Hospital X-rays revealed the child suffered a bruised rib. Hearing officer George Edward Larney agreed that evidence, including testimony from the boy's classmates, indicated the teacher used physical contact. But while the hearing officer said he deplored the physical force allegedly used on the boy, he found insufficient evidence to prove the student's injuries that day were the result of the teacher's abuse. For all anyone knew, the child could have fallen down the stairs or had been hit by the door when leaving the classroom, Larney wrote. Besides, although the boy had above-average reading scores, he had an explosive temper and frequently disrupted class. The teacher, Larney noted, had an otherwise unblemished record and had already "endured a certain amount of anguish" associated with the case. In addition, there was no evidence that Johnson was unable to correct his behavior, a criteria required by law, Larney wrote.[16]

Johnson returned to Ward School in 1990 only to receive another unsatisfactory work notice in 1991 for improper classroom behavior and verbal abuse of students, according to state records. At that point, he took one year's leave of absence, state records show. He returned and received another notice, partly again for verbal abuse, records show. In March 1991, the school board issued a formal warning stemming from a report that Johnson pushed four more children.

Three months later, he was accused of grabbing another student by her throat and pushing her across the classroom, according to testimony given at his dismissal hearing. In short, his seventh-grade classroom was described as being out of control. Fights erupted regularly, including one in which a child hit another student with a window shade. Johnson allegedly had no concept of how to teach and assigned little, if any, homework, testimony showed. He conceded that "he did not make a teaching program, nor keep a record of attendance or grades of his students" but blamed the principal for never telling him to do so. Johnson had worked twenty-nine years in Chicago public schools. His dismissal was upheld by hearing officer Thomas R. McMillen in December 1992, more than six years after the first recorded incident.[17] Parents had petitioned for his removal, which helped the case considerably because it indicated that Johnson's behavior harmed the Northwest Side school, an important criterion for dismissal.

In 1993, a hearing officer overturned the school board's dismissal of Piccolo Elementary School teacher Beverly Anderson for tardiness. Principal Linda Sienkiewicz alleged the teacher was tardy 143 days of approximately 180 days during the 1989–90 school year and 82 days the following school year. Sienkiewicz further charged that Anderson had falsified time sheets. Hearing officer Corinne Hallett recognized, however, that the teacher had greatly improved on-time arrivals, therefore meeting one criterion for reinstatement. The tardies, Hallett concluded, were for good reasons: medical appointments and construction on the nightmarish Dan Ryan expressway. In addition, an engine had blown out in the teacher's new car, and it took her one year because of legal action to get it replaced. In the meantime, she had to rely on friends and fellow teachers to get to school.

Hallett acknowledged the expressway construction as a factor and ruled that since Sienkiewicz had given Anderson an excellent rating in another area, the teacher did not receive sufficient warning that her job was in jeopardy. Repeated verbal and written warnings, including a formal warning resolution adopted by the school board in its monthly meeting, were not enough. Hallett ruled the "excellent" evaluation lulled the teacher into a false sense of job security. "Sienkiewicz could have been more emphatic on the evaluation using words like 'outrageous tardiness' with a detailed explanation under the 'weaknesses,'" Hallett wrote in her decision. In addition, Hallett agreed, as the teacher claimed, that Anderson probably did occasionally stop to talk with parents or colleagues before signing in. Forcing her to sign-in at 8:30 a.m. or before was "an untenable exaltation of form over substance," Hallett wrote. She also noted that "absent her transportation and serious medical problems, respondent may well have made far more improvement." Anderson was reinstated partly because of a "total lack of evidence" that her conduct damaged the students, faculty, or school as required by case law to dismiss a teacher. Although she missed staff meetings, Anderson regularly arrived on time for classes.[18] The ruling was appealed, and the case was pending in 1993, according to union attorneys.

In 1992, Sienkiewicz—who, like Pugh at Truth School and Fields at Ray School, became a principal under reform—took the issue of tardiness even further. She issued warnings and began docking employees a half hour's pay after their tardies accumulated to thirty minutes. The Chicago Teachers Union filed a grievance against her. Although accumulating tardies is not prohibited in the teachers' contract, it does violate a long-standing practice, and changes involving such practices must be negotiated. The contract also specified that any Chicago Teachers Union member who calls in with an emergency but works three-fourths of a day is paid for a full day's work.

When Sienkiewicz arrived in 1990, some staff members, including nonteaching staff, were regularly tardy, Piccolo council chair Pamela Price alleged. "We had people coming in at 9:30, 10 o'clock, 10:30, 11," she said. "Some principals don't dock them, and she did. That's why she's getting all this flak."[19]

Testimony in the teacher dismissal case supported Price's contention: the previous principal was lax about tardiness. Ironically, that was one reason why Sienkiewicz lost her case. The hearing officer ruled that teachers came to view tardies as tacitly approved because of the practice of the previous principal.[20]

The issue of tardiness at Piccolo School stirred great controversy. Some teachers were also unhappy about excessive and unexcused tardiness among colleagues, as teacher Rickie Cochrane explained in a guest column for the *Chicago Sun-Times*. "After all, tardiness impacts not only students but teachers as well. Each time a teacher is tardy, colleagues must cover classrooms in addition to carrying out their regular duties and responsibilities. If a supportive staff member is tardy, teachers miss valuable prep periods."[21] But Cochrane objected to the perception that all tardy Piccolo staff are teachers and that all teachers, some of whom work many extra hours to develop new and innovative curricula, are lumped together.

As Cochrane illustrates, problem teachers influence the entire system. It is not only their ghastly effect on children, who may forever miss out on multiplication tables or key grammar lessons or who may learn to detest school so fiercely they drop out. It is not only society's clear message that these children do not matter. Problem teacher behavior also casts a pall on good teachers, who because of their commitment to city children, refuse to leave for usually better-managed and amply-supplied suburban schools. Tragically, good teachers get swept up in the broad label of bad teaching. More important, they must contend with the aftermath. A diligent sixth-grade teacher who succeeds an apathetic fifth-grader teacher, for example, must try to compensate for lost time. Indeed, a 1993 survey of union delegates shows that teachers understand the injury caused by incompetent colleagues. Seventy-nine percent of the union's own delegates consider removing poorly performing teachers a problem, the Chicago school reform magazine *Catalyst* found. Twenty percent call it a slight problem, 29 percent a moderate problem, 12 percent a definite problem, and 17 percent a serious problem. The only issue considered more serious than dismissing poorly performing teachers is insufficient amounts of teaching materials.[22]

The problem of difficult dismissals applies to more than just teachers. Due process hearings in Illinois also extend to non-teaching employees, ranging from principals to custodians. Imagine trying to reform a long troubled system without the authority to dismiss incompetent employees in a timely manner. At Truth Elementary School, where Pernecie Pugh is principal, a security guard convicted of drug dealing remained on the payroll for months. The school is located in Cabrini-Green, a high-crime public housing development that made national headlines for the 1992 sniper killing of seven-year-old Dantrell Davis as he walked to school. After the guard's conviction, he was moved to a subdistrict office, which meant the job was technically filled. "He's still on the payroll, and we can't replace him," complained council president Wanda Hopkins five months after his conviction in May 1992. "Every time I call the law department, they say, 'We're working on it.' " The board's law department must follow proper procedures, which includes notifying the employee of the charges and asking the state to set up a discharge hearing. The hearing, in itself, involves an additional series of steps.[23]

The school board underwent the hearing process twice for Kathy Erby, a clerk, who was assigned to clerical duties alternately at the central office and in schools. Within four months of being reinstated after her first dismissal for tardiness and absenteeism, Erby faced the same allegations again and was reassigned, according to state records of her dismissal. In May 1991, she was suspended for five days. In the nearly four months that followed, she was allegedly late nineteen times and absent twenty-five days, half of them without notifying her supervisors, even on the days she was supposed to meet with them to discuss her absenteeism, state records show. During her dismissal hearing, Erby offered a litany of excuses: she had to take care of her children, she had strep throat for one week, she had a deaf mother for whom she cared, she had no telephone, and she could not afford money to use the pay phone to notify her supervisor. In addition, Erby resented being assigned to a "very boring" job of alphabetizing overtime reports, a job for which she was not "trained" and one she did not enjoy.

The teachers union, which represents both teaching and some nonteaching employees in legal proceedings before the state, argued that Erby's previous dismissal should not have been entered into evidence because all disciplinary actions are expunged after one year, as required in union agreements. Hearing officer Herbert M. Berman allowed the evidence anyway but only to show that the clerk was given adequate warning about her absenteeism, a key requirement of law. Erby's second dismissal was upheld more than one-and-one-half years after she was reinstated from her first dismissal. During part of that time, she was bounced from one central office department to another, then to a school and back to central office.[24]

The cases that reach hearing status represent only a fraction of the problem, as the principals' survey showed. Many principals and administrators simply do not have the time or energy to fight. When Ray School became classified as a specialty school, it won more freedom to select its staff, allowing it to transfer several teachers to other schools. Some teachers, in the opinion of council president Marcy Schlessinger, were not the best performers. "That's how you always get rid of them: you maneuver and make tradeoffs," she said. "They never went out of the system. They just went to someone who didn't have the energy to fight them."

In defense of the controversial dismissal process, many teachers point to the public school system's long history of employment abuses, such as the practice of firing or demoting whistleblowers. The teachers union—whose attorneys were provided with the author's summary of the findings and declined to comment on specific cases—argues that the job of every union is to protect its members. And, it correctly notes, it has nothing to do with hiring incompetents. "The union doesn't hire them. So we're not going to dwell on it and be held accountable," said the late union president Jacqueline B. Vaughn. Some union members agree. "In my 23 years as a teacher in the Chicago school system, one thing has remained constant: poor management. Education in Chicago is provided in spite of, not because of, management policy. The bureaucracy is more concerned with politics and self-serving image building than with education," wrote Whitney Young Magnet Schoool union delegate Robert Mijou in a letter to the *Chicago Sun-Times*.[25] Says union officer Kotsakis, "The reason we don't get incompetents removed from the classroom—and I'd say it's 1 to 2 percent—is, frankly, principals can't look the person in the eye and do it."[26]

While Republican legislators in Illinois joined in an unlikely partnership with Mayor Daley to advocate changes in the state hearing process, Democratic heavyweight Michael Madigan, speaker of the house, blocked such attempts. Madigan would not let certain bills affecting unions pass unless the unions agreed to them. Proposals to change the dismissal process were among them. "In all these kinds of areas, there needs to be give and take. Madigan's view is he's not for jamming things down people's throats," said spokesperson Steve Brown, who blamed hearing officers, not the law, for the problems. Besides, he pointed out, the union had already

agreed to some changes in law. At the beginn
for example, the union consented to reducing t'
period from one year to forty-five days ev‹
requirement for suburban and downstate distri‹
year. The change, however, does not diminish ‹.‹_
requirements for firing an employee, and 65 percent of Chicago elementary principals still consider removing poor teachers a serious problem despite reform, according to the survey
by the Consortium on Chicago School Research. Only 7 percent believe it is easier to remove a nonperforming teacher.
Due process is still unwieldly, leaving the state's third largest
employer at the mercy of a system that can throw incompetent
teachers back into classrooms because of technicalities.

As a consequence, children suffer.

How serious is the problem of poorly performing teachers in
Chicago public schools? Abysmal test scores may be one indicator. What's more, city principals rank the problem as one of
critical proportions. According to the consortium survey of elementary school principals, one third say that no more than half
their teachers have a good grasp of reading and language arts;
70 percent reveal that at least half of their staffs do not teach
science adequately. If true, such appalling statistics apply to
instructors who teach tens of thousands of children every day.[27]

The findings stand in stark contrast to teachers' views: More
than nine of ten elementary school teachers questioned in a
similar consortium survey are confident in their abilities to
teach basic subjects. Instead, they blame an inadequate home
and community environment for low student achievement.
Nearly 70 percent of teachers say student attitudes and habits
reduce children's chances for success. Even though most
teachers are positive about Chicago school reform, 45 percent
said in 1991 that the movement had no effect on classroom
practices whatsoever.[28]

The survey also indicates that morale is low among thousands of city teachers. Nearly 40 percent say they would not
become a teacher again if they could start over—compared to
5 percent nationally who "certainly" would not and 17 percent
who "probably" would not, according to a nationwide poll
conducted by the National Education Association.[29] Nearly a
quarter of Chicago elementary teachers surveyed say they do
not look forward to coming to school each day. This means

that three thousand teachers—twice that if the survey is representative of the entire teaching work force—stand before one hundred thousand to two hundred thousand children each day but have no desire to be there.

Children understand that. At Goodlow Magnet Upper School, eighth-grader Mark Tabb wrote what he would do if he became superintendent: "I would have a lot of unfit teachers fired because a lot of the teachers come to show off new clothes. That kind does not need to be a teacher. They need to be in a fashion show. Then we have the teachers who come just to get paid, they throw work on the board and figure they're through with that class . . . . We have the ones who don't like kids, and if they don't like them, they should not have become a teacher."[30] Some of the same children subjected to poor teaching today will become teachers themselves. And the cycle will repeat itself.

In fact, it already has.

A number of today's teachers themselves received a poor education in the system after its decline in the 1960s (although, obviously, there are gleaming exceptions throughout the city). Compared with their suburban counterparts, Chicago high schools have been staffed with less educated teachers from less selective colleges, according to a 1984 study by a University of Chicago team headed by then professor Gary Orfield. At that time, one out of four city high school teachers holding bachelor's degrees and one out of three with advanced degrees received them either from Chicago State or Northeastern Illinois universities. The study found that scores of incoming freshmen on the American College Test (ACT) averaged 13 and 14 points, respectively, on a 36-point scale. It is not known, however, how many Chicago public school teachers actually fell into this category. Orfield blamed the inferior education provided by city high schools, some of which did not offer key subjects crucial to college entry, including foreign languages, chemistry, physics, and honors or advanced placement math and science. "We are not saying that professors at less competitive schools are not doing a good job," Orfield said. "But it is not healthy when a school system with the greatest problems relies on colleges that get students with the most educational problems." Orfield called the cycle a "key link in a chain of inequality."[31]

The inequality has deep roots.

Some of the problems stem from the system's inability or unwillingness to meet needs created decades ago by a huge migration of African Americans from the South. Between 1940 and 1950 alone, Chicago's black population increased from more than 282,000 to nearly 510,000.[32] Schools that had six hundred children one year soared to twelve hundred the next. With the immigration came shortages of textbooks, supplies, classrooms, and teachers, which hit the African-American communities hardest.

Benjamin Willis, school superintendent from 1953 to 1966, became a symbol of the bitter feud over segregation in Chicago, then the most racially polarized city in the North. Indeed, the rate of segregation of black children in Illinois schools remains among the highest in the nation, according to a 1993 study conducted by Orfield who, by that time, had become director of the Harvard University Project on School Desegregation.[33] Mobile classrooms brought in by Willis, allegedly to keep blacks in their own schools, were dubbed "Willis wagons." While laws in southern states separating black and white children were ruled unconstitutional by the U.S. Supreme Court, de facto segregation such as the situation in Chicago was found to be equally egregious even though legislators were not guilty of formalizing it into state law. Willis would not bus black children to better-equipped white schools or even to disclose how many empty classrooms those schools contained, according to historian Mary J. Herrick.[34] When he finally did release information, it was apparently inaccurate. Some unused classrooms in white schools were considered filled, even though they were used for special services, such as nursing stations, for which space did not exist in black schools. He calculated the space in white schools based on thirty children in a class; the average was thirty-two and, in many black schools, more than forty.

School days were cut in half in the overcrowded schools— primarily, although not exclusively, in African-American communities.[35] Veteran educator Grace Dawson, a one-time principal and later head of the system's division of dropout prevention, remembers those days: "When I went to grammar school in Chicago, there were forty-eight kids in a classroom. From first to fourth grade, everybody went a half day."

Books and materials were in short supply. Coles Elementary School council member Melvin Johnson recalled getting used books with the math problems already worked out. Johnson wondered why he always received used textbooks, stamped with the names of North Side schools, or no books at all. One day—the memory remains vivid—he visited Disney Magnet School on the primarily white North Side: "I saw with my own eyes brand new microscopes and equipment locked away unused—and I knew of schools on the South Side where entire classrooms of students were sharing one or two microscopes."[36]

The shortages extended beyond textbooks and classrooms. The exodus of teachers and the influx of children created a severe teacher shortage. Moreover, many veteran teachers left as the complexion of Chicago's schoolchildren changed. In 1962, the system employed about 25,000 teachers for 491,000 students. Just four years later, student enrollment had grown by 86,000, but the ranks of teachers dropped by 2,500. In 1967, schools opened 700 teachers short.[37]

The school board's solution partly lay in the hiring of substitute teachers, even those who could not pass a basic competency exam. The system saved money by paying substitutes far less than their tenured counterparts. In 1968, nearly seven thousand substitute teachers—some of whom had already taught for a decade or more—went on strike demanding tenure and comparable pay and benefits. As part of the settlement, substitutes who did not pass the competency exam but had worked for three years with satisfactory ratings within the system were hired permanently and given tenure.[38] While the substitutes deserved to be treated fairly and paid fully—especially since they had taught so long already—the effects were clear, at least in Dawson's opinion. "A lot of bad teachers got into the system then—all they had to do was hang on for three years. Most of the time when new teachers came in, they were either really young or substitute teachers. All the black teachers got black kids. You can see, most of the children in the black community were taught by substitute teachers."

Studies at the time by the Chicago Urban League confirmed that black schools received less money per child than schools in wealthier white neighborhoods, mainly because black schools had proportionally fewer highly paid and experienced teachers and more low-paid substitutes.[39] Years after her graduation from DuSable High School, Dawson discovered that some of her own teachers had been substitutes. "When I started teaching, I realized the teachers who taught me never passed their examination," said Dawson, who holds masters' and doctoral degrees. "I got my certificate before they did."

Not everyone agrees with Dawson's assessment. Political activist Conrad Worrill, a professor and director of inner-city studies at Northeastern Illinois University in Chicago, said the substitute teachers could not pass the oral examination because many came from the South and spoke with a pronounced Southern accent. "They used the oral examination against the blacks by failing large numbers of blacks saying they could not speak properly. That led to the organizing of the black teacher caucus. There were some school board meetings where chairs were actually thrown at school board members over this issue of school certification," Worrill said. In 1967, substitutes charged that both the written and oral exams were based on white middle-class values and, therefore, automatically discriminated against blacks.

The situation worsened as jobs with better salaries opened elsewhere for women and minorities. "If you look at the 1960s, it was the brightest women who went into teaching and nursing," said Margaret M. Harrigan, the system's associate superintendent for human resources. "I don't know that the brightest women are doing that now or have been for the past twenty years. They're going into board rooms, court rooms, operating rooms, but not into classrooms in the same numbers that they did."

The breakdown of families and mounting social problems exacerbated the shortage, making teaching far more difficult than before. "The social conditions have worn out the professional educators," Worrill said. "They're beat down. They're demoralized. They're in war zones."

What is the answer to improving the quality of teaching? Paying teachers well is certainly a significant step. The interim Chicago school board attempted to do just that in 1990 by negotiating a three-year contract promising teachers and other employees 7 percent raises each year. Subsequent financial crises, however, chipped away at the raises when it became clear they cost far more than the system could afford. Nevertheless, beginning pay for a first-year teacher with a bachelor's degree rose from $24,717 in 1990—the first year of the contract—to $29,147, including a pension fund contribution, for a thirty-nine-week work year in 1993.[40] By then, the average pay topped $43,000 for a teacher.[41] But such pay—the tenth highest of forty-seven of the nation's largest school districts, according to one survey[42]—should have been accompanied by requirements for a commensurately higher performance. It was not. In the view of experts, this lack of higher standards bucked a nationwide trend. "Policymakers have made it very clear that they want to grant additional benefits to teachers only in exchange for the creation of a more performance-based profession," wrote Lorraine M. McDonnell and Anthony Pascal in the Rand Corporation's *Teacher Unions and Educational Reform.* "At the same time, rank-and-file teachers have become accustomed to a system that allocates benefits uniformly on the basis of seniority and educational attainment; they expect unions to preserve that system."[43]

Nationwide, states are experimenting with measures to ensure that teachers are qualified. Some states, for example, require teachers to be recertified, for which they must take an exam, do coursework in their field, or undergo classroom observation once every few years. In 1990, states that required a periodic assessment totaled fifteen, according to the Council of Chief State School Officers in Washington, D.C. They consisted of Florida, Georgia, Iowa, Massachusetts, Montana, New Mexico, New York, North Carolina, Oklahoma, Oregon, Tennessee, Texas, Virginia, West Virginia, and Wisconsin.[44]

In Georgia, more than three hundred practicing teachers lost both their certification and their jobs because they failed to pass the state's teacher competency test in 1987, some of them after nine attempts, *Education Week* reported. The test was introduced under a 1985 state reform law that required teachers who wanted to renew their credentials to pass a subject-area test.[45]

Adopting competency exams in Illinois would not likely pass a legislature that is so heavily influenced by union clout and campaign contributions. But many believe such tests would be effective. Margaret M. Harrigan, who once supervised curriculum for the school system, is among them. "There's so much new, and what was adequate ten or fifteen years ago would not be adequate now. Much changes, particularly in the area of science. It would keep teachers better informed, more up to date, more alert."

One way to test teachers would be to base examinations on the curriculum guides that the system prepared in 1990 to describe what students should learn at each grade level. Or, as one teacher suggested, teachers could be given the elementary school version of the same achievement test given to students. Such a test would weed out teachers who do not have basic knowledge, such as the number of states in the union—one teacher's deficiency as recalled by a former student whose mother was so horrified she promptly moved her to a private school.

In 1992, nine Chicago teachers crossed bureaucratic hurdles to form Foundations School, a Chicago public school on the South Side where teachers have developed creative ways to increase both parent involvement and teacher accountability. This was done in many ways, both major and small, which included giving teachers access to classroom telephones, allowing students to visit cultural institutions one afternoon per week, and replacing conventional grading with elaborate exhibitions of students' work.

For their children to be accepted, parents must sign a pact agreeing to several points: 1) to provide their children with quiet places to study, 2) to obtain Chicago public library cards for both parents and children, 3) to read to their children a bedtime story every night and help them with their homework, and 4) to volunteer three hours a week at the school.

For their part, teachers contribute countless extra hours to their regular school schedule and, in an unusual move, leave parents with their home telephone numbers. Teachers must also submit to rigorous evaluations by peers, students, and parents. If improvement is deemed necessary, they undergo training by colleagues; if, after the training period is completed, they still fail peer evaluations, they leave voluntarily. In turn, the school agrees to help the teacher find a job elsewhere in the system under the assumption that only a difference of philosophy may be at fault. Nevertheless, asking a teacher to leave is more difficult than overcoming any bureaucratic obstacle, concedes Foundations teacher Lynn Cherkasky-Davis.

Other ideas to improve teacher competence have been suggested, most of which significantly tread on traditional teachers' rights. To protect children, for example, state law should require police departments to notify school districts when they know they have arrested any school employee for sex, violent, or narcotics offenses. Further, offers school board attorney Joyce Combest Price, teachers fired through the state process should lose the board's contribution to their pension funds. Educational experts may also wish to consider depriving teachers and principals dismissed through the regular channels of their certificates, either permanently or temporarily. Or, as Mayor Daley suggests, perhaps the state hearing process should be eliminated entirely. School districts, in agreement with their unions, could then set up their own procedures for firing employees. In that vein, retired principal William Rankin suggests placing teachers who do not receive excellent or superior ratings on probation. After three years with such a status, they would lose seniority rights and tenure. "A lot of teachers burn out—they truly burn out," he said. "They may have started like a ball of fire but, in the end, some of them are really coasting, and some of them coast for years."

Or, teachers and principals could be held accountable through review boards, suggests Bob Law, a New York City radio talk show host and chair of the Respect Yourself youth organization. "Part of our concern with school systems around the country is how teachers are unaccountable," he declares. "There is no review board. If they were any other licensed professional, you could take them to the Bar Association or the American Medical Association or the Better Business Bureau. There is no one you can take a teacher to, and it's really the result of teacher unions' power." Ridding the system of failing teachers is left to principals or members of the administration, who may or may not be particularly competent or caring themselves. Some principals hire incompetent relatives and friends in order to build their political power bases when it comes to contract-renewal time, some teachers allege. The alternative to nonexistent legal means of protest is civil disobedience. "When there is nothing you can do legally, you have to close the school down and sit in and do all kinds of activism which should not be required of parents," Law remarked.

But there is a gentler way of improving the quality of the teaching work force and that is properly training teachers. Some states recognize that training teachers in today's rapidly advancing technological society is crucial. Under Kentucky's sweeping 1990 reform law, for example, more than $1 billion new state dollars were invested into education, part of which were used for teacher training. Eight regional centers for teachers and administrators were created, and school boards were permitted to allocate as many as five instructional days for staff development. In 1992, individual districts were awarded $17 per student for ongoing training. "We put more training money into this than we've ever had before," Robert F. Sexton, executive director of a citizens' advocacy group, told *Education Week*. "Over all, a remarkable amount. But it's still not enough. The scale and scope of this thing is so huge that there's almost a bottomless pit of need."[46]

In 1990, the interim Chicago school board attempted to address teacher training by providing a $6,000 bonus to teachers who went back to school to obtain more semester hours. The intent was to increase the quality of teaching, but a program that was praiseworthy in concept backfired when it came to the details. The key deficiency was that the courses did not have to relate to the teachers' schoolwork. "It was a joke," says Grace Dawson. "Everybody in the schools was laughing about it. You didn't have to take a sequence of courses. You could get a hodge podge of courses. Some went and took courses like calligraphy [or] business entrepreneurship." More than three thousand teachers applied for the bonus during the first year alone of the contract, at a cost of more than $19 million—triple what the system expected to pay.[47] The $6,000 was to be spread over five years.

In 1993, the school board negotiated a teachers' contract that, while eliminating the incentive for teachers who had not yet begun the additional training, added five fully paid training days to the 1994–95 school year. Until then, Chicago public school teachers had only one day to prepare for the new school year, a practice rated as disastrous in the 1992 principals' survey. Only 3 percent "strongly agreed" with the statement that there was adequate time for teachers' professional development.[48]

In addition to offering the training incentive, the Chicago school system and state law allow school councils to spend poverty funds for teacher training. The system also runs an innovative recruitment program called Teachers for Chicago, partially funded by a five-year $462,000 grant from the Chicago Community Trust. Through participating colleges and universities, the program offers free tuition for a master's degree to liberal arts graduates and professionals from other fields who are seeking a career change. In exchange, participants agree to work in the Chicago public schools. With some twelve hundred applicants, the system selects one hundred candidates per year. As substitute teachers, they receive benefits while attending classes. Interns who have already served under experienced teachers are put in charge of their own classrooms.[49]

The Chicago Teachers Union also set up teacher training programs through its so-called Quest Center, which provides technical assistance and awards grants to model schools. Funded with a $1.5 million MacArthur Foundation grant, it has been singled out by University of Illinois associate professor William Ayers as a reason for hope in otherwise traditionally confrontational union-board relations. The Quest Center, Ayers wrote in *A Union of Professionals, Labor Relations and Educational Reform,* "represents the most visible attempt to promote teacher-led educational change; it is also a counterpower within the union, a force for a new approach to union activity."[50]

There are a plethora of other training efforts launched by outside organizations under Chicago reform. The movement, for example, helped teachers like Sylvester Bradshaw, whose teaching at Emmet Elementary School was hampered by a nagging contradiction between a proposed curriculum and the realities of an inner-city classroom on the West Side. His students had sixth-grade textbooks, but lagged years behind in reading. "If you've got third-grade readers and a sixth-grade curriculum, what do you do?" he asked. "We try to find a curriculum at the lower level, but so far very few publishers have addressed that." His solution is makeshift: "We do a lot of talking."

But under a five-year program funded with $3.7 million from the Kellogg Foundation and $2.4 million from the University of Illinois at Chicago, Bradshaw found access to experts who could address such critical concerns. As the result of collaboration with university faculty, Bradshaw's students began writing their own books and book reviews.

Bond Elementary School on the South Side used grant money from the same program to pay teachers for an additional two days' preparation time at the beginning of the school year. "It's the first time we've ever been able to do it," principal Donald I. Prather said. "Can you imagine coming to school with one day to prepare?" Through the program, named Nation of Tomorrow from a reference made by Theodore Roosevelt to America's children, teachers critique each other through videotapes, providing the type of feedback so desperately needed in Chicago schools. "It's helping to eliminate the terrible isolation that we feel," one teacher told a program evaluator. It was an eye-opener for Mark Smylie, assistant professor of education at the University of Illinois at Chicago. "In some of the schools," he said, "teachers are talking to one another for the first time in their careers."[51]

Chicago school superintendent Argie K. Johnson.

Courtesy *Chicago Sun-Times*. Photo by Rich Chapman.

6

Everybody Passes

The school promotion policy is simple: Everyone passes. I have one child in my room who has never handed in a completed paper—usually not even an uncompleted paper. This child has all F's on his report card. You guessed it: my promotion list came back to pass this child.

A fourth-grade Chicago schoolteacher[1]

It's called *social promotion,* a kind term for a criminal practice: herding tens of thousands of students through a school system without demanding high standards and providing students with the help they need to meet them. "We're still moving kids out of grammar school who come out with a piece of paper saying they're graduates—but they come into high schools with third, fourth, and fifth-grade reading levels," Calumet High School council chairperson Edwin Green declared. "They're destined to fail."

To understand the effect of social promotion—and, frankly, poor education—one need only listen to teacher Jenny Conti recount her teaching debut when she designed a bulletin board for a sixth-grade classroom. Conti recalled: "When I went in the room to hang it up, two students came up to me and said, 'That's pretty . . . . What does it say?'"

At Malcolm X, part of the city's community college system, 40 percent of applicants who held high school diplomas tested below eighth-grade literacy levels while 30 percent tested below sixth grade, according to Joe Layng, director of the college's academic support center. In 1994, the college offered a special program designed to help such students, eight of whom worked on basic word sounds after tests revealed it was necessary—although high school graduates, they read at second grade levels.[2]

If test scores are an indicator, the problem of poor achievement is wider than a handful of anecdotes. It is, in fact, an epidemic. Nearly 60 percent of Chicago public high schools ranked in the bottom 1 percent of the nation on the ACT college entrance exam in 1992—and only 2 of 64 schools surpassed the national average.[3] Only five of sixty-three high schools had average eleventh-grade reading scores above state averages, and only four achieved that distinction in math. Those scores—the likes of which prompted Chicago's monumental reform movement in the first place—reflected the best students since nearly half of the enrollment did not even graduate from high school.[4]

The statistics are equally grim for elementary schools. Only forty-six of nearly four hundred elementary schools that tested eighth-grade reading have levels exceeding the state average in that subject.[5] In Chicago, schools that fare well—and some do extraordinarily well, outpacing even the best suburban schools—are primarily magnet schools, which choose the children they educate.[6] Officials at those schools, which have long waiting lists, fume at labels that lump them together with the "worst in America."

Former school superintendent Ted D. Kimbrough blamed widespread failure on inadequate teaching and poor school management. In 1992, he threatened to close the worst schools: "If there is no improvement, the board has the responsibility to do something about it—fire the principal, remove the local school council, or close the school."[7] Kimbrough was, once again, right. But the takeover threats came from an administration that fostered the school decline partly by demoralizing the workforce.

"Why should we as teachers give a damn about the school system?" That was the pointed question put to *Chicago Sun-Times* columnist Raymond R. Coffey in as disturbing and depressing a letter as had ever come the way of the veteran newspaperman. The following excerpt reveals one teacher's tale of desperation:

Why are we dissatisfied? For some of the following reasons: We are tired of being called [expletive] and everything else you can think of. We are tired of machines that don't work. We are tired of ordering books and getting the wrong ones. Most of us now just let them gather dust in the book room. As a qualified teacher who has to work with a "free ride" principal, I have given up. I have been in her office more times this year than in my previous long career. OK, if she wants the animals passed at any cost, that is what she will get. But the students won't get an education.[8]

Coffey dubbed the letter writer "burnt out teacher" and asked other teachers to comment. Dozens responded.

Our kids do not have the slightest idea about proper behavior in a classroom. They are loud, crude and very often extremely dumb and/or lazy. Most want something for nothing (the welfare mentality). They are street smart and great con artists. They intimidate the teachers. Teachers rarely speak out because they are afraid of repercussions. So, we plod along hating every minute of it and looking forward to the day's end or the weekend or the next vacation. There is no reward being a teacher other than the paycheck. What is still amazing to me is that 99 percent of the teachers I know still go into the classroom each day and try like hell to present lessons.[9]

In their own words, teachers supplied a devastating answer to the vexing question of how a child could emerge from twelve years of schooling as an educational cripple: "Unfortunately, the barbarians have stormed the gates. Most are sleeping or fooling around in my classes," wrote the same teacher who called truancy and tardiness rampant. "The inmates are indeed running the asylum."

The author of the original "burnt out teacher" letter was equally blunt about what occurred in his classroom: "If you think for one minute that I have been doing anything for the past 20 years, you're crazy . . . I save my energy for the second job, as do all teachers who work two jobs."[10]

Other teachers acknowledged similar conditions, but they chided the writer for giving up too easily and not being single-minded enough:

> I'm heartened by today's youngsters. I find great hope in their ability to cope and seek for better answers. A teacher can't let the bureaucratic system cloud the way, or be an excuse for not caring about the students and their future.[11]

> Why don't I feel like 'Burnt Out Teacher?' Maybe it's because I feel that I have been called to teach. Maybe it's because I feel that in some small way, I am making a difference in some child's life. All I know is that I love children . . . and I love teaching.[12]

> Please refer to me as an Urban Missionary. I didn't have to cross the ocean to minister to the less fortunate. They're right here in Chicago. I look to the children rather than the administration for signs of hope.[13]

But hope has a constant competitor; namely, a despair prompted by social and family problems that rob troubled children of the most basic understanding of decency and discipline. One elementary school teacher recalled her horror year—a surprise assignment to a classroom with the school's most difficult children, many themselves casualties of abuse. Strange noises prompted her to open a locker one day only to find two seventh graders having sex. Horrified, she slammed it shut. An eleven-year-old student—who police informed her was a pimp—routinely masturbated in class. The principal responded to the teacher's plea for help by placing a screen around the child's desk.[14]

The system is besieged by deep family problems that mercilessly taunt teachers to surrender to burnout. Children sense their teachers' disdain—sometimes it is combined with the same attitude from their own parents—and find no incentive to produce. The alternative to burnout is assuming the exhausting role of parents to emotionally abandoned children, many parented themselves by equally troubled children. Teachers are forced to battle against social ills—a given in many urban settings—but they also must cope with an unlikely enemy: the system. It is a system that, while spending millions in central office, cut or completely eliminated reading programs, truant officers, alternative schools, librarians, and the critical Head Start preschool program.

Many teachers point to social promotion as another example of how they are at odds with the administration. In surveys by the National Center for Education Information, 74 percent of teachers and 91 percent of prospective teachers believe that children should be required to perform at grade level before passing to the next grade.[15] But citing educational research that says children who are retained do not improve academically and are more likely to drop out, the Chicago Board of Education prohibits retaining a child more than once in elementary school.[16] Some students catch on and understand that once they fail a grade they can slide all the way to eighth-grade graduation with little effort.

In one elementary school class, nine students received Fs and two students received Ds for a five-week marking period. The best student completed eleven of sixteen assignments, but the majority finished between one and eight assignments. "These grades were based on whether or not they even *tried* to do the work. Quality, directions, and anything else were not a factor. If they *don't even try,* I cannot help them," said the teacher who supplied copies of her grade book to *Sun-Times* journalist Raymond R. Coffey. She attached a note from the principal, which said, "There are still too many children failing. Pls. see me on Monday, Jan. 9th to discuss the composition handbook."[17]

"Achievement?" wrote another teacher. "We do the best we can. We are getting very little help from anyone. Many principals blame us and lower our ratings for having a 'high failure rate.' I refuse to pass a student who does not come to school and achieve *something.* I refuse to be bullied or intimidated. I will be a good teacher, or I will not teach at all."[18]

Although Illinois discourages schools from promoting students for social reasons, Chicago's philosophy seemingly stands at odds with the law. The school board requires that all fifteen-year-olds automatically qualify for high school, regardless of whether they receive eighth-grade diplomas. The policy is based on two theories: partly on the premise that fifteen-year-olds would disrupt elementary schools and easily influence younger children in areas such as dating or gang recruitment and partly on the assumption that flunking students does little more than demoralize them.

For DuSable High School principal Charles E. Mingo, the policy meant discovering that a fifteen-year-old student who arrived in the fall of 1992 had only a fifth-grade education. The system, which provided few alternative schools, required she stay in high school. "There are hundreds of kids like her," Mingo said. "In order to get the pattern, you have to get the folder [paperwork], but in high school the folders don't come until eight or nine weeks after the student comes. If I knew I had fifteen or twenty coming in, I'd put them in a special class."[19]

School administrators who developed the promotion policy do not specifically advocate social promotion. Instead, they suggest a host of strategies that can help children catch up with their peers. These include tutoring, special homework assignments, counseling, summer school, reduced class size, an extended school day, praise for student successes, university and business collaboration, and involvement in health services. For parents, they include homework study plans, family counseling, and an outline of expectations for student attendance and behavior. Schools that achieve despite enormous odds against them prove such practices can work. But behind those strategies lies the assumption that every school cares enough to help children. Not all do.

Indeed, obstacles to achievement that originate in the schools themselves are well documented. They range from abuse of funds intended for children to complaints of principals who build patronage armies to ensure that their employment contracts are renewed. A major problem has been the flagrant misuse of study halls, first exposed in 1986 by the Chicago Panel on Public School Policy and Finance. The group revealed that some high schools assigned students to study halls one or two periods a day to meet the state-required three hundred minutes of instruction; 40 percent of students in eight schools received as few as two hundred minutes of daily instruction because study halls were scheduled for first and last period. The panel's study was called "Where's Room 185?" and was based on the three days a researcher spent looking for a room where, according to school records, a study hall was located. In fact, the room did not even exist.[20]

The panel reported that suburban students received, on the average, 20 percent more instruction in subjects such as English, math, and history than Chicago students. Republican legislation proposed in 1993, however, would have prohibited using study halls to fulfill the required three hundred minutes of instruction a day and, coincidentally, would have also banned the system's practice of not assigning new teachers a month or six weeks into the school year. The bill was withdrawn after school systems throughout the state protested that such a change would be expensive and would require renegotiating teacher contracts since teachers, too, used study halls to fulfill state requirements for instruction. In Chicago, however, such legislation is no longer necessary. In 1993, the school board eliminated study halls by mandating that eleven forty-minute high school periods be changed to fifty minutes each, which provided fewer periods in the high school day.

Besides using phantom study halls, schools engaged in other questionable practices in the name of education. Holding retreats at Wisconsin and Illinois resorts was a popular custom among Chicago educators and school council members, who argued that acquainting teachers with one another in a relaxed resort setting improved morale and, in some cases, persuaded them to begin a one-on-one dialogue for the first time in decades. Subdistrict 10 council member Larry A. Nowlin, who participated in ten to twelve resort trips as a volunteer council member during the first three years of reform, had a more interesting defense. In June 1992, about two hundred teachers and subdistrict council members traveled to a Wisconsin resort for a three-day drug abuse prevention seminar at a cost of $50,000. The resort offered horseback riding, boating, indoor and outdoor pools, a health club, tennis courts, miniature golf, swimming, and a marina with boat rentals. When the trip received publicity, Nowlin complained: "We didn't have time to enjoy the horseback riding, all the saunas, or the whirlpools. We have produced dynamite programs that will help reduce drugs, gangs, and promiscuous sex in District 10." Nowlin said it was not the luxuries that drew the Chicago crowd to the Wisconsin resort. It was the last-minute announcement that federal drug prevention money was available but had to be used by the June 30 deadline. "This money was going to go back to the government and then anybody could have gotten it," he insisted.[21] The same type of funds was used elsewhere in the system to work directly with children, helping them write plays, poetry, videos, and music with a drug-free theme.[22] The federal funds are used in some school districts to hire security staff, according to U.S. Department of Education officials.

In other areas that some felt worked against a sound education, many elementary schools adopted a shorter school day that eliminated most recess time for children, giving them a twenty-minute lunch period and a ten-minute recess break. Advantages for educators were great: namely, a workday that ran from 8:30 a.m. to 2:30 p.m. and freedom from the nuisance of settling playground skirmishes. But, in the view of administrator and former principal Margaret M. Harrigan, children lost an important outlet for blowing off steam and the opportunity it brought to arrive ready to learn for afternoon classes.

There were other examples. Principals were allowed to take their vacation at their convenience. Thus, if they wished, they could take weeks off anytime during the school year. Also, because educators were allowed to accumulate sick days from year to year—for a maximum of 275 sick days during the span of their service—some waited until their last year, typically following a routine of four-days-off and one day on. This could continue for months at a time. (A physician's note is required after four days' absence.)

"It's expected," said school social worker Bernie R. Noven, head of the reform group Parents United for Responsible Education. "I was in one school where we had five or six teachers go through a classroom one year." Absent teachers could not be replaced because their positions were technically filled, leaving substitutes to teach the children. To offset this "time-honored tradition," in the words of Lloyd W. Lehman, the Cook County superintendent of schools, the school board eventually agreed to reimburse its employees for as much as 85 percent of their unused sick days.

Elementary schools that have not achieved under reform make up 26 to 35 percent of those in the system, the Consortium on Chicago School Research concluded in a 1993 report. Such schools are typically marked by unfocused reform initiatives, nonsupportive leadership, limited contact with the school community, and an isolated faculty whose members blame school failures on outside factors. "Those schools pursue a generic conception of a 'good school' that may have little relation to local needs," survey authors wrote. "Funds are used to add programs and personnel haphazardly to the periphery of the school. While these add-on programs, such as computer centers and art and music programs, may be valuable additions, they neither enhance the core instruction provided to most teachers nor improve the classroom practice of most teachers." Systemwide, reform is working in 36 to 45 percent of Chicago elementary schools, the consortium concluded. Advancing the premise that improving achievement test scores would take some time, the consortium reported that more than a third of schools are taking a systemic approach and developing programs that are expected to eventually lead to student achievement in those schools. Progress in the rest of the elementary schools is unclear and, as of 1993, a study of Chicago high schools had yet to be done.[23]

"You have to have a plan," said veteran educator Grace Dawson, a one-time teacher, principal, and central office administrator. Dawson believes that antifailure strategies listed in school board policy should be combined with an unswerving commitment to high standards. As the renegade principal of Beethoven School in 1988, she created her own mighty uproar. Working in the decay of the Robert Taylor Homes public housing development—an area torn by urban plagues of violence, gangs, and drugs—Dawson took a stand unheard of in Chicago public schools: she demoted 192 children who scored two or more years below grade level on achievement tests and who needed remedial work. She sent failure notices to another 250 of her 834 pupils, warning they could be set back one grade. A furor ensued, with parents picketing for three days and more than a third of them sending their children to alternative schools in protest of Dawson's radical approach.[24] Ultimately, 190 children were retained in June

Grace Dawson, former teacher, principal, and indefatigible fighter for Chicago school reform.

Photo by John H. White.

1988 and another 90 the following year. "Scores started creep-
ing up immediately," Dawson said. "The children started real-
izing they couldn't get by."

When Dawson made a partial retreat by bowing to parents
who attended personal conferences, *Chicago Sun-Times*
columnist Raymond R. Coffey offered a sarcastic response:

> It was almost scary. Kids attending the school were in
> danger of actually being required to learn how to read.
> Worse than that, some of them were openly threatened
> with being flunked a grade. Now, as we all know, no
> real American kid in any real American big city public
> school has actually flunked a grade since the days when
> Dick and Jane were watching Spot. But here we were—
> in America's heartland, in Chicago, where civic wonders
> never cease, in A.D. 1988—and a school principal was
> announcing the imminent flunking of some 500 of her
> 834 pupils at Beethoven School because of failing grades
> and low test scores. Just imagine, a school wherein the
> fifth graders actually had to be able to read at fifth-grade
> level. It was, in fact, just the sort of thing that could cost
> Chicago its popular designation, by Education Secretary
> William J. Bennett, as proprietor of the worst urban
> school system in the country. In the end, though, the
> forces of ignorance and illiteracy, led by none other than
> the mothers of the Beethoven student body, triumphed
> once again and our reputation was saved.[25]

Educational researchers howled at such commentary, pointing out that schools posted retention rates as high as 50 percent. Among the most forceful opponents of retention was
Designs for Change, a Chicago children's research and advocacy group. "When a pediatrician uses medical procedures
that have been proved ineffective and harmful, it is called
'malpractice.' When a Chicago public school principal employs
methods consistently proved harmful through research, her
superiors call it 'creative and innovative.' Welcome to the
Alice-in-Wonderland world of the Chicago public schools,"
responded Joan Jeter Slay, director of the group's policy who
later became an interim school board member. "Hard research
fails to confirm the popular prejudice that poor black children

will learn best if educators threaten and demean them and their families. The best research about the effects of flunking students clearly indicates that holding these students back does not improve student achievement and dramatically increases the likelihood that they will drop out."[26]

Studies show that children who repeat a grade at least once in elementary school post lower academic achievement, exhibit poorer self-esteem, and lack a sense of control over events in their lives than other students of the same age, race, and economic status. But even the most ardent opponents of retention concede harm is difficult to prove conclusively because children who are retained may be academically less gifted in the beginning. At best, researchers say retention is a highly questionable academic practice.[27]

When well-intentioned theory turns into the mindless reality of social promotion, pressing questions remain unanswered: how is a child's self-image improved by graduating without being able to complete a job application? Or open a bank account? Or give correct change at a grocery store counter? And how can children ever catch up once they have missed learning the basic skills essential to building a sound education?

"Sooner or later our children will be compared to others; by a prospective employer, by a customer, by an agency," notes Herbert Elementary School principal William Rankin. "What do they say then? 'No, I cannot add the numbers on this shipping ticket, but I passed fifth grade; do you want to see my report card?'"[28]

Many believe there is a far more pressing reason for passing children despite low achievement: it saves money. A 1985 study by the Chicago Panel on Public Policy and Finance put the statewide cost of retaining students who were one year or more behind grade level at $255 to $382 million. Undoubtedly that conservative estimate would be far higher today.[29] "It's all about dollars," said West Side activist Coretta McFerren. "Why else would you pass an illiterate child?"

In May 1991, the school system's office of school operations sent a letter urging schools not to fail students because, among other things, it cost money to educate students another year. The memo noted that the failure of high schoolers in nearly 259,000 courses the previous year cost an estimated $68.7 million in salaries for extra teachers. "The emphasis here is not to have a kid come back and do a whole class over if we can prevent it," the letter said. "The research says the all-over-again approach doesn't really give all we are seeking, and it's extremely costly. . . . The emphasis should be not on failing them but addressing them in ways that they won't fail."[30] In response to publicity, then superintendent Kimbrough elaborated: "We do not suggest by any stretch of the imagination that teachers pass students along just because it saves money. We wholeheartedly support alternatives to holding our students back, when those alternatives provide greater results. What we are talking about," he declared, "is saving our children."[31]

Throughout the nation, educators disagree on the issue of failing a child. Some balk at the idea, insisting that it is a sure way toward increasing the number of dropouts. Instead they point to alternatives such as changing the way children are taught and grouped in school. G. Alfred Hess, Jr., executive director of the Chicago Panel, is among them. "Why think of grouping kids by age? Why teach them in the same group with the same teacher for a year, teaching them multiple subjects across a long period of time? Why not concentrate all the math into one three-week period?" he asks.

Others recommend instituting tough requirements for promotion. In the early 1980s, H. Ross Perot, the Dallas billionaire and maverick presidential candidate during the 1992 election, led a campaign to overhaul Texas education. Perot's efforts resulted in the 1984 passage of strict education measures, the most controversial of which was "no-pass/no-play." Under that rule, students who wished to participate in extracurricular activities were required to pass every course during the previous six-week grading period. Six years later, a survey of principals reported mixed results on whether the rule affected graduation rates for students at risk of academic failure. But they did say that students who participated in extracurricular activities such as high school sports worked harder in their classes to remain eligible. They also reported improved communication between teachers and coaches over athletes' academic work.[32]

One thing is certain: high expectations from both parents and teachers, not social promotion, are essential. Children of parents who care tend to stand out. Explained one teacher: "They send their children to school every day that they are not ill. They insist that their children do homework and study for tests. They do not accept poor and failing grades." She estimated the number of such parents in general high schools at 25 to 35 percent.

But in an age of broken families and growing numbers of illiterate adults, teachers must learn to educate the possible two thirds of children whose parents are either not supportive or absent altogether. Low expectations are a sure way to fall short of educational goals. Nevertheless, a shocking one third of Chicago elementary teachers believe their students are not capable of learning the materials they are supposed to teach, according to a 1991 teachers' survey.[33] It is a failure aura, said Margaret M. Harrigan, who assembled the promotion policy when she headed the city's curriculum department. "Our teachers feel the students can't learn. Our students feel they can't learn. It needs to be totally replaced with a success mentality." If teachers and parents do not believe it, what would motivate students to prove them wrong? "I have textbooks, but we don't use them," said Clemente High School senior Raul Rivera, just weeks before his graduation in June 1993. "Most of the books are in my locker. I have a book I haven't opened yet." Rivera said he never opened the book because he never received instruction to do so at the school, a school from which only two out of five students graduate. Even so, Clemente's 1992 graduation rate was 37 percent, a considerable improvement over the previous year's 28 percent.[34] Still, Rivera reported, class sizes were usually down to six or twelve students in nice weather.

Brainwashing. That's what G. Alfred Hess, Jr., calls the popular philosophy that the social and economic status of a student's family are the only factors that matter when it comes to achievement. It translates into dismal teaching. "These teachers, like other urban educators, blame the victims for the failures of urban school systems," Hess wrote in *School Restructuring, Chicago Style,* pointing partly to a 1966 report by educational researcher James S. Coleman who, Hess said, concluded that only a family's socioeconomic status correlates with student achievement. "Confronted in graduate school educational administration courses by the Coleman report, and bolstered by their own disappointing experiences in inner-city schools, a whole generation of school administrators grew up believing there was little [that] school people could do for inner-city urban schools."[35]

When Argie K. Johnson became the Chicago school superintendent, she vowed to challenge that theory. "I have spent my entire life fighting against the vicious practice of 'dumbing down' the curriculum for inner city students," she declared. "I will insist that we review and upgrade the academic standards for Chicago's children."[36]

The idea that low-income urban children cannot learn has been disproven throughout the country by educators who demand that their students excel. Perhaps the most famous example is East Los Angeles High School teacher Jaime Escalante, featured in the movie *Stand and Deliver.* Although his students were primarily from poor, Hispanic families, a large number consistently earned high scores on the Advanced Placement calculus examinations.

In *Escalante: The Best Teacher in America,* author Jay Mathews recounted the teacher's guiding slogan: "Determination plus hard work plus concentration equals success." Mathews explained, too, the celebrated teacher's method of communicating high expectations: He jokingly threatened students with a failing academic grade plus unsatisfactory marks in work habits and cooperation.

One afternoon a bright but poorly achieving student failed to turn in his homework assignment. His excuse? A bad dream. Mathews then described the teacher's reaction:

Escalante recoiled, uncertain how to proceed against the forces of darkness. The excuse only demonstrated, to his mind, how intelligent the youth was. He reached for a dismissal slip. "O.K., all right. This ticket is one way, one way. You got to talk to your counselor, or you bring in the homework. You want to drop the class, you bring in your mom, your dad. They sign the paper and you fly. Then you have to take three buses to get to the other school. Have to wake up about six o'clock. Less time for bad dreams. So you want the ticket? Or are you gonna bring the homework?"

The student promised to bring the homework.

The school psychologist protested, lecturing Escalante that the child's problems would occasionally prevent him from completing assignments. But Escalante was tired of excuses "borrowed from adults." He threatened to transfer to another school, but the principal was unwilling to lose the prized teacher. Listening to the school psychologist, he sighed, "Do what you can, but stay away from Escalante. He has his own school of psychology."[37]

Chicago has its own proof that low-income children can excel. Although 62 percent of its twelve hundred students are from low-income families, Beasley Magnet School consistently scores above city, state, and national achievement levels. More than one thousand children from throughout the city annually vie for the seventy or so open slots at the school near the troubled Robert Taylor Homes public housing development. Parents are required to play a significant role, signing contracts promising that their children will study, do homework, abide by school rules, and conform to a dress code. Students learn one poem per week; open house regularly draws more than one thousand parents. After-school activities, paid for by donations and other fund-raising events, include foreign language and engineering clubs. Significantly, 97 percent of the students who complete eighth grade at Beasley finish high school. Principal Ollie McLemore's work has not gone unnoticed. She was one of President Clinton's fifty American "Faces of Hope" at his inauguration in 1993.[38]

Aldridge School, which serves the far South Side's Altgeld Gardens public housing development, is another school working against the odds. It posted the twelfth-lowest eighth-grade reading scores in the city in 1986. Eight years later, scores reached the top 40 percent. From 1990 to 1992, reading and math scores rose by as many as 23 percentage points in third and eighth grades, depending on the category tested.[39] The following year, scores increased in nearly every category as well.

How did the school improve? It was no accident. Aldridge School instituted measures nationally recognized as hallmarks of good schools everywhere: a new army of parent volunteers, regimented discipline that rewarded students for good behavior, an improved reading curriculum, and increased flexibility to select incoming teachers—a power granted systemwide under reform.

With state Chapter One funds, Aldridge not only hired extra teachers but also bought equipment—such as overhead projectors—for every classroom. The school computerized its achievement test scores to identify students who had fallen behind their peers. Slow learners received special help. "We have a real commitment here that before children leave third grade, they're reading," declared principal George Pazell.

Since the local school council was created under reform, Aldridge School parents participate in school decision making and, for the first time, volunteer in large numbers. Some ensure that the path is clear of gunfire as school opens and closes each day—an unfortunate but necessary duty. Each classroom has the daily services of a parent helper, who may receive a $10 stipend for three hours of grading papers, copying work sheets, and helping students with assignments. Students have more activities, too, including chess and video clubs. "We have a lot of gangs and violence, so we have a lot of programs to keep kids out of the gangs," explained twelve-year-old Robert Thomas, whose experience tutoring younger children at the school has prompted him to consider a career in education. "If I teach, I want to teach little kids, so I can start them off on the right track," he said.

The forty-five graduating eighth graders in 1992 were assigned adult mentors, who promised to keep in contact with their assigned student at least once a month for five years. Each graduate opened a bank account at Chicago's Heritage Pullman Bank, which donated $5,000 to the accounts and waived fees. The money was earmarked only for college.[40]

Despite inner-city odds, superior schools and superior teachers can make a difference with even the most difficult students. In the periodical *Catalyst, Voices of Chicago School*

Reform, Sawyer School teacher Daniel P. Peterson describes the transformation of a "problem" fifth grader. Mike, a pseudonym, had a second-grade reading level when Peterson was assigned to tutor him:

> His main problem was that he hated everyone. He hated his mom, his dad, school and, most of all, his teachers. He constantly assaulted us with the "F" word. Mike told me in no uncertain terms that he did not "do" books. I asked, "How about this book?" "F ——— you," he replied. So we talked instead; session after session we talked.
>
> One day, unbeknown to Mike, I hid a tape recorder under the desk and recorded our conversations for several days. Then I transcribed Mike's words and bound the pages in a booklike manner, adding an attractive cover. At our next session, I told Mike I had a book he might be interested in. I got the usual response: "I told you I don't read no f ——— books!" I said, 'I think you might enjoy this one. Look who wrote it." Mike was amazed to see his name on the cover, but he groused, "I never wrote no book." I countered, "On the contrary, you wrote this one." He opened "his" book and began to read for the first time in a long time.

Peterson used Mike's book, curse words and all, to explain language arts skills such as punctuation and capitalization. Peterson furthered the child's interest by offering a point for every correct answer on quizzes. The points were then deposited in a "checking account" from which Mike could buy items from the Reading Store in Peterson's classroom. At first, Mike always went for the candy. One day he flabbergasted his mother and his teacher by announcing he was saving points for something more expensive: a book. By the end of the year, Mike had disproven the hopeless line of thinking that inner-city children cannot learn—he had made a four-year gain on his reading test. With tears in his eyes, he hugged the teacher and said, 'Mr. P, you are right,'" Peterson recalled. "'Impossible dreams can come true.'"[41]

Charles Mingo, DuSable High School principal.

Courtesy *Chicago Sun-Times*. Photo by John H. White.

7

Discipline Makes a Difference

It's like a war. So many drive-by shootings occur, and so many innocent people get killed. You never know if you'll be next. You can't think straight in class because you've got your mind on the fight or you're figuring out a way to leave school without getting caught in the crossfire.

Fourteen-year-old Maria Rivera, a student at Kelvyn Park High School

During the 1991–92 school year, more than 10,000 arrests were made inside Chicago public schools. Authorities seized 589 weapons, including 122 guns. Despite such horrifying statistics, only nineteen students were officially expelled from the system.[1]

Illinois law does not allow principals to permanently expel students who commit crimes—they have a right to return the following September. In fact, public school principals cannot expel anyone. Expulsion is the responsibility of the school board, which creates a cumbersome and lengthy process in the nation's third largest school system. More often than not, troubled youngsters are sent back to disrupt classrooms and influence their peers. As Dennie E. Johnson, a teacher at Julian High School explains, "We have students who can stay in school until they're twenty-one if they choose to—regardless of what infractions they commit. We have a student who is supposed to get out of jail who will be in school the next day. He's not there for any purpose. For him, school is a place to socialize and a place to sell his drugs. It's a place to reinforce his gang position."[2]

At Amundsen High School, it took five months to expel a sixteen-year-old student for carrying a loaded gun to the school. His status as a ward of the state slowed the process since the school had to deal with the state child welfare agency, another formidable bureaucracy. Two younger boys were expelled for the same offense in shorter time: twenty days. The school system provides few alternative schools for such troubled youth as they wait for the process to be completed; in the meantime, they threaten the safety of their peers and school staff. Consider the message such a policy sends to classmates and teachers: *Your safety is not important. Fend for yourself.* Consider also what it says to offending youth: *Do it again. We do not care enough to stop you.*

In one school, a student put bleach in a teacher's coffee. Fortunately classmates told the teacher before she drank it. The penalty? Only a three-day suspension, which drew the wrath of the late Chicago Teachers Union president Jacqueline B. Vaughn. "He came right back. It made him a big hero in the schools. . . ."[3]

Principals have the authority to suspend offending students for as many as ten days, but then they may return until the expulsion process is complete. Such conditions contrast dramatically with the freedom to discipline enjoyed by private and parochial schools.

"The board policy right now is a joke—a joke to local school councils, a joke to principals, and a joke to kids," said Calvin L. Pearce, a member of the Morgan Park local school council. "Our kids have a right to an environment that is conducive to education, and I would venture to say at least 85 to 90 percent of kids are doing what we are asking them to do. But the bad kids are getting all the focus."

Previous generations benefitted from discipline without it adversely affecting their self-esteem. Yet many modern-day educators fear that strict disciplinary methods will damage fragile young egos. Promoting self-esteem—sometimes at any cost—is a recurrent theme in American public education today. In a 1989 comparison of industrialized nations, American students scored last in math but highest in self-esteem. When asked to rate themselves, their assessments topped those of children from every other nation. South Korean children, who scored four times better in math, rated themselves lowest in math skills. "This country is a lot better at teaching self-esteem than it is at teaching math," concluded former U.S. Education Secretary William J. Bennett, who recounted the comparisons in his book *The De-Valuing of America: The Fight for Our Culture and Our Children.*[4] Some teachers never reprimand a child or lower a grade for fear of damaging a child's pride. An excuse for cowardice, it is a shallow psychology that robs children of a future and cheats them of a more basic tool of life: the ability to cope with criticism and calmly try again. Based on the false premise that improper actions do not warrant correction, it sends unknowing children tumbling into adulthood on a collision course. At some point they will face the reality that, whether they admit it or not, they are responsible for their behavior. Often that lesson comes too late, however—in a prison cell, a drug rehabilitation center, or a funeral home.

Some argue that expelling teenagers, no matter how hardened they may be, only throws them to the streets. Alternative schools, they add, rob students of positive role models among their peers. But the third option—an undisciplined school environment—is worse not only for innocent classmates and teachers but also for the troublemakers themselves, who laugh at the small penalty given for their crimes and are thus encouraged to create even more havoc. Unquestionably, every avenue must be exhausted before drastic measures are imposed. Children should not be shipped away at the first sign of trouble nor should principals use alternatives as an excuse for failing to establish effective discipline in their own buildings. But as a last resort, expulsion must be made available as one step toward reclaiming the schools. Discipline instilled in love and concern, not inconvenience, has turned many a child around. When imposed early, it may well stop disruptive youngsters from the ultimate segregation: prison.

Commonsense approaches, however, belong to another age before the days when violent youngsters with no physical handicaps were called disabled and protected by law from expulsion. Former special education chief Thomas Hehir acknowledged an unwritten rule: students in Chicago schools who are considered dangerous to themselves or to others are categorized as behavior disordered. Under federal law, such students may not be suspended or expelled for more than ten days a year for behavior that stems from their disabilities.[5]

Amundsen High School teacher George Schmidt explains the implications in the case of one child who carried a loaded gun to school. "Part of his 'behavior disorder' was that he sometimes carried a gun and that he also attacked people," he said. "The rights for violent youth are far and above those accorded their peers."

In many cases, the label of behavior disorder would be unnecessary had the school system done the right thing for the child at an early age. Children often bear the brunt of failure imposed by both the system and their parents, some of whom encourage their youngsters to initiate fights at the first hint of insult. "A lot of kids who end up in behavior disordered classes were simply not handled well in the beginning. If you deal with them adequately in the primary level, you won't have a whole lot of problems in the upper grades," said Bernie Noven, a veteran city school social worker and head of PURE. The answer is simple: educators should practice the same kind of discipline practiced by good parents. As Noven explains, such discipline includes acting consistently, teaching children the consequences of misbehavior, and presenting them with alternatives. "We usually don't do that in the schools. We make all the same mistakes a nonfunctional parent makes," Noven concludes.

The effects of an undisciplined school environment on education and attendance are catastrophic. Student disruption, which is often a precursor to violence, is an overwhelming obstacle to educating Chicago's children. More than half of the city's elementary teachers call it the single largest impediment to education; they expressed more concern about student disorder than any other issue in a 1991 survey.[6] Students also want something to be done. "The kids who don't want to learn—they should just kick them out of school and stop wasting money," said Jerome Rogers, a sophomore at Near North Career Metropolitan High School. Legislation considered in the Illinois General Assembly in 1993 would have allowed public school principals to bypass the school board and, after conducting their own hearings, expel students found guilty of offenses involving guns. The bill sponsored by house speaker Michael Madigan did not pass in 1993, however.[7]

Fear of violence prevents some students from getting to the schoolhouse door. According to the same 1991 survey, one third of elementary teachers believe their students do not feel safe coming to and leaving school, a minimal prerequisite for learning, survey authors say.[8] In a 1984 study of 117 Chicago dropouts, fear of gangs was listed by one third of males as the primary reason for not staying in school. It was the first time that the pervasive fear of gang activity emerged as a major cause for dropping out, reported Charles L. Kyle, who conducted the study sponsored by the primarily Hispanic organization, Aspira, Inc. of Illinois. Kyle revealed that the dropout rate at two primarily Hispanic high schools—Clemente and Wells—stood at 75 percent.[9] At the time, the school system underreported its dropout rate dramatically. With that shocking study and others produced by the *Chicago Reporter* and the Chicago Panel on Public Policy and Finance, the board's publicized figures began to unravel. The system has since revamped its reporting method, a factor contributing—to the chagrin of some board members—to a four-year dropout rate of 45.9 percent, the highest of twenty-six of the nation's largest school systems.[10]

With every shooting in the Robert Taylor Homes, attendance drops at DuSable High School, which serves the public housing project situated along the Dan Ryan Expressway on the South Side. Some parents feel the only way to protect their children is to keep them at home. In 1992, the school launched a recruitment program to lure dropouts back to DuSable. The campaign theme would have been foreign in most suburbs: "It's safer in school than it is out there."[11]

Because of Chicago's blustery winters, spring is universally welcomed throughout the city as a relief from the cold. *Almost* universally, that is. In some neighborhoods, warm weather is a threat, conducive to violent behavior—at least that's how student Jerome Rogers sees it. "All the trouble starts when it gets warm. . . ."

Rogers' fear is justified. In 1992, a wave of violence hit Chicago. With 941 murders, it was the second deadliest year on record in the history of the sprawling city of 2.7 million people.[12] In March 1992, when a fourth-grade boy pulled a gun from his bag in school it fired, injuring an eight-year-old classmate, who had to undergo extensive therapy as a result of a bullet lodged in her spine.[13] In November of the same year, a fifteen-year-old was murdered and two classmates at Tilden High School were wounded in a hallway during class break. A gambling dispute prompted the shooting.[14] Also that month, a thirteen-year-old student at Sherman School pulled a gun in math class while a teacher's back was turned as she put up some visual aids. Apparently in horseplay, he put the gun to his head. It fired. To the horror of classmates and his teacher, seventh grader Willie Clayborn slumped over and died by his own hand.[15]

Perhaps no death caused more outrage, however, than that of seven-year-old Dantrell Davis, gunned down by a sniper as he walked with his mother to school one crisp October morning of that same murderous year. The short walk from his home in the Cabrini-Green public housing project to his school is only three hundred yards.[16] Anthony Garrett, a thirty-five-year-old gang member, was later convicted of firing the fatal bullet. The murder touched off a national furor, and both of Chicago's major newspapers responded with extensive coverage. *Chicago Sun-Times* editor Dennis A. Britton wrote a front-page letter to readers and concluded with a call for action, which was followed by a compelling series on violence in the city.[17] *The Chicago Tribune* responded with its own gripping project called "Killing our Children," which marked the violent death of each Chicago-area child and analyzed the causes. The heavy publicity, housing project sweeps, community activism, and a gang truce eventually led to a decrease in violence. In the first four months of 1993, for example, murders in Chicago numbered 247, down 13.3 percent from the same period in 1992.[18]

In September 1990, Mayor Richard Daley responded to city violence by permanently assigning two police officers to each public high school. Under "Operation Safe," arrests rose dramatically to 4,306 in the city's public schools in the first four months alone, a statistic that amounted to nearly fourteen times the drug arrests and nearly twelve times the weapons arrests over the same period the previous fall.[19]

The insignificant amount of crime reported before police officers were assigned to high schools underscores a nagging national problem: many principals do not report student crime even in a nation in which an estimated one million school-aged boys—statistics regarding the practices of girls are not available—carry a knife and another 135,000 carry a gun to school daily, according to a study by the National School Safety Center.[20] Whether reluctant to jeopardize their schools' reputations or unwilling to face the paperwork, educators often seize weapons and drugs without notifying police. Sometimes they even obstruct authorities. In one school, a teacher tipped off a runaway that police had arrived looking for him, according to the Illinois Criminal Justice Information Authority. Another juvenile officer recalled being summoned to a counselor's office at the end of a school year. When the counselor opened a drawer full of marijuana, hashish pipes, and other paraphernalia, he told the police officer: "We want you guys to take this stuff off our hands. It's stuff we've accumulated throughout the year." The officer was so incensed that he considered arresting the counselor for possession of drugs and drug-related paraphernalia.[21]

In June 1992, as violence escalated throughout Chicago and within its schools, the city offered high school principals the option of permanent metal detectors under Daley's expanded anticrime campaign. Previously, the entire system had only three portable walk-through detectors, available on special request. In the first few months of 1992, forty-two schools accepted the offer, but others complained it turned sacred halls of education into prisons and trust into unwelcome authoritarianism. "If learning is going to take place, schools should be kind of like church. Schools shouldn't be turned into a Stateville," said DuSable principal Charles E. Mingo, referring to the high-security penitentiary in Joliet, Illinois. Mingo pointed out that his students from the towering housing developments surrounding DuSable already felt like they lived in cages.[22]

Others warned that logistics are simply too formidable to overcome: some schools have as many as forty entrances, which by fire code cannot be locked from the inside. With the help of a classmate, students can slip in backdoors or sneak guns in through windows. Further, the detectors are so sensitive that even spiral notebooks can activate them. At Tilden High School, the use of metal detectors takes about one-and-a-half hours with ten people working security, making it impossible to provide the state-required three hundred minutes of daily instruction daily, according to principal Hazel B. Steward. She came under fire for not using detectors the day three students were shot in school over a gambling dispute. Two were innocent bystanders.[23]

Englewood High School, which lies in a crime-ridden neighborhood, has the use of walk-through detectors down to a science. Principal Warner B. Birts said students who know they will have to walk through metal detectors every day are discouraged from bringing guns to school. Farragut High School, site of repeated skirmishes that have resulted in dozens of student arrests, had used them on a November day in 1992 when a teenager was shot and wounded about a block from the school. Within fifteen minutes, several fights erupted in the hallways. Principal Steve Newton, Jr., was convinced that if guns had been in the building, the scuffles would have turned into shootings and possible deaths. "The detectors earned their keep on just that one day," he said.[24]

With the aid of portable metal detectors, authorities at Calumet High School recovered a twenty-two caliber pistol with six rounds, a starter pistol, fourteen knives, a meat cleaver, beepers, and Mace—all in one day. "You can't educate if students and faculty don't feel safe," principal Tam B. Hill said. "It's a really sad commentary on our times."[25] By June 1993, arrests leveled off in city schools—about 9,800 for the school year. The number of guns recovered for the entire 1992–93 period amounted to 158, according to Lt. Thomas Byrne, head of the Chicago Police Department's school patrol unit.

In some public school districts in the country—but not, unfortunately, in Chicago—students who carry a gun to school are automatically expelled. Many are placed in alternative schools. "In Gary, Indiana, you don't come back. They are tough, tough, tough," said Grace Dawson, who became principal of Locke Elementary School in Gary in 1992.

After anguishing over the question, the Los Angeles School Board adopted a similarly strict policy in 1993. "It's not an option anymore," said Melody Sullivan, a vice president of a

Los Angeles parent-teacher association. "Now the policy is, 'You're out the door. We don't care if you thought you were carrying this weapon to school to protect yourself.'" Sullivan was one of three co-chairpersons of a Los Angeles safety task force that in 1990 proposed sweeping changes in student discipline policies. At that time, the task force recommended outright expulsion for any student found with a firearm or for any student who seriously assaulted another person, but it took two years and several in-school shootings before the recommendation was actually implemented. In 1989, the number of Los Angeles students caught with weapons was 438; the number of students expelled, 15. Another 147 students remained in regular schools while the rest were sent to alternative schools. "The conclusion seems obvious," wrote the task force. "[The district] is overly concerned with the welfare of its violent offenders and has, consequently, placed the safety of other students and staff in serious jeopardy."[26]

The Los Angeles task force made manifold recommendations, including preventative measures such as metal detectors and conflict resolution curriculum, which teaches students how to resolve arguments. It also urged ending the common practice of simply transferring thousands of students because of disciplinary problems.[27] Nothing changed until two years after the study. "What they [school officials] realized is what the task force realized: they were only moving the problem around. They weren't dealing with it. The idea was the students had a new environment to reform themselves and start fresh where the old patterns didn't have to apply. You had new people, new friends, new teachers. Nobody needed to know—and nobody was told—you were a violent student. If you knifed somebody in the hallway, they weren't told," Sullivan said.

Only after a few transfer students attacked their classmates did the policy of transferring misbehaving students an unlimited number of times begin to change. It became clear that making student records available was crucial in handling discipline. The Los Angeles task force recommended developing a centralized index of student crimes and disciplinary actions and making it available to educators, police, and outside agencies. It also recommended changing state law that kept juvenile criminal records closed. Placing blame partly at the feet of Hollywood and its extraordinarily graphic portrayal of murder, the task force noted that in the late 1980s youngsters began to kill one another at unprecedented rates—averaging one child a day in Los Angeles County.[28] Keeping juvenile records confidential was a notion founded during a gentler age to prevent children from being branded with the permanent label of delinquency.[29] But the well-intentioned goal became twisted by ruthless reality, as juveniles learned how to escape penalty for repeated crimes. Between 1986 and 1991, the arrest rate for juvenile violent crime skyrocketed. Nationwide statistics confirm that in 1991, 130,000 youth arrests were made for rape, robbery, homicide, or aggravated assault—42,000 more than in 1986.[30]

Maintaining confidentiality means that judges, police, probation officers, and teachers know nothing about the children sitting in front of them, even when they have a violent history and may be ready to explode. When adults do not know such crucial biographical background, they cannot provide children with the help they need to confront educational, psychological, or social problems.[31]

It's an old story, but, like many problems, it has at least a partial solution: penalizing youthful offenders for the first transgression before they become hardened criminals. "If we can grab a kid quick enough, when he's just starting to become delinquent, a lot of times we can stop him from repeating," Illinois Juvenile Officers Association president Warren DeGraff told the state Criminal Information Authority. "Too often we aren't able to intervene in time, because we don't get the information. If you wait until they're freshmen or sophomores, it's too late."[32]

The education can start as early as primary school with simple lessons that teach that students who break the rules have to pay a penalty. At Gladstone School on the West Side, students learn those lessons in Microsociety, part of a small but growing nationwide experiment that emulates adult life. Gladstone's program includes a student-run court that places misbehaving peers on trial. Fifth-grader Johnnie White was found guilty by his peers of fighting. He was put on probation—and the entire school knew about it. "I was put on trial for threatening Kimberly Jackson," he later wrote in the school newspaper. "I threatened her for a silly reason. I realize now that was not a good thing to do."[33]

Staffing our nation's schools with truant officers or community liaisons is also critical to catching youngsters before they slip forever through the cracks—or the chasm, as is more often the case. Partly because of an intense program using that philosophy, the San Diego Unified School District's four-year dropout rate fell to 18 percent in 1990–91. Previously, about a third of high school students dropped out. School aides track what happens to children when they leave, and teachers recruit dropouts back to school by camping out in places such as YMCAs and drug rehabilitation centers.[34]

Despite the touted effectiveness of truancy programs and even though the Chicago system receives state dollars based on how many students attend classes each day, the board of education laid off its entire force of 153 truant officers in 1992. Before they were eliminated, truant officers were assigned to visit students' homes, represent the school system in court on truancy and child abuse issues, and track down students' home addresses, a monumental task in a school system with an enormous movement of students each school year. Many principals lamented the loss.[35] But the administration responded by questioning the officers' effectiveness. Some staff members insisted that schools could rehire them with state Chapter One funds. Such a proposal, however, was complicated by factors board members may not have fully considered. Initially, it appeared that using poverty funds for truant officers was improper because the truancy program had been considered a basic expense, that is, it did not meet the criteria of a supplemental program as required by law. The problem was eventually resolved, but principals faced another more troubling dilemma: they could not simply hire the truant officers who knew their children and their communities best. Rather, because of the civil service lists created by the 1990 contract, they had to hire the truant officers with the most seniority systemwide.

The result of the complications, according to former truant officers, was that few were rehired. Some believe the effects were clear. During the 1992–93 school year, Chicago police made nearly seventy-one thousand truancy stops, eighteen thousand more than the previous year. During the 1991–92 school year, the system brought 385 truancy cases to court. The year after the layoffs, however, the number dropped to zero.[36] The Chicago Teachers Union, which represents truant officers, filed an unfair labor practice charge, but the issue had yet to be resolved in late 1993.

One could argue, as author Jonathan Kozol did in his landmark education book *Savage Inequalities,* that any system that assigns only a handful of truant officers to tens of thousands of children could care less about finding them. "When a school board hires just *one* woman to retrieve four hundred missing children from the streets of the North Bronx, we may reasonably conclude that it does not particularly desire to find them. If one hundred of these children startles us by showing up at school, moreover, there would be no room for them. . . . The building couldn't hold them."[37] Eliminating truant officers altogether, as the Chicago Board of Education did, sends an even stronger message.

Besides having support staff such as truant officers and counselors on hand, in-school alternative programs and separate alternative schools for violent youngsters are critical to salvaging at-risk youth. The Los Angeles task force concluded that alternative schools should be highly structured and specially staffed with counselors, bilingual and special education teachers, psychologists, teaching assistants, nurses, and school police officers. Unfortunately, because of a financial crisis and the reluctance to create such "reform-school" programs, no additional alternative schools were created in Los Angeles following the first three years of the 1990 report.[38]

Chicago once had alternative schools for the toughest "socially maladjusted" youngsters. In 1964, then *Chicago Daily News* columnist Mike Royko recalled the Montefiore special school. "The name Montefiore was and is enough to send a twinge of fear through any public school student who takes a day or two off for the movies or to bum the streets. Most Chicagoans think of Montefiore as a dungeon-like place, with barred windows, fist-swinging, club-waving teachers, knocking students down and abandoning any attempt to teach. This is an image, if you'll excuse the tired word, that didn't come about by accident." Royko then explained how Montefiore principal Harry Strasburg worked to change that image and prohibited the use of force. "If I thought force would do any good, I'd be in favor of it," Strasburg told Royko. "But hitting these kids doesn't change them. Some of them have been hit all their lives."[39] Nevertheless, threatened with the prospect of being sent to such places, many students treated teachers and principals with respect.

Today, children are as troubled and challenging as they ever have been, but there are few such alternative schools. Montefiore is the lone survivor of five special alternative schools for disciplinary problems—and now one must be classified as a special education student to be enrolled there.

Although some Chicago officials consider the idea of sending unruly students to alternative schools for disciplinary problems as outdated, schools serving troubled youngsters still exist around the nation. In Kansas City, Missouri, the Fairview Alternative School addresses the needs of about 120 students, sent there by district hearing officers for carrying weapons to school, assaulting other students or staff, destroying school property, fighting repeatedly, and other offenses.

When students first arrive at Fairview, they are required to set two or three goals for improvement in areas such as attendance, behavior, or academics. In an opening conference with the principal, each is informed of the school's strict rules about weapons, stealing, grades, and attendance. "There's no roaming the halls. They have to be on time for all their classes. They have to stay there until the bell rings. That's one of the biggest adjustments for kids: they have to be in classrooms for a full period," principal Curtis Rogers said. "I expect them to walk the line here." Students who do not cooperate can be suspended for ten days and if that is not sufficient, they must answer to a hearing officer who will likely expel them. "My school is the last chance," says Rogers, who boasts special techniques to minimize conflict. To diffuse a scuffle, for example, he hands the antagonists boxing gloves and takes them downstairs to the gymnasium to settle it—without a cheering squad. "It's amazing," he observed, "what you can do when there is no audience."

Running Fairview costs about $400,000 a year. The school requires extra staff to call parents, strictly monitor attendance, conduct psychological exams, and mentor and tutor students. Thanks to a grant, Rogers is able to rely also on the expertise of three counseling firms. Because the school is small, teachers get to know students. In many cases, personal attention and special assistance with schoolwork improves their behavior. "A lot of kids act out. You take a tenth grader who's either not coming to class or, if he comes to class, he's acting out to draw attention away from the fact he can't do the work," Rogers says. Most students at Fairview make a year's gain in math and English achievement tests annually. Helping them move forward reduces the chances they will hide their academic handicaps by disrupting class, Rogers explains.

One study of nearly two thousand boys in Phoenix, Baltimore, and Indianapolis revealed that the odds of being arrested and found delinquent were 220 percent more likely for youngsters with learning disabilities. Not all was lost though. The study concluded that help brought hope. With fifty-five to sixty hours per year of special academic tutoring, learning disabled children made academic progress and, with as few as thirty-eight hours of special tutoring, their delinquent acts were significantly reduced.[40]

North of Chicago in suburban Niles Township District 219 the Off Campus Learning Center serves students with behavior or emotional problems at an annual cost of $7,100 each. Students who "act up" are interviewed to determine the cause of their behavior, which can be something as fundamental as divorce in the family. Students who are considered criminal— as opposed to emotionally disturbed—are expelled. Guns? "We haven't had that [problem]," said Frank Bostic, special education coordinator for the center, which was established in 1971. "We've taken one pocket knife and one fake handgun, but the kid didn't threaten anybody with it."

In Chicago, where the need is greatest, students must be classified as behavior disordered or emotionally disturbed in order to receive such specialized attention. The alternative programs that do exist are not specifically for disciplinary problems, unless the students are already jailed and therefore have access to schools in jail or in the juvenile detention center. Three alternative schools serve pregnant girls, while the acclaimed Urban Youth High School in downtown Chicago caters to older teens—sixteen to eighteen year olds—who dropped out of high school but now wish to return. The High School Re-entry Center also serves former dropouts not enrolled in regular high schools for reasons that range from expulsion to release from jail. One of several programs funded by a $4.5 million state grant, the reentry center is located at 1819 W. Pershing Road, board headquarters as well as neutral territory where gang members from any part of the city can feel safe. Principals, however, cannot send disruptive students currently enrolled in school to the center. Alternative programs do exist within some schools, but they are few and far between.

Despite limitations, many Chicago schools have taken a hard line under reform to keep their schools oases in urban war zones. Some bend the rules to do so. At Calumet High School, principal Tam B. Hill makes discipline a priority. One year, the school simply refused to accept sixty-two returning students. Council chair Edwin Green explained the decision: "They were out of school thirty or forty days of the year. They had gang affiliations. They were known to be dealing drugs. When we have street people in the school, they are not about education. They find the freshmen they can intimidate or who might be in an opposing gang. They may beat them up. Or they may kill them."[41]

Police officers use walkie-talkies at the South Side school and rely on student tips to stop trouble before it starts. School officials also prohibit the wearing of neighborhood gang colors. "If you allow two different colors to get in the school and they don't get rid of them, sometime during the day there is going to be a confrontation," said Green. His philosophy does not always sit well with students and parents who view such rules as restricting their rights.

Strong policies are only part of an arsenal for establishing discipline in schools. In his first three years at Cregier Vocational High School, principal Alfred Clark attended funerals of eight of his students—all murdered in the neighborhoods. But he works to keep his school violence-free. Cregier sits in the ravaged West Side, which still bears the scars of the 1968 riots that erupted after civil rights leader Martin Luther King, Jr., was assassinated. By students' own accounts, teenagers at one time smoked reefers in the bathrooms, took weapons to school, shot dice in the hallways, and cut classes whenever they wanted. But that was all before the school council lured Clark away from a suburban district. With the help of his staff,

Alfred Clark, Cregier Vocational High School principal.

Courtesy *Chicago Sun-Times*. Photo by Amanda Alcock.

the former Army major established order at the school where 95 percent of students arrive with achievement test scores at least six grades below their peers. At 6 feet 3 inches tall and 275 pounds, Clark is an imposing figure. He established respect in his first year when he broke up a fight while several hundred students gathered around. He challenged the largest instigator—a 280-pound youth—and placed him in a head lock.

Under Clark, Cregier created an in-school suspension room—called a Behavior Improvement Center—where disobedient students are required to study all day with few breaks—classical music is frequently piped in as an added attraction. One student who was caught with spray paint was pressed into service as the school's official graffiti-remover. Moreover, Clark removed the school's pay telephone so youngsters in trouble with other students could no longer contact their friends for backup help. Students—some of whom wear jail ankle monitors—welcome the discipline. "He'll suspend you," said seventeen-year-old Richard Toliver. "All that gang fighting is not here. All the beepers, the smoking in the bathroom, the drugs—he eliminated all of that." Clark would like Cregier to be officially declared an alternative school. He insists that extra staff in such critical areas as counseling is needed. "If you put them back in regular high schools, you spend 95 percent of your time with 5 percent of the youngsters, and they need extreme counseling of all sorts, attention of all sorts, exposure of all sorts," he said.

Reform at Phillips High School on the South Side means that fewer students throw food in the lunchroom, carry switchblades or guns to school, or vandalize the walls. Students credit the change to principal Juanita T. Tucker who, like Clark and Hill, was hired as a new principal under school reform. "When I first came here, the kids used to run wild. Graffiti was all over the wall," said eighteen-year-old Joe Davis, a junior at the South Side school in 1991. "It's much cleaner now. You can study in the library without anyone interrupting you."

How did they do it? Phillips High School uses parent volunteers. One stands at the bottom of the stairs; another on the top. Their twenty-member team patrols hallways and bathrooms during classes. They provide a set of extra eyes and ears for the police officers and take pressure off the staff. They know the neighborhood and its families well enough to spot potential trouble. Phillips stands as a safe house in an area scarred by graffiti and crime. It serves seven housing projects and stays relatively graffiti-free through constant efforts to remove students' unauthorized signature work as soon as it appears. "We are appealing to our students' sense of self-respect, self-pride, self-determination, and brotherly love," said Tucker, herself a Phillips graduate.[42]

Reform at Amundsen High School brought an aggressive local school council that waged a battle against student absenteeism, which, as one truant officer observed, is the first act of delinquency. "We have had more parent-teacher conferences in this building in the last couple of years than we've had in the ten years prior to this," said council member Harriet O'Donnell in 1990. The school takes parents of chronic truants to court. In one case, the parents of an Amundsen student were sentenced to one year's court supervision and mandatory attendance at three local school council meetings and two parent-teacher meetings. "People have been waiting for this for a long time to see if we would be able to keep a case in court," said O'Donnell, who signed the complaint against the parents of a fifteen-year-old who had been absent eighty days during one school year. "There has never been any desire or any intent to send any parent to jail. Our intent is to get kids in school so they can get an education." The council's overall campaign, which included repeated warnings to four hundred parents, improved attendance at the school by 10 percent, school officials claimed.[43]

When Charles Mingo became principal of DuSable High School in 1988, teachers were so afraid that they locked their classroom doors when the bell rang. Hallways were in chaos. "The first thing I had to do was get the teachers to let kids in. Then I started walking the halls—and my staff started walking the halls," he said. Mingo laid down the law: no fighting, no hats, no sunglasses, no earrings. Teachers were to take charge of their classrooms, and the principal promised to back them up. In some cases, he informally expelled troublemakers and allowed them to return only if their parents agreed to volunteer in the school.[44] Today, with Mingo's direction and the help of some thirty parent volunteers, DuSable is an oasis in a troubled neighborhood. "These kids had been doing what they had been doing for years, and they acted as though I was cheating them out of their divine right," he said. "My philosophy is, I'm your best friend and, if you're right, I'll be the first to defend you. But if you bring in any narcotics, guns, or knives, I'll be insisting you go."

The Chicago Board of Education frowns on expelling students, and its expulsion policy reflects this reservation. "We try and reach every child. Realities come into play, but that doesn't mean you give up on children," said Joseph A. Ruiz, an administrator in the board's office of school operations.

The issue is a touchy one because of the public school system's traditional obligation to educate all children. Some schools ensure that students enroll elsewhere. Others simply suspend students repeatedly. Principals maintain they offer students every chance, including meeting with parents, before taking drastic measures. "Usually when you get rid of them," Mingo said, "they've done enough that you know and they know it's time to go."[45]

Graffiti-scarred desks at Schurz High School, a landmark
Chicago building. The building subsequently underwent
a facelift.

Courtesy *Chicago Sun-Times*. Photo by Amanda Alcock.

8

Schoolhouses in Disrepair

Dear Mr. Kimbrough:

My school, Van Vlissingen, is very big. It has many flaws. My room 302 has a whole [sic] in the sealing [sic] and when it rains, water comes out of the whole [sic] onto the floor. When it is very cold, it makes it cold in the room. One of our shades is broken and when we try to watch a movie in the room, the light makes it so we cannot see the movie that good. I gust [sic] hope that something will be done about these flaws in my Room 302, and other rooms in Van Vlissingen.[1]

So wrote sixth grader Vernon Worsham to Chicago's superintendent of schools in October 1990. In his own imperfect words, Vernon voiced so purely a national phenomenon: the nation's schoolhouses are in ruins.

The result is that schoolchildren throughout America work in excessive cold and heat. They are injured, inconvenienced, and forced to improvise. They are shortchanged on programs never instituted because of insufficient facilities. They are exposed to asbestos, lead poisoning, and peeling paint. Millions of American public school students go to class in substandard buildings. One in four schoolhouses are shoddy places for learning, according to a study by the Education Writers Association.[2] Another survey, conducted by the American Association of School Administrators, placed the number at one in eight; nearly 5 million students attend classes in inadequate buildings.[3]

"More than half of our school buildings are more than fifty years old, and almost every one is in some state of serious disrepair with problems ranging from leaking roofs to faulty boilers to broken windows," said Robert H. Terte, spokesperson for the New York City school system, which in 1991 had a backlog of thirty-three thousand requests for repairs in eleven hundred schools.[4] The cost? A projected $17 billion, of which only $4.3 billion was available at the time.

Los Angeles public schools need about $3.37 billion to build new schools through 2010, of which $1 billion is available. The maintenance backlog is pegged at $600 million.[5] Detroit has enough money to fill only about 10 percent of its estimated $1 billion capital need. "When you don't have the ability to fix the problem, the shape is obvious," said Darrell Burks, deputy superintendent of fiscal integrity for the Detroit Board of Education in 1991.[6] For twelve years, the Detroit school system performed virtually no maintenance. Only in the 1990s did it begin to make a dent.[7]

Nearly a third of the nation's 110,000 public schools were built before World War II. Another half were built in the 1950s and 1960s, generally a time of rapid and cheap construction, notes the Education Writers Association. While the statistics show a dire need nationwide, Chicago schools are older than average: nearly half were built before 1930 and two thirds desperately need repair. Workers each month respond to some twelve hundred building emergencies that threaten student safety or school operations, including broken boilers, bursting water pipes, and electrical failures.

Even $1 billion would not solve the problem, according to a facilities study commissioned by Chicago's interim school board, which voted to borrow nearly $400 million for building projects. Every time a project is deferred, its cost grows. "This is one of the most disgusting wastes of public money and exploitation of young people," said Chicago alderwoman Mary Ann Smith, who toured every school in her North Side ward and found "crumbling sidewalks, broken fencing, crumbling stairways, and things that were outright dangerous."[8]

Tragically, that proved all too true for Richard Haley in June 1987. The nineteen-year-old, hot and sweaty from playing a game of basketball, stopped by Garvey Elementary School where his father was assistant principal. In an offer characteristic of the good-natured youth, Richard agreed to help his father, Joseph, stamp and sort books at the South Side school. But when the teenager reached to open a window, he was electrocuted. Faulty wiring from a heating unit below sent a current through the metal frame, a lawsuit alleged. "When he touched the window handle, he collapsed," the elder Haley said. Richard died in his father's arms.

The heating unit and others throughout the building were not properly grounded, and a ground wire, designed to absorb shocks, was not connected, a building inspector who visited the site after the accident testified. What's more, there was no record of a building permit for the original heating system. "They probably didn't have a project manager on the job," speculated James P. Harney, then the school system's director of facilities. "Somebody just blew it and figured they had the sense to ground it properly."[9]

Deteriorating schoolhouses throughout Chicago put children in danger. At Clay Elementary School on the far Southeast Side, a six hundred-pound piece of concrete crashed through the roof one day, missing by several yards the glass skylight of a lower lunchroom ceiling, according to school engineer Robert J. Hrnciar. The five-foot long piece of concrete fell in a pocket between a lower roof and the wall.

At Calumet High School, the roof leaked for two decades, rotting paint and plaster. Nature, unchecked, had eaten away at the structure, rendering entire rooms unusable in the once glorious building. In one class, a rain-soaked chunk of thick ceiling plaster crashed between two students sitting only three feet apart. "Lucky again," said teacher Darlene Blackburn, recounting the incident. In a science room, a student escaped injury when a blinding stream of sunlight—like a warning— prompted her to stand up. Seconds later a piece of ceiling hit her desk. "It must have been an act of God she moved," biology teacher Charles Fullman declared. In the gymnasium, rainwater seeped in through a leaky roof, destroying sections of wood floor. "Everything is makeshift," gym teacher John Butler said in 1991. "We are limited to actual use of only half of the gymnasium." The school could not host tournaments for fear of lawsuits.[10]

The precaution was well-founded. At Simeon High School, the family of seventeen-year-old student Christopher Hill sued when he slipped in a puddle on the gymnasium floor while playing basketball. The puddle was caused by a leaky roof, the lawsuit alleged, and Hill tore cartilage in his knee, forcing him to have surgery as a result. In many schools, rotting wood frames leave panes of glass precariously loose. Shards of glass rained down on Mile Manojlovic, a student at Washington High School, in 1987 when he tried to open a window that did not function properly. Manojlovic's hand was gashed, and the school board compensated him with $8,000.[11] A burst of wind broke a pane of glass in 1990 at Van Vlissingen School, narrowly missing a student.[12] And dozens of students at that school's modular building were rushed to the hospital one year because of fumes from an unknown source.[13]

On election day at Graham Elementary School in 1984, poll watcher Kenneth Thompson walked out of the wrong second-story door and onto an unlit landing with no railing, said family attorney Jeffrey M. Marks. He kept walking and ultimately fell to his death. The board agreed to pay a $125,000 settlement. At Peabody Elementary School in 1983, a restroom wall collapsed on the legs of Jose Luis Arellano when, during horseplay, the nine-year-old jumped on the wall. According to a subsequent lawsuit, a contractor apparently left it in poor condition—the wall did not have mortar between its cinder blocks—and the board paid $100,000 as a result. In total, settlements and court fees for accident claims and lawsuits carry a price tag in the millions.[14]

The problem affects not only children's safety and the taxpayer's pocketbook but also the educational process in a myriad of ways. Consider the effect of winter winds extending their icy grip into the classrooms. Children wear coats in class, grip pencils with frozen fingers, and catch colds from constant drafts filtering through broken windows. Clay Elementary School teacher Vivian Cardin was convinced that such conditions at her seventy-five-year-old school increased absenteeism. In winter, her fifth-grade classroom was equipped with a hands-on nature exhibit: it actually snowed *in* class. "It's very depressing," she added. "You can bring in only so many plants and so many posters to cover the holes and falling plaster."[15]

Then there's the other extreme: sweltering classrooms that make the most energetic of students sleepy and unproductive.

"This room was 100 degrees," Kelly High School principal John P. Gelsomino said one January, blaming the antiquated heating system. Such high temperatures—particularly in schools where windows no longer open—can contribute to an overwhelming odor of sweat. One school held gym class in such a classroom.

But it gets worse. At Chicago's Funston Elementary School, nine mobile units—the so-called Willis wagons that were designed to last five years—served as classrooms for decades. Rats occasionally died underneath, producing an unbearable stench that grade school children and their teacher had to tolerate for weeks. Students at Hammond Elementary School were pulled out of a mobile classroom for a week because of the same problem at that Southwest Side school. As principal Julio A. Rivera explained, "Our engineering and janitorial staff did a lot of cleaning, but they couldn't locate any dead animals. They think it was just the wood. It is impregnated with mildew."[16] Such problems can spell misery for students and teachers with allergies.

Disrepair sends our children an astounding message, simple and overwhelming: Nobody cares about you.

In 1991, Schurz High School sophomore Eumir Arreguin slumped in his seat in study hall, nodded toward his surroundings, and declared, "I hate it here." Graffiti was everywhere in the Northwest Side school, a historic landmark. On the walls. On the broken and aging desks. On the auditorium chairs. Even on the study hall blackboard, where the bold work of vandals covered a neatly written explanation of classroom periods. "If you repaint, they'll just put it back on," said Arreguin. "I guess they gave up." Inspectors from the Illinois State Board of Education agreed. "The building is a disgrace," they reported in 1989. "The facilities need to be cleaned thoroughly by the maintenance staff. The school halls are dirty. The floors, walls, windows, stairways, lunchroom, and classrooms are filthy. Painting and repairs are needed throughout the school."[17] After a change in staff, the school received a facelift. In 1994, further renovation was planned, according to Schurz's new principal Sharon Rae Bender.

Still, even though building experts say interior walls should be painted at least once every eight years, the Chicago system discontinued its regular painting cycle altogether—leaving some schools unpainted for two decades. "What does that say to a kid who's here every day?" asked Burley Elementary School principal Barbara L. Gordon, pointing to the peeling paint and plaster at her school. "It's saying we don't care enough about you to have things nice and bright and shiny every day."[18]

At Van Vlissingen Elementary School, vandals broke into the nearly one hundred-year-old building and sprayed black paint high up on a classroom wall. Four years later, in 1991, the ugly scar of vandals had yet to be removed. Fifth-grade teacher Kay Serapin's description was an understatement: "It's not a very pleasant environment for the children."[19] Maintenance crews could not paint over the blotches—apparently because of trade rules that prohibited them from painting above eight feet on a wall—a courtesy to ensure jobs for union painters, school officials said. But board painters have a backlog of work that goes back years. Meanwhile, community members who wish to volunteer their services need special permission, which includes a work permit, an inspection of all materials by central office facilities staff, and a $3 million liability bond. The approval process is supposed to take no more than eighty-three days, but at least one school complained that it took far longer. In addition, volunteers are required to provide their own ladders, scaffolding, drop cloths, extension planks, brushes, and other supplies. A nineteen-page set of procedures from the school board is so specific that it even requires a particular type of drop cloth: a ten-ounce canvas.[20]

The regulations would be understandable for a normal business with professionally maintained buildings in sound condition. But they are absurd considering the desperate state of schools. The Calumet High School greenhouse—trashed by pieces of rotting roof and vandalized in its disrepair—was a prime example. Gym teacher John Butler explained the effect: "When you are in an area that's crumbling all around you, it's hard to command any respect. If you have a nice environment, chances are students will put more effort in." The greenhouse once had been a showcase for the school, among the city's finest, recalled Butler, himself a Calumet graduate.

At McPherson Elementary School on the North Side, pigeons found a home in a vent above the third-floor hallway.

Damaged greenhouse at Calumet High. Local school council chairman Edwin Green looks on.

Courtesy *Chicago Sun-Times*. Photo by Rich Chapman.

Children walked through bird droppings daily until a screen was installed to remedy the problem. "We perpetuate under-achievement," said Tony J. Wall, head of the Council of Educational Facility Planners International. "What we're telling children indirectly is that disrepair is okay."[21]

In a study by the American Institute of Architects, achievement scores rose 20 percent in some schools when students moved to a newly-constructed building. "For many youngsters, the school environment is the only quality space in which they get to spend a significant amount of time," architect Gaylaird Christopher explained. "It should demonstrate to them the values of society. A school that mirrors the slum does not give that youngster a very good message."[22]

Critics of Chicago public schools have long said they should operate like businesses, but in successful businesses employees have adequate supplies and equipment that functions. Chicago school staff often have neither. A plumbing problem at Kelly High School means three of eight sinks in the home economics room have no water. "They 'fixed' it eight years ago by turning it off," teacher Connie Glascow said. Because rainwater from leaky roofs short-circuits light fixtures, some children and teachers are forced to do paperwork amid shadows. McPherson School had no water in student restrooms on three of four floors for a month in 1991, which led principal Camille E. Chase to ask an obvious question: "How can you teach hygiene when you don't have running water in the building and no soap?"[23]

Building disrepair also means that up-to-date technology is thwarted at the front door. Schools built before the turn of the century need both extensive rewiring and air conditioning to keep high-tech equipment from overheating. Water damage in the electrical outlets at Mather High School impaired an acclaimed program in which students used computers to design items they later made. But they could not use a lathe for the manufacturing end of their assignments because the outlets at the North Side school did not work.[24]

At the huge Washburne Trade School, a state-of-the-art machinists' program had all the equipment it needed, but it could not be expanded because the electrical system lacked the capacity. The building had unlimited potential for programs that train carpenters, plasterers, painters, heating repair workers, and other trades. "We have wonderful training, but the building is falling apart," said principal Charles A. Lutzow in 1991. "It needs tuckpointing—bricks have fallen—and new windows practically all over. It's really depressing, but yet the things the students learn are really unbelievable. With a rehab, the potential is unlimited for the type of training needed by the city."[25] Although the potential was great, the school board eventually closed the school and turned it over to the City Colleges of Chicago.

Asbestos is also a major—and expensive—problem in Chicago schools: it would cost $125 million or even twice that amount, depending on the estimate, to remove.[26] At Bowen High School on the Southeast Side, bureaucratic snags in an asbestos removal project delayed expansion of a proposed computer program for two years. "We have money allotted in our budget for computers, but we have not spent it," principal Gloria D. Walker said. "We don't have space for them."[27]

Chicago children—and their counterparts in poorly financed school systems across the country—suffer from other types of building deficiencies. Chicago's $1 billion building program price tag—of which not even half was made available to the schools—does not include having extra rooms for computer labs, reading classes, or a growing number of preschool programs. Nor does it include the bill for building cafeterias, which a number of schools lack, or making buildings accessible to the handicapped. Of 631 facilities run by the Chicago Board of Education, only 39 are wheelchair accessible, according to 1992 statistics. Because of a revolution in special education, far more children with disabilities are sent into regular classrooms. When thousands of children previously schooled in special facilities or programs arrive, however, many buildings are simply not prepared for them.[28]

By and large, Chicago elementary schools are also not ready for the twenty-first century. Most, for example, do not even have science labs. "If we're actually going to give our kids a world-class education, we need science labs," said Patricia A. Harvey, principal of Hefferan Elementary School, where an elaborate lab was donated by Rush-Presbyterian St. Luke's Medical Center and Turner Construction Co. "One of the reasons our children do not do well in high school science is they never have had the experience in the laboratory," said Harvey. "When you're in regular classrooms and you don't have materials to support those activities, too often it becomes too simplified."

Many schools are also overcrowded, which places an incalculable toll on education and, quite often, leads to shortcuts. Kilmer Elementary School teacher Ivan Zapata had forty-four students in his classroom. "My wife sometimes helps me with correcting the tests in my house," he said in 1992. "The best thing is to try to do short tests and multiple choice."[29] Multiple-choice tests speed grading, but they are not ideal learning tools. Sometimes, though, they are the only way to educate large numbers of children. At Carson Elementary School on the Southwest Side, some classes contain forty students. System administrators send extra teachers to the school, but they have no place to teach other than in hallways where disruptions are constant.[30]

Chicago schools were short about three thousand elementary classrooms and thirty-one hundred high school seats during the 1992–93 school year. Amundsen High School was among the schools stretched to the limit. In September 1992, council member Harriet O'Donnell received a number of telephone calls from parents who were angry and upset "and rightly so," she said. Amundsen was built to hold thirteen hundred students, not the seventeen hundred that were enrolled.[31] Because classroom space does not match neighborhood demographics, a surplus of about seven hundred elementary classrooms and twenty-three thousand high school seats exist elsewhere in the city.[32] Once again, management and money could make a difference in educating Chicago's children. "When the public looks at test scores, they say, 'What's wrong with Chicago public schools?'" Carson principal Kathleen Mayer said. "They don't look at each case and see the problems each school is struggling with."[33]

Older generations remember larger class sizes and recall that, backed by solid discipline, teachers were able to maintain control and provide a good education. But what many do not realize is that neither children nor education are the same today. Why don't large class sizes work any more? "You don't have the family backup," said Patricia A. Daley, a former board member and now a teacher at Chavez School. "You don't have the church backup. You don't have the social organizations' backup. You don't have neighborhood structures where everybody is raising the children together. You do have children on drugs. You never had that before. You have children born to drug-addicted parents. You have a vast majority of your population who don't even have a magazine in their homes. Everybody watches television." Shorter attention spans make lecturing less suitable.

"Their educational needs are different from yours and mine," offers Hefferan principal Patricia A. Harvey. America's families have disintegrated, too. Consequently, teachers are left to cope with children from broken homes, children who come unprepared for school, and children weaned on cocaine who fly off the handle at a moment's notice. Violence at home and in the neighborhoods takes an enormous toll on education. As trauma mounts, IQ actually drops, studies show.[34] When death is a daily part of a life, some children find little reason to prepare for a future they know they may never see. Such fatalism is a new phenomenon faced by to-day's educators.

Hands-on science and computer technology require individualized instruction, as does teaching children with special needs in classes typically consisting of five to twelve students. Previously many of these children were segregated into separate schools, but now the low pupil-teacher ratio for special education classrooms requires as much as triple the amount of space as would an equal number of pupils in a regular classroom, the Education Writers Association reported.[35] In addition, some families do not teach the alphabet, colors, or even their own last names before their children enter kindergarten. Further aggravating an already difficult situation is that some parents themselves cannot read.

Breaking through these barriers is left to the teachers, and in a classroom of thirty children it is an overwhelming task. In 1992, first-grade classes in Chicago public schools averaged 24.6, about two more students than the state average. Such figures, however, are deceiving. The number in nearly 115 schools, for example, swelled above twenty-eight—the maximum allowed under contract with the Chicago Teachers Union. One school had an average eighth-grade class size of fifty in 1992. Despite the contract violations, many teachers choose not to file union grievances.[36]

At overcrowded Funston Elementary School, the bathroom serves as an office. Maria Vasquez (right) of the Center for Community and Leadership Development and Bienvenida Nieves, a community school representative.

Courtesy *Chicago Sun-Times*. Photo by Phil Velasquez.

The problems force teachers to work under enormous odds at the expense of staff morale, which is essential in turning around any organization. At Funston School on the Northwest Side, fine arts coordinator Lillian Heminover worked out of a bathroom for more than a dozen years. It functions as her office. There she tapes calendars on a bathroom stall and hangs choir robes from its frame. Rolled-up murals rest atop the stalls, and materials are stored around the toilets. Her desk stands next to a sink. "I don't have space to meet with children because the area doesn't allow it," said Heminover, who nevertheless coordinated an award-winning Academic Olympics program. "I don't have space to store materials, which I desperately need."[37] Heminover recently retired but still works as a volunteer.

Children at Funston take classes in the lunchroom, in hallways, and on the auditorium stage. And they work in the mobile classrooms. Even if computers are donated, they cannot be stored in the classrooms because thieves regularly raid them, stealing calculators and supplies. Teacher Gonzalo Maldonado lost $200 worth of books purchased with his own money.[38] To relieve overcrowding, the school council, under reform, adopted a year-round schedule that allowed alternating shifts of students. An addition was planned in 1994.

Building problems in Chicago public schools have a long history that, like many other obstacles in the system, date back to the 1979 financial collapse. "Since the financial crisis, we have not only not had money for preventive maintenance, we have not had money for repairs," said J. Maxey Bacchus, acting director of Management Information Services. "We come in with a crash program and put $5 million in and move on to another school. And immediately, since you're not providing preventive maintenance, the building begins to deteriorate. We're always falling behind."[39]

It is a matter of priorities. Maintenance has no union lobbying for it; children, no political action organization to send workers into precincts on election day. Buildings do not go on strike. Instead, student safety, day-to-day repairs, and an environment conducive to learning take second seat to political and economic compromises that put labor peace and employee wages first.[40]

It is easy to understand. When cash for public schools is short and programs are essential, cuts are made. But where? Initially, school systems across the country find the least painful place is building repairs. It begins when policymakers, often in strong union towns like Chicago, postpone a year of repairs to squeeze out money for pay raises to prevent a system shutdown. Another year goes by, and the backlog keeps growing. "Then you're so far in the hole that you don't see any way out," said Margaret A. Scholl, maintenance branch director of the Los Angeles Unified School District.[41]

The Chicago Board of Education has been warned repeatedly by its oversight panel not to defer maintenance, but in a world of declining government dollars, taxpayer revolts, and labor unrest the warning falls on deaf ears. In the decade after the financial collapse, the Chicago Teachers Union called five strikes. To return to peace, the cash-strapped school board postponed repair plans to finance pay raises. "The facts are unequivocal," said Jerome Van Gorkom, former chief of the

Chicago School Finance Authority. "In order to get their employees back to work, if they needed $500 million, they'd chop maintenance all over."

In 1990, it happened again. Although the interim school board launched a building effort funded by bonds, it also successfully lobbied the legislature for authority to shift what it publicized as $15 million a year in property taxes from its building fund. In reality, the number was far larger. The law—written in legalese—actually transferred more than $60 million in property taxes in fiscal 1992 from the building fund to the board's general fund. "Why are we taking money out of the building fund to pay salaries if what we're concerned about is fixing buildings?" school watchdog G. Alfred Hess, Jr., asked. "You can't have it both ways. You can't come back and say, 'Well, we're blameless that our buildings are the way they are.' Yes, you are to blame because you went along."

The late Chicago Teachers Union president Jacqueline B. Vaughn believed the solution to be more state funding for both raises *and* repairs. "Yes, we think it's awful, and we'd like to see that not done," Vaughn said. "But until such time that school districts have an adequate source of revenue to run the school districts, then the rob-Peter-to-pay-Paul principle will continue. We're not telling the board where to make the cuts. That's a decision the board makes."[42]

The war between pay raises and buildings plays out across the nation. But in Chicago, there were startling twists to the national problem. Despite the crying need for school repairs, the system was allegedly paying flagrant overcharges to small building contractors for emergency repairs, so much so that if proper procedures had been followed, the board could have saved $7 million of its $35 million budget in contractual services. That conclusion was reached by both the Financial Research and Advisory Committee (FRAC), a group of professionals whose governmental work was donated by the business community, and the accounting firm of Arthur Andersen and Company. In one example, the board paid a contractor $75 for an 80 cent electrical wall plate and, in another, $1,350 for a $247 vacuum cleaner, according to the audit. It also paid $796 for four boiler pressure relief valves that should have cost $123, the audit showed. By studying invoices of contractors, FRAC concluded that the system routinely paid an average of 70 percent more than retail markets when, in fact, it should have spent at least 20 percent less because of volume discounts.

In addition, labor rates were often high compared to industry standards. For example, the board paid $58 an hour for a pipefitter versus the industry average of $40.50. Materials and the amount of personnel time billed to the board appeared also to be inflated. In one case, contractors took 100 work hours to replace an air compressor at Melody School, a job that should have taken 16 hours, auditors said. The cost of the air compressor itself was high—contractors charged $2,850 for a $1,500 piece of equipment, auditors alleged. In addition, although the board requires contractors to list the make and model of parts used and the hours spent on repair jobs, the school system routinely paid invoices that contained no such details. In the case of the $75 wall plate, contractors told the local CBS television news affiliate that the charge was a clerical error and would be refunded to the board. Regarding the 100 work hours at Melody School, a contractor said services not listed on the invoice were included.

The report was kept secret by the system for a year before it was leaked to the Better Government Association. During that time, no one was penalized for the alleged overcharges although system leaders, responding to the subsequent publicity, did announce that they had tightened contracting procedures. In fact, board attorney Patricia Whitten said federal investigators briefly studied the audit and found nothing criminal. "The indication is that it doesn't look like anything's here," Whitten said.[43]

There was another case of bureaucratic bungling of astonishing proportions. During its short tenure, the interim board worked feverishly on a nearly $400 million building bond program to begin addressing building neglect.[44] In 1989 and 1990, bonds were issued—that is, money was borrowed—through the Chicago Public Building Commission, an independent agency headed by an eleven-member board chaired by Mayor Daley.[45] But the borrowed money earmarked to replace and repair the aging schools—more than $300 million of it—sat unspent in financial institutions for years, even while city taxpayers paid interest on it, according to school board and building commission reports. The delays put an additional round of $155 million in public school building projects on hold, projects—including new schools to relieve crowding—that were scheduled to follow the first round.[46]

The commission said it never anticipated how difficult it would be to administer hundreds of contracts to replace fire alarms, tuckpoint buildings, repair electrical systems, fix roofs, and build or buy more than two dozen schools. "When you think about the magnitude of something like this, with hundreds of millions of dollars broken down with so many different sites, it's a major undertaking," said Thomas R. Walker, who was appointed executive director in the fall of 1991 to turn around the agency. The commission was "a complete mess" and "moribund for a long time," a mayoral spokesperson conceded. Eight commission administrators had been assigned to oversee the projects, far too few to handle the program, Walker said. Although hundreds of millions of dollars to help clear up its problems were sitting in the banks, the agency said it lacked personnel and proper coordination with the school system.[47]

One could also argue that it lacked the will. Daley, who had long criticized the school board for not cleaning up the system's bureaucratic mess, himself headed a sterling example of botched opportunities to improve education for Chicago's schoolchildren.

Meanwhile, since the commission's problems were not made public until January 1992, educators and parents—ecstatic when the money was borrowed—were puzzled when architects and workers did not arrive. Among those waiting were schools designated for repairs under the $155 million sequel, which included construction of twelve new schools and major repairs at sixty-nine others. "We were all fairly convinced as much as a year ago that the money was there," said Patrick T. Reynolds, a council member at Murphy School, slated for $1.5 million in repairs in 1992. "We even had an architect out at our meeting because we figured it was time to start making plans."[48]

Reynolds and thousands of other school constituents did not know that the wait would extend for years. By March 1992, nearly $181 million of more than $230 million that was borrowed in 1990 remained unspent or uncommitted to specific contracts. Of seventy-two projects, seven were begun; none was completed. Of 360 projects at 113 schools funded from a 1989 bond issue, 36 were completed by March 1992.[49] With heightened publicity and the contributions of Thomas Walker, projects quickened somewhat. In 1992, construction on twenty-three schools under the 1990 bond issue began and four were finished, compared to three schools begun and zero finished the previous year. The program, however, still lagged years behind its initial conception.

Although amazing in its own right, Chicago's bureaucratic blundering was hardly unique. In 1993, school officials in Dade County, Florida, came under fire for building just half of the schools promised five years earlier when voters approved a $980 million bond issue, *Education Week* reported. School officials blamed most of the delays on damage inflicted by Hurricane Andrew and red tape generated by state laws and agencies governing school construction, according to the education weekly.[50]

The situation was different in New York City where the state legislature in 1988 created the New York City School Construction Authority and instituted a five-year $4.3 billion plan to address the city's school building needs. Although the Chicago building commission had existed for years, its newly formed New York City counterpart quickly outpaced it. In the first three fiscal years of its existence, the three-member board awarded nearly $2.5 billion in construction contracts. New York had another critical element: strict oversight, of which the Chicago public building commission had none. The New York authority had an inspector general's office with strong powers and an internal audit division, two essential units when billions of dollars of public money are at issue.

The oversight proved its worth in 1993, when a bid-rigging scandal unfolded and eleven people were indicted.

There were other questionable practices—the spending plan included more than $1 million to buy and renovate a home for the New York City chancellor of schools. Although marred by such problems, the New York City Construction Authority made progress. It assigned project managers and made them accountable for all details of their projects, including design, construction, safety, and financial management. It established a community relations unit to work with schools and parents who had a stake in the construction. In addition, it set up a number of streamlining procedures, ranging from easy-to-understand bids to prompt payment of vendors to bond waivers for contracts under $50,000, of which the latter gave smaller companies a chance to compete. In its first year, the New York City Construction Authority broke ground on two new schools and launched renovations of several others.[51]

Meanwhile, in Chicago, other governmental agencies failed to contribute to reclaiming the troubled system. The Cook County Circuit Court, for example, allowed code violation cases to languish for years. In 1992, 113 code violation cases were pending against city public schools; only 25 had been filed during that decade. Two of the cases, one from 1986, involved broken windows. Another four were for roof and ceiling leaks. The rest were for fire alarm violations. "Absolutely no case should be allowed to disgrace our courtrooms by sitting there for years," said Cheryl Aaron, a spokeswoman for the Association of Community Organizations for Reform Now, which monitored school repairs. Over five years, 169 fires caused nearly $1.5 million in damage to Chicago public schools, with at least one serious injury in a boiler room fire.[52] At Beethoven Elementary School on the South Side, a fire code case continued in court through more than forty hearings in four years.

It was a typical delay.

Then Cook County Circuit Court judge Morton Zwick was assigned to handle school building cases. In 1992, Zwick ended Beethoven's case by fining the system and forcing the board to install an updated fire alarm system within three months. Schools had been cited for hundreds of fire code violations since a 1985 fire safety law required annunciator panels that electronically pinpoint the location of fires, but Zwick issued the first finding of guilt and the first penalty. "The first time anyone pushed on this was when Judge Zwick put that deadline on Beethoven," said assistant corporation counsel Alexander P. Johnson, who prosecuted board code violations. After that, the city and the schools negotiated an agreement to set deadlines for correcting each case. "It broke the logjam," Johnson said.[53]

Zwick accused school officials of balancing their budget on the backs of children after hearing of handicapped pupils maneuvering wheelchairs and walkers around buckets of water from a leaky roof and eight-year-olds being exposed to fumes from lead-based paint.

"These children are unrepresented. Nobody is championing their cause," he said. In what is believed to be the first ruling of its kind, Zwick appointed the county public guardian to represent the students and ordered lead tests of children at two schools.[54] In June 1992, Zwick made history again by ordering 775 students to be moved from two school buildings at Richards Vocational High School that were not equipped with adequate fire alarm systems. Principal Patrick Noonan said, apparently in all earnestness, that the staff had planned to ring cowbells if fire broke out.[55] Zwick was criticized by school officials for going too far, but his actions set a precedent. He singlehandedly began to reverse a lackadaisical attitude toward building code violations.

Other problems contribute to the overall breakdown in oversight for school buildings. Arguing that the Chicago building department is responsible for city schools, the state legislature exempted Chicago buildings from the state life safety code for schools. The code gives the state the legal right to close suburban—but not Chicago—schools for deplorable building conditions. Meanwhile, the building department that is supposed to oversee Chicago schools overlooks at least one major component: electrical systems.

Following the 1958 fire that killed ninety-two children and three nuns at Our Lady of the Angels Catholic School, the late Mayor Richard J. Daley ordered that school electrical systems be inspected. Inspections had been conducted for more than twenty years but stopped after a corruption inquiry resulted in indictments of twenty-nine building inspectors in 1978. Others retired, and the number of inspectors dropped from eighty-five to sixteen. In the early 1980s, the department fell behind in inspections, but, instead of increasing staff, city budget officials told the building department to set priorities for inspections; thus, schools were cut from the list. The number of inspectors later climbed to forty-one, but annual school inspections did not resume. "It's a question, from our standpoint, of manpower," said Timothy M. Cullerton, the department's chief electrical inspector who provided the statistics. "That breaks down to money—although you would think that's not important when you're talking about the lives and safety of children of Chicago, be they in private schools or public schools."[56]

Today the electrical inspections bureau is required by law to annually inspect day-care centers, hospitals, and nursing homes, but, when it comes to schools, it inspects only new electrical work and responds to complaints. While it cited schools for thousands of boiler code violations over a five-year period, the building department wrote up fewer than three dozen electrical violations despite a well-documented need: electrical emergencies in the schools number about six hundred a month, school board records show. Because of the leaking roof at Kelly High School on the Southwest Side, for example, power was shut off to light fixtures in the school's learning-disabled resource room for years. "Instead of fixing the damage to the roof," said principal John P. Gelsomino, "they shut off the power." Classes were still held there, however.

An electrical fire at Poe Classical School's field house on the far South Side in 1991 caused $35,000 worth of damage. Fortunately, teachers and children escaped unharmed. At Van Vlissingen School, electrical wiring hung from light fixtures, prompting one youngster to write a school essay about being "shocked" when he pulled on the wiring during horseplay. The case of Richard Haley, who died by touching a windowsill at Garvey School, is the most extreme example of the need for regular electrical inspections. Several heaters at Garvey were without ground wires, apparently for years. [57]

Although his father's order prompted the original school electrical inspections, the current mayor, Richard M. Daley, believes they are unnecessary. "We feel it would be redundant to add another level of city electrical staff to those who already exist at the board of education," said mayoral press aide Caroline Grisko. "It would mean more money going into the inspection process when the real problem—as everyone knows full well—is that the board needs more money in its building and maintenance fund."[58] The school system has about seventy electricians, but they spend their time responding to emergencies, not conducting inspections. Meanwhile, the Chicago Fire Department inspects only fire alarms and exit signs for electrical problems. Ironically, if Chicago's school houses were day-care centers or nursing homes, they would be cited for building code violations and forced by the city to make repairs or risk being shut down.

Policies of political expediency and neglect of our nation's school buildings will be far more expensive to rectify in the long run, critics say. "If we wait too long, it's simply going to be too late," declared Murphy School's Patrick Reynolds. "The physical plant can't last forever without these kinds of repairs." Even as far back as 1984, almost two thirds of a $95 million bond issue in Chicago public schools was earmarked for building repairs made necessary because of years of delayed maintenance.[59]

Much of the work was an attempt to catch up on rehabilitation never finished in a previous project in the 1970s. Each annual delay continues to bring higher costs. "When you get into financial problems, you try not to cut back in the classroom first, so building repair is the first place [that is cut], which means a $10,000 repair in 1980 becomes a $100,000 problem in 1990," said Walter Jones, Detroit's deputy superintendent of fiscal integrity. "Small problems become big problems." That is what happened at Calumet High School, which, after two decades and much publicity, finally underwent renovation in the fall of 1992. Basketball players no longer dodge gaping holes in the gymnasium floor. The floor, once rotted away by water dripping from a leaky roof, is smooth—so smooth that the school now hosts grammar school basketball and cheerleading championships. "We never could do any of those things before because of the buckling floors, the leaking ceilings, the falling plaster," council chairman Edwin Green said. "We would have been asking to be sued by everybody."

Although welcomed, the approximately $2.5 million reno-vation was far from perfect. Within months, plaster began to deteriorate and a foot-and-a-half chunk fell in a classroom. Project manager Daniel Scholtes of Michuda Construction of Chicago said the construction company was paid to fix only plaster that had fallen—about 2 percent in the school—not to repair weakened plaster. "The contract did not include pre-ventative maintenance," Scholtes said. "I didn't search out areas I thought were sagging."

Scholtes estimated it would cost about $5,000 and take a week for two workers just to inspect the entire building for loose plaster, much less repair it. To further aggravate the situ-ation, one wall was not tuckpointed because it had already been completed five years earlier. But the work was done so poorly that bricks had become loose and fallen. As another cost-cutting measure, no chairs were installed in the balcony of the auditorium, which means the entire student body can not be seated at any one time. "If you short-cut, at some point you're going to have the same problem again," Green said. "Why does a board go into a job three fourths the way?"

Although the renovation budget was set by the board of education, the Chicago Public Building Commission handled the work. "We can't get in the position of having gone through the first third of schools and doing everything we thought needed doing," commission director Walker said, "and have no dollars left for the remaining schools."[60]

State representatives Clem Balanoff and Ellis Levin, both Chicago Democrats, each proposed legislation to place a tax referendum for school repairs on the city ballot. Such a life safety tax is already authorized for every other school system in the state, amounting to 5 cents per $100 of assessed valua-tion or about $10 a year for the owner of a home with a mar-ket value of $75,000. It also gives school boards the right to borrow as much as 13.8 percent of their tax base for life safety projects, such as renovating buildings to meet fire, safety, and environmental standards, reducing energy con-sumption, and making buildings more secure from intruders. If legislators had the courage to adopt such a tax for Chicago schools, they could also demand that schools meet the life safety standards required of other districts. "It would help the schools in Chicago," said Cook County superintendent of schools Lloyd W. Lehman, whose office worked furiously with the Chicago Board of Education to develop new and more thorough criteria for inspecting city schools. Lehman said it was the first such comprehensive effort in two decades to help schools identify building situations most threatening to students and staff.

Until reform, few outsiders knew of the building conditions, but the entry of thousands of volunteers and community residents brought the situation out of the shadows. Principals who formerly were rewarded for keeping quiet either left the system or now report to councils, many of whom encourage public lobbying for repairs. The unrelenting protests of various heroes eventually prompted some repairs and new building construction. "For so long, people did not know the conditions that existed in the public schools because they were hidden," Green said. "By having the local school councils in the schools, they can speak out and have it exposed." At Kosciuszko Elementary School on the Near West Side, school council president Emma Lozano declared herself on a hunger strike to protest overcrowding. Her six-year-old daughter was repeatedly sick, she said, because she attended classes in a hot boiler room.[61] In 1992, a $5.5 million new school for Kosciuszko was approved. But Lozano's activism did not stop there. She was arrested the following year when, as part of a crowd, she forced her way into a meeting of the Chicago Public Building Commission to lobby for construction of additional schools. The confrontation resulted in a scuffle with sheriff's deputies. The group, estimated at one hundred people, demanded that five new schools be built from the 1990 bond issue, as promised. The scuffle occurred about one week after Mayor Daley announced the first school would be built for $7.2 million—three years after the money was borrowed and deposited.[62]

Other council members assumed the role of lobbyists as well. Take the Van Vlissingen regulars, for example. For months, this indomitable group of parents arrived at the monthly school board meeting armed with protest signs and speeches trimmed to the two minutes allotted each speaker. "Our children are living in a cesspool," Frances Carr, chairperson of the school safety committee, told the board in 1991. The parents regularly attended court hearings when the

school's code violations were the subject. Their persistence—
and the resulting publicity—led to numerous repairs at Van
Vlissingen, which is located in the troubled Roseland neighborhood on the South Side. At one time in the 1970s, the
school was supposed to be replaced. Seventeen homes were
razed to make way for a new building, but the school board
abandoned its plans even after forcing the residents to move
and destroying their homes, school officials said.[63] Reform
brought Van Vlissingen's problems into the spotlight. "We can
put our input in. We have more say-so," Carr said. "The local
school councils can allow the media in."

"These people have been ignored for years," said Kelly
High School principal John P. Gelsomino of the school
activists. "School reform has opened up the can. It's brought
the community in."[64]

Superintendent Ted D. Kimbrough announces his resignation
at a press conference, November 1992.

Courtesy *Chicago Sun-Times*. Photo by Bob Ringham.

9

Revolving Leadership

There is no one trying to help the community . . . I feel as though the world and the people may come to an end. No one seems to care about the children of the future.

Thirteen-year-old Demetrius Jones, a resident of the Washington Park public housing development[1]

In the fourteen years following its financial collapse in 1979, the Chicago school system underwent constant upheaval. Seven superintendents governed. Five union strikes closed down classes, and three quarters of school principals left under reform. A revolving door of people—fifty-five in number—sat on the Chicago Board of Education.

"As soon as you get to know the system, you're gone," said Patricia Daley, a board member from 1990 to 1992. "Too many people waste too much time learning the ropes and—while they're busy learning the ropes—children are growing up, dropping out, getting pregnant, giving up."

In the first eighty years of this century, leadership of Chicago public schools was relatively stable. The system was overseen by 110 board members, averaging about 14 new appointments per decade. But from 1979 to 1992, that rate tripled, according to Thomas J. Corcoran, secretary of the board from 1981 through 1993, when he retired and became a board consultant. "What does that tell you?" he asked. "There is no doubt it contributes to the difficulty of the school system." Corcoran blamed the "change-the-manager" philosophy for the steady flow of mayoral appointments and legislation creating new boards—supposedly to shore up the steadily deteriorating schools. As Corcoran observed, "People are impatient. So we keep starting over."

Newcomers replaced incumbents, often over community protests that instability would kill the system. The protests, of course, depended on who was being replaced. In 1989, the reform law authorized Mayor Richard M. Daley to directly appoint a seven-member interim board to oversee the first year of Chicago's unprecedented education reform movement. Daley could have appointed incumbents, but instead he named only one veteran. "Daley has made the decision of putting a green board over a red-hot school crisis," said the Reverend Jesse Jackson, founder of Operation Push and then national executive director of the Chicago-based Rainbow Coalition.[2]

In 1990, as required by the reform law, the mayor appointed fifteen permanent board members from a pool of candidates selected by a newly formed grassroots nominating commission. Made up of local school council members, the commission gave communities its first real voice in board appointments—the previous commission had been advisory only. The mayor's five-month delay in getting the permanent so-called people's board seated, however, was cloaked in controversy.[3] It allowed Daley's hand-picked interim board to seal generous union contracts and select Ted D. Kimbrough as superintendent—functions, many argued, that should have been performed by the permanent reform board that would have to live with the decisions.

The controversy over Daley's appointments continued two years later when he infuriated the school community by replacing board member Patricia Daley (no relation to the mayor), who had wide community support, partly for exposing waste and partly for asking probing questions on system policy. "Anyone who gets on that board and goes against the status quo will not be there," Calumet High School's Edwin Green said. "Either the mayor gets rid of them, they get removed from certain committees, or they get pushed into the background." The mayor also drew the community's wrath by replacing Illinois Bell employee Grady Bailey, Jr., who headed the finance committee during the chaotic cuts of 1991 and presumably gained some expertise from the experience. Anna Mustafa, a third board member, was not reslated.

The mayor was reportedly angry that the incumbents rejected his advice to close schools. Daley also frequently blasted the board for not streamlining the central office and, therefore, defended his choices by insisting that he wanted more financial expertise on the board. His appointments included John F. Valinote, a thirty-one-year-old IBM manager; James D. Flanagan, a twenty-nine-year-old officer in the commercial real estate division of American Bank and Trust Company, and Charles E. Curtis, Sr., a fifty-one-year-old supervisor for the U.S. Department of Housing and Urban Development. The three formed part of the majority bloc that aggressively approached union negotiations in 1993. The school board's stance resulted in an unprecedented $60 million in concessions from the Chicago Teachers Union that year. "It was important to get some new life and new blood there," Daley said. "There is nothing wrong with that."[4]

The mayor was reportedly angry, too, when the fragmented lame-duck forces gathered on May 27, 1992, in a surprise show of unity to elect Florence B. Cox as board president. She toppled Daley ally Clinton Bristow, Jr., an ambitious administrator at Chicago State University with aspirations of becoming school superintendent. Bristow, who had been president since the reform board was seated in October 1990, sat on the building commission with Daley and sided with the mayor on school closings. Daley addressed the rocky leadership change and school closings in the same breath: "Board members were supposed to close twenty-five schools. [Then] they were supposed to close three. They finally closed one, and they have a moratorium. When you have difficult decisions to make, a lot of people want to make scapegoats of everyone. But if they want to change the leadership, so be it. They know the message they want to send to Springfield."[5]

The school board nominating commission, dominated by anti-Daley forces angry over the school closing issue, apparently retaliated against the mayor the following year by refusing to renominate three members of the original 1990 board: real estate developer Stephen R. Ballis, seen as the mastermind of many board strategies; vice president Juan S. Cruz;

and chairperson of the instruction committee, Saundra Bishop. On May 26, 1993, one day after the three majority bloc members lost their bid to be renominated, the bloc carried through its plans to oust Florence B. Cox as president.

It was a riotous meeting punctuated by threats and taunts as the bloc replaced Cox with another African American, D. Sharon Grant, a forty-three-year-old chief operating officer of a health care sales and marketing company. Grant was little known, but her mother, Illa Daggett, had been an ardent community activist who had supported the late Richard J. Daley. At the meeting, Eddie Read, president of Chicago Black United Communities, walked to the podium and objected to the action. Flanked by members of various street gangs, including the Vice Lords, the El Rukns, and the Disciples—who were becoming increasingly active on the political front that year— Read warned, "Don't make Florence Cox a Rodney King. That is not rhetoric. That is truth." It was a reference to the California man whose beating by police, captured on a home videotape, sparked widespread rioting in April 1992 in Los Angeles, resulting in the deaths of at least forty-one people.

Despite allegations, Mayor Daley insisted he had nothing to do with the board election of Grant, whose company, Concerned Health Care of America, was a subcontractor for the Chicago Transportation Authority and the State of Illinois. "I've worked with Florence Cox, and I can work with anyone over there. It's up to the board," Daley said. "They decided this on their own."[6]

If board appointments were controversial in Chicago, a city once dubbed "Beirut on the Lake" for its city council wars of the 1980s, the selection of superintendents was even more so. The controversies stretched back decades—and they often carried racial overtones.

Benjamin C. Willis, who became superintendent in 1953, built new schools for an additional one hundred thousand children and reduced class size. Many believed his attitude toward integration proved to be his downfall, however. Known for maintaining temporary classrooms—the infamous "Willis wagons"—that prevented blacks from enrolling in white schools, Willis resigned in 1966, a year before his contract expired. He denied he was forced out by an increasingly adversarial board.[7]

His successor, James F. Redmond, was known as a gentleman and a conciliator. Redmond had been an administrator under Willis's predecessor, superintendent Harold C. Hunt (1947–53). Hunt was admired in Chicago for his contributions to the system, not the least of which was introducing ethics standards in such areas as purchasing.[8] As an administrator for Hunt, Redmond knew the Chicago system, an advantage he had over some of those who were to succeed him. In the words of historian Mary J. Herrick, "He had seen the original reclaiming of an administrative staff, the rescuing of a teaching force, and the severance of corrupt business affiliations in the school system of a great city. He had seen the ethnic patterns and conflicts of that city, watched its municipal government in action, and knew the traditions and legal status of its Board of Education."[9]

Redmond also had experience with fierce battles over segregation in his previous post as superintendent of schools in New Orleans. In Chicago, he introduced a desegregation plan that critics said went too far; others said it did not go far enough. Redmond served from 1966 to 1975. He stepped down but sharply criticized the "constant bickering" of board members who, he said, could not work together.[10]

Joseph P. Hannon replaced Redmond and gained the unenviable distinction of presiding over the system's financial collapse in 1979. He stepped down in the midst of it, two months after being awarded a new four-year contract. Angeline P. Caruso succeeded him and served for two years. Caruso, a thirty-five-year veteran of the Chicago public schools, was elected interim superintendent over the objections of Jesse Jackson, who insisted that an African American should be named to the post, not a Caucasian.

Ruth B. Love was the system's first African-American superintendent—a flashy, domineering, and, many say, innovative school chief from Oakland, California, who arrived in 1981. In her first month, however, Love ran into a public relations disaster: she announced that her office, conference room, and car were wiretapped. But her chief deputy, Charles Mitchell, Jr., later backpedaled, saying he concocted the story, according to press reports at the time; consequently, he resigned.

Love was praised for such innovations as the Adopt-a-School program, which built bridges to the corporate community. But while she had strong ideas, some believed she was better at proposing initiatives than carrying them through.[11] She was known, for example, for the controversial Chicago Mastery Learning skills program, a systemwide reading program that required children to learn 283 distinct reading skills. Critics charged that when theory was carried into the classroom, children spent so much time filling in workbooks that many never opened a book. In the words of associate superintendent Margaret Harrigan, who scrapped the program after Love's departure, "One of the joys of our lives is reading, and many children just don't have books in their hands."[12] Love was forced out in 1985 two weeks after the board gave her its vote of confidence. She claimed that Mayor Harold Washington instigated her removal because she was neutral during the 1983 mayoral election. When she left, Love filed suit, charging that her ouster was a politically motivated conspiracy marked by race and sex discrimination. She sought up to $12 million in damages but later agreed to drop the suit.[13]

Manford Byrd, Jr., a deputy superintendent who had served in the school system for decades, had made three unsuccessful bids for the top job before he was chosen to succeed Love. Under Byrd's administration, improvements were visible: new state money was used to restore attendance counselors, reading specialists, after-school social centers, full-time assistant principals, and free summer school for some high school students with multiple failures. (The board no longer funds free summer school. A number of schools, however, have resurrected the program free-of-charge by using Chapter One funds. At the same time, those students who can pay are encouraged to do so.) Byrd's administration hired more substitute teachers, decreased mid-semester teacher transfers, and ordered magnet schools to discipline troublesome students rather than send them back to neighborhood schools.[14] Reading scores improved under Byrd.

Then, in 1987, came the longest teachers' strike in Chicago school history, followed by the reform law calling for dramatic change in the system. Critics charged that Byrd was lukewarm to the effort, a position that ultimately led the board not to renew his contract in 1989. James W. Compton, president of the interim board that selected Byrd's successor, told reporters that Byrd should have been in the forefront of the reform movement, but he was not. "The perception was that he was against it. Had he taken a leadership role in crafting it, he wouldn't have run into what he eventually ran into," Compton said.[15]

But Byrd's self-described style was to work for gradual change. "Somehow in urban centers we've gotten the notion that something cataclysmic must be happening," he said. Byrd's departure coincided with dramatic changes in the racial politics of the city. Chicago's mayoral post in 1989 had been returned to a white man, Richard M. Daley, an Irishman who replaced Eugene Sawyer, an African American who had succeeded Harold Washington after Washington's death from a heart attack on November 25, 1987. Washington was the city's first African-American mayor. Before Byrd's departure, members of the African-American community rallied to retain him. Among them was an association of black business owners who said $150 million in contracts had come their way as a result of his enforcement of affirmative action policies.[16]

Charles D. Almo, a respected and bright veteran administrator in the system, succeeded Byrd—but only for four months—until the interim board chose Ted D. Kimbrough from California's troubled Compton Unified School District to run the nation's third largest school system. Enrollment in the Compton system was about 5 percent that of Chicago; achievement was low and the dropout rate high. What's more, Compton schools had a history of harsh labor strife and student walkouts. In 1987–88, Compton hit the bottom 1 percent of all California schools in state test scores. In addition, Kimbrough's private business interests in California included part ownership in a manufacturing company that declared bankruptcy, according to newspaper reports at the time.[17] "His credentials are nowhere near other educators' right here in this city," said Florence Cox, then co-chair of a coalition of parent advisory councils.[18]

Kimbrough came recommended by then California state superintendent of education Bill Honig. Further, the Compton school chief had a no-nonsense reputation: he reassigned forty top administrators during his first two years in office amidst allegations of altered student test scores, illegal contracts, and nepotism.[19]

The interim board selected Kimbrough hurriedly after other choices fell through. "We flew out to California. We had a whole day of interviews with people who raved about him," said interim board vice president William S. Singer years later. "There was nothing but wild praise for the guy."

From the beginning, the selection was mired in controversy. Kimbrough's $175,000 salary was $75,000 higher than Byrd's. Kimbrough's benefits package included a $25,000 housing allowance, unlimited expenses, and an annuity that provided as much as $30,000 a year for life after age sixty-five.

Community activists objected when Kimbrough stayed in a $650-a-night hotel suite for a reception two months before he took his post, even though a local foundation footed the bill. His image was further tarnished when a doctor of law degree from UCLA that was listed on his resume turned out to be in error after it was challenged. Kimbrough told Chicago reporters he had no idea how the incorrect information got onto a "resume addendum" distributed by the interim board but said it was actually an honorary law degree from the University of West Los Angeles.[20] In February 1990, Kimbrough hosted a dinner at a San Francisco restaurant for superintendents attending a conference sponsored by the American Association of School Administrators. He reimbursed the Chicago school system for the $1,000 restaurant bill but only after the public expressed outrage.

Despite the negative publicity, Kimbrough forged ahead, declaring his intent to reduce the Chicago school bureaucracy and support decentralization. He greeted more than five thousand local school council members at their swearing-in ceremony November 2, 1989, with these words: "A lot of soothsayers and pundits are predicting we will not succeed, that school-based governance is a futile experiment. Well, they will be proven wrong."[21]

One day later, he promised that after his arrival on January 15, he would dismiss any administrator who balked at supplying the newly formed councils with proper training information. "I think it's unfortunate that the councils don't have their materials at this point. I can't go in and order anybody to do anything just yet," he said two months before his term began in 1990. "But I tell you, January 15, if that problem hasn't been taken care of, I'll get some other people who will."[22]

Six months into his new job, Kimbrough agreed that Pershing Road blocked reform. "Certainly that is the case," he wrote in a *Chicago Sun-Times* opinion column. "What those who prefer to criticize neglect to say is that it will take more than a few months to solve problems that have been decades in the making."[23]

But as his tenure lengthened, Kimbrough alienated both the Chicago education community and reformers by not bridling the very bureaucracy he promised to change while making steep cuts in schools as the system's financial picture worsened. He asked employees to accept a pay freeze while insisting he himself was underpaid. When reform groups suggested he take a pay cut to the tune of $60,000 to match the mayor's salary, he called the request insulting. "You ask me to come here to risk my life—take ten years off my life—and you ask me to [take a pay cut]?" said Kimbrough, who had received $108,000 a year in Compton. Describing himself as an executive of what amounts to "one of the biggest businesses in the state," he insisted his work was far more critical to Chicago than that of highly paid presidents of private companies.[24]

Kimbrough's comments did not go over well with community groups. Nor, in the midst of a financial crisis, did *Chicago Sun-Times* reports, that the system's travel and convention bill exceeded $4 million during Kimbrough's first eighteen months in office. Kimbrough himself spent at least $67,000 in travel, convention, and dining expenses, more than six times that spent by Manford Byrd, who insiders said was frugal when it came to his own personal expenses. Kimbrough, on the other hand, spent thousands of dollars for restaurant meals alone. Some meals exceeded $100, and many receipts did not document who was present or why they met. Among the dining charges were $103 for a meal with a businessperson and a television news reporter, $81 to interview a job applicant, and $151 to meet with a cabinet member and a board leader.

"That's highway robbery," said Lu Palmer, chairman of Chicago Black United Communities and a prominent figure in the African-American community. "If he's interviewing people for a job, he doesn't have to take them for dinner. He can have them come to his office."

Kimbrough dismissed the tab as minimal for a system with a $2.7 billion budget and attributed the travel costs to school reform and the necessity of promoting it nationwide. "This is a school district that is in the national eye, and people want to know about it," he said. "Under school reform, it's just so much more demanding. Most people wonder how I do what I do."

Kimbrough also argued that such criticism deflected attention from the real problem: lack of education funding. "If we keep it at the level of looking at every little item—whether I bought a No. 2 pencil or a No. 3 pencil—it diffuses and distracts us from where we ought to be. We need to concentrate on the real problem of sufficient dollars. You can take all this money you're talking about here, it wouldn't make that much a difference."[25]

Some also were angered by reports that Adrienne Y. Bailey, superintendent of instruction, spent more than $1,000 in cab fares in eighteen months, mostly for travel between her home and O'Hare airport. Under reform, Bailey's department expenses in travel and convention costs soared, which she considered an accomplishment and a move toward professionalizing the school system's staff. "Some people see this as being excessive or unnecessary. I don't see it that way as all," she said. "It's the opportunity to network, to not reinvent the wheel, to consider how things can be done collaboratively." But why hold conferences for Chicagoans in hotels and out-of-town resorts? Bailey's response was that the Pershing Road building "is certainly not the kind of environment that is conducive to deliberation, and thinking, and planning. It's being able to feel you're a professional—having decent meals, being surrounded in environments where you can do your work."[26]

Other things angered reformers. Central office administrators received pay raises under the guise of promotions. Principals received none. The school board, upon administrators' advice, cut equipment and supplies for schools by 90 percent while reducing central office supplies by only 25 percent. Teachers on the front lines, many of whom yearly spent hundreds of dollars of their own money for supplies, were insulted. Cuts were steep. They included the full-time assistant principals, reading specialists, and free summer school that Byrd had reinstated. Resentment and power struggles fueled a battle that made children the casualties.

Meanwhile, Kimbrough's administration trimmed the bureaucracy significantly. Unfortunately, critics charged, the trims involved massive last-minute cuts that gave no thought to how the role of administration should be redefined under reform. "There were people who needed to go, but it had to be done on an individual basis, not wholesale throw-all-the-rascals out," said Grace Dawson, who headed the Department of Dropout Prevention at the time. "The Singer board and Kimbrough did more to hurt the system than any one group of people because they did it helter-skelter, without any thought put into it."

Interim board vice president William S. Singer rejected that argument, which was echoed in schools and throughout the reform community: "Clearly that's wrong. There was an enormous amount of thought. We had task forces of people working day and night for three months in May, June, and July before the people were cut. We cut $60 million in expenditures in one year. We cut more out of that system than anyone."

Many complained the central office tried to do the same tasks it always performed, but with fewer people. "The complaints are almost unanimous: All the energies of local school councils are going to fight the central office rather than developing the schools the way they want," said Bernie Noven from PURE.[27] "We went all over the country to find someone who could turn things around, not just to baby-sit or stand by," past school board president George Muñoz, also a critic of Kimbrough, said in 1992. "No one has said we have a better educational system today than we had two years ago. In fact, quite the opposite is true."[28]

Schools and communities were also up in arms about Kimbrough's recommendation to close twenty-six schools in 1991. The plan was based on statistics that the 1990 student enrollment of 409,000 was about 50,000 less than the decade before; yet there had been no corresponding decrease in the number of schools.[29] In both public and private systems nationwide, schools were closing because of declining enrollments. Particularly to the business community, downsizing seemed a sensible beginning toward addressing the system's financial crises.

But educators see it differently. They argue that because of both a proliferation in computer labs and a surge in social problems that create children with special needs, schooling in urban America in the 1990s requires more space than schooling a decade or more ago. Children born addicted to cocaine or learning disabled children, for example, require smaller class sizes. A school serving them, therefore, requires more classrooms, counseling offices, nurse stations, and reading labs than a school filled with children who are less needy.

Closing schools saves little money, critics charged, because union contracts at that time guaranteed most employees their jobs, and the largest part of any school budget is salaries. In addition, most of the schools targeted were for low-achieving or special education students and, therefore, received federal funding. Such savings would not reduce the budget shortfall, which lay in the main fund for day-to-day operations. In fact, the money the school system spent on travel, conventions, dues, and subscriptions during the first eighteen months of reform amounted to more than the annual savings of closing five schools, based on the board's own estimates of savings averaging $726,000 a school.[30]

Perhaps the strongest argument against school closings for economic reasons is that research proves schools with fewer students do better than those with larger enrollments. Closing Chicago schools would enlarge enrollments that already exceed state averages. Besides, students forced to cross rival gang territories to get to their newly assigned schools would feel threatened by gang violence and might give up on school entirely. Such a theory, system veterans say, was apparently proven at Farragut High School, which has been regularly plagued by gang violence since another area school closed.

Board members originally rejected school closings, insisting that the schools proposed by Kimbrough and his staff were ill-chosen; they were not in the worst physical condition nor did they fail to educate. Plenty of schools fitting those descriptions were exempted. However, facing a financial crisis and hoping their action would win mayoral support for more school funding, the board bowed to pressure and reversed its previous vote. Just days before the school year was to begin in 1991, it voted to close thirteen schools. When the tally was taken, some teachers at those schools had already put up their bulletin boards for the new school year.

By July 1992, a war-weary Kimbrough, prompted on his status, confessed he would not return unless the Chicago environment changed. "Anyone who doesn't feel that they're making a difference and that support is not forthcoming would not be very bright to want to stay in a crucible that is hostile," Kimbrough said at a *Chicago Sun-Times* editorial board meeting. A decision to stay "would probably mean a change in the environment—the hostilities that are here, the lack of support, the racist comments that continue to flow out not about me so much but about this district that keep this district from receiving the kind of money it should.

"You can beat up on Kimbrough all day long, but it's not going to make one bit of difference about improving the quality of life or helping these children," he continued. "What ought to be the position of the people in this city is how do we help Ted Kimbrough, this board of education, and the local school councils do their job and do it better."[31]

By late 1992, the controversies had subsided, and, by the time Kimbrough announced his imminent departure in January 1993, his opposition had mellowed. Presumably this was partly because Kimbrough had begun to understand the system and partly because he had changed advisers, insiders said. Kimbrough had been "gobbled up" by guardians of the bureaucracy, the late Chicago Teachers Union president Jacqueline B. Vaughn told the *Chicago Tribune*, but toward the end he began to understand the reform movement.[32] In the same month of his departure, he conceded that closing schools does not necessarily save money and acknowledged the philosophy behind keeping them open. "There's plenty of research out there that says small schools give more individualized instruction to students and also have smaller classes," he said.[33]

Although Kimbrough's tenure was dogged by controversy—part of it for opposing decentralization—there were visible accomplishments, including a nearly $400 million building plan adopted by the interim board for management through the public building commission, introduction of computerized routing in busing students, improvements in purchasing, and the reduction in the number of children awaiting evaluations and placements in special education.

By the time Kimbrough left in early 1993, even some of his fiercest critics had sided with him. Board president Cox was furious at his forced departure. Alderwoman Dorothy Tillman of the Third Ward led a stormy protest and accused Mayor Daley of orchestrating the move. "Four board members made the decision to go to Dr. Kimbrough like gangsters and tell him to get out of town," Tillman said, referring to members of the majority bloc. "The question is whether they were serving the children or the master."[34]

"His first year he got an F, and now an incomplete," said Chicago Black United Communities' Eddie Read in late 1992. "I think he may have become sensitized to the black community and some of the problem areas of the school system and may have started to attempt to turn around and work with it."[35]

"Toward the end, he was the kind of superintendent we should have had, but, by that time, he lost his credibility," said one veteran administrator.

Leadership is key to the success of a decentralizing school system, argued Paul T. Hill and Josephine Bonan in their 1991 report *Decentralization and Accountability in Public Education.* In Chicago, Los Angeles, and Montgomery County, Maryland, schools were "awash in confusion about the goals, boundaries, and permanence of site-based management," wrote the authors, placing the blame on the superintendents of those systems. "A superintendent who sends mixed signals—that site-based management might be abandoned after a while or that he or she may be ambivalent about it—can singlehandedly destroy a site-based management initiative." It may even require a chief executive officer of a school district to turn on his or her own staff: "Only the CEO can persuade central managers to abandon old habits of intervening in local office business and assure them that they will not be punished if a local office makes a mistake."[36]

But to revamp a central office, one had to understand where the problems lay, and constantly changing superintendents prevented a meaningful clean-up from occurring. Kimbrough traveled often and was not a detail man, insiders say, and may simply not have known about the problems. By the time he did understand them, some argued, he was gone.

In February 1993, Kimbrough was replaced temporarily by one-time city principal Richard E. Stephenson, who received widespread support in Chicago. In a historical first, the Chicago Principals Association endorsed Stephenson and said he should be made permanent school chief. Supporters described him as both principled and politically savvy. "I am very much surprised this board chose someone of this character," said Sixth Ward alderman John O. Steele, calling Stephenson "the people's choice" the day he was chosen as interim school chief. "This is a great day for Chicago when the school board can pick a person who has little or no clout but is known throughout his community as a hard worker. In Chicago, the best man doesn't always win. But in this case, the best man won."

"If there is anything he lacks, it's arrogance," then board member Albert Logan said. "And arrogance is what can kill a superintendent."[37]

Stephenson was one of the system's eleven district superintendents charged with helping schools in such areas as local school council disputes, personnel problems, staff training, and distribution of maintenance funds. As subdistrict superintendent, he supervised forty-five principals and fifty-four school sites. Although Stephenson's support apparently ran deep, it was not unanimous. Some complained privately that the thirty-five-year veteran was not tough enough, lacked vision, and had no real accomplishments to his name. Others argued he was a "centrist" who did not embrace school-based management. Stephenson and his supporters denied all charges as excuses to hire someone from outside the system.

Another insider candidate was former board president Clinton Bristow, Jr., the mayor's apparent choice for the position of superintendent.

There was widespread sentiment that the new superintendent should be an insider well versed in system finances, obstacles, and politics. Despite the push for a local choice, an out-of-town search committee chose two East Coast finalists, Argie K. Johnson and Laval Steele Wilson. Johnson, deputy chancellor for instruction in New York City, had earned a reputation for integrity and educational success. A one-time science teacher, she became principal in 1978 of the struggling Ruggles Junior High School 258, which she transformed into a model for the city—partly through curriculum, partly through strong discipline, and partly through a style that included knowing every child by name. Johnson went on to become superintendent of one of New York City's thirty-two school subdistricts. There she doubled the frequency of staff development, increased the number of teacher trainees in math, and expanded the use of computers. She also garnered a reputation as being tough: she had at least four principals removed during her tenure, including a principal convicted of welfare fraud who had been supported by Johnson's own school board. Even the New York school system's critics found a friend in her, including Bob Law, an activist who led boycotts against the schools at various times. "All the people we dealt with prior to Argie were mired in the bureaucracy. They seemed to like to be protected by the bureaucracy," he said. "With Argie, you get more access."[38]

The second finalist, Laval Steele Wilson, was a former school superintendent in Boston who was forced out in 1990. Critics said he alienated communities by his high-handed style, but supporters attributed his ouster to politics. From Boston, Wilson became a consultant and then was hired by the state of New Jersey to assume control of the Paterson school system.

Wilson was far more controversial than Johnson, but he had an extensive resume. In New Jersey, he set up a program that provided nothing but reading, writing, math, and the state-required gym courses for failing students. In Boston, he negotiated a nationally acclaimed 1989 union agreement that shifted authority to schools and provided help where needed while threatening penalties for schools that failed. Wilson also developed a training academy with Boston University for new and potential principals and created all-day early learning centers for three- to six-year-olds.[39]

After unprecedented televised and open community forums featuring both candidates, the school board chose Johnson. She joined the system on August 8, 1993. In selecting an outsider, members of the school board's majority bloc bluntly stated that insider candidates for school chief were not qualified. Board member Stephen R. Ballis explained: "We were required by law to do a national search. We had an honest and clear playing field. And everybody had an opportunity to apply in a fair manner."[40]

Community members argued that the board went outside the system so it could control the school chief since any newcomer would obviously need substantial advice. "Instability means removing all people who have a history of what has happened to date with the Chicago public school system—and once they remove everybody who has a history, then what they say is law," claimed school activist Calvin Pearce. Hiring any outsider as the system headed toward a possible shutdown, he insisted, was just one more nail in the coffin of Chicago public schools, a system long victimized by senseless decisions and practices born often out of lack of knowledge and inexperience.[41]

Insiders have concluded that so many decisions that threaten to sabotage the well-being of Chicago schools cannot be purely accidental. Some go so far as to say there is a behind-the-scenes campaign to persuade the public—unfamiliar with the reasons why the school system is failing—to support a voucher system that would give parents public money for private school tuition. Such a system, community activists insist, would deprive public schools of funding that already has proven inadequate for basic programs. Vouchers would benefit mostly the middle and upper class because the overwhelmingly white private schools would simply raise tuition beyond the voucher amount and, therefore, beyond the price range of low-income, mostly minority families, or so the argument goes. Quotas may exist to serve low-income children, but the number served would pale compared to the number in need of an education.

On the other hand, voucher proponents argue that private school parents pay their share of taxes and should get a fair return on their investment. They also argue that vouchers would allow low-income parents to have the same schooling choices afforded their wealthier counterparts. Most important, they argue that vouchers would stimulate public schools to improve by forcing them to compete.

Public schools, hamstrung by union rules and state regulations on such issues as employee dismissals, respond that since private schools have more advantages than their public counterparts it would be unfair to require public schools to compete against private ones. In truth, public schools could never compete successfully because private schools are not obligated to take every troubled child or those in need of expensive special education services. Private schools could—and do—attract the best students with the most parental support; thus the public school system would be left with the children nobody wants, voucher opponents argue. An already two-tiered system of education—one for the poor, one for the wealthier—would be further ensured.

"This entire school system has been under attack by people who represent concerns outside to take public dollars and funnel those public dollars to private institutions. And it is all being done with the blessings and by the wishes of the Fifth Floor," charged Pearce, referring to Mayor Daley's office on the fifth floor of City Hall.

"A number of years ago you couldn't talk about it. You were elitist, people jumped out and said you were racist—You know, all these other words they used trying to divide people and separate people," Daley said in 1992. "Now it's come to the point where people are looking at education with an open mind."[42]

The controversy over school leadership and politics in Chicago is neither unique nor new. In the nation's forty-five largest urban school districts during 1993, the average tenure of a school superintendent was two years, according to the Council of the Great City Schools.[43]

Joseph A. Fernandez, chancellor of the New York City school system, was fired in a four to three school board vote in 1993 because of his plan to teach children as early as first grade about gay rights and for a policy to distribute condoms to high school students. In Boston, Laval Steele Wilson had the longest tenure of any superintendent in twenty-two years—but he lasted only a stormy five years. Threatened by a $400 million shortfall and teacher walkouts, Los Angeles Unified School District superintendent William Anton left in the fall of 1992. And in Dade County, Florida, three superintendents oversaw the system in the three years after Joseph A. Fernandez left for New York City in 1990.[44]

Urban superintendents are increasingly torn by legislative demands to keep taxes down, by political backbiting over jobs and contracts, by power plays from sometimes novice board members unaccustomed to the prestige of their position, by the soaring toll of societal problems, and by the need to address them. Union demands conflict with school demands to gain more control over hiring practices. Urban school superintendents are caught in the crossfire. Amidst it all is the public pressure to improve failing schools.

Jerome T. Murphy, dean of the Harvard Graduate School of Education, told the *Washington Post* that the high turnover rate for urban school superintendents prevents reforms from taking hold. "It's a 'keep-your-bags-packed' job," he said.[45]

Strikers gather in a display of solidarity at McKinley Park on the Southwest Side, October 1983.

Courtesy *Chicago Sun-Times*. Photo by Richard Derk.

10

Union Might

I hope that in the future when I become a teacher, we will not be in a $415 million dollar debt so that there will be no more problems!

Jessica Pantoja, a fifth grader at Smyser Elementary School [1]

Chronic crises have plagued Chicago public schools for decades: school disrepair, lack of disciplinary programs, budget cuts, large class sizes. They all have their roots in the financial difficulties of the system. In the long and complex history of the crises, the strength of the labor unions has played a key role.

Union strength has many sources. While board members and superintendents came and went, union leadership remained constant and capable. Some school leaders were inexperienced in the vagaries of Springfield, but union officials have warmed the chairs of the house Democratic leadership offices for years. While the unions wrote legislation, some school groups and even some board members failed to read the bills. With the possible exception of a unified battlefront during negotiations in 1993, the fifteen-member board was disorganized and divided. Organization, on the other hand, was the forte of the teachers union, a well-oiled machine whose ability to effectively communicate with its thirty thousand members came in handy during legislative sessions. The union employed telephone hotlines, published its own newspaper, and held regular meetings during the negotiating process to

Teacher union president Jacqueline B. Vaughn and fellow
union members sing "We Shall Overcome" at a Labor Day
parade, September 1993.

Courtesy *Chicago Sun-Times*. Photo by Ellen Domke.

instruct union delegates on matters ranging from complex
issues such as early retirement and pension plans to tasks as
simple as writing thank-you cards to favorable legislators. And
while the late Chicago Teachers Union president Jacqueline B.
Vaughn inspired great devotion among her members—thousands mourned her death on January 22, 1994, after a long,
private battle with cancer—the board had few loyalists in the
schools and among reformers, partly because of an extraordinary lack of communication and the decisions that resulted
from it. Closely allied with Democratic leadership that ensured
recognition of their demands, the unions brought the system
to its knees with nine strikes in two decades.

Union strength, however, was not always so assured.

The Chicago Teachers Union, the largest of twenty in the school system, gained power and momentum from the administration's history of abuse and self-indulgence at the expense of its workforce and its children. In the 1930s, the school administration balanced its budget by cutting teacher salaries dramatically—by 23.5 percent in 1934—and then often paying teachers in scrip, which merchants would not accept at face value.[2] At the same time, the administration passed out jobs to people connected to the Democratic party. In 1933, it fired fourteen hundred teachers five days before school opened, with four months' salary still outstanding.[3] Meanwhile, the janitorial staff—appointed by the ward committeemen of the Democratic machine—remained untouched.[4] In 1936, a scandal involving the principals' one-time only examination broke—favored candidates were coached by the superintendent in a special review course. As a result, the list of 155 people who passed was heavily weighted with relatives and friends of politicians.[5] Tales of job buying echoed through the system for generations. Minorities were traditionally excluded.

In 1937, four smaller unions merged to form the Chicago Teachers Union (CTU).[6] Ten years later, no teacher made more than the poverty level salary of $3,000 per year; therefore, teachers were eligible to live in public housing.[7] In 1953, Chicago teachers had the dubious distinction of having the largest class loads of any major American city—averaging nearly forty children to a room, with some classroom sizes far larger.[8] Studies in the late 1950s and 1960s revealed that some janitors in city schools made more than teachers with thirty years' experience and doctoral degrees.[9] Despite these problems, the term of Superintendent Harold C. Hunt (1947–53) was marked by relative labor peace, a credit to his support of the workforce but also a reflection of the lack of power of the labor union, which had no formal bargaining capability.

Throughout the first half of the twentieth century, unionism in Chicago was traditionally blue collar. Union strength and its traditional ties to the Chicago Democratic machine were forged in Southeast Side steel mills and the famous Union Stock Yards near Bridgeport, neighborhood of the late Richard J. Daley and several other Chicago mayors. Beginning with

Daley's first election in 1955, unions played a critical role in consolidating his political power. The relationship was mutually beneficial: public employees won lucrative job contracts through the mayor's influence, and labor responded by supplying precinct workers and campaign contributions to the Democratic political machine. As *Chicago Sun-Times* investigative reporter Charles Nicodemus explained, "The unions contributed heavily and almost exclusively to the Democratic party and, in particular, to the late Mayor Daley's Cook County Democratic organization. Daley, in turn, was the sole controller of hundreds of thousands of dollars that came into the organization. And he dispensed this money as he pleased in political campaigns. The union leadership was a substantial source of political campaign funds, giving Daley an almost unsupervised political slush fund."

During the 1960s, the white-collar teachers joined with the Democratic machine, and, in December 1966, the Chicago Teachers Union won the right to bargain collectively.[10] At the time, beginning teachers were paid $5,500; after a threatened strike, their first contract increased teachers' pay by $500 a year.[11] This coincided with a surge in new money for education. In 1965, Congress passed the Elementary and Secondary Education Act, sending streams of new federal money into America's schools. On June 11, 1968, Chicago voters passed a property tax referendum[12] and, in 1969, Illinois passed its first state income tax. From 1953 to 1966 the budget had increased an average $17.5 million a year, but these new factors allowed it to expand at a rate of $43.4 million per year from 1966 to 1975, the first four years of James Redmond's term as school superintendent.[13]

Meanwhile, facing turmoil from every angle, Daley had good reason to welcome the white-collar teachers union as an ally. In 1968, Chicago's West Side flared up in race riots. Eleven people died, more than five hundred were injured, and nearly three thousand were arrested. Arson fires destroyed 162 buildings. It was the same summer that ten thousand antiwar protestors demonstrated during the Democratic National Convention.[14] Daley also faced bitter protests and boycotts over the segregation of black and white children. Paul E. Peterson, author of *School Politics, Chicago Style,* described the political environment: "Daley could ill afford to have the CTU, still another political force within the educational arena, actively opposed to his policies. If strikes were added to demonstrations, sit-ins, and boycotts, the turmoil in school politics could possibly once again disturb the stability of Chicago's political regime."[15]

When a teachers' strike loomed in January 1968, the riots of summer had yet to occur, but the climate in the city was unsettling enough to make eliminating conflict a chief goal of the mayor, who appointed the school boards and, at one point, threatened to replace members who did not settle on his terms.[16] Daley declared, "Chicago has never had a teachers' strike, and I'm sure there won't be one now." To avert a strike, the school board responded to the mayor's appeals and made dramatic concessions to the union, including a 12 percent pay raise and ten days of paid vacation.[17]

The union was pleased with the contract, based, as it was, on others from around the nation. Indeed, much of it derived from the Philadelphia model. "Pages and pages of the structure of the union and board agreement came straight out of the Philadelphia contract that had been settled years before," recalled union attorney Lawrence A. Poltrock, who disputed traditional conclusions that Mayor Daley favored the teachers union in negotiations. Others believed that even though money was not available to pay for the contract, labor peace proved to be a more pressing priority than sound financial planning.[18]

In the view of outsiders, the late mayor's ongoing intervention at the expense of the system's financial stability lasted more than a decade. "Daley's relationship with the labor movement and with the school teachers union laid the groundwork for the financial difficulties that would haunt the school system for decades to come," said *Chicago Sun-Times* investigative reporter Charles Nicodemus. The problem was partly that the largesse of Redmond's early years did not last. Voters began to resist higher taxes, state aid did not pour in as quickly as before, and federal money was limited by the Nixon administration's opposition to increased federal aid for urban schools. By 1971, the school board could not afford to pay teachers the raises it promised, so it borrowed from 1972 money to do so and shortened the length of the school year.[19]

In 1972, the board was $125 million in debt and sought to freeze wages in the second year of a contract guaranteeing teachers 8 percent raises per year. In the end, it compromised by raising teacher salaries 5.5 percent, which placed the teacher base at $9,571, the highest of any in the nation's ten largest cities.[20] After a twelve-day strike in 1973, teachers won a 2.5 percent wage increase for a work year that was shortened from forty to thirty-nine weeks—and which also cut instruction time for students. Then came a glowing prediction: for the first time in seven years the district would operate without a deficit. How did it manage such a feat? It borrowed against revenue anticipated for 1974.[21]

Because of the union's increasing political effectiveness, teacher salaries rose an average of 11 percent per year from 1966 to 1972.[22] During that period there were two strikes, followed by a twelve-day strike in 1973 and an eleven-day strike in 1975. The latter resulted in a 5 percent raise, a dental care plan, and increased medical coverage. "The board voted $79.6 million it did not have, providing such a cash crunch that schools closed early the following spring when the board ran out of money," wrote Charles L. Kyle and Edward R. Kantowicz in *Kids First—Primero Los Niños: Chicago School Reform in the 1980s.*[23]

Not long after Mayor Richard J. Daley died in office in 1976, the financial gimmickry of earlier years came to a head. The system tumbled into financial collapse in 1979 under Mayor Jane M. Byrne, when lending institutions discovered the maneuvering of money they lent, and teachers suffered their first payless paydays since the Great Depression.[24] As Nicodemus recalled, "Daley's role in persistently settling the contracts on terms favorable or acceptable to the teachers union finally caught up with the city during the Byrne administration. And the kinds of accounting sleight of hand and money juggling and fiscal accounting practices that Daley originated and used came to light." Such juggling included paying for day-to-day operations using money reserved to repay loans and borrowed against future revenues.

The system was bailed out with a combination of state money, union concessions, the system's own cash reserves, and $573 million in loans over two years, most of which taxpayers still had not paid a decade and a half later.[25] The bailout legislation created the Chicago School Finance Authority through which bonds were issued. Through 1988, this oversight panel possessed stringent powers, which included the authority to force the board to reject union contracts.[26]

Teachers repeatedly went on strike—in 1980, 1983, 1984, and 1985.[27] Then came the longest walkout: nineteen days in 1987. Weary of disruption, parents rose up in protest and banded together in a "children's army" to demand the legislation that eventually created the unprecedented reform movement. After much haggling and an education summit convened by the late Mayor Harold Washington, the reform legislation was signed on December 14, 1988, and a new interim school board was formed in 1989. By that time, the strictest of the finance authority's powers had lapsed, and it could no longer force the board to reject union contracts. It still, however, required the board to submit a balanced budget for each coming year.

Mindful of the new age of reform, the interim board—with vice president William S. Singer as the key negotiator—set about bargaining three-year contracts and ended up agreeing to 7 percent pay raises for each of the three years, with the first raise delayed several months into the school year. The teachers' contract preserved generous provisions from the past, including the board's shouldering 100 percent of health-care coverage for all employees and their dependents and granting teachers a workday an hour shorter than that of their suburban counterparts—although city teachers were quick to point out they worked in inferior working conditions. Two new provisions were added: 1) fully appointed and certified teachers were guaranteed jobs for life, and 2) teachers were to be paid tuition bonuses as well as raises for advancing their education.

The contract was announced with great fanfare in July 1990. Superintendent Kimbrough, fresh from Compton, California, where he had been school chief only six months earlier, declared: "We're placing a new emphasis on teacher education. With the more attractive salaries, we will begin to bring the best to our schools."[28]

Perhaps not coincidentally, the contracts guaranteed labor peace for the 1991 reelection of Mayor Richard M. Daley, son of the Democratic machine boss who had built a political empire decades earlier. Combined with the euphoria of reform, this made teachers exuberant. They could focus on the classroom for three years without having to worry about walking out and disrupting the education of more than four hundred thousand children. The crippling instability of the decade before had ended—or so it seemed.

———————

Not long after, however, things began to unravel. In May 1991, Kimbrough announced the system faced its largest budget shortfall to date: $315 million for the upcoming year. It was followed by steep cuts in programs directly affecting children, about one thousand layoffs of jobs not guaranteed by union contracts, and more financial gimmickry, including dipping into future reserves to balance the budget and winning gubernatorial permission to receive some early state aid.[29]

The labor contracts were estimated at $250 to $270 million, but they contained contingency clauses that allowed pay increases to be renegotiated if money did not become available. In down-to-the-wire contract talks during 1991 and 1992, union workers forfeited part of their promised raises. In the end, teachers received a nearly 18 percent raise over three years while other employee groups—such as engineer-custodians—received 14.5 percent.[30]

In the short run, money for the contract was available: the school reform legislation diverted building fund money and property taxes intended for the teachers' pension fund. Both measures were shortsighted and born of political expediency. Meanwhile, the legislature placed a sunset clause on the pension fund provision, which supplied $55 million per year for employee pay raises and was due to expire in 1993. "The contract was built on financial quicksand from the very beginning," wrote Kyle and Kantowicz.[31]

In August 1993, employee contracts expired. Worse, the year brought financial troubles unprecedented since the collapse in 1979. It began with a $415 million budget hole, which fell to $298 million. The shortfall clouded the entire first semester and threatened the system with financial instability for years to come. Week by week, teachers, students, and parents wondered if schools would stay open. About one thousand jobs were cut after classes began. Budgetary information was not entered into the mainframe computer, preventing schools from having access to money for supplies, equipment, and other budgeted items for the new year. Some schools refused to allow students to bring home textbooks, a tradition during threatened school closings, because of the potential loss of tens of thousands of dollars worth of costly books that could disappear if students did not return.

What happened in the fall of 1993? The years of financial wizardry and built-up salary increases collided with the reality of state aid and property tax revenue diminishing, not to mention the hole created by the loss of pension funds.[32] As for the pay raises, they amounted to more than twice the estimates— accumulating into $560 million over three years. When questioned, interim board vice president William Singer said the original estimates assumed that employees would otherwise get reasonable 5 percent raises. The $250 million estimate was *in addition* to the raises employees would normally receive, explained Singer, who as an alderman in the 1970s worked on a task force to investigate school fiscal operations. "No one believes there would be a situation where salaries would be frozen for three years. The schools wouldn't be operating," he said. Of course, such caveats were never made clear on press releases when the so-called $250 million package was signed.[33]

Because of other provisions in the contract, 40 percent of teachers received raises for seniority and educational advancement beyond the 7 percent rate in the first year. In addition, tuition bonuses amounted to more than $19 million over five years—triple what the system expected to pay. In response to *Sun-Times* disclosures, union vice president Thomas H. Reece declared, "[The teachers] deserve what they're getting. And anybody who doesn't believe that should go work in a classroom in the city, and not just for a day, but for a few weeks, and see how they like it. It's a tough job."[34] Besides, he argued, many Pershing Road employees received comparable increases.

By 1992, with an average teacher salary of $43,096 for a thirty-nine week work year, Chicago ranked 96 of 261 districts in average teacher pay in the six-county Chicago area. The beginning salary for a first-year teacher with a bachelor's degree was $29,147, including a 7 percent contribution toward the teacher's pension.[35]

From the 1989 to the 1994 fiscal year, the total tab for salaries increased by more than 30 percent while revenues rose by only 24 percent. Such conditions resulted from both pay raises and great increases in staff, hired mostly with Chapter One funds.[36] "It's not that teacher salaries have been outrageous, by any means, it's simply they were larger than we had money to support," notes G. Alfred Hess, Jr. During that period, the city was reassessed for tax purposes, and the school system received massive increases in revenue from property taxes, but it was not enough. Although Mayor Daley proposed raising property taxes for city operations, he killed all legislative attempts to raise the tax rate limit for the school system, a separate taxing body. Nearly 80 percent of Chicago public schoolchildren are poor and, therefore, comparatively few families own homes on which property taxes can be assessed. For this reason, Daley rejected suggestions that the matter be put to a referendum. As former mayoral press secretary Avis LaVelle remarked, "What you have would be a very outraged segment of people who are directly affected by the outcome. It's easy for me to vote to raise somebody else's taxes."[37]

By the spring of 1993, the school board was headed for another catch-22 situation. If it balanced its budget by cutting teacher salaries by the necessary 22 percent, it faced a strike. If it did not, it faced a shutdown. A shutdown differed from a strike because, by law, the system could not extend even the most miniscule of funds to resurrect the system, pay school bills, or keep school buildings secure from vandals. With no new state aid on the horizon—coupled with the loss of financial gimmicks, state aid, and property taxes—the board faced an impending disaster. "Unilaterally, the board's hands are tied," chief financial officer Charley Gillispie declared. Throughout the continual crises, the school board turned to the state for additional money, acting on the mistaken assumption that new state revenues would eventually follow the reform legislation. In the first four years of reform, however, this never happened. The state, hit hard by the nationwide recession that resulted in thousands of job losses, had financial troubles of its own.

Meanwhile, legislators accused the school board of lacking a workable legislative agenda and credibility. Time and again, Chicago school leaders cried "wolf," projecting overwhelming deficits that dropped by tens of millions of dollars in the eleventh hour without any cuts or new revenues. In 1993, Jacqueline Vaughn described the annual ritual: "The problem is we have a lot of people new to the process who have been misinformed and misled and told if you project a very, very serious deficit, then the legislature will be provoked and moved to do something for Chicago only." (A year earlier, the school system's budget for central and subdistrict administrations was $106 million—or was it $104 million? It depended on which page of the budget documents one looked. Officials attributed the discrepancy to different computer software used for different sections of the budget summary.)

There were other questions raised about the system's credibility. While its leadership boasted deep cuts in central administration jobs, it quietly resurrected and reclassified many of the same positions under the label of "citywide services," replacing employees with consultants or budgeting employees in schools and district offices while stationing them at Pershing Road. In 1992, the business-backed reform group Leadership for Quality Education reported that nine out of ten consultants in the Department of Research, Evaluation, and Planning were full-time staffers laid-off during a much publicized cut of 404 central office employees. "The evidence, although anecdotal, points to patterns that reinforce the difficulties we have in achieving credible numbers from the board," said Diana L. Nelson, president of the reform group. Despite a fiscal crisis and an administrative pay freeze, the board granted $545,000 in yearly pay raises to 299 central and district office employees that fiscal year. Administration officials insisted they never meant to imply that a pay freeze would hold the line on salary increases for seniority and educational advancement. Kimbrough called the pay-raise issue "garbage" and said the reform group's report was another strategy to shift focus from the lack of classroom achievement.

Pay raises became an issue again in 1994 when Leadership for Quality Education reported that the administration distributed nearly $1 million in raises during the 1993 financial crisis.

Some administrators received raises of 20 or 30 percent, others even higher. High travel expenses also did little to help the board improve its credibility rating with either legislators or reformers. "When you got people in the administration wasting thousands and thousands of dollars on travel, and you're going to cut programs that keep children in school and off the street, then something is definitely wrong with the credibility of the administration," declared school reformer Kathryn Kuranda.

By 1993, the school board—which had been paralyzed by internal bickering and rivalries for years—managed to unite to propose some changes. For the first time in decades, unions faced opposition from every corner. Partly because of the poor economy, the depth of the financial crisis, and a change in leadership in the Illinois Senate, the political climate had changed. Consequently, the Chicago Board of Education adopted a plan called SAVE (Sacrifice Plus Added Value Equals Empowerment) and demanded dramatic concessions from the union. Written by member Stephen R. Ballis, SAVE proposals included: placing principals in charge of all school workers (reflecting a long-running controversy in the the system), lengthening the school day and school year to allow for more teacher training, and streamlining and shortening the time it takes to dismiss an employee. The SAVE plan became the first legislative agenda the board had produced in years. Some board members felt it was worth pushing even if it meant a system shutdown and the possibility of a projected 22 percent pay cut for teachers or a strike to break union might. As board member John "Jack" Valinote, part of the majority bloc, explained, "If we can't move toward better student achievement without a strike, it's better to have a strike. We must spend our money in support of student achievement. If we need work rule changes to do that, if we need legislation to do that, so be it. People must realize we're not in the business of opening schools or signing contracts or having a jobs program. If all we wanted to do is open schools, we would have a different strategy." Chicago Teachers Union spokesperson Jackie Gallagher responded by asking: "What are they going to teach those children, and with whom, if the schools aren't open?[38]

The proposal that teachers work longer was based on national comparisons indicating that Chicago teachers spend less time in the classroom than do teachers elsewhere. Under contract rules, teachers were required to work 406 minutes—6.7 hours—a day compared to the national average of 7.1 hours, reported the National Education Association, the nation's largest teacher union. In addition, Chicago teachers had a longer duty-free lunch period each day, amounting to forty-five minutes for elementary teachers and forty minutes for high school teachers. The national average for both was only thirty minutes, the NEA said.[39] (Of course, none of the comparisons consider the countless volunteer hours teachers spend correcting papers or contacting parents, nor can they compare inner-city school conditions with those in suburbia or rural America.)

The SAVE plan asked teachers to tack on four weeks to the typical thirty-nine-week work year and half an hour to the workday. The four additional work weeks would be used for badly needed training, Valinote said, adding, "They want to get paid for it. We're saying they get paid enough."[40] Enraged, teachers, in turn, recalled the time when the school board paid Valinote $5,000 as a consultant before he became a board member. In response to questioning at his confirmation hearing before the city council, Valinote publicly conceded that the fee covered only two days of notes he took at a closed-door board retreat although, when questioned months later, he said the fee also covered his work on a long-range plan for the board.[41]

Mayor Daley became an unexpected ally in the school board's struggle to win union concessions and the first mayor in decades to stand up to the unions. Leonard Dominguez, his deputy mayor for education, called Daley "a bold hero in American education." He continued: "Essentially it's very straightforward: we worked hard for them over the years in terms of providing a living wage, and now we're asking for flexibility on some items and we feel it's appropriate to ask. They need to understand it's a new era."

Since unionism's decline in the 1980s with the loss of man-ufacturing and steel mill jobs, some saw Daley's position as an attack on the last bastion of organized labor: government workers. "He doesn't see it as antiunion," Dominguez responded. "It's a matter of them understanding it's a difficult time, and unless they're willing to come to the table with a flexible attitude, there's no way the governor or the mayor will have any support for them."

Governor Jim Edgar and the Senate Republicans declared that the system should learn to live within its means. For months the legislators refused to approve a bill that would have allowed the system to borrow money to make up its budget gap—and they certainly had no intention of giving the system additional state funds. Instead, they demanded changes in union work rules, among them the elimination of job guarantees for supernumeraries, those teachers whose jobs were cut because of changes in enrollment or programs. Equally determined, Democrats resisted such moves, and some even insisted that the state should offer additional funding to ease the crisis. Meanwhile, children were held hostage by the uncertainty.

Jacqueline Vaughn was livid over proposals that infringed onto traditional union turf. In the CTU newspaper, *Union Teacher,* Vaughn told her members: "Everything we have in our contract, we fought for. They didn't give us [preparation] periods, a ten-minute break, personal days, accumulated sick days, job security, step increases, or anything else willingly." The paper published photographs of teachers walking a picket line and said, "Ask yourself and the people in your school if they're willing to take [a 20 percent pay cut] or if they're willing to fight to keep intact one of the best contracts of any public school system. In an era when consensus and cooperation are the order of the day, a board that offers a 'SAVE' plan designed to skin the employees is counter-productive and sets the stage for unnecessary conflict and confrontation."[42] The union took out full-page newspaper ads to protest the attacks.

Negotiations that began in April dragged on bitterly through September and into October. Toward the end, the teacher talks were held at city hall and mediated by the mayor, House speaker Michael Madigan, Senate minority leader Emil Jones, Jr. (D-Chicago), and Alderman Patrick J. O'Connor, head of the city's education committee.[43] After more than sixty bargaining sessions held over a period of six months, the mayor, negotiators, and mediators emerged with the long-awaited news of a settlement. It was announced at 5:45 a.m. on October 9, following sixteen hours of continuous talks.[44] Ultimately, teachers agreed to make $60 million in concessions rather than strike in response to what Vaughn described as the most acrimonious negotiations in union history. "This is not like the good old days when we had the option of going back for more and doing better," she later explained. Vaughn convinced her members that the political powers badly wanted a strike to break the union. According to conventional wisdom, the board could break the union by bringing in replacement workers or by garnering enough public support to divide the system into smaller districts. This, in turn, could encourage the rival Illinois Education Association to draw members away from the Chicago Teachers Union and its parent organization, the Illinois Federation of Teachers. A strike could also conceivably build public support for a voucher system.

"Remember PATCO?" Union leadership posed that question to its members in urging their passage of the hard-won contract. It was a reference to the ill-fated 1981 strike of the Professional Air Traffic Controllers Association in which 11,500 members were fired by then President Ronald Reagan. The literature continued: "The air traffic controllers rejected their leadership's recommendation and went on strike. Their union was destroyed and they all lost their jobs. Don't let that happen to us." It was enough to convince 63.6 percent of the voting union members—15,765— to vote in favor of the contract.[45]

The teachers' contract froze base pay but included raises for seniority and educational advancement. Maximum class sizes in January 1994 were rolled back to 1993 levels—typically twenty-eight to thirty-one students in elementary schools and twenty-eight students in high schools, depending on the grade and subject. Such a measure restored five hundred jobs. In addition, teachers and other employees agreed to contribute 1.5 percent of their salaries to health-care premiums for an estimated savings to the system of $20 million over two years. Principals were allowed to fill assistant principal and head teacher vacancies with their own appointments. Supernumerary teachers were reclassified as "reserve teachers," and their job guarantees were shortened to a maximum of twenty-five months. High school class periods remained at fifty minutes—up from forty minutes previously—for a savings of $36 million over a two-year period.[46]

With the contract out of the way, there was still one more major hurdle to resolve. The General Assembly had to approve legislation conforming to the pact and make up the budget hole that still remained. Although teachers reluctantly agreed to allow $110 million to be borrowed from the teachers' pension fund over two years with strict guarantees that it be repaid, Republicans opposed the measure. Retired Chicago teachers—many of them suburban residents and constitutents of Republican legislators—lobbied heavily against dipping into pension money, arguing in part that the political powers had no track record of keeping their word. In addition, Republicans proclaimed there were not enough work rule changes; most Democrats, whose representatives served in the city hall talks, wanted the contract and the proposed legislation that accompanied it to pass the way it stood.

The only thing keeping the system open during this time was a series of waivers of the balanced-budget requirement, first by the legislature and then by the federal courts. For the first time since the requirement was instituted after the 1979 collapse, the entire school system shut down September 1–3, but on the third day, the legislature granted a ten-day waiver. On September 13, the system shut down a second time. Meanwhile, the school board went to court and claimed that the budget requirement violated the rights of minority children whose interests were protected by a 1980 federal desegregation consent decree. As a result, on September 13, U.S. District judge Charles P. Kocoras imposed a temporary restraining order to reopen the system, declaring that the board could not satisfy its constitutional obligation to minority students with shuttered schools. Since the courts traditionally leave such matters to the legislature, the ruling came as a surprise. Said Governor Edgar, "That's the first time I know of that the federal courts have come in and kind of swept aside state law in dealing with the schools here in Illinois."[47]

For all but eleven year-round schools, which were already in session, classes began one week late on September 15. Superintendent Argie K. Johnson, who announced the decision to delay the opening, explained that the system needed an extra week to prepare because of vacancies caused by early retirement. The legislature, the board, and the unions still had no agreements when the waiver expired. Subsequently, Judge Kocoras granted a second ten-day waiver on September 23, insisting that "innocent and powerless children should not be held hostage to the inability of our governmental and educational leaders to agree on a solution to the present crisis." The Chicago School Finance Authority objected to the waiver, pointing out in its court brief that the action would lead to financial disaster and, ultimately, to a second financial collapse.[48]

On October 4, Kocoras extended the waiver again and, at the authority's urging, set deadlines for the union and the legislature to act.[49] Then, over objections of the finance authority, he added another ten days but warned that granting more than two waivers stretched his legal authority. On November 10, in response to the school finance authority's plea, a federal appeals court threw out Kocoras's fourth waiver. At the same time, it shattered all hopes for a long-term court-ordered solution, which the school board had also originally requested. A panel of the 7th Circuit U.S. District Court of Appeals ruled that Kocoras had no jurisdiction and that the board's suit was entirely a matter of state and local law and politics to resolve.[50]

Although a long-term solution was discarded, the court's action proved to be just the push legislators needed to end months of posturing. The legislature was forced to act or risk the political fallout of a school system shutting down just as campaigns were beginning for the state elections of 1994, including the governor's seat. One day later, Governor Edgar and legislative leaders announced a compromise settlement, which was approved by the legislature late Sunday evening of November 14.

The legislature agreed to authorize $427 million in borrowing to provide an infusion of new money over two years— as much as $49 million of it would be used toward merely processing the bonds, that is, paying the fees of attorneys and

Demanding to be heard. Jackie Rodgers, a student at Julian High School, protests the latest change in Chicago public school policy during the 1993 crisis.

Courtesy *Chicago Sun-Times*. Photo by Robert A. Davis.

bond houses. The legislature also withheld for over two years $32 million in state Chapter One funds that the schools would have received in the final payment of the transfer from the board's basic 1993–94 budget. It eliminated permanent job guarantees for supernumerary teachers, slightly strengthening the agreement between the board and the union.[51] It created an inspector general's office to operate within the Chicago School Finance Authority, which was closely aligned with the business community. It also dramatically expanded the powers of the finance authority in governing such areas as closing individual schools for economic reasons and staffing plans. It gave principals the power to approve school contracts of as much as $10,000 with local school council permission alone. On the other hand, it cut into principals' rights to appoint teachers by authorizing the school board to fill vacancies temporarily with its own appointments for the first sixty days and permanently thereafter if principals did not make appointments of fully certified staff in the meantime.

The legislature further required the board to adopt its budget by August 15 each year, instead of August 31, thereby giving schools an additional two weeks to discover last-minute budget cuts. Finally, it authorized the board of education—or the city council, if the school board failed to do so—to place a school property tax referendum on the ballot in the first half of 1995.[52] Such a referendum would fall during the primary reelection bid of Mayor Daley, a move that the mayor said was intended to embarrass him. Conspicuously absent, however, were any provisions to change the criteria for dismissing school personnel or to give principals control over selecting staff such as clerks and engineers.

The head-on collision in Chicago mirrored clashes elsewhere in America over reform measures that granted more power to schools while trampling traditional union domain. In Detroit, three school board members who sought to empower schools by transferring money and authority to local school jurisdiction were ousted at the polls in 1992, partly because of union opposition, according to *Education Week*. The members of the so-called HOPE team, an acronym loosely based on the last names of the candidates, lost their reelection bids allegedly because they advocated reform measures—although the election also followed a twenty-seven day employee strike over salary issues and what workers viewed as assaults on their contract.[53] As part of the effort to transfer more power to schools, twenty-one Detroit schools received 8 percent of the normal per-pupil allotment—averaging $70,000 a year—and were free to use that money to buy services, textbooks, and equipment from outside vendors. Unions, however, reasoned that services purchased elsewhere than from central office could, in the long run, threaten union jobs, and they heatedly opposed the measure.

In Chicago, the war over union versus school power extended not only to the teachers unions but also to the trades and other nonteaching unions. When the 1988 reform legislation was written, the engineers union managed to preserve an old union rule: engineer-custodians are equal in rank to principals. Through allies in the legislature, the traditionally Irish Catholic union ensured that engineers would report to supervisors in the system's subdistricts instead of to principals. Thus, principals had no control when custodians failed to work or when engineers balked at requiring certain chores, such as special cleanups before parent meetings. In the view of Ben E. Graves, head of Educational Planning Consultants in Austin, Texas, that was a mistake. "If a parent group wants to have a meeting that afternoon and the principal wants the cafeteria nice and neat and the custodian says 'I'll get to that tomorrow morning,' the principal has no control. There has to be someone in charge."[54] Engineers, who manage custodians (not to be confused with those who hold engineering degrees), responded that they cannot fire poorly performing custodians. Unless a custodian agrees to resign uncontested, a due process hearing is necessary.

Union contract and central office rules also require that an engineer, not a lower-paid custodian, be present any time anyone other than the principal is in a school building. As a result, a principal is required to obtain a central office permit and approval to pay an engineer overtime if an employee or council member stays late, typically past 4 p.m. in elementary schools and 6 p.m. in high schools. This rule led to a showdown at Prescott Elementary School in 1992, when engineer

Robert O'Dowd threatened to call police and evict local school council members working past the 4 p.m. deadline without prior approval. "I handed him the phone and said, 'Go ahead,'" principal Karen Carlson declared. "It's our building. It belongs to our community, and if we need it, we're not going to be kicked out. You cannot come in at 8:30 a.m. and leave at 2:30 p.m. and do a good job."

O'Dowd, on the other hand, noted that he had every right to file such a trespassing complaint—and the central office agreed. O'Dowd explained: "I never threatened her. I said as a last alternative, if she did not follow the rules and regulations, that the last alternative open to me after expiring all the others is, I would call the police and have the people evicted from the building—not her, other people. There were children in the school—adults, teachers—all out past the 4 o'clock time element that the board of education set up."[55]

The rule that an engineer must be present during school operating hours dates back to a time when schools had high-pressure boilers, and they required an experienced watchful eye, according to the Citizens Schools Committee, which lobbied zealously to change the rules. By 1993, only a few high-pressure boilers remained in the system.

Without overtime, head engineers' pay averaged $44,800 in Chicago public schools, according to a 1991 study by the Hay Group, which ranked the pay of Chicago engineers second among seven major cities studied at that time. At $57,000 a year, only New York City head engineers were paid higher. Unlike Chicago, however, the New York City school system does not pay overtime. (The custodial system in New York City, however, did provide enormous benefits that came under sharp criticism for other reasons.) In 1992, eighty Chicago engineers made more than $57,000 a year, with overtime.[56] Principals, meanwhile, averaged about $66,000, despite far more taxing roles.

The engineer issue dogged the reform effort from the beginning. Local school councils and engineers first locked horns in early 1990, after newly elected councils learned they would have to pay as much as $300 for engineer overtime per evening to hold meetings at their schools after hours. In council start-up kits issued in January 1990, the interim school board allocated two free meeting nights a year. Thereafter, councils were required to use scarce school funds, hold fundraisers to raise the money, or "be sharp enough to find free public places," as one board member put it. Reform groups were appalled. School reform leader Coretta McFerren, then a spokesperson for the Peoples Coalition for Educational Reform, explained: "It's been a tremendous problem. It caused some councils not to be able to meet at all because the school was the safest place."[57] As Delores Fitzpatrick, a council member at Doolittle East and West Schools, said: "They are locking out the parents. The only people who can meet during school hours are teachers. What this is saying is 'the heck with school reform.' What was our fight for?"[58]

After heated public protest, Local 143 of the International Union of Operating Engineers compromised on the issue, allowing councils to meet far more frequently. Under the agreement with the interim school board, engineers would receive overtime for six council meetings a year and compensatory time for twenty-six meetings. Herbert School principal William Rankin later observed that the "free" meetings simply gave engineers more vacation days.[59] Engineers were allowed to work as substitutes during those days off and get paid twice for the same day—once for compensatory time and once for their substitute labor, according to the union contract signed by the interim board.

A look at the budget of a Saturday high school social center in 1992 amply demonstrates the differences in salaries. Popular with teenagers, social centers provided such student activities as swimming lessons, weight training, and basketball workouts. By school system rules, three types of maintenance workers had to be present during the social center operating hours: a custodian, an engineer, and a maintenance assistant to monitor the swimming pool and, in cold weather, the boilers. Thus, $13,000 of the $29,500 annual social center budget paid for maintenance crews, according to a memo circulated by the board. The money was distributed as follows:

- Program director: $12.91 per hour (no overtime);
- Teacher: $11.30 per hour (no overtime);
- Engineer: $26.51 regular rate (plus overtime, which included $35.26 time and a half and—after 12 p.m. on Saturdays—$53.02 double time);

- School maintenance assistant: $19.73 (plus overtime);
- Custodial worker, $10.70 (plus overtime)

The unions reacted to negative publicity about such matters with anger. "It's a money problem. It's not a union problem," said John Code, chairman of the coalition of nineteen non-teaching unions. Coalition members, he noted, gave up pay raises completely during one year of the three-year contract. "As far as the work rules, all those things are negotiated there for a reason," he declared. "Our employees have lives, and they have rights, too. The unions have been blasted enough. It's unconscionable."[60]

As for the principal-in-charge issue, Donald J. McCue, president of local 143 of the operating engineers union, argued that the 1988 reform act introduced accountability by allowing principals to bring problems to an engineer's off-site supervisor, of which twenty-three existed in the city. Although criticized by some as cumbersome, the process worked, McCue maintained. "If the principal comes to me and says, 'I want the toilets cleaned on the second floor right now,' I'm accountable," he said. McCue insisted that building maintenance should be handled by licensed engineers who have training in such areas as pest control, swimming pool operations, and asbestos management. In many schools, in fact, the relationship between principal and engineer runs smoothly. Ignoring union contract rules, some conscientious engineers clean and make repairs themselves, although it is not required. Many dig into their own pockets for repair money. Some even allow teachers to enter before the 8 a.m. starting time, again bending the rules of the contract signed by the interim board.

In addition, engineers asked, who were principals to talk? Most schools failed miserably in educating children. What made anyone think principals would do any better in an area for which they were not trained? The new demands of school reform left principals little time to oversee engineers or lunchroom supervisors, another post operating independently of the principal. "The whole idea of school reform was to turn out kids who can function and earn a living," McCue said. "The principals' goals should be to move kids up to reading national averages. With this type of problem facing them, how do they have time for these additional duties?"[61]

Moreover, engineers were often left to deal with the after-math of poorly disciplined children who, when left to their own devices, vandalized property and ran wild in some schools, they argued. "If they cannot control their faculty, how are they ever going to take on the maintenance and lunch-room departments? Their faculty cannot discipline the kids," said O'Dowd, who pointed out that engineers also informally acted in a security capacity for their buildings.

The powerful Michael Madigan, speaker of the Illinois House who protected the lines of authority involving engineers, agreed. As Madigan spokesperson Steve Brown explained: "There's a flawed premise to begin with. You tell me any one individual thing—like changing engineers-in-control—that test scores will get better and the dropout rate will improve? I doubt that anything that relates to principals and operating engineers will lower the dropout rate, which is a tragedy, or improve test scores, which is where the school reform people should aim themselves. I don't think you can blame the operating engineers for dropout rates and test scores."

As a matter of fact, principals responded, the issue did have a bearing. "It has a lot to do with education," countered Aldridge Elementary School principal George Pazell. "If the maintenance is poor, that affects the school environment. You want a nice clean environment. You want a building with good upkeep." Allowing principals to schedule staff hours would also mean keeping buildings open later. As churches and YMCAs lost their prominence in American society, schools emerged as focal points of the communities and, especially in violence-prone areas, became recognized as safe houses. Keeping doors open past 4 p.m. would provide access not only to children but also to working parents who cannot visit during day-time hours. It would also enhance teacher training and allow councils to work late on school plans. Moreover, allowing principals to schedule and stagger staff as needed would free money for educational purposes, such as reducing dropout rates by rehiring truant officers. Kilmer Elementary School paid $370 in overtime to open the building for its volunteer painting party, according to council member Carlos Malave. Multiply that across the city and the money amounts to millions.

In Chicago, overtime for head engineers, custodians, watch-men, and school maintenance assistants totaled $8 million for the 1990 fiscal year. Because of a massive renovation project for which he was required to be present at all times, one engineer received $43,000 in overtime pay. Although reimbursed by the contractor—who was, in turn, paid through building funds—the overtime boosted his annual salary beyond $90,000. Trade workers also receive overtime wages. One asbestos worker made $89,439 in 1990, another $80,635—more than double their regular $37,960-a-year salaries. Some turned in work claims of twenty hours a day. A foreman of electrical mechanics increased his regular salary of $45,700 to $81,627 through overtime.[62] In his third month on the job, Superintendent Ted Kimbrough himself was shocked by trade prices. Because it was done on a weekend to avoid disruption, renovating his office cost $20,542. "I don't know why it would cost that much to add doors, move a wall, and paint," Kimbrough said. The materials alone cost $1,710.[63]

Engineers argued that attacks on their union were nothing but a ploy by principals to get more pay and expand their political power base. Principals' salaries rise according to the number of people they supervise, which may be one reason 5,802 staff were hired mostly with Chapter One funds during fiscal years 1989 to 1994, but only 1,395 of them were teachers, critics charged. The rest were mostly lower-paid employees.[64] Reform groups responded that principals did not ask to run the maintenance program, only to have those who did report to them.

Reformers found other trade customs offensive. Long-standing division-of-labor practices prohibited tradespeople from crossing too many lines. Custodians, for example, were not supposed to install a door lock. That was a locksmith's job. They could not paint over graffiti above eight feet on a classroom wall. That was a painter's job. And they could not replace a window pane. That was a glazier's job. Although the system did not have enough tradespeople to paint all the schools or install all the necessary locks, the rules remained.[65] After three years of reform, volunteers were allowed to paint the schools, but central office continued to stipulate that each school must follow its guidelines on paint color and type, obtain a central office permit, and secure a $3 million liability bond.

Union laborers in the Chicago system benefitted in other ways from their cozy relationship with the Democratic political machine. In the private sector, tradespeople were paid extra to compensate them for the transient nature of their jobs. Often their work was only seasonal. Chicago, however, paid its public employees the same prevailing wages—the basic pay rates set by representatives of construction industry management and their unions—even though work was guaranteed year around. Such employees may have deserved their wages but in increasingly tight financial times educators and school councils resented the favorable treatment given maintenance management.[66]

After a summer of heated rhetoric on both sides, a compromise was reached in August 1993. Engineers would still receive overtime and occupied schools would still require an engineer to be present, but principals were granted greater authority over maintenance staff. In addition, staffing of engineers could be staggered to prevent paying overtime in all but the smallest schools where it was not feasible. The legislative compromise of 1993 placed principals in charge of engineers, subject to union contracts and law. For example, according to the new legislation, if an engineer believed that an order of a principal violated the law, the engineer could appeal to the system's director of facilities.[67] Taken together with the dramatic concessions made by the teachers union, the changes represented a chink in the traditionally impenetrable union armor. Some politicians basked in the school board's success of winning concessions unprecedented in thirty years.

But not everyone was so sure the days of using taxpayer money to further political purposes were over; instead they feared that only the method had changed and a new era had begun. *Pinstripe patronage*—that is, awarding contracts to politically connected firms in professional services such as law, auditing, insurance, and consulting—may have become the preferred method. Expenditures for "professional services" soared in Chicago public schools, from $27.9 million in fiscal year 1988 to $65.3 million several years later.[68] Unlike traditional patronage, pinstripe patronage is more difficult to track because the use of subcontractors obscures the beneficiaries of such contracts. Further, since consultants and equipment are often lumped into one sum, price comparisons are not feasible. Professional services are typically exempted from bidding requirements and public disclosure laws, making it impossible to determine how much specific individuals are being paid. What's more, the civil rights gains made in the public sector have rarely been duplicated in the private sector.

As school reformer Calvin Pearce said, "They use privatization for everything. They say it's faster, it's more efficient, they're able to downsize. They say it doesn't break the union, but it does. And it doesn't do a thing to establish any accountability whatsoever." Pearce argues that the new patronage—privatization without stringent disclosure requirements—opens the way for improprieties. "When you privatize public services and public dollars and give the benefactor of a contract the right to use proprietary information as the reason not to disclose and not be accountable," Pearce concluded, "that is a license to steal."

Chicago students and teachers protest school policies during the 1987 strike.

Courtesy *Chicago Sun-Times.* Photo by John H. White.

11

No Accountability, No Controls

I really get mad. I see my little sister and my cousin going to school. I don't want them to see what I see.

Clemente High School senior Raul Rivera on gangs and drugs in school

Each year millions of dollars in student funds pass through the hands of principals, teachers, and school clerks—and tens of thousands of it disappear. The money—collected from pop machines, fundraisers, and student fees—is supposed to finance strictly student activities.[1] Ideally under decentralization, schools would be given the authority and meaningful guidance on how to spend these and other monies—and schools that fail would be called into account. This has not happened under Chicago school reform, which instead has created an environment ripe for waste, fraud, and abuse. While most schools act responsibly, there is little penalty for those that do not.

At Gage Park High School, teacher Stephen Levine said he heard rumors of teachers receiving brown envelopes for "doing a good job." Then he himself received $225 for extracurricular work he said he did not perform.[2] He reported it to authorities and to his state senator, William G. Mahar, a Republican from south suburban Orland Park, who subsequently introduced a senate resolution asking for an investigation into what became known as "brown envelope day." The resolution alleged it was common knowledge at the school that teachers received pay for work they did not perform.[3] In an internal investigation, school board auditors agreed, eventually concluding that more than two dozen Gage Park High School employees were overpaid $45,000 during an eighteen-month period. Teachers were compensated for sponsoring student clubs and visiting so-called vocational education sites, such as fast-food restaurants that did not exist, or supervising after-school activities that actually took place during regular school hours, auditors alleged. Auditors also charged that student records related to vocational educational programs were disposed of immediately before their review.[4]

Carol A. Faulk, who was principal of Gage Park High School at the time, attributed the problems to bookkeeping errors and blamed the lack of oversight on the elimination of the assistant principal's position. In the audit section earmarked for her response, Faulk said system rules gave her leeway to award some extracurricular monies at her discretion, and she noted that previous audits found no major violations of board rules.[5] When the payroll problems became public in 1992, Faulk told a reporter, "I do not know what I am being accused of and who is accusing me officially. It will all get straightened out. . . . There is no wrongdoing. There is no manipulation of funds."[6] Apparently no teacher was penalized in the probe, and Faulk herself retired in an agreement with the school system, according to school board attorney Joyce Combest Price.

In another example, internal auditors alleged that Crane High School principal Reginald V. Brown used $5,216 from student accounts for a personal loan. Then when ostensibly repaying it, he bounced six personal checks, auditors said. Brown, who in 1993 sought the superintendency of Chicago schools, declined to comment. But in a section of the audit reserved for the principal's response, he said that the money was used for "students activities" [sic] after a payment for an adopt-a-school partner did not materialize. At the same time, Brown said that he made restitution, including $150 for overdraft charges on the school checking account.

While investigating Crane High School accounts, auditors also concluded that two pop machine sales came up more than $2,500 short. In 1991, auditors reported that nearly $12,000 of Crane High School student funds were allegedly spent on items prohibited by system rules, rules that many principals complained were extraordinarily tight. (Some state officials, however, had another view: they praised the internal accounts system as particularly thoughtful and fair when followed correctly.) Auditors also reported that Brown, a former subdistrict superintendent whose job it was to follow through on reports of corruption, hired a fellow Crane teacher's decorating firm and spent more than $2,000 of student money to redecorate his and other offices in violation of system rules. He later became principal of Washington High School.[7]

At Henderson School, $27,380 was spent on dinners, a $50 ticket to a Casino Night, a resort trip for some local school council members and their guests, and repairs for windows damaged on then principal Milton W. Hall's car, auditors alleged in 1992. Hall also reportedly used $240 to pay back a loan he took from a school council member. (Hall responded that the council member was confused: the money was actually reimbursement for items she had purchased for the school.) In addition, concession sales posted an unexplained shortage of more than $2,000. As for the Wisconsin retreat, a school check made payable to the resort and amounting to almost $1,500 toward the $2,100 bill bounced and still had not been paid more than seven months later, auditors reported.[8] Hall attributed the problems to clerical errors and said that training funds and student account money were commingled before he arrived at Henderson in 1991. The training funds had fewer restrictions, he argued, although school board lawyers disputed that claim. Hall further attributed the accusations to a bias in the school community against central office administrators because he had previously served as a project manager in dropout prevention where he handled some $10 million in grants. Although he admitted to attending the resort trip, Hall said he only followed the instructions of his council—that is, his employer—when he signed the check. He was subsequently fired through a state hearing process that took nine months. Although he said he had appealed the case, school board attorneys found no record of it.[9]

For years internal auditors at the board of education meticulously documented missing and misused student funds, each time giving principals a chance to respond to their allegations and gaining a reputation among insiders for thorough work.

But these audits were kept secret until the *Chicago Sun-Times* sued the school system in 1992, arguing that internal audits are public documents. The school board released the audit reports—which document payroll discrepancies as well—in a settlement. The findings were astounding:

- At Austin High School, auditors in 1988 uncovered "monetary discrepancies" of $73,625, including more than $20,000 in missing money;
- At Beale Elementary School, a staff member cashed a school check for $7,000 and made it payable to herself, auditors charged in a 1990 audit report;
- At Bowen High School, concession sales and bank deposits were short $6,022 in 1990. About $240 was used for liquor, movies, and long-distance calls at a hospitality suite for teachers on prom night. Describing discrepancies in how concession sales were run, auditors reported "a serious lack of controls at the school that is conducive to misappropriation of funds";
- At Bryn Mawr Elementary School, $2,445 of student money was used for a faculty social fund that paid for flowers, staff parties, and fruit baskets for staff, a 1990 audit alleged;
- At Chicago Vocational High School, auditors in 1990 reported shortages of nearly $12,000 in graduation fees, ticket sales for the 1990 class luncheon, concessions, and vending machine sales;
- At Esmond Elementary School, the general ledger had not been maintained for five years, auditors reported in 1991. More than $2,100 in checks were written to staff members with no explanations;
- At Lane Technical High School, a school jewelry sale and a spice sale came up $1,730 short in 1990. A teacher told the principal he felt responsible and agreed to repay all but $100 of it, auditors said;
- At Schurz High School, auditors in 1992 disclosed concession sales shortages of $7,443, of which $248 was repaid. Ralph J. Cusick, principal at the time, attributed about $5,200 to students' theft of soda pop, malfunctioning machines, and erroneous billing. [10]

Because of the massive turnover that occurred under reform and the changes wrought by the early retirement program, most schools hired new principals after the above audit reports were made. Those implicated were usually asked to repay missing funds although apparently few employees ever did. From 1985 through 1987, the latest years for which overall repayment figures were available, school employees repaid $6,600 of $217,000 in shortages in student funds at eighteen schools. Taxpayer money made up another $89,000 of the losses; $121,000 was not recovered, school board documents show.

No principal was ever prosecuted as a result of the audits, although in an unprecedented crackdown during the 1992 school year, four Chicago school principals were forced to resign, according to Price. For board lawyers, the alternative is to seek dismissal procedures through lengthy due process hearings. As board attorney Janet Johnson-Vinion explained, "The principal finds out orally that there is a suspicion they have done something. Ninety-nine percent of the time, it doesn't get as far as a hearing. They resign. Part of the agreement is that they resign and anything in their personnel file is removed." It is an arrangement common in private industry, where internal audit divisions function as branches of management. Uncovering and quietly cleaning up internal problems takes precedence over preparing cases for prosecution. Sometimes, too, agreements have already been reached, which further hampers prosecution.

In one incident, Sayre Language Academy principal Eileen M. Gallagher denied wrongdoing when more than $15,000 in student funds disappeared in 1992. Gallagher agreed to resign without a due process hearing and to pay back part of the money: $6,000 up front and the remaining $4,000 in paycheck deductions, board attorney William J. Quinlan said. After her resignation, she was rehired as a teacher in another Chicago public school. "If they are certified by the state, we put them on an eligibility list, and we don't overrule the choice of principals," said Quinlan, explaining the concept of local control under reform.[11]

Forcing compromises and encouraging settlements are the lengthy due process hearings that soak up hours of precious time and thousands of dollars in legal fees. In the case of

Marshall High School, concession and vending sale receipts came up $30,000 short and nearly $30,000 in bank account money was missing in 1985, according to state records of the principal's dismissal hearing. School checks were overdrawn by $16,000. At one point, $46,000 was owed on a school checking account that had a balance of $18.71, auditors reported. As a result, the school board attempted to fire principal Carl A. Van Kast, but the Illinois Appellate Court reversed its decision and ruled in favor of Van Kast, who said other staff members were responsible for the shortages. One basis of the 1993 ruling: Van Kast had not been warned to improve his conduct. The court noted that the board had not cracked down on pervasive shortages at other schools where principals—who were among several people responsible for co-signing checks and whom system rules claimed were legally responsible for the funds—went unpunished. Van Kast also argued that he had received inadequate training to comply with the complex accounting requirements.

In examining other criteria for dismissal, the court concluded that the school's reputation remained untarnished, partly because hotels continued to do business with the high school even after two checks for more than $15,000 written to the Westin Hotel, apparently the site of a student prom, bounced. In addition, the court ruled, no teachers were harmed by the shortages because none lost pay or quit after disclosure of the problems. Students were not harmed either, the court concluded—two student witnesses testified as such and a third called Van Kast an excellent principal. Van Kast, who was hired under reform as principal at Garvy School on the Northwest Side, said he was entitled to back pay for the time he was inappropriately fired.[12] "The appellate court upheld my exoneration," Van Kast said in 1993. "I expect we'll be settling for compensation now."[13] The dismissal attempt took seven years.

How widespread are shortages of student monies? Documented shortages alone amounted to a half million dollars over a seven-year period from 1985 to 1992 and nearly $82,000 in 1991–92 alone—although small change when compared to $1.2 million in taxpayer funds lost by the Pershing Road headquarters in one bus contract kickback scheme alone. In that scandal, a Pershing Road administrator was sentenced in 1989 to three-and-a-half-years in prison for accepting payoffs.[14]

Although small amounts of student money are documented as missing each year, the internal audits undoubtedly point to a far larger problem. Why? First, the number covers only schools that were audited, not the dozens that waited for audits because of changes in administration or complaints of improprieties. Traditionally, the school system audits what are referred to as *internal accounts* every five years for elementary schools and every three years for high schools, except when specific allegations are made or when a new principal arrives. Consequently, internal account money is audited at fewer than 20 percent of schools each year. In those schools where audits are conducted, however, the number with shortages is a fairly high percentage. From 1985 to 1992, for example, 17 to 30 percent of the schools audited had shortages in concession money, 3 to 20 percent in bank deposits, and 8 to 19 percent in student fees.[15]

Second, books are in such disarray in many schools that estimating missing money is impossible. Sometimes records of various fundraisers are incomplete or nonexistent; in other cases, schools have not kept their financial books current for years. Auditors said their estimates were based only on what they could prove.

Finally, the estimates do not include tens of thousands of dollars spent on items prohibited by system rules or overpayments for hours that employees could not document. Nor do they include instances in which employees held onto thousands of dollars of student money for months at a time—the equivalent of interest-free loans. "The withholding of monies from deposit for extended periods of time raises serious questions as to the probability/possibility of these funds having been diverted to personal use during the period withheld," auditors remarked in one case.

Failing to penalize theft and to punish wasteful spending practices demoralizes honest workers and robs students of both the money they contribute and the education they deserve. If funds are misspent in one area, one can reasonably assume they are misspent elsewhere.

Such a system has a devastating effect.

"The waste is so rampant it breaks my heart," said one teacher in a letter to *Chicago Sun-Times* columnist Raymond R. Coffey in 1991. "There are hundreds of teachers and administrators getting paid for doing absolutely zero. Useless Mickey Mouse programs abound. Pershing Road is a standing joke."[16]

"Our principal forces us to misrepresent facts on paper," wrote another teacher. "We must issue grades for subjects, such as physical education, not offered our students. The LSC is not disciplined enough even to meet, effectively giving the principal carte blanche. The principal now regards himself as a politician and behaves accordingly."[17]

"We are a school with more than a $3 million budget and a student enrollment of approximately nine hundred plus students," wrote one school council chairman who unsuccessfully sought an audit. "We are concerned that it appears to be more and more cushion jobs opening up for a small special interest group of people." He complained that teachers had only seven reading books for a class of more than twenty students. "We believe that our budget is sufficient to educate our children if allocated properly."[18]

With no independent office to investigate charges of corruption or improper practices and an understaffed internal audit staff, complaints mounted. Dozens of letters and telephone calls to the *Chicago Sun-Times,* for example, contained allegations of everything from ghost payrolling to inside job equipment thefts. Some letters were accompanied with warnings in capital letters: "DO NOT USE MY NAME AS I HAVE 3 YEARS TO RETIREMENT." Others also requested anonymity: "For God [sic] sake don't mention my name, should you desire to print anything I have to say. I collect a pension and I don't want anybody even *thinking* about my pension."[19]

In writing the dramatic 1990 Kentucky school reform act that called for decentralization and the creation of hundreds of school councils, Kentucky legislators understood that creating site-based management posed inherent dangers of financial and other types of abuse. For this reason, it created an Office of Education Accountability and charged it with, among other things, investigating complaints of corruption.

In just one case, the office's investigation led to the suspension of a county school superintendent for allegedly using school equipment and persuading school employees to work on his farm, violating bidding law, and retaliating against enemies by demoting or firing them. He also allegedly used school lunch money to reward supporters with trips to an amusement park and to Cincinnati Reds games, Kentucky's *Courier-Journal* reported. When an interim school superintendent planned to rehire the ousted superintendent as a teacher, education commissioner Thomas Boysen threatened to seek his removal, too.[20]

In July 1993, Boysen went even further: he recommended removal of the entire school board for failing to prevent the superintendent's abuses. Board members—who eventually resigned—allegedly neglected to ensure that expenses were properly documented, that bidding laws were followed, and that school equipment and employees were used for work-related reasons. The board also allegedly approved minutes of meetings containing blank spots to be filled in later with the amount of money to be spent.[21]

In Boysen's view, mismanagement and corruption can be deadly to reform in two ways: "One is it drains off resources . . . . The other one, which I view as more serious, is it drains off public support."

In 1992, the state of New Jersey created a special commission to uncover corruption and abuse on school boards throughout the state. According to *Education Week*, the New Jersey School Ethics Commission in its first year responded to twenty complaints or requests for advisory opinions and examined some twenty-two thousand public disclosure forms that asked board members about sources of income and substantial gifts and whether or not relatives worked for the school system. Of a total of ten thousand people, a dozen refused to complete the forms. They were stripped of office.[22]

Charges of corruption within the New York City school system also emerged around this time in a 107-page report published by the office of Edward F. Stancik, special commissioner of investigation. One of the most egregious examples involved two custodial employees who allegedly bought and sold semiautomatic firearms, sometimes at school. One of the employees reportedly told an undercover police officer he was available if the officer needed assistance in performing a contract killing.[23] At another school, an engineer-custodian, despite being paid $83,000 in 1990, spent considerable time on his thirty-four-foot yacht during sixteen school days while under surveillance by investigators.

The report was shocking: one engineer-custodian regularly piloted corporate aircraft during school hours while operating a pay telephone company from his school office in the little time he was there, according to Stancik. Another engineer-custodian was a real estate attorney who allegedly practiced law during school hours—both at a law office and on school grounds. He even purportedly brought his law office secretary to school to perform work for his private practice. A custodian with a criminal history of drug dealing allegedly smoked marijuana and practiced target shooting in his school's basement. Despite the allegations, many of the accused had received satisfactory or good ratings for years, partly because their pay and promotions depended only on the ratings of outside supervisors who rarely visited the schools. As a result of the probe, all eleven people investigated were either fired or forced to resign; seven were prosecuted.[24]

Among special agencies that investigate allegations of school corruption, the New York City Office of the Special Commissioner is unique: it has subpoena and arrest powers and is independent of the school system.[25] Created by an executive order of the mayor with the approval of the New York City Board of Education, it replaced what formerly had been the inspector general's office. "We had a series of scandals in the late '80s and the inspector general's office was found to be too much of an inhouse operation and didn't have the confidence of confidential sources in the board of education community," said Stancik. "What that comes down to is there's nobody at the board who can call me up and say, 'Don't do that investigation or don't release it now.' We make the decision, for better or for worse, what are the most significant things to investigate in the school system."[26]

The $3 million-a-year investigatory post has a number of important strengths. First, it has time and resources to investigate what prosecutors cannot—and its results prove that. During its first three years, its investigations led to the arrests of twenty-two pedophiles and the resignations of an additional eighteen people suspected of child abuse, compared to the previous three years when no suspected child molesters were removed from the system. "That's not because we suddenly had an epidemic of sexual abuse," Stancik said. "It's because we're bringing in experienced people who are serious about their work to the area."

Second, investigators are steeped in the internal culture, structure, and mentality of America's largest school system, no small accomplishment for an $8 billion-a-year operation.

Third, unlike criminal prosecutors, Stancik can recommend changes in management practices. In the probe of the engineer-custodians, for example, the office recommended restructuring a system that permitted fraud and abuse. Among other things, Stancik suggested that engineers report to principals.

Fourth, the office is able to enter previously taboo areas, such as politics, and show how practices—although not always criminal—undermine education. In a probe of the city's thirty-two subdistricts, for example, investigators provided a fascinating but appalling study of how politics cripples education. Common sense would dictate that abuse cannot be limited to New York City alone.

In Community School District 12, some employees were promoted not for how well they educated students but for how well they politicked for school board members in ways that included collecting petitions, handing out leaflets, attending fundraisers, and even performing personal favors, Stancik alleged.[27] By having school board members secretly record conversations, investigators learned how some members swapped and negotiated schools among themselves to determine who would control what patronage hall. Elementary schools with strong parental involvement and after-school activities were considered the political plums, they said. The reason? Parents who came to pick up their children after school represented potential votes that could be swayed by principals indebted to board members who placed them there. Conveniently, many schools served as polling places. In some cases, principals were given vote quotas—minimum numbers of votes they were required to provide for their benefactors' campaigns for reelection or higher political office, Stancik alleged. School board members employed an unusual vocabulary in this sordid political world. *Godfather* or *godmother,* for example, referred to a school board member who obtained principalships or other jobs for people. A *piece* was someone who could be counted on to perform legwork to get candidates elected to school boards. According to a 1993 commissioner's report, the system worked this way:

> Some pieces have particular roles to play. Someone working in the printing office can print campaign litera-ture free of charge. A secretary at the district office is well situated to distribute fundraiser tickets and collect money from those who sell them. Listening to all the talk about pieces in District 12, the overall effect is of board members playing a game—acquiring pieces, losing pieces, trading pieces—all in an effort to improve their position in the game. The game can be played fiercely, as our investigation demonstrates, and it is played on a political board. Education is at best a minor considera-tion when godfathers and godmothers get together to talk about their pieces.[28]

As a New York school principal, Virginia Noville was forced to resign in 1989 because she allegedly sold junk food to youngsters at a considerable profit, Stancik's office reported. But four years later, Noville attempted to make a comeback. She paid a school board member $4,000—the down payment toward a promised bribe of at least twice that much—to become a principal again, Stancik's office alleged based on secretly tape-recorded conversations. Noville preyed on the desperate poverty of parent activists by giving Christmas gifts to teachers and PTA members in the school whose principal-ship she sought, Stancik's office further alleged. She also reportedly offered a parents association president a $300 "loan" to secure both her allegiance and support of her par-ents' group.[29]

Such legwork helped candidates for principal pass muster of parent committees responsible for screening candidates. Godfathers and godmothers also worked for candidates by offering jobs or money to screening committee members to sway their decisions. At one point in their probe, investigators watched as a PTA president and vice president who sat on a screening committee changed midstream their ardent support of a candidate. Investigators knew that, behind the scenes, the pair won better job offers by sponsoring a rival applicant.[30] In their report, investigators posed the question of why someone with no children in a school district would want to be a school board member for a mere $125 per month. Their conclusion is frightening. The potential for accumulating income from bribes was part of the lure, they surmised, but there apparently was a stronger, more powerful reason. "The motivation we found most often is the acquisition and expansion of political power. At the school board level, the ability to hand out jobs generates enormous influence, particularly in a community where jobs are hard to come by. It also brings a member into contact with other elected officials, the seductive world of political conferences, and the promise of higher office."[31]

Such a system demoralized those educators who truly wanted to educate but who could not advance without politicking for candidates. Making the findings public was crucial toward improving morale and deterring further abuse, Stancik believes. "We took this dark corner of the political world of New York education and we shined a bright light into it. We showed people exactly how politics was hurting education in New York," he said.

Unlike their New York counterparts, Illinois legislators made few provisions for oversight of Chicago public schools. In a state with a long and colorful history of corruption in high places, no such office for investigating schools existed until 1994, five years after the reform movement began. Even then legislators provided no specific funding for it and loudly stated to voters they had no wish to create a new government bureaucracy. Part of the reason was a long tradition of local control of schools, based on the premise that individual school boards are accountable to their communities primarily because citizens can raise havoc if members do not act responsibly. Of course, unlike other school boards in the state, the Chicago Board of Education is not elected, so voters have no way of holding members directly accountable.[32] Even if they were, New York City's system illustrates how the electoral process can be thwarted and abused. In addition, the sheer size of the system, its unwillingness to release some public documents, and the complexity of its operations poses significant obstacles for citizen watchdog groups.

Local school councils are supposed to oversee the schools and, in a growing number of cases, they actually do. At Sayre Elementary School, the council initiated the probe of more than $15,000 in missing funds and tirelessly pushed for an investigation after suppliers complained their checks bounced. "If it weren't for school reform, this never would have come to light," school council member Susan Klonsky said.[33]

But oversight by councils is difficult—and the legislature does not offer much help. It turned down requests to grant councils specific authority over internal accounts following complaints that some principals refused to provide those documents to their council members. Unbelievably, some councils—which control employment contracts of principals and thus have the power to grant contract renewals—did not even receive audit reports that were critical of their principals' work.

The actual job of overseeing the Chicago public schools is left to the volunteer fifteen-member Chicago Board of Education. But that revolving body of lay people has little or no training in budgets, contracts, or bids. Even if they had, the board as a whole chose to adopt a hands-off approach. In August 1992, for example, the board voluntarily reduced the amount of information it received on finances, limited the financial matters on which votes were recorded, and adopted a strong stance against micromanagement.

Micromanagement has been faulted in education literature as an ineffective intrusion by board members into the day-to-day affairs of school systems. "There's a basic philosophy that says the board should stay out of micromanagement. It presupposes the administration will take its fiduciary responsibility seriously," said Stephen Ballis, the powerful head of the Management Services Committee, who engineered the move away from micromanagement. "The whole point was that board members spend their time on policy, not counting toilet paper." Board member John "Jack" Valinote argued that addressing abysmal education, poorly performing teachers, high dropout rates, and the real possibility of another financial collapse in 1995 were far more important issues than monitoring whether individuals overspent in various areas or exploring cozy relationships with vendors that may have contributed to the overruns.

But taking such a stance means that the school board approves purchasing reports—often millions of dollars at a time—with no discussion and little background information (a page of backup data is available if board members request it.)[34]

Furthermore, in 1992, the board cut its internal audit staff in half and farmed out the work to private companies at a higher cost. Such a system complicated an already cumbersome method of channeling charges of corruption since council members did not know what firms were handling the complaints. As proof, private auditors found fewer than a handful of problems in 1993—a fraction of what had been reported by the board's own auditors in previous years, a comparison of the audits showed. A spokesperson for the auditing firm of Arthur Andersen and Company, which held the bulk of the $515,000-a-year contract, explained that because the private firms performed audits according to a set schedule, they did not receive tips concerning impropriety.

To obtain a special audit for a school, council members were often told to go through an administrative chain of command within the system's subdistricts. Some complained about the ineffectiveness of this procedure because in the internal culture of the massive system, allegations occasionally took a backseat to long-time friendships between supervisors and veteran principals. Anonymous allegations were not accepted.

———————

The accomplishments of the New York City commissioner's office proved it made little sense to let a multibillion-dollar agency police itself. If there was any doubt, the Chicago school system offered its own conclusive evidence in 1992. During that year, the board spent twice its $15 million budget for central office computer equipment and services with no specific school board authorization to do so.[35] Internal procedures were so lax and the computer system so obsolete that even the chief financial officer did not know about the overrun, which quietly appeared on an obscure financial report made available to the state. "They can overspend in certain departments with impunity—without people raising the question of why," said Toni Hartrich, senior research associate for the Civic Federation, a Chicago taxpayers' watchdog group that recommended ways to make the school system's financial procedures less complex and more accountable. "To control costs, one absolutely has to have that." The extra computer money was used partly for consultants and partly to pay off loans early to save $3 million in interest, officials said.[36]

The overrun came to light three months after Kimbrough disclosed an internal investigation and an FBI probe into the board's computer department. The accounting firm of Washington, Pittman, and McKeever reported alleged cost overruns and other questionable practices, including invoices paid to Unisys Corporation outside its contract period and a five-year lease to IBM without school board authorization. In a closed-door meeting, Kimbrough told board members that, all in all, irregularities and overcharges could amount to more than $1 million.[37]

The lack of oversight in Chicago public schools allowed the system to bypass competitive bidding on tens of millions of dollars in computer contracts before the no-bid practice was made legal by the Illinois legislature in 1992. While school systems across the nation regularly bid computer purchases, the Chicago school board authorized as much as $163 million in no-bid computer contracts in the five years before Illinois law allowed the practice, school board reports showed. (Most of the contracts were "requirements agreements," which merely set a cap on purchases with a specific vendor. Consequently, less than $163 million was spent. Board officials, however, could not produce the actual dollar value of computer equipment and service contracts for both classroom and administration use.) Minority contracting requirements were overwhelmingly waived in most central office computer purchases, sending city dollars to Chicago's wealthiest suburbs.[38]

The only way to force the board to comply with bidding law was, in some cases, to file a lawsuit. In 1990, Compass Health Care Plans of Chicago charged that the school board illegally shut it out of $484 million in no-bid health-care contracts. Lower and appellate courts agreed with the company and ordered the school board to competitively bid the three-year health-care package. The interim board, which negotiated the contracts, could have saved an astounding 15 to 20 percent had it done comparison shopping from the start, wrote

Appellate Court Justice Mary Ann G. McMorrow in 1992.[39] In arriving at her decision, she quoted the expert testimony of David Dranove, then codirector of the graduate program in health administration at the University of Chicago Graduate School of Business, who testified in an affidavit that "when purchases exploit the competitive thrust of selective contracting, they are able to obtain significant and substantial discounts—as high as 15 to 20 percent."[40] School board officials and a spokesperson for health-care giant Blue Cross-Blue Shield of Illinois—whose company, HMO, Illinois, received the bulk of the business—said the court did not understand some details of the complex health-care industry. "I'm not sure the justices of the Illinois Appellate Court were looking at the financial and network agreements," said Blue Cross spokesperson Dennis Culloton. "They may have been just saying it's the board's responsibility to put HMOs out for bid."

After the ruling, the successor school board twice extended the health-care contracts in question, arguing that it made a verbal commitment to do so with Blue Cross-Blue Shield, which received the bulk of the business. Board president D. Sharon Grant later said she made the commitment in the heat of 1993 negotiations with the Chicago Teachers Union; retaining the same health-care providers was part of the deal. Some board members explained they did not want to anger the union.

Ironically, while the board publicly trumpeted an end to micromanagement by board members, Grant came under fire for her front-line roles in negotiating a separate no-bid health-care contract with a Blue Cross-Blue Shield company involving a slightly different type of health-care insurance.[41] On the one hand, Grant's health-care company had been hired by a Blue Cross-Blue Shield company to provide services to the Chicago Transportation Authority, a government agency. On the other hand, Grant helped negotiate on behalf of the school board a contract with a Blue Cross-Blue Shield company, even after the appellate court decision required bidding for a similar—although not identical—type of health insurance. Blue Cross-Blue Shield spokesperson Dennis Culloton credited Grant's negotiating acumen for forcing the company to cut $13 million a year from its previous contract. Talks on the school board contract were held, in part, at Grant's offices at Concerned Health Care of America. Grant said she entered the talks when

Blue Cross-Blue Shield executive Cleveland A. Tyson—who previously had headed the school board's insurance department—complained that board staff members were not negotiating in good faith. Once involved, Grant said she insisted on negotiations that would save the school board money.

Meanwhile, another vendor complained of being shut out of the process. American Health Care Providers said it provided evidence that it could have saved the system $28 million a year. Nevertheless, the school board refused to consider its proposal and awarded an eight-month, no-bid contract to a Blue Cross-Blue Shield company. Although the contracts involved complex and difficult procedures, all evidence pointed to one conclusion: Much of the 1993 crisis in the city's high schools could have been averted if only good management had prevailed. "Look what's happening in our high schools—this money could have solved the crisis," said board member Ashish Sen, who unsuccessfully argued to consider American Health Care. "How do you justify giving a more expensive contract when someone says you can do it for less and we're short of money?"[42]

The central office itself proved that employing proper bidding procedures could save money. In 1992, it rewrote the specifications on its massive food contract and invited competitors to bid where they had been conspicuously absent before. Changing the specs and streamlining distribution saved $3 million on the $14 million contract. Nevertheless, Preferred Meals Systems, a suburban Schaumburg company that had received the annual contract for about a decade, won it yet again.[43]

Simple mathematics indicates that the school system could save hundred of thousands of dollars—if not far more—by bidding computers. When legislators exempted computer and and computer-related products from bidding—ostensibly because it would be difficult for the system to make all computer equipment compatible—they opened the way for administrators to use more questionable methods of deciding what to buy. During 1991 and 1992, at least one hundred Chicago principals, teachers, and central office administrators were treated to out-of-town trips on computer vendors' tabs, according to school system records of employee leaves granted for conferences. In one month alone, at least sixteen principals and teachers attended free computer conferences in Houston, Orlando, San Francisco, and Atlanta. Principals, who did not need local school council approval to attend, said the conferences familiarized them with products they could later recommend for their schools. They claimed that the system provided no other alternatives to guide them through the complicated task of choosing computers. (Chicago's decentralization plan, it must be remembered, assumed that school officials could handle budgeting and purchasing with little guidance.)

The free-trip marketing strategy—encouraged by the lack of central office guidance—sent the sales of one Arizona company skyrocketing. Begun with four employees in 1989, Educational Management Group of Phoenix sold $6.7 million in computer packages to Chicago schools in one fourteen-month period during 1992 and 1993, a feat achieved with no advertising. Dozens of Chicago principals, teachers, and administrators took the company's offer of free trips to sunny climates during Chicago's freezing winters. "Chicago is not one Chicago school district anymore," explained Gail Richardson, then the company owner. "It's 609 school districts. We have found a much better way to tell our story, and it's less expensive than the way many companies market."[44]

Richardson also hired former Chicago school board employees, a practice vendors in many industries found productive because it gave their staff intimate knowledge of the market, and it put Chicago educators in the comfortable position of negotiating with someone they knew. Among those hired by Educational Management Group was Robert A. Sampieri, the school board's chief operating officer. Sampieri became the company's vice president for operations in 1993, although he left that position later the same year.

The Phoenix company made its name on the Accelerated Station 2000, a package that impressed Chicago educators who for years had lacked basic supplies, let alone technology. Educational Management Group tailored AS-2000 to accommodate Chapter One funds. At Randolph Magnet School on the South Side, a $65,500 package consisted of hardware, including a twenty-seven-inch computer monitor, two computer disk drives, a fax machine, a color and a black-and-white printer, a laser disc video recorder, a scanner, and a camcorder to videotape students. Richardson conceded that the cost of the hardware plus installation amounted to no more than $28,000.[45] The $65,500 package also included repairs, the services of a consultant who visited every two weeks, and an educational computer software program that in one seventh-grade language arts classroom was used to quiz students and keep score in a game called "Knowledge Champs." A typical sampling of questions included:

- How many states are there in the United States?
- As the earth begins to turn away from the sun, what time of day will it soon be?
- What will a caterpillar turn into: a frog, a butterfly, or a lizard?
- What day do we honor Americans who have served in the Armed Forces? Name the holiday and the date.

Teacher Joyce Dunson raved about the computer service. A single phone call to Phoenix would bring quiz questions and lesson suggestions via fax. Principal Theodore Washington, Sr., also a convert to the service, explained his own philosophy of education and technology's role in it: "I think eventually textbooks will be on the way out. The day where every child has to have a book—that teaching is out of date." The AS-2000—shared by the entire classroom—contrasted with other computer packages in which students worked in labs at their own pace, each assigned their own computer.

The board of education employed a purchasing practice that, theoretically at least, should have led to reduced costs, but many believed it only raised them. The board purchased computers and services in "bundles"; that is, packages that included consultants and maintenance, whether or not a school wanted them. "If I'm buying my software from you, there's a built-in service where I have to use your consultants to come in and give me periodic lessons and update me on what's on the market," Westcott School principal Michael Woods explained. "Why do I have to have them as consultants? If I need them, let me pay them." It often made it impossible to determine what price the school paid for specific components. In the case of the $65,500 package mentioned above, not one purchase order listed specifics about the equipment or the services.

Chicago compares unfavorably with the Hawaiian school system, which refuses to buy bundled items, according to Philip J. Bossert of the Hawaii Department of Education. "It's so you know exactly what the stuff costs. That's the way the state bids in order to be able to compare prices among all the people bidding. Otherwise, it would be very difficult." New York City schools also discontinued the practice after concluding it was not cost effective.

The stakes in spending money on computers are extraordinarily high in a multibillion dollar industry. In the first three years of reform, the Chicago school system spent more than $120 million on computer equipment and services, about twice as much as the previous three years. Roughly 70 percent went toward classroom computers, most bought with poverty funds.[46] The numbers, however, are only ballpark figures because, ironically, the mainframe computer system is not designed to make such a simple calculation. Despite the $30 million reportedly spent on computer headquarters in 1992, the system could not perform even the most basic functions. "It's an amazing problem," Toni Hartrich, of the Civic Federation said. "What we have are antiquated systems in which checks and balances are fairly minimal—in fact, in some places, we think they're nonexistent." Chief financial officer Charley Gillispie blames a band-aid approach and a lack of planning in a central office repeatedly hit by personnel cuts and not-so-subtle encouragement by outside forces to favor privatization. The practice of pinstriped patronage—some private companies receive as much as $250 per hour—is common to all levels of government. Consultants, some argue, have replaced the traditional form of job patronage. More than $12 million of the $30 million spent by the Chicago school system on central office computers in 1992 went for "purchased services" such as consultants.

How could so much money be spent on a system that cannot perform basic functions? "No one has done a complete study of what's needed. It's sort of like if you decide to buy furniture for your home and you buy one living room piece at a time. You're going to pay more than if you buy it all at one time," Gillispie said.

The extra money did not avert delays and rationing of computer time during the enrollment crunch of September 1992, however, when school staff needed to enter information on everything from immunizations to free lunch figures for Chicago's 411,000 students. "It's having an impact on the system—this sort of expansion without a plan," said J. Maxey Bacchus, who temporarily took over the computer department after former head Clifford Cox left for a job with the Detroit school system. The administration's eighteen-year-old mainframe system is reportedly so obsolete that it needs an additional $10 to $30 million to update it. "If someone asked you how much money do you have today and you couldn't get a verifiable answer for two months, you'd be somewhat alarmed, too," interim superintendent Richard Stephenson once said. The board's 1994 tentative budget proposed increasing central office computer expenditures by nearly $12 million although later budget cuts reduced that figure.

The problem, however, is not only a matter of technology. It is the way in which it is used: payment information entered into the system is so vague that pencils cannot be distinguished from disk drives. Computer purchases are listed under various categories in different funds and labeled in different ways. For example, IBM is listed five ways in the computer—IBM, IBM Corp., IBM Corporation, International Business, and International Business Machine—each time under a different vendor number. Auditors who tried to link purchase orders with contracts in 1992 came away scratching their heads. They could not confirm whether vendors were paid more than their contracts allowed because purchase orders were not marked with contract numbers. "It appears there are no control mechanisms in place to keep track of purchase orders pertaining to a particular contract," the report by the accounting firm of Washington, Pittman, and McKeever stated.[47] In fact, various computer contracts made with different companies over several months all had the same contract number. The new purchasing director, McNair Grant, Jr., could not explain the reason for the convoluted procedure nor did he wish to defend it. Asked how it came about in the first place, Grant consulted with his staff and came to only one conclusion: "It's always been done that way."[48]

Students give the Illinois legislature failing grades.

Courtesy *Chicago Sun-Times*. Photo by John H. White.

12

A Legislative Will

It's not racism due to race. It may come from people being isolated.

> Whitney Young High School student Benny Hunt
> about the lack of funding for Chicago schools [1]

Given the legacy of waste and inefficiency in Chicago public schools, it would be tempting to argue against giving the system another dime. But the solution is not to abandon the schools—as, in many ways, the Illinois state legislature has done—but to correct the system and spend the necessary capital on it.

To do otherwise is to relinquish hope of an educated and productive society. It means depriving hundreds of thousands of children of the well-financed education provided their wealthier suburban peers. It sentences Chicago schoolchildren to classes in boiler rooms and hallways, to elementary schools without science labs, and to teacherless classrooms well into the school year. It assigns students to burnt-out teachers who have little incentive, support, or training to improve. It robs children of after-school activities, such as school musicals, language clubs, and band. For those who go astray or are violent, it ensures that they will never see a truant officer and that the first "alternative school" they may ever know is prison, where lessons are of the harshest reality.

For taxpayers across the state, it means paying more for prisons, welfare, literacy programs, and the loss of a thriving economy as manufacturers and corporations move elsewhere in search of a suitable work pool and good schools for children of job applicants they wish to recruit. It means that fewer people will shoulder the tax burden as the population of those lacking basic skills and dependent on government handouts—which are derived, after all, from the working American's pocketbook—continues to grow. It means today's adults, when elderly, will depend on a generation unskilled and ill-equipped to handle the needs of an aging population. It means increased violence, taking not only an incalcuable emotional toll but also sending health-care costs soaring.

Illinois legislators should address public education with the same sense of urgency they give to building premier ballparks and convention centers. The investment, although less tangible, will nevertheless yield as real a return. Clearly the solution is not only a matter of money. The system itself must be repaired. Some say that will never be done and, in a state that lacks the political will to do so, they are tragically correct—unless voters unite and give politicians an incentive to do otherwise. The experiences in other states have already indicated that Chicago's structure—in which reform, after all, proved to be a step in the right direction—can be vastly improved if care and common sense prevail.

When the state supreme court in Kentucky ruled its school system unconstitutional, it mandated that the state not only overhaul public school education and properly fund it but that it be continually monitored "so that there is no waste, no duplication, no mismanagement, at any level."[2] In response, Kentucky legislators passed strict ethics laws, prohibiting board members from attempting to influence the hiring of any school employee other than the superintendent and the attorney. They limited campaign contributions for local school board races to $100 from any one individual and $200 from any one political action committee. They prohibited candidates from soliciting or accepting money or services from school district employees. In addition, they barred school superintendents from hiring their own relatives or those of board members.[3]

The Kentucky legislature also provided a mechanism, the Office of Education Accountability, to enforce the enacted rules. The office verifies the accuracy of school district and state performance and investigates charges of corruption. Not surprisingly, it ran into stiff opposition, especially in areas where schools had been used for years as patronage hiring halls. As Kentucky education commissioner Thomas C. Boysen explains: "Economic development and education reform are two sides of the same coin. The people are not about to come up with an extra half-billion dollars a year—the people are not about to make that investment—and see it squandered. The only way to keep reform alive is to insist on competence and honesty." Boysen rates investigating mismanagement and corruption as the second most important element of reform. "The most important thing is to have a very strong system of assessment and accountability," he notes. "You can do everything by the book and not get results. That's the most powerful part of our reform."

It was also the most controversial. The state of Kentucky provides penalties for poorly achieving schools and incentives for good ones based on specific criteria, such as improvements and declines on test scores, attendance, and graduation rates. Schools are given twenty years to bring all students up to a prescribed level of proficiency, but, at the same time, they are required to improve at a certain pace every two years or be penalized. Under the plan, schools that do achieve are given more money to spend as they wish—even for staff pay raises. Failing schools have to provide an improvement plan. They then receive state money and aid in the form of an experienced teacher or administrator. Kentucky schools whose ratings decline by more than 5 percent eventually may face probation, threatening the principal with dismissal or transfer. Parents will then be able to remove their children from those schools.

Holding schools accountable for performance is meaningless, however, without state support. Consequently, the Kentucky legislature funded the overhaul of its schools with a $1.4 billion tax increase to finance the first two years of reform. The state pays preschool expenses for all three- and four-year-olds with disabilities and for four-year-olds from low-income families. It provides money for tutoring and for family centers for schools whose student populations are at least 20 percent low income. It pours money into teacher and principal training. Funding for computers and other technology amounts to $35 per child with the important stipulation that schools match the funds and link them to a $400 million statewide technology plan. This conflicts sharply with the hodgepodge of conflicting and sometimes overpriced computer technology introduced into Chicago schools in the name of academic freedom. Kentucky found a way to encourage schools to use compatible technology without trampling on freedoms granted under site-based management. Moreover, the Kentucky computer purchases were competitively bid, according to Stephen K. Swift, the state education department's director of public information.

Such sweeping changes were not easy to implement, especially in a state where no school district spent as much as the national per-student average before reform, primarily because of low teacher salaries. According to *Education Week,* the most opposition came not over a sales tax increase from five to six cents and an increase in income tax revenue,[4] but over more fundamental changes, such as dropping traditional grading and combining primary grades to allow children to be taught at their own pace. Resistance also has grown as Kentucky teachers, whose pay ranked thirty-first in the nation in 1990–91,[5] have become exhausted as greater demands and additional training have been imposed on them. In its first three years, more than ten court cases were filed challenging various portions of the Kentucky Education Reform Act, or KERA, as it is called. By the third year, continued increases in funding were threatened by other state government costs.[6]

Nevertheless, in its first three years, education funding in Kentucky increased by 36 percent, and the gap between the state's richest and poorest districts was reduced by one third. The results in student achievement were mixed: statewide, performance test scores rose 53 percent in fourth-grade reading from 1992 to 1993. Other scores—twelfth-grade social studies, for example—dropped significantly.[7] The Business Roundtable, made up of the chief executive officers of more than two hundred of America's largest corporations, declared Kentucky well on its way to creating an education system based on the nine essential components of school reform: higher expectations for students, performance-based education, better assessment strategies, rewards for successful schools and penalties for failing ones, school-based management, additional staff development, high-quality preschool programs, better health and social services in schools, and greater use of technology.[8]

Contrast Kentucky's carefully conceived plan to the effort rushed through the Illinois legislature to reform its largest public school system. The Illinois legislature eventually adopted a plan that held schools accountable for failure—not achievement—but did not take any responsibility itself for its role in the system's failure. Illinois legislators acted wisely when they adopted Chicago school reform at the behest of a massive parents' movement. Beyond the cameras and the spotlights, the legislature guaranteed that the system would fail. How? For one thing, it placed enormous burdens on rookie councils, requiring each to choose a principal, write a long-range plan, and decide how to spend tens of thousands of dollars in poverty funds during the first year. In doing so, it provided no money for training and no time for planning, leaving little reason to wonder why schools did not improve initially. While the state of Kentucky required each council member to have a high school degree or a G.E.D. high school equivalency certificate, the Illinois legislature set no such standards.

In Chicago, some council members cannot even read. Such an inadequacy may work in schools where principals are competent, honest, and caring enough to explain every document that requires a vote, but it can be a critical deficiency in schools where principals are less than capable and honest. Although nonreading parents may be invaluable in other areas of school work, it is difficult to comprehend how they can ably select a competent principal and set educational policy that will turn a failing school around.

In a critical failure that doomed the system to inadequate funding caused by a lack of public support, the legislature also refused to institute controls early. Something as logical as creating a special school post to investigate charges of corruption did not exist until senate president James "Pate" Philip pushed it through the legislature in November 1993. The office was established as part of the Chicago School Finance Authority, which is closely aligned with the business community. This significant step was a credit to Republicans, who gained control of the Senate in January 1993 for the first time in two decades. But there were flaws: while the work of other inspector generals was made public, only the vaguest information about findings of the Chicago schools inspector general was to be reported.[9] More important, the legislature provided no specific additional funding, hardly laying the groundwork for the top-notch investigative unit that was so badly needed.

There are other ways the legislature could address abuses in a system with a long legacy of mismanagement. It could require and pay for annual or biennial audits at each school. Further in the multibillion industry of technology, it should reverse itself and require that computers be bid—as many states do. "From the beginning of school reform, I have said until you deal with theft, fraud, and deception, this system will never change," said school activist Calvin Pearce, who sought a special legislative commission to determine ways of addressing corruption in the system. "We can start with the internal accounts and then talk about people who have been running off the board of education's wax, people who have never bought milk for themselves or their families for decades because they get it off the board for free, and others who are throwing computers in the trunks of their cars. We don't want to turn it into a blame game, but we need to get good ideas from people—people who are on the front lines."[10]

The legislature also set no requirements for criminal background checks on council members. "How do we know we don't have drug dealers, felons, and child molesters on our LSCs?" school reformer Kathryn Kuranda asked. Although an expensive proposition, background checks may be necessary as street gang members, for example, become politically active and realize the potential of local school councils to advance their "positions." No one would deny or would want to discourage the power of a person turning one's life around, but, in some cases, the activism lacks credibility when no denouncement of drugs or forfeiture of illegal weapons accompanies it.

In passing the reform law, Illinois legislators did not carefully consider possible ethics legislation, such as strengthening conflict-of-interest laws, prohibiting the school board from doing business with employees or board members within a year or more after they leave the system, or barring principals from hiring relatives of local school council members, an easy way for principals to garner support when their four-year contracts are about to expire. Kuranda believes that such a practice should be illegal, even though her husband has a $13,000-a-year job in Kelly High School where she is council president. She also believes the legislature should consider requiring non-English-speaking council members to take English courses to better equip them to deal with the system.

The legislature created a revolving door of leadership by changing school boards every few years and by requiring that the board president be elected annually by peers. Legislators scorned the ineptitude of the volunteer Chicago school board members, some of whom, to be sure, often failed to scrutinize the expenditures they approved or to understand the full effects of their votes. Legislators themselves ensured that once board members grasped aspects of the $2.7 billion system, including such areas as assessing and placing blame for wasteful practices, they would soon be gone and powerless to effect the lessons they had learned.

Until the fall of 1993, when Republicans pushed through the measure, the legislature had refused to grant principals control over staffing their schools even though it was a logical step toward holding principals accountable. The legislators gave principals increased authority over supervising engineers and granted them the power to appoint assistants and head teachers, but they made it more difficult for principals to assign their choice of teachers. Principals should be held accountable for their schools' failure to improve, but only if they can select their staff.

The legislature created grave problems for the 1993 school year by allowing early retirement for hundreds of Chicago teachers and principals. The move in itself was—from an economic standpoint at least—a way to allow the board to negotiate fewer jobs through attrition, rather than layoffs, and to bring new blood into the system. But the same legislature that gave suburban school districts at least a four months' notice set August 15 as the deadline for Chicago. Further, it gave suburban teachers two years to decide and allowed suburban school districts three years to phase-in retirements but told

Chicago educators they would have only one chance to make a decision, just weeks before school began. The move showed disregard for children forced to sit before a string of substitutes or teachers with no expertise in their assigned courses. One cannot help but wonder what outcry would result if the legislators' own children or grandchildren were to miss a month of biology and then sit for the rest of the year in science class before a teacher whose specialty was math. Veteran Amundsen High School English teacher George Schmidt, for example, was abruptly transferred in midsemester 1993 to teach math at Bowen High School. "Our state legislators treat non-Chicago districts first class and the Chicago district second class. Jim Crow is supposed to be dead," notes DuSable High School principal Charles Mingo. "I feel people are trying to go out of their way to paint the public system as a buffoon."

How could the legislature and the teachers union, whose clout resulted in passage of the bill, reasonably expect the school system to reschedule thousands of teaching jobs so quickly? "It's an issue that's been pending for two years," Madigan spokesperson Steve Brown responded. "They knew this day was coming. This wasn't a surprise development." Of course, knowing such a bill might pass was much different than groping with thousands of retirements just four weeks before school opened. Top job applicants understandably accepted firm offers in the suburbs, which also had vacancies because of early retirement, before waiting for Chicago positions to open. In some cases, Chicago schools were left to select from a pool of less qualified teachers.

The legislature also guaranteed that the Chicago school system would be unable to cleanse itself of poorly performing workers. Although there was much discussion on the topic in political circles, legislators barely modified the lengthy and costly dismissal process for teachers, principals, and other staff, a problem affecting suburban districts as well. Most important, they did not address changing the criteria for dismissal.[11] Lawmakers also took no measures to ensure the basic competency of the teaching workforce. Nor did they establish parent centers to address the cycle of poverty and the effects of poor education on previous generations. Despite failing to confront such issues, the legislature refused to shoulder blame for the lack of measurable progress in Chicago schools under reform or for waste in the system. On the contrary, it used these deficiencies as chief reasons for not funding the schools.

Although the interim board was certainly responsible for binding the system to labor contracts it could not afford, the legislature itself bears a large role in the financial failure of the schools. For example, it transferred $250 million in poverty funds from the basic budget to schools—a logical move, in itself—but provided no money to supplement that budget. Legislative leaders would accept reform only if it were "revenue-neutral." When reform was adopted under the administration of then Governor James Thompson, house speaker Michael Madigan blocked an income tax increase. Madigan feared that the money would be used toward expanding the state bureaucracy, according to spokesperson Steve Brown. At the same time, legislators in effect negotiated union contracts for the board by writing into law permanent job guarantees for most teachers from their first day on the job—although, in November 1993, the guarantees were shortened to a maximum of twenty-five months.

The legislature also guaranteed the system's financial failure by approving short-sighted gimmicks—such as temporarily using pension money and transferring millions of dollars from the building fund—to give employees pay raises. In 1993, it laid the groundwork for another financial collapse by approving the issuance of $427 million in bonds to rescue Chicago schools from a deficit that would otherwise have kept them closed. Everyone even remotely connected to the schools knew that the solution would only delay the problem until 1995, when the funds would be consumed and the budget hole would be far larger. Relying on borrowing—which school systems throughout the state are forced to do—mortgages the future of America's children.[12] Paying for education up front is far less expensive than adding to the price tag of schooling millions of dollars in interest and bonding costs that go to private companies—the same phenomenon that has given America its national debt. For example, the School Finance Authority issued $573 million in bonds to bail out the system in its 1979 financial crisis; five years later, it issued $114.5 million more for building repairs. As of 1993, the amount still owed was $795 million—$322 million of it in interest, enough to educate more than fifty thousand students for one year.[13] But that was before the legislature authorized the 1993 borrowing.

The Illinois legislature has failed its children in other ways. In 1973, legislators created the state lottery. To overcome moral arguments against legalized gambling and concern that the poor would be exploited, lawmakers promised gambling profits would help education. The law passed, but without any requirement that lottery profits be used for schools. Most of the money, therefore, went into the state's general revenue fund. Under criticism for not fulfilling promises, lawmakers in 1985 agreed to devote proceeds of the state lottery to education. Slick advertisments trumpeted the change. While then Governor Thompson was running for reelection against former Senator Adlai E. Stevenson III (D-Illinois), the lottery ran a $481,000 television commercial. According to the *Chicago Sun-Times,* the script ran as follows:

> The Illinois state lottery is happy to announce that we are investing all of this year's profits, over half a billion dollars, in the schools of Illinois. After all, doesn't it make sense to invest your money where it will bring the greatest possible returns?[14]

The commercials were misleading. While the lottery profits—amounting to $610 million in 1992[15]—technically went into the education fund, they did not increase money for schools. Instead, the lottery money replaced general revenues that the legislature, in its annual budget process, diverted from education to pay for other state costs. In other words, for every lottery dollar put into éducation, another was taken out for other purposes.[16] Meanwhile, the poor—some of whom bet their last dollar on the remote chance of leaving poverty behind—send lottery profits soaring. A 1988 *Chicago Sun-Times* study revealed that the ten zip codes with the lowest household incomes averaged per capita lottery sales of $221 per year—compared to the $76 per capita sales in the ten zip code areas with the the highest household incomes and populations exceeding ten thousand.[17]

The save-the-schools argument that sold Illinoisans on the lottery was used again in 1993 to promote riverboat gambling. The idea was that Chicago schools could close their annual budget gap partly by paying back what they borrowed with riverboat gambling proceeds. It is ironic that both state and city seek to fund troubled schools by promoting one of society's vices, which will undoubtedly yield enormous profits for investors. The more sensible approach toward funding education—without hollow promises built on gambling—is through a graduated income tax combined with property tax relief, school finance experts conclude.

The shell games involved not only the lottery but also other revenues, such as riverboat gambling approved outside of Chicago and an income tax increase pledged to go to education, according to Illinois comptroller Dawn Clark Netsch, the Democratic candidate for governor in 1994. In 1989, the state enacted a .5 percent income tax surcharge and pledged one half of the proceeds to increase school funding. While the immediate benefits increased education spending 16 percent in 1990, the legislature eventually eliminated other income tax receipts from education, according to Netsch. Mike Lawrence, a spokesman for Governor Jim Edgar, responded that education funding increased in 1994 while funding for other state agencies was cut during the state's financial crisis. Over Edgar's four-year term, beginning in 1990, education spending increased 3 percent, according to the Illinois State Board of Education.[18]

In a 1992 statewide referendum, 58 percent of voters agreed that the state should pay the primary share of education. The ballot question did not specify that income taxes would rise if the measure were approved, but proponents argued that voters were sophisticated enough to understand the consequences. The measure to amend the Illinois constitution failed because it required a 60 percent majority,[19] but it nevertheless indicated that voters may be more concerned about education than some politicians are willing to believe. A 1993 poll put public education as the top concern of Illinois voters, with 54 percent saying they would be willing to pay higher state income taxes for education, according to the Coalition for Consumer Rights, which conducted the poll.[20]

Nationwide, critics of increased funding for education say America has invested enormous amounts in schools with no tangible returns in student achievement. They point out that education spending in the United States rose 50 percent in one ten-year period, after adjusting for inflation, for a total of $493.3 billion in 1992–93. But a closer examination of that figure gives it more meaning: the number is based on both public and private schools in elementary through higher education, where enrollment grew during that period by nearly 6.5 million students. When only expenditures for public elementary and secondary education are considered, per pupil spending rose 29 percent over ten years, adjusted for inflation. In constant dollars, the average per-pupil cost rose from $4,577 in 1983–84 to $5,920 ten years later. What made up the increase? Certainly rectifying the decades-old practice of underpaying teachers contributed. The largest portion of any school budget is staff and, nationwide, teachers' salaries rose 16 percent after adjusting for inflation during that period—from $31,637 to $36,700 a year, again in constant dollars. In addition, the number of teachers rose by 335,000.[21]

Meanwhile, the cost of nurses, counselors, psychologists, social workers, and occupational therapists, not to mention the cost of textbooks—sometimes priced as high as $40 each—has also increased the expense of educating America's children. The price is small compared to the cost of doing otherwise. As social worker Bernie Noven put it, "It's not a matter of what to do—we know what to do. It's so clear to me that with these kindergartners coming to schools speaking like three-year-olds, we really need classes of ten and fifteen in the primary grades. If we don't do it, we'll be spending at least $20,000 per year when they go to jail—for the same kid."

In Illinois, the state income tax is a comparatively low 3 percent for individuals and 4.8 percent for corporations. Republican Governor Jim Edgar made good on a campaign pledge in 1990 not to raise those rates although he fulfilled another campaign promise to make permanent a temporary surcharge reflected in them. In 1991–92, the state picked up only 35 percent of public education costs, down from a high of 48.4 percent in 1975–76.[22] Although it ranks eleventh in wealth—as measured by buying income per household—Illinois is an abysmal forty-fifth in the state per-person contribution toward education, according to a report by the National Education Association.[23] Property taxes make up more than their share.

Illinois is unsupportive of education in other ways, too. In 1993, the *Chicago Sun-Times* disclosed that Chicago schools lost more than $36.1 million in federal school breakfast subsidies for poor children over a twenty-year period because of a bureaucratic breakdown. The state board of education apparently never notified the Chicago system of a special eighteen-cent-per-breakfast stipend for schools with large numbers of low-income students. The state, which is responsible for channeling federal funds to both public and private schools, responded that neither the Chicago school system nor any other school system in Illinois applied for the federal money. Even though schools in every other state in the nation received the subsidy, Illinois officials said they assumed that Chicago schools did not need the money.[24] (The snafu deprived schools in the Archdiocese of Chicago as well.)

Misunderstandings about the Chicago system are fostered by a wide gulf between the city and the rest of the state. Edgar and senate president Philip of wealthy far west suburban Wood Dale justify the level of school funding by pointing out that Chicago schools spend more than the state average in education. In 1992, Chicago schools spent $5,700 per pupil, compared to the state average of $5,066 and the $6,404 average in Cook County outside of the city. Chicago officials argue, the numbers are skewed by several factors. First, they are based on attendance, which is lower in Chicago than statewide. They further argue that they must provide staff and supplies based on enrollment, even if 11 percent of the students do not show up for classes each day. Second, expenses in Chicago are significantly higher than downstate. Finally, they say, Chicago's spending is offset by the high number of special funds set aside for such purposes as educating poor children. When the numbers are based on enrollment and essential program funding, Chicago actually has one third less money for basic education than does the average suburban district. And it falls nearly 12 percent below the average cost in Illinois.[25]

Educating America's urban children requires appropriate treatment. Consider the costs of special and bilingual education, poverty programs, free lunches, and even special education for private school students (which public schools are required by law to provide). The Chicago school system each year spends almost half a billion dollars on special education alone. Its expenditure in 1992 totaled $447 million, of which the state—despite being a source of the special education mandates—contributed only $121.6 million. Transportation costs of special education children exceeded $50 million. Chicago spends approximately 15 percent of its overall budget on special education, compared to 13.5 percent in Los Angeles and 20 percent in New York City.[26]

Another example is school lunches, which cost more than $113 million a year.[27] Meanwhile, some wealthy suburban districts spend more than $10,000 per child without having to provide services for high numbers of poor, bilingual, or special education children. Some are also debt-free. "It makes no sense that in Oak Brook or New Trier Township, you are spending more per pupil than in Chicago, where the need is greater," said United States senator Paul Simon (D-Illinois), referring to some of Chicago's posher suburbs.[28]

Simply put, it costs more to educate children born in poverty. "If children have health problems, you have to provide for those health problems. If children don't get fed at home, they have to be fed at school. There's the additional cost of psychologists, social workers, special education, therapists, doctors, nurses if necessary, food services, counseling," said Bruce Marchiafava, director of the Chicago system's bureau of research and public services. "Those things cost money."[29] The cost of maintaining hundred-year-old buildings and keeping them secure from vandals also far outdistances such costs at suburban schools, where youngsters often have the added benefits of well-maintained parks and libraries.

Chicago's expenses also include $82 million a year in transportation costs, partly because of a federal desegregation decree that requires busing, even though desegregation is an unrealistic goal in a system that is 89 percent minority.[30] A 1991 school system report concluded that although the segregation program reduced the number of schools with large enrollments of white children—an important goal in itself—the busing did little to improve achievement.[31]

Excluding busing, lunch programs, and central administration, 21 Chicago public schools had budgets of less than $3,000 per pupil during the 1992–93 school year, 244 between $3,000 and $4,000, and 204 between $4,000 and $5,000. In sum, three fourths of Chicago public schools were budgeted below $5,000 per child. Schools serving special education children spent $15,000, $20,000, or even twice that amount per student.[32]

Schools that lost ground under reform were those that serve primarily middle-class children. Basic budgets were cut by as much as a third when reform legislation shifted $250 million in poverty funds to the schools over what was originally to be a five-year period—extended to seven years because of 1993 legislation. The transfer rectified a tradition of robbing Chicago's poor children of funds to which their schools were legally entitled. At the same time, the shift left schools, particularly those in wealthier neighborhoods, with spartan budgets. While some elementary schools spent more than $200,000 on computers during the first three years of reform, for example, Ray Elementary School in Chicago's wealthier Hyde Park neighborhood spent less than $6,000, because only a quarter of its children were low-income students.

At Lane Tech the per-pupil budget was an astounding $3,288 during the 1992–93 school year. The city's premier high school, Lane is one of only two schools in the city—the other being Whitney Young—that scored above national averages on the ACT college entrance examination.

The Lane Tech statistics prove, some would argue, that schools do not need money to achieve. Perhaps that is partly true of schools, such as Lane, that select their students and fill classroom seats with children motivated to learn and whose parents support them. Undoubtedly Lane Tech students would have benefitted from improved facilities, updated textbooks, more supplies, and better-trained teachers.

Some argue that socioeconomic factors of a child's family are the biggest predictor of test scores—therefore, schools with poor children will not benefit from more money. If this is true and education funding plays no role in student achievement then, one could argue, wealthy suburban schools with the highest test scores should not mind relinquishing some of their funding. In short, such a questionable argument is never used to justify taking funding away from wealthy suburban schools, whose legislators often author the pronouncements that values and good teaching—not money—will solve education woes. Surely, all three are needed.

For Aldridge School teacher Mary Gay, the influx of poverty funds had a direct effect in her Chicago classroom: the number of pupils dropped from thirty to nineteen under reform. "I can tell you what every child in this room can do," Gay said. "With much larger class sizes, I couldn't always do that." The school's scores continued to rise under reform.

Throughout Illinois, schools are run primarily on property tax revenue, which means that the funding of a child's education depends on the school district in which he or she lives. Those who live in suburban Winnetka, one of the nation's wealthiest communities, for example, have well-funded schools. Those who live in south suburban Ford Heights, the nation's poorest suburb, on the other hand, have poorly funded schools.

The disparities are so severe that some of Chicago's better suburban districts are hiring investigators and truant officers to stem the tide of out-of-district students illegally trying to enroll. They send staffers to some train stations looking for students with book bags. They threaten parents with criminal penalties for seeking something that should be the child's right in the first place: a good education.

———

Across America, reforms to equalize disparities and properly subsidize education have grown not out of legislative vision but from lawsuits charging that such school funding is inequitable and unconstitutional. More than two dozen law-suits have been filed nationwide since two cases, *Serrano v. Priest* (California, 1971) and *Rodriguez v. San Antonio* (Texas, 1973) set the precedent. As of April 1993, supreme courts in eleven states had ruled state-funded education systems uncon-stitutional.[33] An educational equity suit was dismissed in the lower court of Illinois, where judges have repeatedly remanded school issues back to the legislature. As of 1993, the case was under appeal. "The courts ought to be a last resort but in this situation, it seems to me, we're [already] at that point," said Paul C. Marengo, attorney for the Committee for Educational Rights, which filed the lawsuit on behalf of more than fifty Illinois school districts.

The suit seeks to close a funding gap that allows some schools to build swimming pools while others cannot afford even textbooks. "I have teachers trying to teach American his-tory and American geography using maps that still show the 'territory' of Alaska, the 'territory' of Hawaii," committee chair Edward L. Olds III said. "Students born to districts that have a large property wealth can have the best that money can buy. Students born in districts with lower assessed valuations are forced to get by on minimal standards with old textbooks and decrepit buildings."[34] Assessed valuation is based on a percent-age of property value against which property taxes are applied.

A case in point, cited in the committee's lawsuit, is that of the Mt. Morris and the Byron community school districts, neighbors in northwestern Illinois. In the mid-1970s, the Illinois electrical company Commonwealth Edison built a nuclear plant in the Byron district, expanding the district's tax base by more than a half billion dollars. As a result, the Byron school district had one of the lowest tax rates in the state in 1990 and one of the highest rates of revenue, $10,085 per pupil. Mt. Morris residents paid twice the school taxes but their students received only $3,483 each in education funding, the lawsuit charged.

Such discrepancies mean that in one year Mt. Morris High School offered 113 courses; Byron on the other hand, offered 187, including courses in computer technology, journalism, college literature, agriculture, home economics, and industrial arts. Byron attracted more experienced teachers by offering higher wages. Its textbooks were also relatively current, compared to the fifteen- and twenty-year-old textbooks at Mt. Morris. Byron had a relatively new high school and was renovating its elementary and junior high schools. Mt. Morris High School was built in 1951 and had a leaky roof.[35]

Educational equity, nevertheless, is complicated by many factors. Some schools become the exception and do very well on few funds, presumably because they use sound teaching methods, instill discipline, and stress the basics. Usually such schools are small—another predictor of achievement. Other schools waste taxpayers' money through fraud and ignorance—and measures must be taken to correct that.

Voters in some districts pass tax referendums and willingly levy additional taxes on themselves—and can afford to do so—in order to secure good schools. Other districts do not or cannot levy high taxes. Although unsuccessful in winning increases in state aid, the Chicago Board of Education had not placed a property tax referendum on the ballot in twenty-five years. The proposal is fiercely opposed by Chicago politicians who correctly argue that property taxes should not be the main vehicle for funding schools.[36] But Chicago's lower tax rate for schools makes suburbanites—hit by rising property taxes themselves—resentful and reluctant to pay higher income taxes to support the city's schools.

Although no referendum was passed, Chicago taxpayers continued to shoulder an increasing share of school expenses through higher property taxes. Because of a city-wide reassessment, property taxes increased 58 percent—a whopping $429.4 million—from fiscal years 1989 to 1994, according to the Chicago Panel on Public School Policy and Finance. Over that same period, state aid dropped by 5 percent.

Nationwide, states provided an average 48 percent of educational funding during 1990–91, but Illinois provided only 35 percent, which dropped to 32.8 percent in 1993–94.[37] As proven by the outcome of the education amendment and several polls, some voters do not necessarily mind paying more funds for schools, but they want assurance that their money will not be wasted. What even the best-intentioned critics do not realize is that all the handwringing in the world about Chicago school corruption and inefficiency will not get the money to the children who really need it. That is not to say that nothing can be done. Addressing waste and abuse in the system is possible, but it requires thoughtful, responsible, and fair legislation that imposes strict controls. Otherwise mismanagement will drain resources and public support from Chicago's schools forever.

Edison Comprehensive Gifted Center on the far Northwest Side, one of the success stories in the Chicago public school system.

Photo by June S. Sawyers.

13

Heroes on the Front Lines

*At my school, you see my principal everywhere. She's in the
lunchroom. She's out patrolling. She's respected.*

> Farid Muhammad, a Lindblom High School student
> referring to principal Ethelynn St. James [1]

It was another raucous Chicago Board of Education meeting,
and school council activists John and Kathryn Kuranda were
again in the thick of it. Hundreds of angry parents and school
staff tried to enter the boardroom, but administrators pleaded
that the house was full and that too large a crowd would pose
a fire hazard. A lone security guard tried to restrain the bulg-
ing, shouting throng, furious over proposed school closings.
With the Kurandas in the forefront, the crowd broke through.
"We wanted to show that day we were united," Kathryn said.

They won the right to stay.

It was a small victory in a long line of battles waged by the
Kurandas, parents of three children. Whether they are struggling to get gangbangers off school turf, lobbying legislators in
Springfield, or fighting administrative red tape, the Kurandas
devote endless unpaid hours to area schools. "Without people
like the Kurandas throughout the city, reform might have been
a dead issue," said John P. Gelsomino, principal of Kelly High
School, where Kathryn is council president and John a
$13,000-a-year community liaison.

If obstacles facing Chicago public schools seem extraordinary and overwhelming—and they are—so do the efforts to
overcome them. Amidst the constant clash of wills, heroes—

thousands of teachers, principals, parents, and others from every race, neighborhood, and income level—battle to reclaim the schools.

There was the time Kathryn confiscated seventy-five peanut butter-and-jelly sandwiches that, despite being discolored and stored at room temperature for five hot September days, were served to children. After a school official refused to replace them, Kathryn seized them and plopped them down on the desk of an alderman. "What did you have for lunch today?" she asked. "Because this is what our kids are eating." She packed a community meeting with residents and showed photos of dumpsters filled with food thrown away by youngsters. She summoned the television crews while the alderman called the health department. The next day the school received coolers and fresh ingredients to replace the sandwiches.

The Kurandas were among those who convinced the system to lease a former Catholic school to ease crowding on the Southwest Side, where kindergartners numbered forty-two to a classroom. Getting the new building refurbished and stocked required repeated trips to central office headquarters. A break came when Kathryn spotted a going-out-of-business sign at a neighborhood department store. The Kurandas negotiated, and they and other volunteers cleaned out the store— coated with decades of dirt—in exchange for truckloads of tables and counters.

In summer 1991, the Kurandas joined another fight. One night at 10:30 p.m., they learned that the legislature intended to allow the central administration to keep $53 million in state poverty funds instead of transferring them to school councils as the 1988 reform law required. The administration had long argued that it needed the money to balance its budget. By midnight, the Kurandas were on the road to Springfield, more than a three-hour drive. They arrived at the state capitol with only a few hours' sleep. Because of their and other reformers' lobbying efforts, the legislature defeated the bill. "We were the happiest people in the capitol," John Kuranda said.[2]

A community meeting at a local church convinced Carlos Malave, owner of a Northwest Side gas station, to run for the first council elections in 1989. Malave recalled his debut: "I talked with my wife. I thought we could donate a couple hours a week, and I said, 'I'll give it a try.' I had never publicly spoken. I had never been in front of an auditorium or a microphone. I wrote a two-minute speech. Half way through the speech I couldn't remember what I was saying. I was very nervous." Malave's message focused on the fine education offered at Kilmer Elementary School. "One of my campaign promises was to continue the good work being done at Kilmer," he said.

Not long after he was elected, Malave realized he was wrong on both counts: the volunteer work averaged twenty exhausting hours a week and the school that his son had attended for nine years was not up to expectations. Malave became an unrelenting crusader on issues ranging from increasing minority representation on the staff to reclaiming a neighborhood public school leased to an influential Jewish community despite severe crowding in public school classes.

Under reform, educators and parents—as well as other staff and community members—have fought relentlessly to move forward and, given control over state poverty funds, they began the long climb up. They created parent patrols, reduced class sizes, expanded libraries, instituted school uniforms, held painting parties, and turned students into entrepreneurs through innovative curriculum.

Before the historic movement arrived, Hefferan Elementary School student Jason Ferguson went home every day for an evening of television or housework. But two years into reform, the eighth-grader was staying after school to work on a solar collector project. He joined Hefferan's science club, one of thirty-five after-school activities. "In the past two years, we used to complain about not having any programs. Now that's changed," said Ferguson, whose achievement test scores rose in 1991.

Reform for Hefferan, among the one hundred lowest-achieving schools in the city in 1990, began with an aggressive local school council and its willingness to change principals. The school council hired Patricia A. Harvey, a central office administrator, and focused on building a science and technology curriculum. It used Chapter One funds to buy thirty-five computers, and then it sought corporate sponsorship. Rush-Presbyterian-St. Luke's Medical Center and Turner Construction Company stepped forward and donated a science lab that became the focal point of the school. In the

"Turner Club," students and Turner Construction workers built a wall, complete with plumbing, electricity, and window.

Volunteers at Hefferan increased to seventy-five, assisting in nearly every classroom and club. Each quarter, a group of African-American men tour the West Side school and participate in "Proud to Read Aloud." They serve as role models and mentors. At one parent's suggestion, the school adopted blue and gold gym uniforms to spur pride and teach responsibility. It created a Blue and Gold Club to honor students who achieve all A's and B's on their report cards and no check marks for poor behavior. Parent volunteers and students learn to computerize inventory in the school's store.

Hefferan also hired a human relations specialist to coordinate family services and community involvement. "We were trying to do as many things as possible for 90 percent of students," said Harvey, explaining the rationale behind the decision. "We felt we were making inroads in their educational program, but there was a group of children just falling through the cracks—foster children, those whose parents were incarcerated." The school also changed its curriculum, which, before Harvey's arrival, was presented at three or four grades below level.[3]

Did test scores rise at Hefferan? The answer is mixed. In some areas, students made fifteen months of progress within a year; in other areas, they averaged only nine. Progress depends on both the quality of the teacher and the type of test material given to students. Mobility also plays a significant role—at Hefferan, nearly a third of students arrive or leave after the school year begins. "Scores are definitely on the way up for the students we keep," Harvey said.

Across the city, schools—still struggling against systemic obstacles—are making inroads under reform. "It is only because of the tenacity and commitment of the people out there on the LSCs that we have moved as far as we have in the past two-and-a-half years in the reshaping of our public schools," long-time activist Coretta McFerren, executive director of the West Side Consortium Organization, said in 1992. "We have a law with the potential to unleash energy, creativity, and hope."[4]

Staff and council members of Wilson Occupational High School lobbied for three years to move their small North Side school for children with mental disabilities to a spacious building that they had selected. They won $70,000 in grants, including a new training kitchen. Thanks to teachers who drill job-seeking skills into youngsters' heads, the school places half of its seniors in jobs. The school persisted despite off-and-on-again threats by the administration of closure, based on arguments that the mentally disabled students were not being stretched to their capabilities, that they should receive more academic courses, and that they should be educated in regular high schools.

The problem facing Wilson was the mixed messages sent by the administration. While the department of facilities approved the purchase of a new building, the department of special education threatened the school with closing over several years, casting doubt on school plans and lowering morale of the staff, even after remodeling of the new building was underway. Each time the school appeared on a proposed closing list, teachers and parents marshalled forces. At one point, administrators recommended that the new building be given to another school. "It was a matter of faith that, under school reform, hard work in a good cause pays off," principal Jay F. Mulberry said.[5]

Some schools, although not in need of reform, welcomed the movement nevertheless. When it comes to student achievement, the Edison Comprehensive Gifted Center on the far Northwest Side consistently outscores or keeps pace with the best elementary schools in the wealthiest suburbs—so much so that one suburban couple paid nearly $4,200 a year in nonresident tuition fees to send their child there in 1993. At Edison, kindergartners learn the alphabet and their colors in French. Sixth graders take ninth-grade biology; seventh graders, ninth-grade algebra; and eighth-graders, eleventh-grade geometry. By the time they graduate, all students are expected to be fluent in French and able to read music.[6]

What could reform do for such a high-achieving school as Edison? As principal Sheila R. Schlaggar explained, reform heightened its sense of community: "It's a family. It's our school now. It isn't the board of education's school." For one thing, the school has its own principal—which it did not have before reform when schools with branch facilities were consolidated under joint administrations. Second, the loosening of

restrictions on engineer overtime pay made the school building more accessible, allowing for night meetings, which, in
turn, encouraged working parents to participate not only in
traditional fund-raising roles but also in school governance.
"Here we have an opportunity to share decision making,
advice, consultation, help in running a school. It becomes the
community raising the child," Schlaggar said.

Efforts in schools under reform came not only from educators and councils but also from those outside the system. In
1990, the John D. and Catherine T. MacArthur Foundation
launched a $40 million grant program to span a decade of
supporting education. Dubbed Chicago Education Initiative, it
focuses on four areas: restructuring schools and training
teachers, researching what methods work and monitoring the
progress of reform, drawing parents into education, and helping Pershing Road revamp itself.

In the first two years, the foundation concentrated on
increasing community involvement and training local school
councils, but, as governance issues subsided, it switched its
focus to the classroom—devoting half of its $4 million annual
budget to changing schools. The foundation sponsored everything from a television forum on the reform movement to a
high school day care center for children of students. It chose
experts to work with seventy neighborhood schools in greatest need. It also funded the $1.1 million Quest teacher training
center, which is run by the Chicago Teachers Union and
which shares expertise on such issues as combining school
grade levels and dividing large schools into smaller schools
within the same building.[7]

MacArthur grants included $450,000 for the West Side
Consortium Organization, which worked feverishly to field
candidates for school council elections, among other things.
The foundation also worked with schools to help parents play
a more intensive role at home and at school. "We're finding
that is possible even in the most devastated areas," said Peter
Martinez, senior program officer for the education initiative.
Systemwide, nearly 40 percent of teacher union delegates and
45 percent of school council chairpersons say that parent
involvement has increased at their schools because of reform,
according to a survey by the school reform magazine *Catalyst*.[8]

In the first year of reform, Dulles Elementary School parent Barbara Fraley reported that her first grade son's homework did not mysteriously "blow out the window" any more. His arsenal of excuses vanished when his mother began volunteering full time at the South Side school located in the shadow of the Washington Park public housing development. Inside Dulles, parents guided lunch lines, photocopied homework assignments for teachers, and monitored once chaotic hallways.[9]

Despite the burdens of poverty, O'Toole Elementary School on the Southwest Side drew sixty parent volunteers, some of whom worked in classrooms full time. Others served on committees, monitored hallways, and supervised playgrounds. "We couldn't function without our parents," principal Mary Hornung said. "They're our arms and legs."[10]

Emmet Elementary School on the ravaged West Side—at one time, designated for closing—drew twenty-five parent volunteers. "It's just nice to have that extra support," said principal Jacqueline A. Robinson. "Teachers from time to time will have a project to do, something as basic as completing a bulletin board or assisting in cutting out letters or sitting with a child with special problems. The parents are filling in." After the school board cut a systemwide remedial reading program, the parents ran a bake sale to raise money to purchase books. "We want to raise the reading scores of our children," Robinson said. "You can't do that without books."

Emmet was one of four troubled schools that received aid under the Nation of Tomorrow program, sponsored by the Kellogg Foundation and the University of Illinois at Chicago. Begun in 1989, the program concentrated on teacher training and operated under the philosophy that children learn better when they are healthy, warmly clothed, and settled in their home lives. At Emmet School, an environment conducive to learning meant running clothing drives and providing emergency utility payments to families, access to health care, after-school programs, and even adult aerobics classes. With health and family advocates hired under the program, Emmet School distributed Thanksgiving baskets to needy families and held blood pressure screenings for parents on report card pickup day. It raffled off grocery store gift certificates to attract parents. Many parents were children themselves when they had their babies, and memories of bad experiences with school fuel their reluctance to visit. Such incentives begin to reverse a long cycle of family alienation from education.

The four schools in Nation of Tomorrow each received a full-time nurse to address student problems ranging from stomachaches to pink eye. Although the system supplies nurses to schools, they typically visit only one day a week—barely enough time to cover even the most basic paperwork on immunizations. Under its special program, Emmet School offered vision screenings to students and ensured that those who needed eyeglasses received them.

Bond School, a South Side school that also participated in the Nation of Tomorrow, helped make families more aware of community services, such as health clinics, day-care programs, and counseling. "A lot of people just don't know and not knowing has kept them from making use of services they could have been using for years and years," principal Donald I. Prather said. Bond also instituted a fine arts program and ten after-school activities in drama, math, dance, and gymnastics. Perez Elementary School on the near Southwest Side used its grant money for an arts program, teacher training, and a soccer camp.[11]

In general, schools that make the most progress under reform are aided by outside organizations, Designs for Change reported in 1993. Of the 105 organizations that the reform group listed in its 1993 school guide of outside resources, 85 became involved after the reform law passed. Designs calls the influx of outside support unprecedented. "Reform has done what it set out to do, which was to liberate the schools—people at the local level—so they could identify their needs and then find creative ways for solutions," associate director Joan Jeter Slay said. Reform brought in nationally known educators to help heal Chicago schools. "What reform was designed to do was to allow that kind of creativity and expertise into the actual schools—not only at the top, but in the schools where the kids are," Slay said.

In wholesale efforts to support reform, Illinois Bell funded a three-year $1.2 million program that gave dozens of school councils $10,000 each in discretionary money. Winners made a broad range of accomplishments:

- Darwin Elementary School on the Northwest Side moved off the list of the one hundred least-achieving schools by introducing a number of programs, including Junior Great Books, a Young Authors program that encourages student writing, IBM's computer writing-to-read program, and science, drama, and computer clubs. Twelve teachers received special training at six Saturday classes and, in a separate effort, teachers took Spanish courses. With an 82 percent Hispanic population, Darwin hired a parent education coordinator in a parent-teacher resource center that offered materials in both English and Spanish.
- Calumet High School set up a Saturday Academy for three hundred students, who were given up to five hours of instruction in math and language. Consequently, their test scores have improved. Meanwhile, Chicago State University provided students with an introduction to the health professions through Club Pre-Med. Students participated in sessions reviewing algebra, biology, and study skills; they visited medical schools and other institutions with health-care programs. A partnership with St. Xavier University offered Calumet students tutoring services, seminars, and workshops on improving study habits, test-taking skills, and time management strategies.
- Earle School launched a Parent Homework Training program and opened the computer lab to parents at least two periods a week, allowing them to receive basic training. It also created special instruction for students lagging behind in school. After-school instruction in math and reading was made available four days a week.[12]

School achievement was recognized through other programs, including the Whitman, the Golden Apple, and the Illinois Distinguished Educators awards. The latter were sponsored by the Illinois State Board of Education and the Milken Family Foundation.

Yvonne Minor, principal of Dyett Middle School, was among those named a distinguished educator for instigating

Yvonne Minor, principal of Dyett Middle School, talks to one
of her pupils.

Courtesy *Chicago Sun-Times*. Photo by Rich Hein.

the school's turnaround. When she arrived at the school,
which is located near the Robert Taylor Homes, and watched
a student assembly, she was appalled. Students stammered
their lines, mumbled, appeared lethargic, and dressed inappropriately. Minor told teachers to demand excellence or cancel
assemblies. Six years later, the school boasted choir uniforms
and color guards. Programs were performed with pride. "I
grew up in the projects. I attended public high school, and I
was inspired by teachers and parents who believed in me,"
said Minor, also named a top educator by the National
Association of Secondary School Principals. "If I hadn't had
someone who inspired me, I wouldn't be here now."[13]

Before a child enrolls at Dyett, Minor requires a meeting
with parents to spell out the rules: girls may not wear makeup; boys may not wear earrings or caps. With poverty funds,
Dyett hired more teachers and bought computers for every

room. It adopted the increasingly popular school-within-a-school philosophy, which believes that small schools educate better partly because every child is known by name. Breaking larger schools into smaller units establishes the "small school" environment. At Dyett, which serves sixth through eighth grade, each grade has its own section of the building and its own lunch area. Students are taught by teams of three teachers who stay with them through all three grades. The school also established committees of parents and educators to work on school beautification, student and staff morale, discipline, and staff development.[14]

For the first time, schools have the power to devise their own curriculums under reform. Gladstone Elementary School on the West Side, for example, adopted Microsociety, part of a small but growing nationwide experiment to introduce students to the workings of adult life. For an hour each school day, children bank make-believe money by writing deposit slips and calculate interest earnings on savings accounts. Using computers, they edit and publish a newspaper and peddle its ads. They fill out applications for school jobs. Junior scientists design projects to compete in science fairs and illustrate their findings on graphs.

With hard-earned Gladstone "dollars," students buy calculators, puzzles, and basketballs. They understand the significance of losing possessions and of being fined if they misbehave. Under the science segment of Microsociety, one student who often was in trouble with both the school and the law was assigned to take care of a park. What was previously irrelevant to him suddenly became interesting. "Up until now, I've been in charge of making that park look good, and he's done a better job than I have," science teacher Paul Gilvary remarked. "I think what hooked him was having school not be so darn abstract, having it be something real, not just listening to a teacher ramble on." The student even lobbied to recycle trash from the site, which students weeded and readied for sod. For the first time, the student found success in school. "If he's looked up to on the street as the best fighter, the most useful to the drug dealers, and then he comes to school and we said, 'You failed,' we lose him," Gilvary said. "Now nobody is judging him except to say, 'Good job.'"

Microsociety is modeled after trailblazing projects in Lowell, Massachusetts, and Yonkers, New York. Founder George Richmond, an acclaimed educator who conceived the idea as a new teacher in Brooklyn in 1967, was so appalled by his students' contempt for education that he began paying them in make-believe money to complete assignments. Gradually a microsociety evolved. Its origins are documented in Richmond's *The Micro-Society School: A Real World in Miniature.*

Gladstone principal Gary Moriello appreciated its vision and, with other staff members, visited the East Coast programs, courtesy of the North Central Regional Educational Laboratory, a suburban group that also offers staff training. Without reform, Gladstone probably would not have been able to adopt Microsociety. "If we were still under the board's curriculum department, I don't think they would allow anything like this to go on," Moriello said.[15]

In 1993, Gladstone won a five-year $1 million federal grant to open a nursing clinic on its first floor. In a joint project with St. Xavier University's School of Nursing, Gladstone made plans to recruit nurse practitioners, registered nurses, and nursing students to provide immunizations and physical examinations to the school's 529 students at no cost for the first five years.[16] The clinic was more evidence of how Gladstone, which opened in 1884, was working to overcome overwhelming odds: all of its students are from low-income families, its mobility rate is 43 percent, and its average eighth-grade class size is thirty-one students, compared with the state average of twenty-two. To increase achievement and raise test scores is a challenge. Even so, the percentage of Gladstone students scoring above national norms on the Iowa Test for Basic Skills rose from 8.5 percent in 1989–90 to 12 percent in 1991–92. In math, it rose from 16.2 to 21.6 percent, Moriello said. In other areas, however, test scores have either remained stable or declined. Of course, because of its high mobility rate each year many students tested were not at Gladstone the previous year.[17]

In Chicago, one special school has an almost daily turnover of students. The Max McGraw Learning Center is housed in the state's biggest emergency shelter for abused and neglected children, a former hospital. The school is the brainchild of Brennemann Elementary School principal William J. Haran, who discovered that the shelter's children were not being educated at all. The center is intended to be a temporary stop, but, because of a shortage of foster homes, children often stay for months. The McGraw Learning Center, named for its benefactor, began with two classrooms on the second floor and three windowless rooms in the basement next to what was once a morgue. Thanks to donors, the school was moved upstairs to newly remodeled classrooms, where a steady stream of children attend. "It's completely opposite of what you do in a normal school," Haran said. "You don't know on any given day what kids will be there. It requires incredible flexibility." With the help of experts from National-Louis University, the school structures subjects—math, science, reading, and others—around themes, such as recycling. Classes span a range of grade levels. "It makes it challenging when you have fifteen preadolescents between the ages of six and twelve," math teacher Dana Hoover confessed. "It's hard to find activities that interest both a six-year-old and a twelve-year-old."

Haran finds special joy in the center. Sometimes he slips away to the nursery that houses infants and toddlers, many of whom were born with cocaine addictions. In the nursery playroom, staff and volunteers sit with the tots and soothe their symptoms with hugs and caresses. There one Chicago hero rests from his labors and finds comfort in the company of like-minded workers. "When I need resolve and energy to battle the bureaucrats and naysayers," offers William Haran, "this is where I go."[18]

Julianna Garcia listens intently at Funston Elementary School.

Courtesy *Chicago Sun-Times*. Photo by Rich Hein.

14

Conclusion: Chaos and Hope

*We saw God perform a miracle in the hearts of those legislators.
They didn't want to hear us, they didn't want to see us, many
of them ignored us. But as the days went on, I knew that the
Scripture which said, "The heart of the king is in the Lord's
hands and he turns it wheresoever he will" is absolutely fac-
tual. The disdain turned to regard. The disregard turned to
attention. And we began to get their ears. . . . We walked the
halls, and we prayed, night and day, and we got the bill
passed.*

*School organizer Coretta McFerren on passage
of the 1988 Chicago School Reform Act[1]*

When the first immigrants arrived on American soil more than
three centuries ago, visionaries among them viewed public
education nearly as crucial to survival of the young democracy
as a faith in God. Education was "a kind of sacred rite that
could overcome evil, heal class and ethnic divisions, reform
domestic life, moderate greed, and, finally, insure its subjects
of a head start in their 'pursuit of happiness,'" wrote historian
Page Smith in *The Shaping of America*.[2] The creation of common, or public, schools was based partly on the premise that
a literate and educated society benefitted every member. For
the most part, the founders rejected the idea of a tiered culture
that consigned generations born in poverty to remain there
while perpetuating the privilege of the rich. Throughout the
nation's history, America's family albums contain portraits of

individual men and women who emerged from deep poverty with the advantages that a good education can bring.

For years, Chicago public schools have been a major battleground in the national struggle for improving education. For those working to overhaul a failing system, school reform of the 1990s was a turning point. Under reform, parents and educators began to wrest control of schools from the bureaucracy and the corrupt politics of self-preservation. Signs of progress—although far short of what they should be—are evident. State Chapter One funds proved to be a key. For example, during the first year of reform, Foreman High School hired a new dean to concentrate on discipline, two additional security aides, and a math tutor. It also created an in-school suspension room. "In the old days," said principal John Garvey, "it would have been virtually impossible to pull that off with board of education funds without years of effort."[3]

Reform introduced a new set of watchdogs who exposed conditions long hidden from public scrutiny. Volunteer council members have nothing to lose if they blow the whistle on building dilapidation, the use of spoiled food in the cafeteria, a teacher's incompetence, or financial mismanagement of a principal. Heroic advocacy brought problems to light under the premise that exposure and recognition are the first steps toward solving them.

While valuable principals were fired, others who should have been dismissed years before were finally forced out by newly empowered councils. Before school reform, only two principals were fired in the history of the system, according to school board attorney Joyce Combest Price. During the 1992–93 school year, however, eight principals and two top administrators were forced to resign before their contracts expired. "Parents and community people are not as tolerant as the board was. We have gotten eight resignations of principals in the past year, and I attribute it to school reform," said Price, who herself left the system in 1993.[4]

In addition, a great number of practical matters have been addressed by school councils. As G. Alfred Hess, Jr., explained four years into the movement: "The first few years, people were pretty much just addressing the practical issues of getting discipline established, getting roofs repaired, and dealing with overcrowding—lots of practical questions the board neglected for years and years. Now people feel they're getting control of those things, and they're starting to look at how teachers and children learn."[5] Unprecedented outside help was poured into Chicago public schools because of reform. Although test scores dipped initially after the riotous start of the movement, they began to rebound in 1993.

Services provided by Pershing Road, even though subject to cutbacks in all the wrong places, showed improvement in some areas. Such signs of decentralization—again far from adequate—are a testimony to the intense public pressure put on the central office, to the goodwill of emerging leaders within the system, and to the even role assumed by the Chicago School Finance Authority under the leadership of venture capitalist Martin "Mike" Koldyke, who became a forceful mediator on school issues between Democrats and Republicans. As University of Illinois at Chicago associate professor William Ayers explained, "In a sense, school reform is Chicago's *perestroika*. As in Europe, a command system central authority has collapsed practically of its own weight, and a radical democracy is proposed as a solution to years of stagnation and backwardness. A previously insulated and impenetrable central office accustomed to unquestioning obedience has lost its authority, bringing down to human size those who were once omnipotent."[6] The central office undertook a wholesale effort to restructure itself, which had not been attempted since 1975. Problems, of course, still remain. "As bad it is, it's so much better than it was going back three or four years," admitted McCutcheon Elementary School principal Edward A. Ploog.

Reform, however, has not been all good news. Bureaucratic dinosaurs die hard, and the movement has proved to be a whirlwind combination of chaos and hope, struggle and exhilaration, fatigue and victory. It has been undermined by senseless decisions, some born out of financial crises. For all the incomprehensible flaws of the system, however, Chicago school reform proved a point: change is possible when citizens care enough to demand it.

The seeds of reform were planted in 1987 when demonstrations and protests helped end a record nineteen-day teachers' strike. The People's Coalition for Educational Reform held a rally outside board headquarters on September 18 and days later demonstrated in the city's business district, linking arms in a rally called "Hands Across the Loop." As Leon Finney, director of The Woodlawn Organization (TWO), recalled, "Everybody all over the city was raising hell. We didn't have to organize them. They organized themselves. We just networked with the hell-raisers."[7]

On October 2, some two thousand protesters marched on city hall.[8] "Everybody had this energy and they didn't know what to do with it. They came together from all over the city. It was just like going back to the 1960s," said Bernie R. Noven, whose Parents United for Responsible Education (PURE) helped organize the Friday march. As a result, Mayor Harold Washington intervened, and the 1987 strike was settled the following Monday.

The strike led to unprecedented reform legislation. Mary O'Connell, then editor of a community publication called *Neighborhood Works,* chronicled how the strike electrified parents, who became a new force in Chicago education. "Something snapped during the strike, something that broke up the business-as-usual mood . . . Nobody can pinpoint exactly what it was or when it started: everybody agrees that it was the accumulation of anger and frustration built up during the previous strikes, combined with the increasingly depressing evidence of reading scores, dropout rates, financial misdealings, and yet more strikes."[9] Community groups such as United Neighborhood Organization, a primarily Hispanic body led by the gifted organizer Danny Solis, and the People's Coalition used the strike to build alliances that ultimately led to reform.

———————

Although reform is underway, there is no time for complacency or for public vigilance to subside. On the contrary, tremendous amounts of work in overhauling Chicago public schools need to be done. The most monumental task is forging a legislative will to create a system that functions effectively and efficiently. Until that happens, the best efforts of educators will be thwarted by lack of funding and continued senseless decisions.

How must this be done? One answer is through the creation of a citizens' political movement that informs voters on education issues. A national model already exists. Consider H. Ross Perot, a master at organizing apolitical citizenry into a powerful political organization. Although disdained by some intellectuals, the Texas billionaire capitalized on a deep-seated disgust with American government when he ran for president in 1992 and created United We Stand, a nationwide lobbying organization. Politicians listened, and some still vie to associate themselves with this new force in American politics. The same kind of mass lobbying efforts that appeal to common sense can revolutionize education in Illinois and other states where legislators have a history of ignoring the plights of urban public schools.

Much can be learned from the hard-fought lessons of unions, which have built their strength through stable leadership, unmatched political organization, unity, professional and informed lobbying, and campaign contributions derived from members' donations. Unions should not be blamed for doing extraordinarily well what they are designed to do: protect their workers. But legislators must be held accountable when they put those interests above those of the commonweal; that is, the public good on which the principle of "common schools" was founded.

For such a political movement, reform has laid invaluable groundwork: it brought in countless parents, community members, and businesses to work side by side with educators. Although a handful of reformers lobby tirelessly in the state capitol of Springfield, there is no area-wide political lobbying organization that keeps thousands of people informed on educational issues. In order to make an impact, a "children's army" must be formed, drawn from every neighborhood, every race, and every socioeconomic level of society. It must include people with disabilities (who already have a well-organized network). It must also include suburbanites. After all, suburban residents have a financial and societal stake in urban public education as well. Many suburban and downstate districts face the same problems as Chicago.

An education organization that focuses on political lobbying could work something like this. The organization could poll candidates for elective office on specific education issues and make report cards available to the media on a regular basis. In the maze of last-minute legislation that emerges from Springfield, it could keep tabs on every education vote and distribute the information and voting records to the public swiftly. How? Through telephone hotlines that would provide callers with immediate updates, through press releases, through newsletters, and through computer mail.

Such an organization would obviously form a liaison with or emerge from the dozens of school reform groups that already exist. Even if disagreements over education policy arise, as they inevitably will, distributing the information alone will make a significant contribution.

To win credibility, an education movement must not merely advocate granting more funding to education. It must first address the source of reluctance to provide those funds; namely, the level of waste and corruption in the system. Holding a summit on the issue—as school reformer Calvin L. Pearce has suggested—is one step toward purifying the system. Ideally, such a summit would be sponsored by the legislature itself.

Once the political will exists to educate Chicago's children, educator-led efforts coupled with accountability can take root and eventually produce fruit. Whatever answers emerge, they must begin with culling the expertise of proven educators, of whom there are many in Chicago and in the administration of the Illinois State Board of Education. Reform was correctly based on the premise that those closest to the problem know the solution. It must be allowed to go farther.

What can legislators do? Experts generally agree that schools should be given greater guidance and latitude in spending money on education but then be held to high financial and academic standards.[10] The state of Illinois already has enacted academic standards that place failing schools on "academic watch lists" with penalties as severe as eventual closure of those schools that do not improve. There are other measures of holding schools accountable that can be considered. The following are some suggestions:

1. The office of the inspector general at the Chicago School Finance Authority, although in its infancy in

1994, should be strengthened, funded, and focused on corruption. Its powers should extend to investigating school board and council members. The absence of such authority and funding are glaring deficiencies that raise the question of whether legislators really want the office to serve as more than mere window dressing. In addition, the office's authority should extend to the school projects that are handled by the little-known Chicago Public Building Commission, which oversees hundreds of millions of dollars of building contracts for public agencies.

2. The powers of the inspector general should be broadened to investigate child abuse allegations, as is the case for New York City's special commissioner of investigation. In fewer than three years, the New York office removed forty suspected child abusers from the system. In Illinois, no agency is addressing child abuse specifically in schools, a critical detriment not only to education and children's lives but also to the future of society. Such evil multiplies.

3. A Chicago school inspector general's office may not be sufficient to root out all those who abuse the system and its children. For all schools in the state, the Illinois State Board of Education should be equipped with its own investigatory office, as in Kentucky. Again, launching a statewide—even nationwide—effort to address child abuse in schools should be part of it. The names, photographs, and fingerprints of convicted abusers should be placed on a master list. In addition, Illinois and all states should require police departments and prosecutors who know that a school employee has been charged with child abuse in their jurisdiction to notify the appropriate school authorities.

4. State law should be expanded to provide for automatic dismissals of all school employees who are convicted of certain violent, sex, and drug crimes.

5. A legislative summit, task force, or committee should address issues involved in firing school employees. New York City activist and radio talk show host Bob Law suggests review boards similar to those governing other

licensed professionals, such as medical doctors and attorneys. Retired Herbert Elementary School principal William Rankin recommends that teachers who do not receive excellent or superior ratings should be placed on probation. After three years with such a status, they should lose seniority rights and tenure. Others suggest that teachers and principals fired through the state process should lose the system's contributions to their pension funds and that teachers and principals fired through the dismissal process be deprived of their certificates, either permanently or temporarily. In any system, however, safeguards must exist to ensure that whistleblowers are not victimized. One way is to create a mechanism, such as a review board of some sort, through which teachers can bring their complaints and be assured they are acted upon if the allegations prove true. A principal, for example, who demotes or transfers whistleblowers must be brought to justice for doing so. In too many instances, the system penalizes honest teachers instead.

6. The same legislative summit or committee that addresses the dismissal process should examine ways to improve teacher competency. Additional training is one obvious solution, but if legislators really want children to be educated, teachers should also be required to pass periodic basic competency exams—perhaps the same exams that elementary school students are required to take.

7. The practice of housing children in teacherless classrooms should be illegal. Prohibiting schools from using study halls to fulfill the required three hundred minutes of daily instruction would be one way to address the problem (with the understanding that districts could phase in the policy.) Like other mandates, such a rule would be meaningless without greater funding and enforcement—two elements grossly lacking in Illinois education policy.

8. The legislature or school board should consider eliminating the requirement that nonteaching positions be assigned to schools by seniority only—a measure that

undoubtedly would be opposed by the unions. Principals should be allowed to hire anyone—other than their own relatives or relatives of council members— who meet set criteria, and then they should be held accountable for their schools' progress or lack thereof, with leeway given to factors beyond their control, such as student turnover and teacherless classrooms.

9. Council members should be required to have high school diplomas or general equivalency certificates.

10. The legislature should explore the cost of criminal background checks for council members and consider instituting them.

11. State law should provide for removal of council members who knowingly violate the law in any area, including expenditure of funds. The authority to remove members should be the responsibility of an outside agency, such as the Illinois State Board of Education or the Cook County Superintendent of Schools, an office that the legislature moved to phase out in 1993. Steeped in controversy that ended with the resignation of the former superintendent, the office should now be strengthened, not abolished.

12. Negotiations between the school board and the teachers union are typically hampered by the board members' lack of understanding of the system. The school board should permit a representative of principals to sit in on negotiations that affect their schools.

13. Board of education members should be paid full salaries and elected with campaign contributions capped at reasonable levels so that the rich do not have extraordinary advantages. An alternative suggestion: Chicago could be the site of a pilot experiment in public financing of campaigns, with every candidate given an equal amount. Maintaining ethics and legislative safeguards are critical; otherwise, children's welfare will yield to political self-interest. For example, board members should be prohibited from accepting money or services from school district employees for their campaigns. Electing a school board would hardly be a panacea, as other states have proven, but it would allow voters to

hold board members accountable—and if board members fail to provide the oversight required, voters would have only themselves to blame.

14. To increase stability in leadership, board presidents should be elected by their peers for at least a two-year term. Currently, the board selects its leadership yearly.

15. System ethics rules must be strengthened. For example, the school board should be prohibited from doing business with board members or with employees for one to three years after they leave the system. Such rules would apply to those former employees who were in the position of influencing the awarding of contracts and would prevent individuals from putting concerns of companies that might later employ them above the interests of children. Principals should be barred from hiring relatives of council members.

16. State law should prohibit board members from influencing or attempting to influence the hiring of school employees other than the superintendent and the attorney. Penalties for doing so should be written into law. Again, enforcement is essential.

17. State law should include penalties for principals who refuse to provide schools with internal audit information. In addition, councils should be granted authority to prevent principals from spending student money on items that violate school board rules. State law should explicitly make internal audits subject to public disclosure. In 1993, the school board argued that such information was exempted from state freedom of information law although it agreed to release the documents to the *Chicago Sun-Times* after the newspaper's attorneys argued otherwise in a lawsuit.

18. The legislature should require and fund annual audits at every school. The legislature should also respond to school board wishes to set aside one half of 1 percent of the $250 million in Chapter One monies for audits.

19. State law should allow public school principals to bypass the school board and, after conducting their own hearings, expel students found guilty of offenses involving guns. Alternative schools should be created to accept them.

20. The legislature must mandate that the Chicago school system follow the simpler budget format required of other schools. Instead, Chicago's budget adheres to its own indecipherable format, a considerable obstacle to citizen watchdogs who wish to read it.[11]

21. Bidding laws should be tightened. Computers, for example, should be competitively bid, as is done in school systems across America. Bundling—that is, combining equipment and services so prices cannot be itemized—should be prohibited. Penalties should be instituted for board of education members who knowingly flaunt bidding, open meetings, or other laws. Under the current system, the only way to force a school district to bid is to sue them—unfortunately, the school board's legal bills are paid by the taxpayer. State law does not penalize—not even by removal—board members who fail to bid, thus shielding those who violate the law from the consequences. Such a system puts contracts ahead of the interests of the children.

22. State law is currently ambiguous regarding whether school board members must vote on contracts of more than $10,000. The ambiguity should be removed, thus putting board members on the record.

23. If private companies want to compete for public dollars, they should be required to disclose what has been shielded from the public in the name of proprietary information. For example, past business dealings, subcontracts, and wages of consultants paid by taxpayers should be disclosed as should, in the complicated area of health care, the discounts that health insurance companies receive from doctors and hospitals for giving them high-volume business with public funds. In this way, citizen watchdog groups can determine if public dollars are being drained at great profits to private companies.

24. The legislature took a positive step in 1993 by moving the deadline for the board's budget from August 31 to August 15, thus allowing principals two extra weeks to learn of budget cuts. The legislature should go even further and move its own June 30 budget deadline back. Currently schools in Illinois are not given enough time

to plan because they do not know until July what their
state revenues will be for the upcoming school year.

25. If it wants to buck tradition and transcend politics, the
legislature should require—and fund, as would be necessary—electrical inspections of Chicago schools. It
should also require Chicago schools to comply with the
life safety code that applies to other school systems to
ensure that buildings are safe and secure.

26. Although it is rather like closing the proverbial barn
door after the horse has left, the Chicago system should
address the use of technology and provide incentives
for schools to use compatible computer systems.
Perhaps programs could even be extended statewide.

With such controls and a mechanism to enforce them in
place, the legislature must begin to actively support public
education in Illinois. Proper support will require raising the
income tax to address inadequacies and disparities in the
funding of education. How should the money be distributed?
Again, educators can negotiate the specifics, but a number of
issues might be addressed:

1. *Teacher training and recruitment.* When one third of
elementary school principals say that no more than half
their teachers have a good grasp of reading and language arts while 70 percent lack proper science skills,
something is terribly wrong. Even if such statements are
incorrect, as the teachers union claims, the fact remains
that the average age of a Chicago public school teacher
in 1993 was forty-seven-years old. No matter how competent, any teacher who has been away from higher
education for twenty-five years or more would likely
benefit from additional training. One type of training
could be in the form of "master teachers." To attract
individuals with the proper credentials, these teachers
could be offered higher salaries.

2. *Principal training.* Since most principals who have
arrived under reform are new, they should be supplied
from the start with information on writing budgets and
equipped with the proper leadership skills. As reform

progressed, outside agencies and universities began to address this area of critical need. Some school districts have taken the issue further and already provide mandatory training academies for principals. This should be encouraged.

3. *Local school council training.* Outside groups have poured great effort into local school council training, but the board has provided no mandatory council training in such areas as principal selection, budgeting, and law. This should be remedied. If nothing else, anyone involved with local school councils should be familiar with *Roberts' Rules of Order,* the standard handbook on how to run a meeting.

4. *Early childhood education.* Providing strong early-childhood education is one proven method of closing the poverty gap. Children who arrive in kindergarten knowing their full names, primary colors, numbers, and the alphabet have an enormous advantage over those who do not. State and federally-funded preschool programs should be expanded.

5. *Summer staffing of district offices and schools.* Allowing students to enroll during the summer would reduce the problem of teacherless classrooms. The school system should assign teachers based on projected enrollment. Schools that inflate their student bodies should be penalized. A principal and administrative task force should be formed to determine the most equitable way to staff schools from the beginning of the school year.

6. *Lower class sizes.* Small class sizes are necessary in today's age of technology and severe social problems. Chicago class sizes should be no higher than the state average, preferably lower.

7. *Reading programs.* Many children might not need costly special education if they had received remedial reading classes early in their schooling. This area should be explored further.

8. *Facilities and new buildings.* Facilities, including science labs, lunchrooms, and gymnasiums as well as air conditioning for unventilated year-round schools, should be provided. Basic repairs must be completed,

including the necessity of making schools accessible to people with disabilities.

9. *Supplies and equipment for teachers.* In a city with massive dropout and truancy problems, teachers should have access to telephones in order to contact parents when necessary. Teachers should also be provided basic supplies, such as tissues, toilet paper, pens, pencils, and copying paper.

10. *Support staff.* Children with health, mental, and discipline problems have difficulty learning; thus the need for nurses, counselors, and social workers. Chapter One funds are designed to address such needs, but when they are constantly being diverted to pay for the essentials, they can sometimes fall short. Studies must be made to determine whether reform addresses these supplemental needs.

11. *Libraries.* Chicago school libraries, by and large, have fewer and older books than those in many Chicago suburbs. The libraries must be updated and expanded.

12. *Highly structured alternative schools.* Alternative schools have been used successfully in other districts as last resorts for disciplinary problems. They are important tools toward creating a disciplined environment.

13. *Special education.* In a problem shared by schools throughout Illinois, the state mandates that school districts provide special education services—even private out-of-state homes for disruptive and damaged children—but it does not fully fund them. The state should provide complete funding for special education programs.

14. *Dropout prevention programs.* Crucial in a district with a 50 percent dropout rate, dropout prevention programs send staff or volunteers into the community to recruit students back to school. Truant officers, now absent in Chicago schools, should be reinstated to work with students on the verge of dropping out.

15. *Vocational schools.* In 1993, the Chicago Board of Education voted to transfer its premier trade school, Washburne, to the City Colleges of Chicago. The school served individuals seventeen and older in such trades as carpentry, air conditioning and heating, chef's train-

ing, and upholstery, among others. Though they may aim for a younger crowd than Washburne, comparable alternative schools should be replicated throughout the city, not shut down.

16. *Incentive pay for principals and teachers.* Incentive pay is generally considered more successful when given in lump sums to schools that show signs of improvement. Some argue that this is because awarding individuals extra compensation builds resentment among front-line workers. Under reform, Chicago principals were paid not for how well their schools functioned but partly by the size of their staffs. Critics suggest this is one reason for the enormous growth in school staffs—particularly the lower paid nonteaching staff—while some classrooms lack basic supplies. Nevertheless, incentive pay for both principals and teachers should be considered.

17. *Summer school and after-school programs.* Gifted and remedial programs and extracurricular activities such as drama clubs, chess clubs, Spanish clubs, and intramural sports are among the means for reclaiming city children from the streets. They should be encouraged.

18. *Family resource centers.* The state of Kentucky created 373 such centers in 639 schools at a $9.5 million investment. The centers provide health, social, and even legal services for families of 241,000 children. Chicago schools, which have nothing similar, should establish their own equivalent.

19. *Computerization.* Although it is incomprehensible that the central office spent $30 million on computers in one year alone and has little to show for it, the system needs to modernize its computer headquarters. Using computer technology, teachers should have access to files of children who have special but unseen needs, whether that be the child who has been bounced from home to home or high schoolers with fifth-grade reading levels. Background information should be made available to principals and teachers before the students walk in the schoolhouse door.

Some may question why those who have no children in the school system or have not contributed to the social ills that devastate the schools should feel obligated to pay for their extraordinarily expensive healing. The answer lies in the fabric of society. If public schools fail, eventually we all will.

"We've already lost a couple of generations," notes Amundsen High School teacher Janet Fennerty. "Eventually, we're going to be asking other people for aid and financial support just to survive. It's the future of our country that is ultimately being sacrificed."

Certainly government cannot solve all of society's ills. It cannot instill values in its people that it often does not have itself. However, if visionaries emerge and take leadership roles, government can contribute. Rooting out inefficiency and corruption are important first steps. If some legislators are unwilling to educate Chicago's children, voters must assume their own responsibility and elect representatives who will. Voters should no longer allow legislators to simply throw up their hands in helplessness and despair, flippantly dismiss Chicago schools as a "black hole," and rob thousands of children of the basic education that is already provided to their wealthier peers. Who must bear ultimate responsibility for the failure of public institutions? We must—for government, after all, is a reflection of ourselves.

Sign of the times, door to the future.

Photo by June S. Sawyers.

Appendix

Every November the Illinois State Board of Education releases "state report cards," an annual indicator of each school's strengths and weaknesses as measured in achievement test scores, attendance and graduation rates, demographics, and financial information. What follows is a comparison of Illinois and Chicago averages.

Comparison of Statistics

	Illinois Averages		Chicago Averages		
	1992–93	1991–92	1992–93	1991–92	
Student Demographics					
Total Enrollment	1,835,740	1,815,128	401,445	401,898	Note: Enrollment does not include preschoolers or students at some special education schools.
% Low Income	30.3	32	68.1	79.2	
% Limited English Proficiency (LEP)	5	4.8	13.7	12.6	
Instruction					
One-Year Dropout Rate	6.2	NA	14.8	NA	Note: Dropout rates can be reported as one year or four year. While the state report cards list the one-year rate, Chicago's graduation rate of 50.3 percent indicates the four-year rate would also be slightly less than 50 percent.
Daily Attendance	93.4	93.6	89.1	89.8	
Mobility	20	20.4	32.8	33.5	
Chronic Truancy Rate	2.2	NA	4.7	NA	
High School Graduation Rate	81.4	80.8	50.3	50.7	
First-Grade Average Class Size	22.8	22.7	24.2	24.6	
Average Years Teaching	16	15.8	16.6	16.6	
Teachers with Master's Degree	46.5	45.5	42.9	42.5	Note: State averages include Chicago.
Number of Pupils to Teacher (High School)	17.5	17.5	18.6	18.7	
Number of Pupils to Teacher (Elementary School)	19.7	19.8	20.3	20.9	
Pupil/Administration Ratio	260.2	251	430.1	376.2	Note: Spending per pupil figures are reported a year behind to ensure only audited numbers are used. The report card figures for 1990–91 were $5,066 for the state and $5,675 for Chicago. State average is for unit districts (K–12) only.
School Spending					
Average Teacher Salary	$38,809	$36,508	$43,086	$39,966	
Average Administration Salary	$61,128	$58,540	$63,590	$61,968	
Spending Per Pupil	NA	$5,327	NA	$6,031	

(Comparison of Statistics continued on next page)

Test Scores

	Illinois Averages			Chicago Averages		
(ACT) Score	21		20.9	17		17
Percent Tested	62.2		61.9	59.5		58.8

American College Testing Program

Illinois Goal Assessment Program (IGAP)

Grade / Subject	Illinois Averages	% Exceeding State Goals		Chicago Averages	% Exceeding State Goals	
Third Grade: Reading	245	21	247	154	6	170
Math	268	24	261	187	7	167
Writing	17.7	20	17.7	16.2	12	15.6
Science	NA	NA	250	NA	NA	166
Fourth Grade: Science	250	38	NA	165	10	NA
Social Science	250	30	NA	162	7	NA
Sixth Grade: Reading	259	27	244	184	9	179
Math	257	17	251	192	5	185
Writing	21.4	25	22.3	19.6	10	20.1
Science	NA	NA	250	NA	NA	168
Seventh Grade: Science	250	34	NA	178	10	NA
Social Science	250	31	NA	182	10	NA
Eighth Grade: Reading	258	24	248	206	11	200
Math	266	19	250	204	5	187
Writing	23.7	22	24.4	21.9	8	22.2
Science	NA	NA	250	NA	NA	174
Tenth Grade: Reading	250	32	NA	182	11	NA
Math	250	23	NA	176	5	NA
Writing	25.1	14	NA	22.6	3	NA
Eleventh Grade: Reading	NA	NA	243	NA	NA	190
Math	NA	NA	251	NA	NA	185
Writing	NA	NA	26.1	NA	NA	23.8
Science	257	23	250	195	6	183
Social Science	250	24	NA	184	8	NA

Source: Illinois State Report Cards

Note: Except for writing, all scores are reported on a 500-point scale. Writing tests are based on a 32-point scale. The percent of students exceeding state goals is new in 1993.

The first year a subject is tested, the state arbitrarily sets 250 as the state average.

NA means not applicable.

Definition of Comparison Statistic Terms

Average Class Size: For elementary schools, average class size refers to the total enrollment for the first grade divided by the number of classes on the first school day in May.

Average Composite ACT: Average composite score for all students taking the American College Testing college entrance exam. The ACT has a 1–36 point range. The composite score includes the ACT's four parts: English, math, reading, and science reasoning.

Dropout Rate: New in 1993, the report card lists the number of students in grades 9–12 who dropped out during that school year. The one-year rate should be distinguished from the four-year rate, which in 1992 was 45 percent. The four-year number was not available for 1993.

% Graduated Rate: Percentage of students who enrolled in high school in 1989 and graduated in 1993. The rate excludes transfer students, students who died during the school year, and students who took more than four years to graduate.

Illinois Goal Assessment Program (IGAP): Statewide achievement test scores reported on a 500-point scale, except for writing tests, which are based on a 32-point scale.

% Limited English Proficiency (LEP): Percentage of students with Limited English Proficiency—the percentage eligible for bilingual education.

% Low Income: Percentage of low-income students, ages 3–17, living in institutions for neglected or delinquent children, being supported in foster homes with public funds, eligible to receive free or reduced-price lunches, or from families receiving public aid. Chicago's low-income population was counted earlier in the school year in 1993 and therefore is underreported, according to Chicago school officials.

Mobility Rate: Percentage of students who arrive or leave their schools after the school year begins.

Pupil/Teacher Ratio: Fall enrollment divided by number of teachers or full-time equivalents. Excludes special education classes.

Spending Per Pupil: Operating cost of the district divided by average daily attendance. Excludes summer school, adult education, payment on debt, and capital expenditures such as building renovations, additions, or new schools. The numbers are reported one year behind to ensure that only audited numbers are used.

Average Teacher Salary: Sum of all classroom teachers' pay divided by the number of full-time equivalent teachers.

Source: Chicago Sun-Times *based on state report card results supplied by the Illinois State Board of Education.*

Resources

Access Living of Metropolitan Chicago
310 South Peoria Street, #201
Chicago, Illinois 60640
312-226-5900

For children with disabilities. Staff members work with special education teachers-in-training at several Chicago universities Also focuses on issues of inclusion and integration through Independent Living Skills curriculum for high school students.

Art Resources in Teaching (A.R.T.)
18 South Michigan Avenue, Suite 1108
Chicago, Illinois 60603
312-332-0355

Nonprofit visual arts organization. Its mission is to enhance the education of every Chicago public elementary school student through art while meeting the State Fine Arts Goals.

Aspira, Inc. of Illinois
1567 North Milwaukee Avenue, 2nd floor
Chicago, Illinois 60622
312-252-0970

Runs drop-out prevention program involving math and science centers at two elementary schools and one-on-one contact with Roberto Clemente High School freshmen. Math/science centers provide tutoring to students in second through eighth grade.

Center for Inner City Studies
700 East Oakwood Boulevard
Chicago, Illinois 60653
312-268-7509

Helps schools focus their learning programs from an Afrocentric perspective.

Center for Neighborhood Technology (CNT)
2125 West North Avenue
Chicago, Illinois 60647
312-278-4800

The center's Schools and Energy Project works with several LSCs to reduce school system energy expenses. Analyzes the school's energy budget and helps create an energy conservation strategy. Publishes *Neighborhood Works*.

Chicago Area Writing Project
National-Louis University
Reading and Language Department
2840 Sheridan Road
Evanston, Illinois 60201
708-256-5150, x2577

Provides intensive training for teachers in the area of writing instruction.

Chicago Panel on School Policy (formerly Chicago Panel on Public School Policy and Finance)
220 North Michigan Avenue, Suite 501
Chicago, Illinois 60601
312-346-2202

Coalition of twenty organizations that advocates on behalf of students in Chicago and across Illinois through testimony and collaboration with other reform groups. Also provides training and assistance to LSCs in budget, school improvement planning, needs assessment, and other issues.

Chicago Urban League
4510 South Michigan Avenue
Chicago, Illinois 60653
312-285-5800

Offers several programs to students, LSCs, and parents, including SMART (Science and Math Advocacy for the Recruitment of Teachers), which works with about sixty talented high school students from DuSable, Phillips, and Kenwood.

Citizens Schools Committee
36 South Wabash Avenue, #1028
Chicago, Illinois 60603
312-726-4678

Resource center carries literature on Chicago school reform, reform initiatives, and innovative programs. Also runs a weekly Education Hotline televised on Cable Access.

Community Renewal Society (CRS)
332 South Michigan Avenue
Chicago, Illinois 60604
312-427-4830

Ongoing Principals/Teachers Dialogue project on matters related to Chicago Teachers Union rules. Also organizes bimonthly Principal Workshops and provides workshops for teacher instructional aides that cover reading, spelling, mathematics, and science instruction at both elementary and secondary school levels. Publishes *Catalyst: Voices of Chicago School Reform.*

CPAs for the Public Interest
222 South Riverside Plaza
Chicago, Illinois 60606
312-993-0407, ext. 259

Coordinates the efforts of volunteer CPAs and other business professionals with financial experience to help LSCs prepare their school budget and develop a plan to monitor their schools' finances throughout the school year.

Designs for Change
Network for Leadership Development
220 South State Street, #1900
Chicago, Illinois 60604
312-922-0317

Works with all key groups in a school community to assess school needs, develop realistic plans, and mobilize leaders from the entire school community. A two-person team assigned to each school interviews school council members, convenes focus groups, observes in classrooms, and facilitates planning for school improvement. Each LSC receives a computer, printer, and modem for in-school projects and to connect to the Network bulletin board. A resource center provides computer training, meeting space, and a resource library.

Effective Schools Institute
53 West Jackson Boulevard, #918
Chicago, Illinois 60604
312-435-0505

Introduces teachers, administrators, and LSC members to the Effective Schools approach through a series of research and practice seminars.

Family Resource Center on Disabilities
20 East Jackson Boulevard, Room 900
Chicago, Illinois 60604
312-939-3513

Provides information and referral to families of children with disabilities. Also provides free training workshops. Serves families throughout Illinois.

Golden Apple Foundation
8 South Michigan Avenue, #2310
Chicago, Illinois 60603
312-407-0006

Promotes excellent teaching through programs for teacher recognition, recruitment, and renewal. Each year, Golden

Apple Awards are presented to ten outstanding teachers in the Chicago area. Winning teachers are featured on a WTTW television special and receive a paid, tuition-free semester at Northwestern University; an IBM computer; a cash award; and membership in the Golden Apple Academy, an educational improvement think tank. Golden Apple Scholars of Illinois recruits and prepares students from primarily low-income minority families to teach in urban schools. The Golden Apple Science Program offers a hands-on summer workshop for Chicago elementary school teachers.

Illinois Alliance of Essential Schools
Illinois State Board of Education
100 West Randolph Street, #14-300
Chicago, Illinois 60601
312-814-1487

Fosters high school restructuring within a framework of Nine Common Principles around which curriculum and teaching methods are shaped. In order for schools to participate in this five-year process, which was developed by Dr. Theodore Sizer of Brown University, there must be commitments from the local school council and at least 75 percent of its faculty.

Illinois Fiesta Educativa, Inc.
1921 Blue Island Avenue
Chicago, Illinois 60608
312-666-3393

The only Latino statewide advocacy and training organization focusing solely on the needs of Latino individuals with disabilities and their families.

Illinois Writing Project
9423 Lincolnwood Drive
Evanston, Illinois 60203
312-341-3860 or 708-475-1100, x2136

Trains teachers in the area of writing instruction.

Latino Institute
228 South Wabash Avenue, 6th floor
Chicago, Illinois 60604
312-663-3603

Focuses on Latino schools, works with LSCs to provide technical assistance and training in planning, conflict resolution, team building, and group dynamics.

Lawyers' School Reform Advisory Project
17 East Monroe Street, #212
Chicago, Illinois 60603
312-332-2494

Provides LSCs with impartial legal assistance and advice on issues, including the powers and responsibilities of LSCs, principal selection and performance contracts, writing LSC bylaws, applying the Open Meetings Act to LSCs, problem solving and dispute resolution, monitoring internal accounts, and board of education rules and resources.

Leadership for Quality Education (LQE)
29 South LaSalle Street, Suite 200
Chicago, Illinois 60603
312-629-3300

Advocacy organization formed by Chicago's business community that works with various school reform groups to ensure the successful implementation of the school reform law.

North Central Regional Educational Laboratory (NCREL)
Urban Schools Action Project
1900 Spring Road, #300
Oak Brook, Illinois 60521
708-571-4700

NCREL directs this national project, which works with fifteen urban schools, two of them in Chicago. Through a five-day summer institute, audio "seminars" on the telephone, and computer linkups, NCREL helps schools adapt and implement proven research-based methods for academic improvement. Also publishes a magazine on urban education issues.

Parent/Community Council (PCC)
1603 South Michigan Avenue, #301
Chicago, Illinois 60616
312-427-8999

Emphasizes the necessity of parent involvement in decision-making processes at all levels of the school system. Also provides technical assistance/training to local school council members. Connected with the lauded Chicago Algebra Project.

Parents and Community United for Safe,
Honest, and Educational Schools (PAC-U)
P.O. Box 199
Chicago, Illinois 60629
312-785-5861

Formed in 1993 to address corruption in the schools.

Parents United for Responsible Education (PURE)
1145 West Wilson Avenue, Box 398
Chicago, Illinois 60640
312-989-6091; 312-784-PURE

PURE informs parents about educational issues and acts as an advocate for parents in their relationships with the school administration. Offers individual advocacy and free workshops for LSCs and other interested people on school budgets, school improvement plans, and principal evaluations.

Quest Center
Chicago Teachers Union
222 Merchandise Mart Plaza, #400
Chicago, Illinois 60654
312-329-6210

The Quest Center, a three-year, $1.1 million initiative by the Chicago Teachers Union, provides teacher training conferences, workshops, courses, and school-site presentations. It also funds proposals for innovative teaching methods at ten to fifteen schools each year. Schools receive an initial grant of $3,000 and three years of intensive support, training, and technical assistance. Schools that achieve their goals receive a $6,000 bonus, or the equivalent in services, per team member.

Schools First
220 South State Street, #1900
Chicago, Illinois 60604
312-922-0550

An alliance of LSC members and parent and community volunteers that provides up-to-date information on issues and
events that affect schools on a systemwide and local school
level through its regular informational meetings, the Schools
First Hotline (554-4LSC), and its newsletter, *Schools First Focus.*

Schools United for Better Education (SUBE)
United Neighborhood Organization (UNO) of Little Village
125 North Halsted Street, #203
Chicago, Illinois 60606
312-441-1300

SUBE, a partnership of United Neighborhood Organization of
Little Village and seven neighborhood schools, hosts events
that bring community resources into the school buildings.
Includes hands-on math and science activities for students;
proposal writing, parenting, and financial counseling for families; and curriculum workshops for teachers.

Small Schools Workshop
University of Illinois at Chicago
Department of Education
Chicago, Illinois 60680
312-996-9689

Helps large schools organize into smaller units of students and
teachers, called "schools within schools."

Southeast Asia Center
1124 West Ainslie Street
Chicago, Illinois 60640
312-989-6927

Provides information to Asians and LSCs on bilingual education rights and other issues.

University of Chicago School Mathematics Project
Department of Education
5835 South Kimbark Avenue
Chicago, Illinois 60637
312-702-9770

Provides mathematics training.

Urban Gateways: The Center for Arts in Education
105 West Adams Street, 9th Floor
Chicago, Illinois 60603
312-922-0440

Provides performing and visual arts programs in the schools.

Voices for Illinois Children
53 West Jackson Boulevard
Chicago, Illinois 60604
312-456-0600

Provides information and assistance to schools and programs interested in relocating a preschool from a regular public school, has also issued several reports on what makes a good preschool.

West Side Schools and Communities Organizing for Restructuring and Planning Progress (WSCORP)
c/o Malcolm X College
1900 West Van Buren Avenue, #1209
Chicago, Illinois 60612
312-850-7116

Conducts Saturday field trips, workshops, and family events to help build family involvement at West Side schools. Two outreach workers help LSCs organize and train parents with an emphasis on school improvement plans, budgeting, and problem solving.

Youth Guidance
53 West Jackson Boulevard, #950
Chicago, Illinois 60604
312-435-3900

Private social service agency for disadvantaged inner-city youth. Provides mental health, educational enrichment, job development, and social services.

For a complete listing, including many programs operated by Chicago's universities, see *School Help: 105 Resources for chicago School Improvement,* Designs for Change, 1993.

Notes

Note: Quotations that are not annotated in the text were taken directly from the speaker for this book.

Introduction

1. William J. Bennett, Letter to the Editor, *Chicago Sun-Times*, 4 October 1993, 26.

2. Mary J. Herrick, *The Chicago Schools: A Social and Political History* (Beverly Hills, Calif.: Sage Publications, 1971), 43.

3. Ibid., 44.

4. Ibid., 45.

5. Ibid., 174.

6. Ibid., 260. A precinct is a voting district that is also used by political parties as a unit of organization to turn out the vote. Precinct captains are responsible for building local organizations to distribute campaign literature, to telephone voters on election day, and to canvass voters door to door.

7. Of the nearly 273,000 people receiving public assistance in 1962, all but 10 percent were African American. See Herrick, *Chicago Schools*, 305.

Chapter 1: The Stakes, the Obstacles

1. Linda Waldman, *My Neighborhood: The Words and Pictures of Inner-City Children* (Chicago: Hyde Park Bank Foundation, 1993), 58.

2. Maribeth Vander Weele, "Most Chicago Schools Fail College Test," *Chicago Sun-Times,* 30 November 1992, 18. Based on annual state report cards, which are statistical reports available for all public schools in Illinois. Source: Illinois Department of Education.

3. Linda Lenz, "City's Schools Called 'Worst,'" *Chicago Sun-Times,* 7 November 1987, 1. "You've got an educational disaster on your hands. You need something radical," declared William J. Bennett. The controversial secretary of education promoted vouchers to send public funds to private schools although critics feared that would exacerbate a two-tiered educational system—one for the rich and one for the poor. "When you've got a dropout rate of 45 percent, and when half of the high schools score in the bottom 1 percent (on the ACT college entrance exam), is there a worse case? Tell me if there is. I haven't seen it."

4. Isabel Wilkerson, "New School Term in Chicago Puts Parents in Seat of Power," *The New York Times,* 3 September 1989, 1.

5. Maribeth Vander Weele, "School Reform Survives, Climbs to a Higher Grade," *Chicago Sun-Times,* 21 October 1990, 1. The first council election turnout of 15 percent surpassed a suburban Cook County average of 11 percent for school board elections, according to the reform group Designs for Change. Chicagoans, however, had an advantage: the school reform law was not written to conform with regular election law, allowing nonregistered voters to cast ballots. Nevertheless, the turnout for such a special election was higher than expected. It dropped to 8 percent in 1991.

6. Roger Flaherty, "Educator Says Current Remedial Program Works," *Chicago Sun-Times,* 16 February 1992, 5.

7. Maribeth Vander Weele, "Failing Grades for City Schools, Chicago Rated as Worst," *Chicago Sun-Times,* 23 September 1992, 1. Statistics were compiled from the following report: Council of Great City Schools, *National Urban Education Goals: Baseline Indicators, 1990–91* by Michael Casserly (Washington, D.C., September 1992). The report indicated that while systems in Detroit, New York City, San Diego, Dade County, and Houston improved dropout rates through aggressive programs, Chicago's worsened. Chicago's rate was 45.9 in 1990, meaning that nearly half of the freshmen who began school in 1986 dropped out by their senior year. Readers should understand there are numerous caveats when considering dropout rates and achievement test scores. Districts calculate dropout rates differently and not all forty-three systems, which included Los Angeles— undoubtedly a rival to Chicago's disheartening status—reported the four-year rate for the survey. Another point to keep in mind is that Chicago defines students taking high school equivalency examina-

tions as dropouts while some districts do not. Furthermore, testing is never completely scientific because of wide variances in the types of students tested, the timing of the tests, the group that is used for national comparisons, or "norming," and economic bias. Although some districts do not test special education students whatsoever, Chicago does to some extent. In issuing the report, the authors cautioned that all schools do not administer the same test. Chicago test experts do note, however, that all districts use achievement tests that divide children's scores into four quarters nationally and, therefore, conclusions can be drawn from how many students score in the bottom quarter of the nation, the bottom half, the top half, and the top quarter. Despite the caveats, no one disputes that objective indicators for Chicago public schools are indeed abysmal.

8. According to the Council of the Great City Schools, Chicago had the fifth poorest student population (70.1), as measured by those eligible for free and reduced-price subsidized lunches. Systems with the poorest student populations include St. Louis (86.8), Atlanta (74.8), New Orleans (74), and Boston (72.9).

9. See "At a Glance: Chicago Public Schools," a March 1993 fact sheet issued by the Chicago Board of Education.

10. Maribeth Vander Weele, "More Students Found to Lack English Skills," *Chicago Sun-Times,* 10 August 1992, 3.

11. In 1992, the largest foreign-speaking groups of Chicago public school students enrolled in special programs included Spanish, 43,601 students; Polish, 2,759; Arabic, 1,033; Chinese, 821; Vietnamese, 794; Urdu, 786; Rumanian, 690; Assyrian, 499; Khmer, 437; Korean, 416; Russian, 400, and Filipino or Tagalog, 328. Source: "News and Notes," *Chicago Public Schools, Department of Language and Cultural Education,* School Year 1992–93, 6.

12. Vander Weele, "More Students Found to Lack English Skills," 3.

13. Larry Weintraub, "Voices from the Front, Teacher Troubles: Violence, Funding," *Chicago Sun-Times,* 26 March 1993, 7.

14. Obviously, New York City has a higher cost of living, which magnifies the difference in spending.

15. National Education Association, *Rankings of the States,* 1993 (Washington, D.C., September 1993), 58. Numbers include per capita state government expenditures for all education during 1990–91, the most recent year available. In 1989–90, Illinois ranked forty-eighth.

16. Vander Weele, "Failing Grades for City Schools," 1.

17. Maribeth Vander Weele, "Pocketfund Blues: Study Predicts Huge School Fund Deficit," *Chicago Sun-Times,* 12 May 1992, 1. Based on the report issued by Booz-Allen and Hamilton and Washington, Pittman, and McKeever, *Financial Outlook for the Chicago Public Schools* (Chicago, 14 May 1992), II–4, III–7.

18. G. Alfred Hess, Jr., *School Restructuring, Chicago Style* (Newbury Park, Calif.: Corwin Press, 1991), 25.

19. Ibid., *xi.*

20. Denis P. Doyle, Bruce S. Cooper, and Roberta Trachtman, *Taking Charge: State Action on School Reform in the 1980s* (Indianapolis, Ind.: Hudson Institute, 1991), *v.*

21. Maribeth Vander Weele, "Chicago's Schools: An 'Impossible Job'? *Chicago Sun-Times,* 8 November 1992, 4.

22. Vander Weele, "Failing Grades for City Schools," 1.

23. Maribeth Vander Weele, "Parents Enlist as Aides," *Chicago Sun-Times,* 21 October 1990, 17.

24. Vander Weele, "Chicago's Schools: An 'Impossible Job'?", 4.

Chapter 2: A Whirlwind Start

1. Tom Seibel and Tracey Robinson, "Parents Say Cops Beat Schoolkids; Fourteen Injured," *Chicago Sun-Times,* 11 April 1990, 3

2. Neil Steinberg and Tracey Robinson, "Shouts Erupt Over Firing of Principal at Burns School," *Chicago Sun-Times* 14 March 1990, 3. Parents accused the primarily Hispanic council of discriminating against the principal because he did not speak Spanish.

3. Seibel and Robinson, "Parents Say Cops Beat Schoolkids," 3.

4. Frank Burgos and Philip Franchine, "Principal's Ouster Protested; Students, Police Clash in Morgan Park Walkout," *Chicago Sun-Times,* 2 March 1990, 1.

5. Rosalind Rossi and Mary A. Johnson, "White Principal Wins Lawsuit, Council that Fired Him Ordered to Pay," *Chicago Sun-Times,* 5 May 1992, 3.

6. Daniel J. Lehmann, "Principal Loses in Bias Suit Appeal," *Chicago Sun-Times,* 28 August 1993, 5. The Illinois Appellate Court ruled: "The

only way to conclude based on this paltry record that he was discriminated against because he was white is to make the illogical and insupportable assumption that every time a black council member votes against a white candidate, the decision is motivated by race. This is impermissible. The notion that all black decision-makers are driven by this single issue rests on just the type of stereotype the civil rights laws were designed to prevent from infecting decisions; it would be painfully ironic if those same laws were here used to perpetuate such stereotypes."

7. Designs for Change, *Closer Look, First Year of School Reform in Chicago* (Chicago, January 1991), 3. Nevertheless, 29 percent of elementary principals say there is more conflict in their schools under reform. Fourteen percent of the system's elementary school principals rate internal conflict on their councils as a serious problem.

8. Consortium on Chicago School Research, *Charting Reform: The Principals' Perspective; Report on a Survey of Chicago Public School Principals* (Chicago, December 1992), 13.

9. Maribeth Vander Weele, "End Comes Quickly for School Veterans," *Chicago Sun-Times,* 17 August 1993, 3.

10. Maribeth Vander Weele, "Many Factors Translate into Lower Test Scores," *Chicago Sun-Times,* 30 November 1992, 21.

11. Pierre LeBreton, Letter to the Editor, "Let's Follow Our Neighborhood Heroes," *Chicago Sun-Times,* 30 September 1993, 32.

12. Floyd M. Banks, Letter to the Editor, "Longer Classes Block Progress in High Schools," *Chicago Sun-Times,* 13 October 1993, 36.

13. Rosalind Rossi, "Uncertainty Breeds Anger at Lane Tech," *Chicago Sun-Times,* 16 September 1993, 6.

14. Maribeth Vander Weele, "Class Schedule Edict Mystifies School Brass," *Chicago Sun-Times,* 18 September 1993, 4.

15. Maribeth Vander Weele, "Central Office Frustrations Continue," *Chicago Sun-Times,* 6 September 1992, 4.

16. Paul T. Hill and Josephine Bonan, *Decentralization and Accountability in Public Education* (Santa Monica, Calif.: Rand Corporation, 1991), 25.

17. Principals' loss of tenure was the primary reason the Chicago Principals Association sued, claiming that the 1988 reform law was unconstitutional. The suit focused on the obscure method of electing

council members, insisting it violated the one-person, one-vote rule because parents voted for six parents' seats, community members voted for two community member seats, and teachers voted for two teacher seats. In a stunning decision, the Illinois Supreme Court agreed with the principals about the voting structure but not about their tenure rights. The decision, handed down just weeks before Christmas 1990, declared Chicago school councils unconstitutional. Under subsequent legislation that changed the voting structure, parents and community members vote for each other, with some limits, but the council makeup remains the same. Teachers are appointed after a poll of each school's staff. Still hoping to get compensation for its fired members or to gain tenure, the principals' association sued again in 1992, claiming that the new structure is also unconstitutional. "We were not particularly interested in tackling the School Reform Act because it does make us the bad guys in black hats," said Bruce Berndt, head of the Chicago Principals Association at the time. "However, if the method of selecting councils is illegal—and I think it is—if that is what we have to do to obtain compensation for the principals who were illegally fired, we have no choice. They could have found all kinds of ways to change the guard. They didn't have to fire nearly 100 people and force another 150 into early retirement. They could have offered early retirement incentives that would have not been so brutal to the guard that was being changed." In 1993, the suit was still making its way through the federal courts.

18. Chicago Board of Education purchase order files.

19. Chicago Board of Education, *Board Reports Re: LSCs Sign-Off* (Chicago, 1991).

20. Maribeth Vander Weele, "School Reform Report Card," *Chicago Sun-Times,* 21 October 1990, 17.

21. Maribeth Vander Weele, "Seminars Here Cost Bundle, Too," *Chicago Sun-Times,* 21 July 1991, 16.

22. Tracey Robinson, "$37,500 Paperweight Tab Jars School Councils," *Chicago Sun-Times,* 26 October 1989, 3.

23. Consortium, *Charting Reform: The Principals' Perspective,* 4.

24. Audit from the Internal Audit Department of the Chicago Board of Education.

Chapter 3: Chaos on Pershing Road

1. Maribeth Vander Weele, "Classroom Chaos Seen as Possibly Worst Ever," *Chicago Sun-Times,* 1 October 1991, 1.

2. Maribeth Vander Weele, "Pershing Road Bottleneck, Headquarters Snafus Deny Schools Crucial Funds," *Chicago Sun-Times,* 21 October 1990, 17.

3. Ibid.

4. Maribeth Vander Weele, "School Board Reform Plan Shot Down; Finance Bosses Brand It a 'Let's Pretend' Agenda," *Chicago Sun-Times,* 15 August 1991, 5.

5. Maribeth Vander Weele, "Shape Up, Schools Told; Kimbrough Warns of Takeovers, Closures," *Chicago Sun-Times,* 26 March 1992, 1.

6. Hill and Bonan, *Decentralization and Accountability,* 14.

7. Although the state legislature waived the balanced-budget requirement for ten days on September 3, 1993, schools opened one week late. Superintendent Argie K. Johnson concluded the system was not prepared to open because of thousands of staff vacancies created by a last-minute early retirement program adopted by the legislature.

8. Maribeth Vander Weele and Phillip J. O'Connor, "Sick of Cuts, Julian Teachers Stay Home," *Chicago Sun-Times,* 19 October 1993, 1.

9. Maribeth Vander Weele, "Computer Chaos; City Schools Can't Get Access to Available Cash," *Chicago Sun-Times,* 12 October 1993, 1.

10. Maribeth Vander Weele and Rosalind Rossi, "Budget Funds Finally Available to Schools," *Chicago Sun-Times,* 28 October 1993, 20.

11. Maribeth Vander Weele, "At Funston, Teachers Take a Gamble for Preschoolers," *Chicago Sun-Times,* 12 October 1993, 6.

12. Maribeth Vander Weele, "Reeling from Budget Blitz, Schools Open," 5 September 1991, *Chicago Sun-Times,* 24.

13. Chicago Board of Education, *State of Illinois Annual Financial Report* (Chicago, fiscal year 1991–92).

14. Tracey Robinson, "Widespread Waste, Foul-ups Uncovered at School Board," *Chicago Sun-Times,* 29 June 1990, 38. For information on overcharges on facilities repairs, see chap. 8.

15. Maribeth Vander Weele, "Schools in Debt, Execs Travel More," *Chicago Sun-Times,* 21 July 1991, 1.

16. Michael Briggs, "Feds Hit Schools on Food Safety; Supplies Kept Past Expiration," *Chicago Sun-Times,* 26 September 1993, 1.

17. Harlan Draeger, "School Board Drops Ball on U.S. Help, Surplus Equipment," *Chicago Sun-Times,* 19 April 1991, 1.

18. Lou Ortiz, "Appeals Court Voids School Board Health Pact," *Chicago Sun-Times,* 25 August 1992, 5.

19. Maribeth Vander Weele, "Monahan Is Latest Exec to Leave School Board," *Chicago Sun-Times,* 18 September 1992, 16.

20. Maribeth Vander Weele, "Special Advocate," *The Executive Editor* (May 1992): 30.

21. Maribeth Vander Weele, "School Costs Do Not Compute, Outdated Systems, Chaotic Procedures Lead to Overruns," *Chicago Sun-Times,* 12 April 1993, 6.

22. Maribeth Vander Weele and Rosalind Rossi, "Schools Scramble to Fill Key Posts," *Chicago Sun-Times,* 9 August 1993, 1.

23. Raymond R. Coffey, "Stalking the Pershing Road Monster," *Chicago Sun-Times,* 20 May 1990, 50.

24. Maribeth Vander Weele, "Half a Loaf for School Execs, 50 Percent of Principals Grade Them Highly," *Chicago Sun-Times,* 25 August 1992, 5.

25. Charley Gillispie, *A Proposal for an Organizational Analysis and Restructuring of the Chicago Public Schools* (Chicago, June 1993), 3.

26. Maribeth Vander Weele, "Board Cuts Red Tape to Ease Supply Purchases by Schools," *Chicago Sun-Times,* 21 December 1992, 14.

27. Survey results, *Financial Research and Advisory Committee (FRAC) Initiative* (Chicago, June 1993).

28. Vander Weele, "Pocketfund Blues," 1.

29. Ted D. Kimbrough, The Forum, "Student Grades, Not Governance, Need Attention," *Chicago Sun-Times,* 1 August 1992, 20.

30. Vander Weele, "Shape Up, Schools Told," 1.

31. Maribeth Vander Weele, "School Councils Seek New Powers," *Chicago Sun-Times,* 6 August 1992, 11.

Chapter 4: Governance Affects Kids

1. Maribeth Vander Weele, "Late Teacher Hirings Add to Student Woes," *Chicago Sun-Times,* 29 September 1992, 4.

2. Maribeth Vander Weele, "Plight of Two City Schools: No Teachers in Twenty-two Classes," *Chicago Sun-Times,* 27 September 1991, 24.

3. Maribeth Vander Weele, "Students Await Teachers as Schools Shuffle Staffing," *Chicago Sun-Times,* 14 September 1992, 4.

4. Vander Weele, "Many Factors Translate into Lower Test Scores," 21. Based also on additional author conversations with Zavitkovsky.

5. Maribeth Vander Weele, "Audit: School Data Faked; Orr High Allegedly Inflated Student Count," *Chicago Sun-Times,* 20 January 1994, 1.

6. Council of the Great City Schools, *National Urban Education Goals,* 130, 174.

7. Vander Weele, "Students Await Teachers," 4. Statistics provided by Margaret M. Harrigan.

8. Ibid.

9. Vander Weele, "Late Teacher Hirings," 4. Graduation rate taken from 1992 state report cards, obtained on computer disk from the Illinois Department of Education, Springfield, Illinois. Statistics for each school were printed in charts accompanying the following story: Vander Weele, "Most Chicago Schools Fail College Test," 18.

10. Vander Weele, "Students Await Teachers," 4.

11. Vander Weele, "End Comes Quickly for School Veterans," 3.

12. Maribeth Vander Weele, "Teachers Face Freeze on Hiring," *Chicago Sun-Times,* 23 August 1993, 1. Although school superintendent Argie K. Johnson later announced there was no hiring freeze, her puzzling statement contradicted both the experience of principals throughout the system and confirmation of the freeze by Margaret M. Harrigan.

13. At the end of the 1993 union negotiations, the board agreed to restore one hundred jobs immediately and four hundred more in January 1994, thereby rolling class sizes back to the levels of spring 1993. The savings from one semester of higher class sizes amounted to $8 million, according to budget officials.

14. Vander Weele and O'Connor, "Sick of Cuts," 3.

15. Zay N. Smith, "Cuts Deal Setback to Magnet School," *Chicago Sun-Times,* 26 October 1993, 6.

16. Vander Weele, "Late Teacher Hirings," 4.

17. Vander Weele and O'Connor, "Sick of Cuts," 3.

18. Maribeth Vander Weele, "Good News Soured by Court Ruling," *Chicago Sun-Times,* 11 November 1993, 14.

19. Vander Weele, "Late Teacher Hirings," 4.

20. Maribeth Vander Weele, "Young Teacher 'In Shock' Over Shift," *Chicago Sun-Times,* 15 September 1991, 5.

21. Maribeth Vander Weele, "Schools Struggle to Juggle Jobs," *Chicago Sun-Times,* 15 September 1991, 5.

22. Charles N. Wheeler III, "Cut in State Aid Cited in School Layoff Notices," *Chicago Sun-Times,* 4 June 1988, 40.

23. Vander Weele, "Young Teacher 'In Shock' Over Shift," 5.

24. Hill and Bonan, *Decentralization and Accountability,* 20.

25. Maribeth Vander Weele, "School Board Pushes for Longer Teacher Workday," *Chicago Sun-Times,* 8 April 1993, 1.

26. William Rankin, The Forum, "Bureaucracy Smothers True School Reform; Principals Lack Meaningful Control," *Chicago Sun-Times,* 5 December 1992, 18.

27. Chicago Board of Education report, 27 March 1991.

Chapter 5: Caretakers of Our Children

1. "Kids Tell How to Fix Things," *Chicago Sun-Times,* 26 March 1993, 7.

2. Under reform, a principal had to win another principal's acceptance of a transferred teacher. *Chicago Sun-Times* writer Alf Siewers called the shifting of poorly performing teachers from school to school "the dance of the lemons" in a May 1988 series entitled "Search for Solutions." See Alf Siewers, "Bad Teachers a Sour Spot," *Chicago Sun-Times,* 5 May 1988, 7.

3. Margaret M. Harrigan, interview with author, spring 1993.

4. Edwin M. Bridges, "Commentary: Coping With Incompetent Teachers," *Education Week,* 20 November 1985, 24.

5. The Illinois State Department of Education each year provides a summary of dismissal hearings. Information includes case number, hear-

ing officer charges, decision, and date. In addition to tenured teachers, ten probationary Chicago public school teachers—those with three or fewer years of experience—were fired during the 1992–93 school year, according to school board attorney Joyce Combest Price.

6. Maribeth Vander Weele, "Principals Report Teachers Lacking," *Chicago Sun-Times,* 2 December 1992, 3.

7. *Gilliland v. Board of Education of Pleasant View,* 67 Ill. 2d 143, 8 Ill. December 84, 365 N.E. 2d 84 (1977). The Illinois Supreme Court stated: "The test in determining whether a cause for dismissal is irremediable is whether damage has been done to the students, faculty or school, and whether the conduct resulting in that damage could have been corrected had the teacher's superiors warned her. Uncorrected causes for dismissal which originally were remediable in nature can become irremediable if continued over a long period of time."

8. Decision of hearing officer Ellen J. Alexander, 10 February 1992. Alexander wrote that although Smith was extensively briefed, either informally or verbally, on her areas of weaknesses, "the statute requires a final evaluation to be written, covering strengths, weaknesses and rating. The Chicago Board's own official plan does also. The Board does not have discretion to omit a written evaluation following completion of a remediation period."

9. Decision of hearing officer Harvey A. Nathan, 15 July 1990.

10. Ibid.

11. Decision of hearing officer Allen D. Schwartz, 25 May 1989.

12. Linda Lenz, "Social Worker's Persistence Led to Moffat Conviction," *Chicago Sun-Times,* 6 June 1987, 41.

13. Linda Lenz, "No Firing in School Sex Case; Ruling Backs Kelvyn Park Principal Accused of Relations with Students," *Chicago Sun-Times,* 4 November 1986, 3.

14. Decision of hearing officer Julius Menacker, 9 January 1992.

15. Case 92 CH 1623 in Cook County Circuit Court, 6.

16. Decision of hearing officer George Edward Larney, 19 January 1988.

17. Decision of hearing officer Thomas R. McMillen, 3 December 1992.

18. Decision of hearing officer Corinne Hallett, 30 March 1993.

19. Maribeth Vander Weele, "Teachers Union Objects to Docking Late Workers," *Chicago Sun-Times,* 8 December 1992, 6.

20. Decision of hearing officer Corinne Hallett, 30 March 1993.

21. Rickie Cochrane, Personal View column, "Piccolo Teachers Aren't Tardy," *Chicago Sun-Times,* 28 January 1993, 28.

22. Lorraine Forte, "Bad Teachers Worry Teacher Leaders," *Catalyst, Voices of Chicago School Reform* (May 1993): 1. *Catalyst* provided author with additional breakdown of survey information.

23. Maribeth Vander Weele, "Convicted Guard on School Board Payroll," *Chicago Sun-Times,* 29 October 1992, 6.

24. Decision of hearing officer Herbert M. Berman, 16 May 1992.

25. Robert E. Mijou, Letter to the Editor, "Chicago Teacher Flunks Schools' Management," *Chicago Sun-Times,* 5 July 1991, 30.

26. Vander Weele, "Principals Report Teachers Lacking," 3.

27. Consortium, *Charting Reform: The Principals' Perspective,* 11.

28. Consortium on Chicago School Research, *Charting Reform: The Teachers' Turn, Report No. 1 on a Survey of CPS Elementary School Teachers* (Chicago, September 1991), 11.

29. National Education Association, *Status of the American Public School Teacher, 1990–1991* (Washington, D.C., 1992), 64.

30. "Kids Tell How To Fix Things," 7. Author uses a more complete quote than originally published in the *Chicago Sun-Times.*

31. Gary Orfield used ACT scores to determine the selectivity of area colleges. See Howard Witt and Jean Latz Griffin, "City Colleges Focus of Study on Minority-Student Failures," *Chicago Tribune,* 9 September 1984, sec. 2, p. 1. See also Linda Wertsch, "City's Teachers Are Less Educated–Study," *Chicago Sun-Times,* 9 September 1984, 2.

32. Alan B. Anderson and George W. Pickering, *Confronting the Color Line—The Broken Promise of the Civil Rights Movement in Chicago* (Athens, Ga.: University of Georgia Press, 1986), 54.

33. Lynn Sweet, "Illinois Schools Among Most Segregated in U.S.," *Chicago Sun-Times,* 14 December 1993. The study was prepared for the National School Board Association's Council on Urban Boards of Education.

34. Herrick, *The Chicago Schools,* 312.

35. Although "Willis wagons" were associated primarily with African-American communities, they were placed in overcrowded white neighborhoods as well. Television commentator and attorney Joel Weisman, host of WTTW's *Chicago Week in Review,* recalls attending school half days in mobile classrooms in one North Side neighborhood.

36. Again, it is not an exclusively African-American phenomenon. The author's mother recalls her Fenger High School biology teacher in 1940 telling students that money for new microscopes had disappeared. "She said the politicians took the money," Elizabeth Vander Weele recalled. "They were promised, but someone absconded with them."

37. Nicholas R. Cannella, *171 Years of Teaching in Chicago, 1816—1987* (Chicago: Chicago Teachers Union, 1987), 29.

38. Paul E. Peterson, *School Politics, Chicago Style* (Chicago: University of Chicago Press, 1976), 196. In 1967, full-time basis substitutes—called FTBs—constituted a full 28 percent of the work force, according to Peterson, 204.

39. Herrick, *Chicago Schools,* 195.

40. Maureen O'Donnell, "$250 Million School Contract; On-Time Opening 'Guaranteed,'" *Chicago Sun-Times,* 31 July 1990, 1. See also 1993 Chicago Teachers Union contract.

41. Information provided by the Chicago Board of Education.

42. Council of Great City Schools, *National Urban Education Goals,* 131.

43. Lorraine M. McDonnell and Anthony Pascal, *Teacher Unions and Educational Reform* (Santa Monica, Calif.: Center for Policy Research in Education and the Center for the Study of the Teaching Profession, Rand Corporation, 1988), *vii.*

44. Council of Chief State School Officers, *State Education Indicators, 1990, For the School Year 1989-1990* (Washington D.C., 1990), 28–30.

45. "States News Roundup," *Education Week,* 9 September 1987, 3. The teacher testing program was later modified.

46. Lynn Olson, "From Risk to Reform: Kentucky Moves to Enact Reform Plan," *Education Week,* 21 April 1993, S4–S11.

47. Maureen O'Donnell, "$19 Million Tab on Bonus for Teachers Jolts Board," *Chicago Sun-Times,* 3 May 1991, 5.

48. Consortium, *Charting Reform: The Principals' Perspective,* 12.

49. Maribeth Vander Weele, "New Program Gets Would-be Teachers into Class," *Chicago Sun-Times Education Guide,* 3 March 1992, 2.

50. Charles Taylor Kerchner and Julia E. Koppich, *A Union of Professionals, Labor Relations and Educational Reform* (New York: Teachers College Press, 1993), 188. William Ayers, an associate professor of education at the University of Illinois at Chicago, wrote the chapter on Chicago and its school labor relations.

51. Maribeth Vander Weele, "Enrichment for Mind, Body Shores Up Four City Schools," *Chicago Sun-Times,* 8 December 1991, 5.

Chapter 6: Everyone Passes

1. Anonymous letter written by a fourth-grade teacher to *Chicago Sun-Times* columnist Raymond R. Coffey, 11 June 1991.

2. Roger Flaherty, "Learning Drills Get Students Caught Up," *Chicago Sun-Times,* 20 February 1994, 6.

3. Vander Weele, "Most Chicago Schools Fail College Test," 18. Based on annual state report cards, which consist of statistical reports available for all public schools in Illinois. Source: Illinois State Board of Education. The two schools that surpassed the national ACT average of 20.6 on a 36-point scale were Whitney Young Magnet High School and Lane Technical High School. Lincoln Park High School scored at the national average.

4. Based on 1992 annual state report cards. In 1992, the seven-year-old Illinois Goals Assessment Program tested public school students in reading mathematics, writing, and science in grades three, six, eight, and eleven. Science was a new category in 1992. The state changed its writing scale, so only reading and math scores were comparable over three years. Chicago public school students fared worst in science during 1992. Depending on the grade tested, city averages ranged from 166 to 183 in that subject—250 was set as the state average.

5. A number of elementary schools do not have eighth grades. Specifically, the Chicago school system has 473 elementary schools, including 392 regular elementary schools, 8 middle schools, 35 magnet schools, 23 community academies, 1 upper grade school, and 14 special schools, such as those used for special education purposes. The system also has 78 secondary schools, including 38 general high schools, 2 technical, 8 vocational, 9 magnet, 6 community academies, and 15 special high schools, primarily for children with disabilities and special needs students but also for adult education and appren-

tice programs. See "At A Glance: Chicago Public Schools," a 1993 fact sheet issued by the Chicago public school system.

6. The system has nine magnet secondary schools and thirty-five magnet elementary schools.

7. Vander Weele, "Shape Up, Schools Told," 1.

8. Raymond R. Coffey, "Is 'Burnt Out Teacher' Alone in Despair?" *Chicago Sun-Times,* 6 June 1991, 3. Column is slightly abridged.

9. Letter, 10 June 1991. Because of the personal nature of the letter, author has chosen to maintain teacher's anonymity.

10. Coffey, "Burnt Out Teacher," 3.

11. Anonymous letter, 11 June 1991.

12. Anonymous letter, 9 June 1991.

13. Anonymous letter, 10 June 1991.

14. Based on author's conversation with the former teacher.

15. C. Emily Feistritzer, *Who Wants to Teach?* (Washington, D.C.: National Center of Education Information, 1992), 25.

16. The 1990 Chicago Board of Education Promotion Policy reads: "A student who becomes 15 during the school year or during the subsequent summer shall be graduated from elementary school to high school in June or at the end of the summer session in August . . . A student shall not be retained or demoted more than once in kindergarten-grade 8."

17. Letter from South Side elementary school teacher, 21 December 1990.

18. Anonymous letter, 9 June 1991.

19. The promotion policy also reads: "The high school must enroll any student who has official documentation of successful completion of elementary school, whether or not the student has an elementary school diploma. The high school must also enroll any student who is 15 at the beginning of the school year, regardless of number of years spent in elementary school, and provide a suitable program."

20. Hess, *School Restructuring, Chicago Style,* 126.

21. Maribeth Vander Weele, "Costly School Conferences Tied to Idle U.S. Funds," *Chicago Sun-Times,* 24 June 1992, 22.

22. Maudlyne Ihejirika and Maribeth Vander Weele, "Critics Knock Schools for Wisconsin Retreat," *Chicago Sun-Times,* 21 June 1992, 22.

23. Consortium on Chicago School Research, *A View from the Elementary Schools: The State of Reform in Chicago* (Chicago, July 1993), 14. Designs for Change, a reform research and advocacy group, produced a study in November 1993 showing that when all achievement tests taken by Chicago schoolchildren were considered, 72 percent of available scores in various grades and categories rose between 1990 and 1993.

24. Don Hayner, "192 Students at Beethoven Not Promoted," *Chicago Sun-Times,* 1 July 1988, 3.

25. Raymond R. Coffey, "Whew! Ignorance Has Close Call," *Chicago Sun-Times,* 28 February 1988, 12.

26. Joan Jeter Slay, guest column, "Demotion Fuss: Who's Right? Critics Charge 'Creative' Idea is 'Malpractice,'" *Chicago Sun-Times,* 28 February 1988, 7.

27. Samuel J. Meisels of the University of Michigan and Fong-ruey Liaw of Columbia University, report, "Failure in Grade: Do Retained Students Catch Up?" (March 1991): 22.

28. William Rankin, Letter to the Editor, "School Promotion Policy Fails," *Chicago Sun-Times,* 3 March 1993, 30.

29. Chicago Panel on Public School Policy and Finance, *What Are We Willing to Pay for School Reform? An Analysis of the Costs of Educational Reform in Illinois,* by F. Howard Nelson and G. Alfred Hess, Jr. (Chicago, May 1985), 6, 13.

30. Maribeth Vander Weele and Tim Gerber, "Flunk Fewer to Save Cash? School Official's Idea Draws Fire," *Chicago Sun-Times,* 4 June 1991, 3.

31. Ted D. Kimbrough, Letter to the Editor, "Plan Focuses on Saving Students, Not Money," *Chicago Sun-Times,* 11 June 1991, 26.

32. Texas Education Agency, *Impact of Educational Reform on Students in At-Risk Situations, Phase III, Interim Report, Executive Summary* (Austin, Tex., May 1992), 6.

33. Consortium, *Charting Reform: The Teachers' Turn,* 11.

34. Annual state report card statistics.

35. Hess, Jr., *School Restructuring, Chicago Style,* 126.

36. Written statement by Argie K. Johnson, 18 June 1993.

37. Jay Mathews, *Escalante: The Best Teacher in America* (New York: Henry Holt and Company, 1988), 202–3.

38. Andrew Herrmann, "South Side 'Face of Hope' Gets Inauguration Call; Clinton Gives Free Trip to Beasley School Principal," *Chicago Sun-Times,* 30 December 1992, 5.

39. No Chicago school improved in all grades tested.

40. Maribeth Vander Weele, "Reform Efforts Are Paying Off on Far South Side," *Chicago Sun-Times,* 30 November 1992, 22.

41. Daniel P. Peterson, "First Person: 'We Must Do Whatever It Takes to Turn Our Students On,'" *Catalyst, Voices of Chicago School Reform* (October 1991): 8.

Chapter 7: Discipline Makes a Difference

1. Chicago Board of Education statistics.

2. Maribeth Vander Weele, "Readers List Their Beefs," *Chicago Sun-Times,* 26 March 1993, 8. Unless they graduate sooner, students have the legal right to stay until they are twenty-one years old. Students may quit after turning sixteen, however.

3. Comments by Jacqueline B. Vaughn on WMAQ-AM radio program *The Reporters,* 20 June 1993.

4. William J. Bennett, *The De-Valuing of America: The Fight for Our Culture and Our Children* (New York: Simon and Schuster, 1992), 42–43.

5. Illinois Criminal Justice Information Authority, *Trends and Issues 91: Education and Criminal Justice in Illinois* (Chicago, 1991), 59.

6. Consortium, *Charting Reform: The Teachers' Turn,* 8.

7. Illinois House Bill 2073.

8. Consortium, *Charting Reform: The Teachers' Turn,* 8.

9. Charles L. Kyle and Edward R. Kantowicz, *Kids First—Primero Los Niños: Chicago School Reform in the 1980s* (Springfield, Ill.: Illinois Issues, 1992), 85.

10. Council of Great City Schools, *National Urban Education Goals: Baseline Indicators,* 130.

11. Maribeth Vander Weele, "Teacher-Student Link Key to Fewer Dropouts," *Chicago Sun-Times,* 23 September 1992, 38.

12. Fran Spielman and Jim Casey, "Murders Down 13 Percent in Chicago this Year," *Chicago Sun-Times,* 6 May 1993, 16.

13. Jim Casey and Andrew Herrmann, "Fourth-grader Shot by Classmate at Northwest Side School," *Chicago Sun-Times,* 11 March 1992, 3.

14. Gary Wisby and Jim Casey, "Boy, Fifteen, Shot to Death in Tilden High Scuffle," *Chicago Sun-Times,* 21 November 1992, 4.

15. Maureen O'Donnell and Lee Bey, "Seventh-grader Kills Himself with Handgun in Class," *Chicago Sun-Times,* 11 November 1992, 4. Willie's mother, Edna Clayborn, later filed suit against the Chicago Board of Education alleging the school was negligent for allowing Willie to have the gun on the premises.

16. Phillip J. O'Connor and Tom Seibel, "Rifle Kills First-grader Enroute to School," *Chicago Sun-Times,* 13 October 1992, 1.

17. Dennis A. Britton, "Seven-year-old's Death at Cabrini Stuns Chicago," *Chicago Sun-Times,* 15 October 1992, 1.

18. Spielman and Casey, "Murders Down 13 Percent," 16.

19. Maribeth Vander Weele, "School Arrests Hit 4,306 in Four Months," *Chicago Sun-Times,* 16 January 1991, 1.

20. Illinois Criminal Justice Authority, *Trends and Issues 91,* 39. Estimates taken from the National School Safety Center in Encino, California.

21. Ibid., 50.

22. Maribeth Vander Weele, "Safety Issue Puts Chicago Schools Under the Gun," *Chicago Sun-Times,* 9 January 1992, 1.

23. Tom Seibel, "Tilden Calm; Detectors Win Praise," *Chicago Sun-Times,* 24 November 1992, 3.

24. Ibid.

25. Vander Weele, "Safety Issue Puts Chicago Schools Under the Gun," 1.

26. Board of Education, Los Angeles Unified School District, C-10, *A Start on Stopping School Weapons and Violence,* recommendations proposed by the Schools Safety and Security Task Force (22 March 1990), 10.

27. Ibid., C-7. According to the task force: "Altogether, somewhere between 2 to 3 percent of the 250,000 secondary students (7-12) were . . . transferred for disobedience, violence and protection reasons to other regular schools; in most instances, these transferees continued to disturb the educations of the other 97 to 98 percent of the students."

28. Ibid., A–2, 10. By the age of eighteen, an average American teenager will have witnessed two hundred thousand acts of violence on television, including forty thousand murders, according to the National Coalition on Television Violence.

29. Ibid., G–1. Ending the confidentiality of juvenile records was promoted in model legislation in "The Need to Know" report (Encino, Calif.: National School Safety Center, 1989).

30. Center for the Study of Social Policy, *Kids Count Data Book—State Profiles of Child Well-Being* (Washington, D.C., 1993), 12. The data book was sponsored by the Annie E. Casey Foundation.

31. Los Angeles Unified School District, *Stopping School Weapons and Violence,* G1.

32. Illinois Criminal Justice, *Trends and Issues 91,* 48. Warren DeGraff is a police sergeant in South Holland, a suburb of Chicago.

33. Maribeth Vander Weele, "Hallway Mischief Becomes Primary Lesson in the Law," *Chicago Sun-Times,* 25 October 1992, 38.

34. Vander Weele, "Teacher-Student Link Key to Fewer Dropouts," 38.

35. For example, Madeleine Maraldi, principal of the acclaimed Washington Irving School, objected when the job of truant officer Joseph Guido was cut. She noted that among Guido's duties were visiting children's homes and talking to neighbors and relatives to track down emergency information in cases where address and telephone information was invalid. At Irving, that involved 30 percent of the student body.

36. Maribeth Vander Weele, "Truant Stops Up Eighteen Thousand in City Schools," *Chicago Sun-Times,* 23 June 1993, 5.

37. Jonathan Kozol, *Savage Inequalities* (New York: Crown Publishers, 1991), 115.

38. As in Chicago, the trend was toward consolidating and eliminating alternative schools rather than creating new ones, according to Melody Sullivan, co-chair of the Los Angeles Safety Task Force.

39. Mike Royko, "You Have to Try—That's Principal of Tough School," *Chicago Daily News,* 13 March 1984, 18. The schools that handled troubled boys were Montefiore, which then stood at Thirteenth Street and Ashland Avenue, and Moseley, at Fifty-seventh Street and Lafayette Avenue. The girls' schools were Motley, 739 North Ada Street and Haven, a branch of Motley at 1472 South Wabash Avenue. Montefiore, located at 1310 South Ashland Avenue, now serves behavior-disordered children. In 1973, the $32 million Cook County Juvenile Temporary Detention Center at Ogden Avenue and Roosevelt Road replaced the former Audy Home, considered by some as a dumping ground for wayward youth. Another school, the Chicago Parental School at 3600 West Foster Avenue, was a boarding school for troubled children.

40. Ingo Keilitz and Noel Dunivant, "The Relationship between Learning Disability and Juvenile Delinquency: Current State of Knowledge," *Remedial and Special Education (RASE),* no. 3 (1986): 22. Description is taken from the Illinois Criminal Justice Information Authority's 1991 report, 57.

41. Maribeth Vander Weele, "Some Schools Halt Violence at Front Door," *Chicago Sun-Times,* 22 September 1991, 1.

42. Maribeth Vander Weele, "Phillips Parents Are Extra Eyes and Ears," *Chicago Sun-Times,* 22 September 1991, 18.

43. Maribeth Vander Weele and Maureen O'Donnell, "A Truant's Parents Put Under Court Supervision," *Chicago Sun-Times,* 9 November 1990, 1.

44. Art Golab and Maribeth Vander Weele, "Du Sable, Crete Principals Win $25,000 Awards," *Chicago Sun-Times,* 4 November 1993, 72.

45. Vander Weele, "Some Schools Halt Violence at Front Door," 1.

Chapter 8: Schoolhouses in Disrepair

1. Maribeth Vander Weele and Maureen O'Donnell, "Schools in Ruins: Sixth-grader Pleads for Repairs to Classroom," *Chicago Sun-Times,* 16 April 1991, 1. This chapter is based largely on the 1991 *Chicago Sun-Times* series entitled "Schools in Ruins."

2. Education Writers Association, *Wolves at the Schoolhouse Door—An Investigation of the Condition of Public School Buildings,* by Anne Lewis, David Bednarek, Linda Chion-Kenney, Charles Harrison, Janet Kolodzy, Kathleen McCormick, Jerry Smith, Don Speich, and Lisa Walker (Chicago, 1989): 1.

3. Tamara Henry, "Schools in Ruins Nationwide, Survey Finds," *Chicago Sun-Times,* 20 November 1991, 19. The numbers are imprecise for good reason: no national inventory of school buildings is maintained.

4. Maribeth Vander Weele, "Schools in Ruins: Troublesome National Trend: Putting Off Repairs," *Chicago Sun-Times,* 14 April 1991, 14.

5. Information supplied by the Los Angeles Unified School District.

6. Vander Weele, "Schools in Ruins: Troublesome National Trend," 14.

7. Ibid.

8. Vander Weele and O'Donnell, "Schools in Ruins: Sixth-grader Pleads for Repairs to Classroom," 1.

9. Maribeth Vander Weele, "Schools in Ruins: A Tragedy and a Lawsuit; Son's Death Blamed on Faulty Wiring," *Chicago Sun-Times,* 14 April 1991, 13.

10. Maribeth Vander Weele, "Schools in Ruins: Calumet Students 'Lucky Again'—None Hurt by Falling Ceiling," *Chicago Sun-Times,* 14 April 1991, 13.

11. Maribeth Vander Weele and Maureen O'Donnell, "Schools in Ruins: City Puts Off Repairs, Puts Children at Risk," *Chicago Sun-Times,* 14 April 1991, 1.

12. Ibid.

13. Vander Weele and O'Donnell, "Schools in Ruins: Sixth-grader Pleads for Repairs to Classroom," 1.

14. Ibid. For the years 1986 through 1990, the board expected to pay at least $1.7 million in settlements and court fees for accident claims and lawsuits resulting from dangerous building conditions, according to an incomplete summary of board projections.

15. Maribeth Vander Weele, "Falling Concrete, Rotting Wood Still Greet Students," *Chicago Sun-Times,* 10 May 1992, 13.

16. Ibid.

17. Maribeth Vander Weele, "As Upkeep Lags, Campus Vandals Have a Field Day," *Chicago Sun-Times,* 17 April 1991, 16.

18. Vander Weele and O'Donnell, "Schools in Ruins; City Puts Off Repairs," 1.

19. Vander Weele and O'Donnell, "Schools in Ruins: Sixth-grader Pleads for Repairs," 1.

20. Chicago Public Schools, *Procedures and Guidelines: Interior Painting of School Facilities by Volunteers* (Chicago, May 1993), 1, 13.

21. Vander Weele and O'Donnell, "Schools in Ruins: Sixth-grader Pleads for Repairs," 1.

22. Ibid.

23. Ibid.

24. Ibid.

25. Ibid.

26. Maureen O'Donnell, "New Fund Woes Hit City Schools; Huge Asbestos Removal, Treatment Bill for 560 Units," *Chicago Sun-Times,* 23 April 1991, 1.

27. Maribeth Vander Weele, "Classes Enter Computer Age; Poverty Funds Help Schools Buy Equipment," *Chicago Sun-Times,* 21 March 1993, 22.

28. Maribeth Vander Weele, "Special Advocate," *The Executive Editor* (May 1992): 30.

29. Maribeth Vander Weele, "City Teachers Struggle With Crowded Classes," *Chicago Sun-Times,* 30 November 1992, 21.

30. Ibid.

31. Vander Weele, "Late Teacher Hirings," 4.

32. Maribeth Vander Weele, "Around the Schools," *Chicago Sun-Times,* 24 January 1993, 22.

33. Vander Weele, "City Teachers Struggle," 21.

34. James Garbarino, Nancy Dubrow, Kathleen Kostelny, Carole Pardo, *Children in Danger* (San Francisco: Jossey-Bass Publishers, 1992), 3.

35. Education Writers Association, *Wolves at the Schoolhouse Door,* 2.

36. Vander Weele, "City Teachers Struggle," 21.

37. Maribeth Vander Weele, "Activists Say Schools Are Bursting at Seams," *Chicago Sun-Times,* 9 May 1991, 3.

38. Ibid.

39. Maureen O'Donnell and Maribeth Vander Weele, "Board Delays Maintenance to Fund Labor Contracts," *Chicago Sun-Times,* 15 April 1991, 1.

40. Vander Weele and O'Donnell, "Schools in Ruins; City Puts Off Repairs," 1.

41. Vander Weele, "Schools in Ruins: Troublesome National Trend," 14.

42. O'Donnell and Vander Weele, "Board Delays Maintenance," 1.

43. Maribeth Vander Weele, "Audit: School Board Overpaid Contractors," *Chicago Sun-Times,* 5 February 1994, 3.

44. The money came from $145 million borrowed in 1989 and $230 million borrowed in 1990.

45. Maribeth Vander Weele, "School Repair Snag; $300 Million Idled by Agency Snafus," *Chicago Sun-Times,* 6 January 1992, 1.

46. Ibid.

47. Ibid.

48. Ibid.

49. Maribeth Vander Weele, "School Repairs: Long Way to Go; A Year After Series, Some Progress," *Chicago Sun-Times,* 10 May 1992, 1.

50. Peter Schmidt, "Dade Officials Under Fire for Slow Pace of $980 Million School-Construction Effort," *Education Week,* 24 March 1993, 26.

51. New York City School Construction Authority, 1990 annual report.

52. Vander Weele and O'Donnell, "Schools in Ruins: City Puts Off Repairs," 1.

53. Maribeth Vander Weele, "Schools in Ruins: City Code Violation Cases Get Bogged Down in Courts," *Chicago Sun-Times,* 10 May 1992, 13.

54. Lou Ortiz, "Judge Calls Two Schools Unsafe for Students," *Chicago Sun-Times,* 5 March 1993, 5.

55. Ray Long, "Students Ordered Out After Alarm Violation; 775 Students Affected at Richards," *Chicago Sun-Times,* 6 June 1992, 3.

56. Maribeth Vander Weele, "Electrical Woes Jolt City Schools; Despite Gripes, Systems Not Regularly Inspected," *Chicago Sun-Times,* 13 May 1991, 1.

57. Vander Weele, "Schools in Ruins: A Tragedy and a Lawsuit," 13. Other types of buildings were inspected for fire and shock hazards. A typical inspection checked electrical distribution panels, emergency backup systems, backup system switches, auditorium aisle lights, and fire alarms; spot checks determined if extension cords were used properly. The Chicago Fire Department checked for fire violations.

58. Vander Weele, "Electrical Woes Jolt City Schools," 1.

59. O'Donnell and Vander Weele, "Board Delays Maintenance," 1.

60. Maribeth Vander Weele, "$2.5 Million Later, Plaster Still Falls," *Chicago Sun-Times,* 10 May 1992, 13.

61. Tracey Robinson, "Mom Fasts to Protest School Overcrowding," *Chicago Sun-Times,* 19 April 1989, 58.

62. Ray Long, "Four Charged After Dispute on Little Village Schools," *Chicago Sun-Times,* 10 March 1993, 14.

63. Maribeth Vander Weele, "Van Vlissingen Militants Keep Up the Pressure on a 'Cesspool,'" *Chicago Sun-Times,* 17 April 1991, 18.

64. Maribeth Vander Weele, "Councils Put Problems into the Spotlight," *Chicago Sun Times,* 14 April 1991, 14.

Chapter 9: Revolving Leadership

1. Waldman, *My Neighborhood,* 50.

2. Tracey Robinson, "Activists Rip Singer, School Board at Hearing," *Chicago Sun-Times,* 18 July 1989, 7.

3. Ray Hanania and Tracey Robinson, "Daley Names Seven to School Board; Choosing Last Eight Could Take Long, He Warns," *Chicago Sun-Times,* 12 May 1990, 1. Mayor Daley was reportedly angry that the slates picked by the nominating commission were packed with school activists who opposed him. In addition, a background check ordered by the mayor disqualified twenty-four of the forty-five candidates for reasons that included failure to meet state residency and voter registration requirements, arrest records, and questionable resumes, the *Sun-Times* reported.

4. Mary A. Johnson and Fran Spielman, "Daley Cuts Two Dissidents in School Board Revamp," *Chicago Sun-Times,* 21 May 1992, 4.

5. Fran Spielman, "Daley Rips School Board on Moratorium, Ouster," *Chicago Sun-Times,* 3 June 1992, 10. In November 1993, the legislature gave the Chicago School Finance Authority a significant amount of power on the school closing issue—but for a limited time only in 1994. The panel was given the right to recommend the so-called consolidation of attendance centers to the school board, which then had the right to explain why any specific school should remain open. The law gave the oversight panel the authority to reject the school district's budget if it was not satisfied with the board's response.

6. Maribeth Vander Weele, "School Board Ousts Cox, Faces a Furor; Activists Threaten Boycotts," *Chicago Sun-Times,* 27 May 1992, 1.

7. Scott Fornek, "City School Chiefs Have Taken Heat for Decades," *Chicago Sun-Times,* 6 November 1992, 5.

8. Herrick, *The Chicago Schools,* 281.

9. Ibid., 340–41.

10. Fornek, "City School Chiefs," 5.

11. Steve Sanders, "Some Loved Love; Some Didn't," *Chicago Tribune,* 24 July 1984, 1–2.

12. K. O. Dawes, "Reading Revamp Urged to City School Board," *Chicago Sun-Times,* 25 July 1985, 2.

13. Don Hayner, "Love Lawsuit Is Resolved," *Chicago Sun-Times,* 1 October 1985, 12.

14. Linda Lenz, "Byrd's Stamp Is on Chicago Schools," *Chicago Sun-Times,* 23 March 1986, 40.

15. Maureen O'Donnell, "Sizing Up Schools' Chiefs," *Chicago Sun-Times,* 5 August 1990, 30.

16. Linda Lenz, "Byrd Demands $25,000 Raise for Short-Term Pact," *Chicago Sun-Times,* 14 February 1989, 22.

17. Gary Putka, "Combatting Gangs: As Fears Are Driven from the Classroom, Students Start to Learn," *Wall Street Journal,* 23 April 1991, 1. See also Tracey Robinson, "School Board Sees No Conflict in Kimbrough's Activities," *Chicago Sun-Times,* 9 December 1989, 8.

18. Tracey Robinson, "Incoming School Chief Reported Asking $1 Million," *Chicago Sun-Times,* 1 November 1989, 1.

19. Tracey Robinson, "New School Chief to Earn $250,000; Package of Perks Reported Added to $175,000 Salary," *Chicago Sun-Times,* 21 October 1989, 1.

20. Linda Lenz and Tracey Robinson, "New School Chief's 'Doctor' Degree Fades to Honorary," *Chicago Sun-Times,* 19 October 1989, 35.

21. Tracey Robinson and Gilbert Jimenez, "Five Thousand Kick Off School Reform with High Hope," *Chicago Sun-Times,* 3 November 1989, 7.

22. Tracey Robinson, "Kimbrough Favors School Cops, But New Chief Scoffs at Metal Detectors," *Chicago Sun-Times,* 4 November 1989, 7.

23. Ted D. Kimbrough, Personal View, "Critics Should Help with School Reform," *Chicago Sun-Times,* 21 July 1990, 12.

24. Maribeth Vander Weele, "Take a Pay Cut? Kimbrough Insulted," *Chicago Sun-Times,* 18 May 1991, 1.

25. Maribeth Vander Weele, "Schools in Debt, Execs Travel More," *Chicago Sun-Times,* 21 July 1991, 1.

26. Maribeth Vander Weele, "Administrator Says Travel and Meetings Help Staff 'Feel Like Professionals,'" *Chicago Sun-Times,* 21 July 1991, 17. In the 1990–91 school year, Bailey's office spent $20,617 on travel, compared to $2,831 for the entire twelve months of the previous year.

27. Maribeth Vander Weele, "Kimbrough Lists Pluses as He Faces Second Review," *Chicago Sun-Times,* 13 February 1992, 4.

28. Maribeth Vander Weele, "Daley Seen Backing Kimbrough Rehiring," *Chicago Sun-Times,* 25 February 1992, 12.

29. Maribeth Vander Weele, "Kimbrough Added Up Numbers," *Chicago Sun-Times,* 7 July 1991, 5.

30. Only $300,000 of the $726,000 average were from general funds, where the board's annual shortfall lay. The rest came from categorical money, that is, from specific grants to be used for specific purposes.

31. Maribeth Vander Weele, "Kimbrough Hints He May Bow Out; School Chief Cites 'Hostile' Situation," *Chicago Sun-Times,* 24 July 1992, 1.

32. Christine Hawes, "Teachers Union President Opens Doors to Compromise," *Chicago Tribune,* 10 August 1992, 1.

33. Vander Weele, "Around the Schools," 22.

34. Maribeth Vander Weele, "Team to Run City's Schools; Board Delays Choosing Interim Superintendent," *Chicago Sun-Times,* 29 January 1993, 1.

35. Maribeth Vander Weele, "How Others Grade Kimbrough," *Chicago Sun-Times,* 6 November 1992, 4.

36. Hill and Bonan, *Decentralization and Accountability,* 14.

37. Maribeth Vander Weele, "Hardworking Stephenson Described as 'Hidden Jewel,'" *Chicago Sun-Times,* 2 February 1993, 16.

38. Maribeth Vander Weele and Rosalind Rossi, "Not Just a Bureaucrat; Argie Johnson Gets High Marks for Work in New York," *Chicago Sun-Times,* 25 May 1993, 5.

39. Rosalind Rossi and Maribeth Vander Weele, "Solid But Controversial: Wilson's Record," *Chicago Sun-Times,* 24 May 1993, 4. In New Jersey, Wilson presided over a school district that was home to East Side High, made famous by one-time principal Joe Clark, who fought a state takeover and whose unorthodox disciplinary methods included patrolling the school's hallways with a baseball bat. Nevertheless, after the controversial principal's departure, the state did assume control. Clark's story was dramatized in the movie *Lean On Me.* Meanwhile, Wilson became one of two superintendents in the country to function with only an advisory school board.

40. Maribeth Vander Weele, "Turmoil Plagues School Board; Controversy Over Cox Is One Symptom," *Chicago Sun-Times,* 30 May 1993, 6.

41. As evidence of how inexperienced leadership can kill a system, community activists pointed to the negotiation of the 1990 contract that three years later threatened to send the system spiraling into a shutdown. It was an old problem, stemming back to negotiation of the first union contract under new superintendent James Redmond in 1967, fresh from a small and prestigious Long Island suburb. "In the first negotiations, the system was particularly ill-prepared; the new superintendent had arrived in Chicago in October, and a contract was to be signed by January," wrote Paul E. Peterson in *School Politics, Chicago Style* (Chicago: University of Chicago Press, 1976, 205). "Lacking experience, he settled many minor issues having to do with grievance procedures in ways much more favorable to the union than at least one experienced negotiator felt was necessary."

42. Maribeth Vander Weele, "The Private School Difference—As Public Schools Falter, Debate Over Choice Grows," *Chicago Sun-Times,* 27 July 1992, 5.

43. Mary Jordan, "City School Chiefs Learn to Keep Bags Packed," *Chicago Sun-Times,* 14 February 1993, 12.

44. Ibid.

45. Ibid.

Chapter 10: Union Might

1. Jessica Pantoja, letter to state representative Roger P. McAuliffe (R-Chicago), spring 1992.

2. Herrick, *The Chicago Schools,* 219.

3. Cannella, *171 Years of Teaching in Chicago,* 12.

4. Kyle and Kantowicz, *Kids First,* 21.

5. Cannella, *171 Years of Teaching in Chicago,* 13.

6. Ibid. The four unions that merged were the Men-Teachers Union No. 2, Federation of Women High School Teachers No. 3, Elementary Teachers Union No. 199, and Playground Teachers Union No. 209.

7. Herrick, *The Chicago Schools,* 292.

8. Ibid., 286.

9. Steven Pratt, "Strike Club Gains Teachers Highest-Paid Status," *Chicago Tribune,* 26 September 1974, sec. 6A, p. 6.

10. Peterson, *School Politics, Chicago Style,* 191. New York City teachers won the collective bargaining right five years earlier.

11. Cannella, *171 Years of Teaching in Chicago,* 29.

12. Maribeth Vander Weele, "Schools May Seek Property Tax Hike in '95," *Chicago Sun-Times,* 15 November 1993, 3. The 1968 referendum asked voters to increase the education tax rate 15 cents from $1.86 to $2.01 per $100.00 equalized assessed valuation, according to the Chicago Board of Elections. It passed 52 to 48 percent or 242,530 to 224,613 votes.

13. Peterson, *School Politics, Chicago Style,* 194.

14. Don Hayner and Tom McNamee, *Metro Chicago Almanac* (Chicago: Bonus Books and Chicago Sun-Times, 1991), 260–61.

15. Peterson, *School Politics, Chicago Style,* 192.

16. Harry Golden, Jr., "School Terms His Idea, Daley Says," *Chicago Sun-Times,* 27 January 1973, 10.

17. Cannella, *171 Years of Teaching in Chicago,* 29. See also Pratt, "Strike Club Gains," 6.

18. Kyle and Kantowicz, *Kids First,* 30.

19. Peterson, *School Politics, Chicago Style,* 198.

20. Pratt, "Strike Club Gains," 6. See also "City's Teachers Salary No. 1 in U.S.," *Chicago Tribune,* 11 January 1973, 5. Report was based on October 1972 salaries studied by the Civic Federation. Chicago also had the highest starting salary—$10,224—for teachers with master's degrees.

21. Delia Pitts, "Schools to Open Wednesday," *Chicago Sun-Times,* 2 September 1973, 3.

22. Cannella, *171 Years of Teaching in Chicago,* 29. Peterson's figures were slightly higher: he reported the average yearly increase over that period at 12 percent.

23. Kyle and Kantowicz, *Kids First,* 30.

24. Ibid., 33. Between the time of Mayor Richard J. Daley's death in 1976 and the 1989 election of his son, Richard M. Daley, five mayors served: Michael Bilandic (1976–79); Jane M. Byrne (1979–83); Harold Washington (1983–87), the city's first African-American mayor; David Orr (1987), who acted as interim mayor; and Eugene Sawyer (1987–89).

25. The antiestablishment newspaper *Substance* complained that millions of dollars that should have gone to schools were siphoned off instead to pay back interest on bonds owed the financial sector. In 1993, the finance authority still owed $473 million in bond principal alone, according to the Chicago Public Building Commission's report on building revenue bonds, series A of 1993, which summarized work of the various agencies involved with the schools.

26. Two members of the five-member panel were appointed by the governor and two by the mayor. The chairperson was a joint appointment. The law granted the oversight panel the power to reorganize the board's financial accounts, management, and budget systems "in whatever manner the authority deems appropriate to achieve greater financial responsibility and to reduce financial inefficiency according

to the reform legislation." Some felt the panel's right to approve or reject all contracts to be a bit excessive. Those strict powers were fiercely opposed by some segments of the African-American community because, as one veteran insider put it, it was seen as a way for the white business structure to retain control of jobs and contracts in a system lead by African Americans.

27. The time and length of Chicago teachers' strikes and highlights of the settlements can be summarized as follows:

> May 1969: two days, $100 a month, 725 new jobs (in the following year, there was no strike but teachers gained an average 14 percent pay increase);
>
> January 1971: four days, 13.5 percent pay raise over two years, 600 new jobs, early closing;
>
> January 1973: twelve days, 2.5 percent raise, 210 new jobs, shortened work week translating into another 2.5 percent wage increase;
>
> September 1975: eleven days, 5 percent raise, schools closed sixteen days early;
>
> January 1980: ten days, 8 percent raise, 504 workers rehired;
>
> October 1983: fifteen days, 5 percent raise effective midyear, 2.5 percent bonus pay;
>
> December 1984: ten days, 4.5 percent raise effective midyear, 2.5 percent bonus pay;
>
> September 1985: two days, 9 percent raise over two years;
>
> October 1987: nineteen days, 8 percent raise over two years.
>
> Beginning pay for a first-year teacher with a bachelor's degree rose from $5,500 in 1966 to $8,400 in 1970 and to $11,000 in 1975. It rose from $13,770 in 1980 to $17,137 in 1985 to $26,447 (including a 7 percent contribution to the pension fund) in November 1990. The 1993 rate was $29,147, which included a pension fund contribution, for a thirty-nine week work year. See Cannella, *171 Years of Teaching in Chicago*. See also "Past Teacher Strikes," *Chicago Sun-Times*, 30 September 1987, 4.

28. Maureen O'Donnell, "$250 Million School Contract; On-Time Opening 'Guaranteed,'" *Chicago Sun-Times*, 31 July 1990, 1.

29. Dipping into reserves was accomplished through easing the so-called restriction calculation, which set the minimum to be kept in reserves to pay bills. In 1992, the finance authority gave the school board approval to use $21.7 million of such funds. The so-called speedup of state aid was possible because the state's fiscal year began two months before the school year, allowing 1993 state money to be spent during the board's 1992 fiscal year. The governor had to approve such action, which, in 1992, amounted to $42.3 million. The board routinely counted on both avenues to reduce its annual short-

fall, but the results of such measures usually came through only in the last days of August.

30. Chicago Board of Education statistics.

31. Kyle and Kantowicz, *Kids First,* 307.

32. The state aid formula is written so that when a school district's property tax wealth increases, state aid decreases. State aid for Chicago schools, therefore, dropped by $80 million on the heels of a large increase in property tax revenues after the city was reassessed in 1991 for tax purposes. At that time, the value of Chicago property increased 18.6 percent. State revenue also dropped because the 1990 census counted far fewer poor children in the city than a decade earlier. A number of urban school districts disputed similar census findings. In the 1994 fiscal year (September 1, 1993 to August 31, 1994), property tax revenue for Chicago schools also dropped by $35 million. Meanwhile, the transfer of state Chapter One funds to schools created a $38 million hole in the 1994 basic budget, while the loss of pension funds that were previously channeled to the basic fund led to another $55 million gap. The system also was due to lose the traditional speedup of state aid—although the governor eventually agreed to continue it. In addition, the finance authority eased the restriction calculation as it had done in the past to $21.7 million, but until that amount was approved, the number was part of the $415 million shortfall. See Greg Richmond, "Senate Democratic Concurrence Analysis, 88th General Assembly," Senate Bill 132, 2. The Chicago Panel on Public School Policy and Finance noted also that federal funds dropped by $22.9 million in 1994, partly because of the lower calculation of low-income students.

33. Maribeth Vander Weele and Maureen O'Donnell, "School Bill Soars; Board Unveils Shortfall Today; Union Pact Cost Takes a Leap," *Chicago Sun-Times,* 1 May 1991, 1. At least ten thousand teachers received seniority increases of an additional 5 percent in the first year of the contract. Further, nearly three thousand teachers received increases of as much as $1,700 for completing postgraduate work for advanced degrees.

34. Maureen O'Donnell, "40 Percent of City Teachers Got a 12 Percent Raise; Board Pegs Hikes at $76.7 Million," *Chicago Sun-Times,* 29 May 1991, 1.

35. Maribeth Vander Weele, "Lake Forest District First in Teacher Pay," *Chicago Sun-Times,* 16 November 1993, 15.

36. Chicago Panel on Public School Policy and Finance statistics.

37. Maribeth Vander Weele, "Schools Hoping to Bag $1 Billion; Board Asks Big Hike in Property Tax Levy," *Chicago Sun-Times*, 9 December 1991, 1. Because Chicago property owners have always paid less for schools than their suburban counterparts, the Chicago Panel on Public School Policy and Finance was among the groups that advocated a property tax increase for education. "The mayor has committed the board of education to spend what it doesn't have," argued executive director G. Alfred Hess, Jr. "Unless he wants to repeat the fiscal fiasco of his father, which led to the collapse of 1979, he's going to have to come up with new revenues for next year. And the property tax is the only viable source." Hess pointed out that it was Daley, after all, who directly appointed the interim board.

But interim board vice president William S. Singer blamed the problems on the reform act provision itself that, over a period of five years, transferred control of an estimated $250 million in state Chapter One poverty funds to schools without replacing it. The transfer was supposed to address an old injustice—previously money had been used for general purposes and controlled by the administration. It was, in fact, intended to supplement the education of poor children, not provide basic education for all children. The legislature mandated the transfer, but it did not replenish funds lost to the basic program. Years later, Singer would explain, "The law was imperfect. It shifted money out. It locked people in like supernumeraries, and the tradeoff was to get the concept passed. All we are four years later is at a point where those actions—particularly shifting supplemental out of basic—is an enormous burden." As Hess pointed out, however, the property tax increase—amounting to twice the loss in state Chapter One funds from the basic budget—would have solved the monetary crunch if that had been the only problem. Instead, Hess blamed the 1990 wage settlement for "bankrupting the system."

38. Maribeth Vander Weele, "Board Member Wants Focus on Student Gains," *Chicago Sun-Times*, 14 May 1993, 12.

39. National Education Association, *Status of the American Public School Teacher*, 43.

40. Vander Weele, "Board Member Wants Focus," 12.

41. John "Jack" Valinote confirmation hearing before Chicago City Council, 2 June 1992.

42. Maribeth Vander Weele, "Teachers, Board Set for Battle Over Cuts," *Chicago Sun-Times*, 7 April 1993, 1.

43. No Republican legislators were invited to the city hall talks.

44. Rosalind Rossi, "School Breakthrough; Leaders Agree on Pact; Focus Shifts to Springfield," *Chicago Sun-Times*, 10 November 1993, 1.

45. Maribeth Vander Weele, "Teachers Accept Contract; Leaders Thought Strike Too Risky," *Chicago Sun-Times,* 22 October 1993, 6.

46. "Highlights of Tentative Pact," *Chicago Sun-Times,* 10 October 1993, 4. There were other contract provisions. Beginning in fall 1994, teachers are allowed to work and receive full pay for five additional days per year for work-related training, at a cost of $10 million. Schools can waive any contract provision if 63.5 percent of the individual school's union members approve, down from 70 percent previously—a provision that was changed to 51 percent by 1995. The provision affected such issues as school starting time and structuring. A second early retirement program for teachers was also created.

47. Rosalind Rossi and Ray Long, "Court Order Opens Schools; Teachers Return Today, Students Tomorrow," *Chicago Sun-Times,* 14 September 1993, 1.

48. Maribeth Vander Weele and Rosalind Rossi, "Teacher Talks at Impasse as Closing Deadline Nears," *Chicago Sun-Times,* 9 October 1993, 1.

49. Daniel J. Lehmann and Rosalind Rossi, "Schools Ordered: Stay Open Ten Days; Progress Reported in Pact Talks," *Chicago Sun-Times,* 9 October 1993, 1.
    On October 8, 1993, U.S. District judge James H. Alesia authorized a separate ten-day waiver after three mothers of six Hispanic and African-American children filed suit challenging the constitutionality of the Illinois School Code that required a balanced budget for Chicago schools alone. Attorneys for the students argued the law violated the children's constitutional rights to equal protection since nearly 90 percent of the city's school population is a protected minority class. No predominantly white school districts—more than one hundred of which were also forced to borrow money to operate—faced similar restrictions, they maintained. Four days later, as it appeared that Kocoras would continue to keep the schools open, the plaintiffs withdrew the suit.

50. Rosalind Rossi and Daniel J. Lehmann, "Schools to Face Monday Closing; Federal Ruling Puts Pressure on Legislature," *Chicago Sun-Times,* 11 November 1993, 1. Chief Justice Richard A. Posner and former Chief Justice William J. Bauer made the ruling. As for a permanent solution, the Chicago Board of Education, through desegregation attorney Robert Howard, asked Kocoras to permanently solve the matter by giving the system authority to issue bonds, divert $55 million from teacher pension funds for two years, and use $18 million in poverty funds for basic programs. See Lee Bey and Rosalind Rossi, "School Shutdown Up to Judge Now," *Chicago Sun-Times,* 23 September 1993, 1.

51. Senate Bill 132, which emerged as the legislative compromise, addresses the issue of newly named "reserve teachers" as follows: If principals fail to fill vacancies with fully certificated teachers within sixty days after their positions are created or become vacant, the board shall appoint reserve teachers to the positions. This measure prohibits principals from appointing any teacher with less than a full certificate. If no vacancy exists in the reserve teachers' areas of certification, they shall be appointed on an interim basis to teaching positions as long as they begin retraining in areas of special need (typically bilingual or special education). Reserve teachers retain all rights, salaries, and benefits for twenty school months. At that point, they have completed retraining and, therefore, are eligible for permanent appointments; however, if they are not appointed within twenty-five months, they will be discharged.

52. In 1992, the education tax rate was $2.427 per $100.00 equalized assessed valuation and the total tax rate—excluding separate taxes for the Chicago School Finance Authority—was $4.222. See Board of Education, *1992 Annual Financial Report* (Chicago, 23 December 1992), 56.

53. Peter Schmidt, "Voters Oust Three Reformers from Detroit School Board," *Education Week,* 11 November 1992, 5.

54. Maribeth Vander Weele, "Trying to Engineer Upkeep, Principals Are Powerless to Order Repairs," *Chicago Sun-Times,* 18 April 1991, 19.

55. Maribeth Vander Weele, "Union Rules Don't Stop Principal," *Chicago Sun-Times,* 28 March 1993, 26.

56. Maribeth Vander Weele, "Overtime for Maintenance Staff at City Schools Tops $6 Million," *Chicago Sun-Times,* 11 August 1991, 35.

57. Tracey Robinson, "Engineers, School Board Okay Access for Councils," *Chicago Sun-Times,* 25 January 1990, 76.

58. Tracey Robinson, "School Councils Get 'Rent' Jolt; Must Pay to Meet at Schools After Hours," *Chicago Sun-Times,* 8 November 1989, 7.

59. William Rankin, The Forum, "Bureaucracy Smothers True School Reform; Principals Lack Meaningful Control," *Chicago Sun-Times,* 5 December 1992, 18.

60. Vander Weele, "Chicago's Schools: An 'Impossible Job'?" 4.

61. Vander Weele, "Trying to Engineer Upkeep," 19.

62. Maribeth Vander Weele, "Schools Also Pay OT for Trades Work," *Chicago Sun-Times,* 11 August 1991, 36.

63. Tracey Robinson, "School Chief 'Appalled' at Office Renovation Tab," *Chicago Sun-Times,* 31 March 1990, 4.

64. First Chicago Capital Markets, Inc., *The Chicago Board of Education, May 1993,* by Ronald Heller (Chicago, May 1993), 2.

65. Maribeth Vander Weele and Maureen O'Donnell, "Schools Stretch Union Policies to Get Repairs Made," *Chicago Sun-Times,* 18 April 1991, 19.

66. The school system also had several hundred "firemen" on the payroll, positions created decades ago to care for coal-burning furnaces that had long been made obsolete before the arrival of school reform. Their job titles were changed to school maintenace assistants, and their duties were somewhat similar to custodians although their salaries were higher. Eliminating their positions or converting their job titles to custodians was prohibited by union contract, but it would have saved more than $20 million a year, according to the Citizens Schools Committee.

   According to the 1990 union contract, the duties of a school maintenance assistant include the following: start boilers and heating and air conditioning systems manually or automatically; ensure proper heat in a building; maintain mechanical equipment throughout the building; record indicator readings of building temperatures, pressures, lubrication, and safety inspection dates; perform emergency and preventive maintenance services; clean internal and external boiler surfaces, combustion chambers, breechings, mechanical equipment areas, and equipment; shovel snow, clean, and maintain building grounds, as assigned by the engineer custodian; and monitor the operation of compressors, pumps, heaters, feed-water tanks, and other mechanical equipment.

67. Senate Bill 132 changed the Illinois School Code (chapter 122, section 34–8.1) to read as follows: "Principals shall be employed to supervise the operation of each attendance center. The authority of the principal shall include the authority to direct the hours during which the attendance center shall be open and available for use provided the use complies with Board Rules and Policies and collective bargaining agreements . . . In recognition of the need for continuity of service and safety of pupils, personnel, and the general public, the Engineer In Charge is responsible at all times for the proper operation and maintenance of the physical plant and grounds to which he is assigned. So that educational programs may operate successfully, the engineer in charge for each attendance center shall be under the general supervision of the principal subject to other provisions set forth in collective bargaining agreements, the policies, rules, and regulations of the board, and all applicable federal, state, and local law. If the engineer in charge reasonably believes that an order of the principal may require him to violate the provisions of federal, state, or local

law, the engineer in charge may refer the matter to the director of the department of facilities, whose decision shall be final."

68. *1992 Annual Financial Report,* 56.

Chapter 11: No Accountability, No Controls

1. The money comes from pop machines; candy, doughnut, and photo sale fundraisers; athletic events; student fees; school publications; club fees; and donations from foundations and businesses. Examples of purposes for which the money may be used include classroom materials other than textbooks; school publications; plays and productions; sports equipment; student activities such as dances and musicals; science, math, and history fairs; student groups such as band, ROTC, and science clubs; supplies for removing graffiti; and furniture. Examples for which the money may not be used include memberships in professional organizations that directly benefit individuals; payments to educator groups such as the Chicago Principals Association; luncheons to celebrate retirements or promotions; faculty socials; floral pieces; contributions to fund-raising drives; and expenditures for which there is inadequate or no documentation. Source: *Chicago Board of Education Internal Accounts Manual* (Chicago, June 1987).

2. Larry Weintraub, "School Faces Payroll Probe; Gage Park Teacher Cites Extra Check," *Chicago Sun-Times,* 4 June 1992, 3.

3. Senate Resolution S87.

4. Chicago Board of Education audit of Gage Park High School, 15 July 1992. See also Maribeth Vander Weele, "Allegations by Auditors at Three Schools," *Chicago Sun-Times,* 21 November 1993, 14. In the audit, then principal Carol A. Faulk responded in part that the auditor was confused about the work sites and that she would have provided the proper addresses had the auditor only asked. The auditor responded that there was no confusion. "The sites (five of ten) simply do not exist," the report stated.

5. Faulk also reported in the audit that many of the activities were never logged "even though auditors confirmed during student interviews that these activities were an integral part of the program and the teachers had 'put in the time.'" Auditors responded that no students were able to so confirm and, in fact, they insisted that certain extracurricular activities occurred during the regular school day.

6. Mary A. Johnson, "Gage Park Principal Denies; 'Brown Envelope Day' Called Untrue," *Chicago Sun-Times,* 5 June 1992, 18.

7. Chicago Board of Education audit of Crane High School, 26 March 1991. See also Vander Weele, "Allegations by Auditors," 21.

8. Chicago Board of Education audit of Henderson Elementary School, 10 April 1992.

9. Vander Weele, "Allegations by Auditors," 21.

10. "Examples of Auditors' Conclusions," *Chicago Sun-Times,* 21 November 1993, 14.

11. Maribeth Vander Weele, "Schools' Missing Money: Audits Find Improper Student Fund Use," *Chicago Sun-Times,* 21 November 1993, 1.

12. In 1992, Garvy Elementary School was one of nearly twenty Chicago schools that declined or failed to improve from 1990 to 1992 in both math and reading test scores in every grade tested. See "Chicago Schools in Decline," *Chicago Sun-Times,* 30 November 1992, 21.

13. Vander Weele, "Schools' Missing Money," 1.

14. Lillian Williams, "School Board Ex-aide, Bus Operator Get Three-and-one-half Years in $1 Million Swindle," *Chicago Sun-Times,* 9 May 1989, 67. The payoff scandal involved charges against two bus companies and Donald Sparks, a former administrator in the board's department of management. Sparks was sentenced to three-and-one-half years in prison after pleading guilty to accepting payoffs for assigning favorable bus routes to Northtown Bus Service. Company owner Julius Polan received the same sentence after admitting he received money for bus services never provided. He agreed to repay the board $1.2 million.

15. Chicago Board of Education audit summaries, 1985–92.

16. Anonymous letter, 10 June 1991, to Coffey.

17. Anonymous letter, 11 June 1991, to Coffey.

18. Author has chosen to keep the council chair's name confidential.

19. Letter, 12 July 1991, to *Chicago Sun-Times* columnist Raymond R. Coffey. Author has requested confidentiality.

20. Mark Schaver, "Boysen Calls for Board's Removal," *Louisville Courier-Journal,* 8 July 1993, 1.

21. Ibid.

22. "State Journal: Kentucky Finger Pointing; Brisk Ethics Business," *Education Week,* 23 June 1993, 29.

23. Special Commissioner of Investigation for the New York City School District, *A System Like No Other: Fraud and Misconduct by New York City School Custodians,* by Suzan R. Flamm, Regina A. Loughran, and Leah Keith (New York, November 1992), 5.

24. Ibid.

25. Stancik claims it is the only school post like it in the country.

26. Maribeth Vander Weele, "New York's Crackdown; Powerful Unit Ferrets Out Scams," *Chicago Sun-Times,* 21 November 1993, 16.

27. In one example, a principal who was skilled in electrical work responded, though begrudgingly, to a school board member's repeated requests to do work around her home, including checking electrical wiring, putting up a chandelier, and moving boxes of a tenant, Stancik alleged. See Special Commissioner of Investigation for the New York City School District, *Power, Politics, and Patronage: Education in Community School District 12,* by Lydia G. Segal, Donald F. Schwally, Jr., and Tracy Kramer (New York, April 1993), 85.

28. Ibid., 8–9. One school board member pulled no punches about the education offered in that district: "Nobody in their right mind is gonna send their kids to District 12. I didn't send mine to District 12 . . . Uh-uh, you're not retarding my children."

29. Ibid., 2.

30. Ibid., 42.

31. Ibid., 10.

32. School board members are selected as follows: Chicago's eleven sub-district councils—comprised of local school council members—send representatives to sit on a nominating commission. The commission is made up of two subdistrict council members from each elementary district and three from the lone high school district, plus five mayoral appointees. Further, the commission screens applicants for the school board and submits to the mayor three names for every opening. The mayor chooses one name from each slate or rejects the slates. The appointments require ratification by the city council.

33. Maribeth Vander Weele, "Principal Linked to Missing Funds Will Be Able to Teach," *Chicago Sun-Times,* 25 June 1992, 12.

34. Maribeth Vander Weele, "Few Were Aware Spending Exceeded the Budget," *Chicago Sun-Times*, 12 April 1993, 6.

35. Ibid.

36. The board authorized specific computer purchases but was not told they exceeded the budget, school officials said. After researching the unusual overruns, Charley Gillispie attributed some of them to a change in accounting practices after accountants compressed $4.8 million of long-term contracts into one year. School officials said overruns were recommended by outside auditors because the computer department had stretched out its consultant contracts over several years in order to make its immediate budget appear smaller at a time when massive cuts to central office were taking place.

37. In early 1994, the matter was still the subject of an FBI investigation. See Maribeth Vander Weele, "Audit Finds Schools Lost $156,000 in Overcharge," *Chicago Sun-Times*, 31 December 1992, 1. IBM officials maintained that they did not know the unauthorized contract was improper. "We believed we were doing business in good faith with the people authorized to do it," said Kathy Riemer, a spokesperson for the computer giant.

38. Based on *Chicago Sun-Times* analysis of Chicago Board of Education spending reports.

39. Ortiz, "Appeals Court Voids School Board Health Pact," 18.

40. Maribeth Vander Weele, "Court Ruling Backs Bidding for Health Care," *Chicago Sun-Times*, 5 December 1993, 6.

41. The type of insurance that the court said should be bid involved services provided by a health maintenance organization (HMO). The type of insurance for which Grant negotiated—and school officials said did not need to be bid—was a preferred provider organization (PPO). Under an HMO, employees are limited to the doctors provided by the HMO. Under a PPO, employees have a second option: choosing their own doctors for a higher price. Board officials originally argued the HMO was not subject to bid because they viewed the contracts as professional services, and professional services are exempt from bidding because they demand specific skills that cannot be considered in cost comparisons. Based on the testimony of David Dranove the court ruled that HMOs are not exempt because they do not provide medical services directly but only administer them and, therefore, the question of medical skill was not involved. Why would PPOs then be exempt? Because the lawsuit that generated the appellate court ruling, the board argued, was filed by an HMO and, therefore, the question of bidding PPOs was never addressed.

42. Maribeth Vander Weele, "Aggressive Spirit Runs in the Family," *Chicago Sun-Times,* 5 December 193, 6. See also Maribeth Vander Weele, "School Benefits Director Jumps to Blue Cross Job," *Chicago Sun-Times,* 5 June 1991, 4.

43. "How you write the specs can determine who gets the bid," explains board member Stephen Ballis, who pushed for the move. "You can write so only one person can be the vendor." See Maribeth Vander Weele, "Schools Save $3 Million on Food Deal," *Chicago Sun-Times,* 28 December 1992, 4.

44. Through discount airline and hotel rates, Richardson estimated the company paid about $700 per person for one conference in Phoenix. See Maribeth Vander Weele, "Trips Lure School Cash; City Educators Fly Free; Computer Firms Get Sales," *Chicago Sun-Times,* 21 March 1993, 1.

45. The list of individual pieces was confirmed with Educational Management Group officials.

46. Maribeth Vander Weele, "School Costs Do Not Compute; Outdated Systems, Chaotic Procedures Lead to Cost Overruns," *Chicago Sun-Times,* 12 April 1993, 6. The estimates are based on a summary of purchase order reports of major computer vendors and on board of education reports that set an upper limit on computer spending.

47. Washington, Pittman, and McKeever, *Chicago Board of Education Agreed-Upon Procedures* (Chicago, 23 November 1992), 7.

48. Maribeth Vander Weele, "It's Always Been Done That Way," *Chicago Sun-Times,* 12 April 1993, 6.

Chapter 12: A Legislative Will

1. Maureen O'Donnell, "Students Want Less Talk, More Action from Summit," *Chicago Sun-Times,* 28 March 1993, 25.

2. Legislative Research Commission, *The Kentucky Education Reform Act of 1990, A Citizens Handbook,* by Mary Helen Miller, Kevin Noland, and John Schaaf (Frankfort, Ky., September 1991), 1. Excerpt from Supreme Court opinion *Rose v. Council For Better Education, Inc.* KY 790 S.W. 2d 186 (1989).

3. Ibid., 14, 15. Admittedly, some researchers questioned whether barring relatives from working together was a good idea. In some towns with largely blue-collar populations, only a few educated families worked in education—and such a rule limited their employment,

harming both the families and the school districts that benefitted from their expertise.

4. The state of Kentucky increased its income tax revenue by eliminating the deduction taxpayers could claim for paying federal income tax. Thus, individuals could no longer deduct their federal income tax payments on their state income tax returns, according to public information officer Stephen K. Swift.

5. National Education Association, *Rankings of the States,* 21.

6. Olson, "From Risk to Reform," S4–S11.

7. In spring 1993, 140,000 Kentucky students in fourth, eighth, and twelfth grades took statewide tests in four subject areas. Comparisons between the 1991–92 and the 1992–93 school year are as follows:
   Fourth grade: reading, up 53 percent; mathematics, up 15 percent; science, down 2 percent; social studies, no change. Eighth grade: reading, up 10 percent; mathematics, up 8 percent; science, up 25 percent; social studies, down 7 percent. Twelfth grade: reading, up 17 percent; mathematics, down 1 percent; science, down 6 percent; social studies, down 26 percent.
   Source: Kentucky Department of Education, Office of Communications press release, 27 September 1993.

8. The Business Roundtable, *The Essential Components of a Successful Education System: Putting Policy into Practice,* by Terri Bergman, Frederick S. Edelstein, and Maria B. Lloyd (Washington, D.C., December 1992), 14. See also Mark Walsh, "Business Group's Reforms Need Long-Term Backing, Report Says," *Education Week,* 13 January 1993, 21.

9. Senate Bill 132, adopted in November 1993, reads as follows: "The [finance] authority shall appoint an inspector general who shall have the authority to conduct investigations into allegations of or incidents of waste, fraud, and financial mismanagement in public education within the board's jurisdiction by an employee or contractor of the board. The inspector general shall make recommendations to the authority about its investigations. The inspector general shall be appointed for a term of four years. The inspector general shall be independent of the operations of the authority and the board and perform other duties requested by the authority. The inspector general shall have access to all information and personnel necessary to perform the duties of the office. If the inspector general determines that a possible criminal act has been committed or that special expertise is required in the investigation, he shall immediately notify the Chicago Police Department and the Cook County State's Attorney. All investigations conducted by the inspector general shall be conducted

in a manner that ensures the preservation of evidence for use in criminal prosecutions. At all times the inspector general shall be granted access to any building or facility that is owned, operated, or leased by the authority or the board. The inspector general shall have the power to subpoena witnesses and compel the production of books and papers pertinent to an investigation authorized by this code. Any person who fails to appear in response to a subpoena, to answer any question, to produce any books or papers pertinent to an investigation under this code; or knowingly gives false testimony during an investigation under this code is guilty of a Class A misdemeanor. The inspector general shall provide to the authority and the Illinois General Assembly a summary of reports and investigations made under this section for the previous fiscal year no later than January 1 of each year. The summaries shall detail the final disposition of those recommendations. The summaries shall not contain any confidential or identifying information concerning the subjects of the reports and investigations. The summaries shall also include detailed recommended administrative actions and matters for consideration by the general assembly."

10. Maribeth Vander Weele, "Legislature May Probe Missing School Funds," *Chicago Sun-Times,* 25 November 1993, 22.

11. Technically, suburban and downstate schools had a longer process. Instead of providing forty-five days of remediation—the opportunity given Chicago teachers to improve—schools outside Chicago are required to give teachers one year before the dismissal process can begin. The rigid criteria for dismissing a teacher, however, apply equally in all areas.

12. From 1989–90 to 1991–92, Illinois districts issuing bonds to raise money for day-to-day operations numbered 217, according to the Illinois State Board of Education. Source: Molly Dunn and Lorraine Forte, "Districts Take On More Debt than Chicago," *Catalyst* (November 1993): 1.

13. Arthur Andersen and Company, *Board of Education of the City of Chicago, 1992 Annual Financial Report* (Chicago, 23 December 1992), 24.

14. Lynn Sweet, "Lottery's Profits: School Bonanza or Shell Game?" *Chicago Sun-Times,* 29 March 1988, 4.

15. Lynn Iglarsh, "Elementary and Secondary Education in Illinois," *Comptroller's Monthly Fiscal Report* (March/April 1993), 3.

16. Lynn Sweet, "Myth that Won't Die: Lottery Boosts Schools," *Chicago Sun-Times,* 5 May 1991, 5.

17. Lynn Sweet, "Are the Poor Being Taken By Lottery?" *Chicago Sun-Times,* 27 March 1988, 4.

18. Dawn Clark Netsch, *The Netsch Plan: Dawn Clark Netsch for Governor* (Chicago, February 1994), 18–29. See also Maribeth Vander Weele, "Fighting for the Schools; Voters Want Answers on Reform," *Chicago Sun-Times,* 13 February 1994, 14.

19. Because the amendment did not spell out the implications, Republicans who opposed it argued that the public did not understand that the measure would have increased state income taxes.

20. In an annual "worry index" compiled each year by the Coalition for Consumer Rights in Illinois, public schools in 1993 scored the highest worry average in the four years of the poll; public education also carried the No. 1 rank in every region of the state. See Zay N. Smith, "'Worry Index' Up; Education Is Illinois Voters' Top Concern, Poll Finds," *Chicago Sun-Times,* 25 October 1993, 1.

21. U.S. Department of Education, National Center for Education statistics. Based on information released 3 September 1993 by the communications office.

22. Iglarsh, "Elementary and Secondary Education in Illinois," 5. Numbers provided also by the Illinois State Board of Education.

23. Numbers are actually for the 1990–91 school year. See National Education Association, *Rankings of the States,* 58.

24. Maribeth Vander Weele, "School Meal Funds Fall Through Cracks; Up To $36 Million Unclaimed By City," *Chicago Sun-Times,* 3 May 1993, 1.

25. Chicago Board of Education, Department of Financial Planning and Budgeting, *Comparisons of Per Pupil Spending,* by Buzz Sawyer (Chicago, 29 March 1993), 3.

26. The numbers of special education children have risen from 40,428 in the 1989–90 school year to 46,880 in the 1992–93 school year. See Chicago Board of Education, *Report to the Budget Committee on Serving Children with Disabilities,* by Charlene A. Green (Chicago, 1993). Green is the associate superintendent of the Department of Special Education and Pupil Support Services.

27. Andersen and Company, *Board of Education, 1992 Annual Financial Report,* 52.

28. Maribeth Vander Weele, "Alter School Work Rules, Funding, Simon Says," *Chicago Sun-Times,* 27 July 1993, 10.

29. Maribeth Vander Weele, "The Private School Difference; As Public Schools Falter, Debate Over Choice Grows," *Chicago Sun-Times,* 27 July 1992, 5.

30. Chicago Board of Education, *Board of Education of the City of Chicago, 1992 Annual Financial Report* (Chicago, 1992), 59.

31. Chicago Board of Education, Department of Equal Educational Opportunity Programs and Department of Research, Evaluation, and Planning, *Special Report on Busing, Presented at the Request of Board Member Albert Logan* (Chicago, 6 December 1991).

32. Based on the author's analysis of the "Plan for the Improvement of Instruction for Disadvantaged Students in the Chicago Public Schools," *Chicago Public Schools,* July 1993.

33. Education Commission of the States, *School Finance Litigation: A Historical Summary,* by Mary Fulton and David Long (Denver, Colo., April 1993), 1. They include Arkansas, California, Connecticut, Kentucky, Montana, New Jersey, Tennessee, Texas, Washington, West Virginia, and Wyoming. Another twelve states upheld their systems as constitutional, including Arizona, Colorado, Georgia, Idaho, Maryland, Michigan, New York, Ohio, Oklahoma, Oregon, Pennsylvania, and Wisconsin.

34. Ray Long and Maribeth Vander Weele, "A Squeeze Play for School Bucks; Luxuries v. Outdated Texts Cited in Suit," *Chicago Sun-Times,* 14 November 1990, 1.

35. *The Committee of Educational Rights et al v. James R. Thompson,* governor of the State of Illinois; *Illinois State Board of Education;* and *Robert Leininger,* state superintendent of education, 35–37.

36. There's more to it. Chicagoans paid a greater percentage of their property tax bills to city and county services, such as the county hospital, museums, and police. Perhaps one explanation for the reluctance to increase property taxes was that the influential business community would take the brunt of the increase. In Cook County—unlike elsewhere in the state—commercial and industrial property is valued for taxation purposes at a higher rate and homes taxed at a lower rate than their collar-county counterparts. Still, this did not stop Mayor Daley from proposing additional property taxes for the city while using his influence to kill property tax increases for the schools.

37. Iglarsh, "Elementary and Secondary Education in Illinois," 5. The 1993–94 budgeted figure was provided by the Illinois State Board of Education.

Chapter 13: Heroes on the Front Lines

1. O'Donnell, "Students Want Less Talk, More Action," 25.

2. Maribeth Vander Weele, "Parents Turn Activist for School Councils," *Chicago Sun-Times,* 13 October 1991, 4.

3. Maribeth Vander Weele, "This School Reform Gets High Grades," *Chicago Sun-Times,* 30 November 1991, 1.

4. From a written statement presented at a 9 March 1992 legislative hearing sponsored by State Rep. Ellis Levin (D-Chicago), to discuss the school superintendency.

5. Maribeth Vander Weele, "Plea After Plea Hits School Board; Testimony Outlines Effects of Closings," *Chicago Sun-Times,* 23 May 1991, 3.

6. Rosalind Rossi, "Edison's Gifted Pupils Glow Brightest in the City," *Chicago Sun-Times,* 17 November 1993, 5. Edison has about 17 percent low-income students; roughly a third of its student population is white, not quite a third is Asian, and the remaining students are Hispanic, African American, and Native American.

7. Vander Weele, "New Program Gets Would-be Teachers into Class," 2.

8. Forte, "Bad Teachers Worry Teacher Leaders," 1.

9. Vander Weele, "Parents Enlist as Aides," 17.

10. Editorial, "O'Toole School Shows Success Starts at Home," *Chicago Sun-Times,* 18 April 1993, 43.

11. Maribeth Vander Weele, "Enrichment for Mind, Body Shores Up Four City Schools," *Chicago Sun-Times,* 8 December 1991, 5.

12. Illinois Bell, Ameritech Foundation and Chicago Public Schools Alumni Association, *Local School Councils' Ideas and Successes; Chicago School Reform: Year Three* (Chicago, 1992).

13. Maribeth Vander Weele, "State Gives Twelve Educators 'Distinguished' Honors," *Chicago Sun-Times,* 15 November 1990, 4.

14. Maureen O'Donnell, "Principal at Dyett Pushes Teamwork," *Chicago Sun-Times,* 28 March 1993, 27.

15. Maribeth Vander Weele, "Class Gives Kids a Dose Of Real Life In Miniature," *Chicago Sun-Times,* 25 October 1992, 3.

16. Scott Fornek, "Free Nursing Clinic to Open on West Side," *Chicago Sun-Times,* 19 October 1993, 16.

17. Vander Weele, "Class Gives Kids a Dose of Real Life," 3.

18. Maribeth Vander Weele, "School at Shelter Makes Sure Kids' Education Not Neglected," *Chicago Sun-Times,* 29 November 1991, 3. Haran retired in 1993.

Chapter 14: Conclusion: Chaos and Hope

1. See Kyle and Kantowicz, *Kids First,* 264.

2. Page Smith, *The Shaping of America: A People's History of the Young Republic* (New York: Penguin Books, 1980), 360. The roots of such idealism are largely European. In the sixteenth century, Protestant reformer Martin Luther labored to promote schooling for the common people—regardless of gender or social class—at public expense. His goal was to enable all classes to read the Bible. Roman Catholic educators responded. The Spanish nobleman Ignatius of Loyola, for example, pioneered the Jesuit system of education, a system that incorporated teaching methods dependent on questioning, memorization, and competition—mainstays of education today.

3. Maribeth Vander Weele, "Suspension Room Cuts Class-skipping," *Chicago Sun-Times,* 21 October 1990, 17.

4. Vander Weele, "Schools Missing Money," 1.

5. Maribeth Vander Weele, "A Look in the Mirror; Schools Prepare for Self-examination at Summit," *Chicago Sun-Times,* 26 March 1993, 6.

6. Kerchner and Koppich, *A Union of Professionals,* 178. Ayers wrote the chapter on Chicago and its school labor relations.

7. Mary O'Connell, *School Reform, Chicago Style* (Chicago: Center for Neighborhood Technology, 1991), 3.

8. Andrew Herrmann, "Lane Grid Team Cheers for an End to the Strike," *Chicago Sun-Times,* 3 October 1987, 4.

9. O'Connell, *School Reform, Chicago Style,* 2.

10. Academic standards should always take into consideration factors beyond school control, such as sudden increases in the enrollment of bilingual students, teacherless classrooms, or enormous student turnover.

11. For additional ideas of budget management, see the Civic Federation, *Reforming the CPS Budget System: A Tool for Effective Management and Accountability,* by Denise McAllister, Mark Paul, David Moore, and Roland Calia (Chicago, October 1993).

Bibliography

Anderson, Alan B., and George W. Pickering. *Confronting the Color Line—The Broken Promise of the Civil Rights Movement in Chicago*. Athens, Ga.: University of Georgia Press, 1986.

Arthur Andersen and Company *Board of Education of the City of Chicago, 1992 Annual Financial Report*. Chicago, 23 December 1992.

Bennett, William J. *The De-Valuing of America: The Fight for Our Culture and Our Children*. New York: Simon and Schuster, 1992.

Board of Education, Los Angeles Unified School District. *A Start on Stopping School Weapons and Violence*. Recommendations proposed by the Schools Safety and Security Task Force. Los Angeles, 22 March 1990.

Booz-Allen and Hamilton and Washington, Pittman, and McKeever. *Financial Outlook for the Chicago Public Schools*. Chicago, 14 May 1992.

The Business Roundtable. *The Essential Components of a Successful Education System: Putting Policy into Practice*. By Terri Bergman, Frederick S. Edelstein, and Maria B. Lloyd. Washington, D.C., December 1992.

Cannella, Nicholas R. *171 Years of Teaching in Chicago, 1816–1987*. Chicago: Chicago Teachers Union, 1987.

Center for the Study of Social Policy. *Kids Count Data Book—State Profiles of Child Well-Being.* Washington, D.C., 1993.

Chicago Board of Education. *Board Reports Re: LSC's Sign-Off.* Chicago, 1991.

──────. *Chicago Board of Education Internal Accounts Manual.* Chicago, June 1987.

──────. Department of Equal Educational Opportunity Programs and Department of Research, Evaluation, and Planning. *Special Report on Busing, Presented at the Request of Board Member Albert Logan.* Chicago, 6 December 1991.

──────. *Financial Research and Advisory Committee (FRAC) Initiative.* Chicago, June 1993.

──────. *State of Illinois Annual Financial Report.* Chicago, 1991–92.

Chicago Panel on Public School Policy and Finance. *What Are We Willing to Pay for School Reform? An Analysis of the Costs of Educational Reform in Illinois.* By F. Howard Nelson and G. Alfred Hess, Jr. Chicago, May 1985.

Chicago Public Schools. *Procedures and Guidelines: Interior Painting of School Facilities by Volunteers.* Chicago, May 1993.

──────. *A Proposal for an Organizational Analysis and Restructuring of the Chicago Public Schools.* By Charley Gillispie. Chicago, June 1993.

Civic Federation. *Reforming the CPS Budget System: A Tool for Effective Management and Accountability.* By Denis McAllister, Mark Paul, David Moore, and Roland Calia. Chicago, October 1993.

Staff of the *Chicago Tribune. Chicago Schools: "Worst in America": An Examination of the Public Schools that Fail Chicago.* Chicago: Chicago Tribune, 1988.

Consortium on Chicago School Research. *Charting Reform: The Principals' Perspective; Report on a Survey of Chicago Public School Principals.* Chicago, December 1992.

——————. *Charting Reform: The Teachers' Turn, Report No. 1 on a Survey of CPS Elementary School Teachers.* Chicago, September 1991.

——————. *A View from the Elementary Schools: The State of Reform in Chicago.* Chicago, July 1993.

Council of Chief State School Officers. *State Education Indicators, 1990, for the School Year 1989–1990.* Washington, D.C., 1990.

The Council of Great City Schools. *National Urban Education Goals: Baseline Indicators, 1990–91.* By Michael Casserly. Washington, D.C., September 1992.

Designs for Change. *Closer Look, First Year of School Reform in Chicago.* Chicago, January 1991.

——————. *School Help: 105 Resources for Chicago School Improvement.* Chicago, 1993.

Doyle, Denis P., Bruce S. Cooper, and Roberta Trachtman. *Taking Charge, State Action on School Reform in the 1980s.* Indianapolis, Ind.: Hudson Institute, 1991.

Education Commission of the States. *School Finance Litigation: A Historical Summary.* By Mary Fulton and David Long. Denver, Colo., April 1993.

Education Writers Association. *Wolves at the Schoolhouse Door—An Investigation of the Condition of Public School Buildings.* By Anne Lewis, David Bednarek, Linda Chion-Kenney, Charles Harrison, Janet Kolodzy, Kathleen McCormick, Jerry Smith, Don Speich, and Lisa Walker. Chicago, 1989.

Feistritzer, C. Emily. *Who Wants to Teach?* Washington, D.C.: National Center of Education Information, 1992.

First Chicago Capital Markets, Inc. *The Chicago Board of Education, May 1993*. By Ronald Heller. Chicago, May 1993.

Garbarino, James, Nancy Dubrow, Kathleen Kostelny, and Carole Pardo. *Children in Danger*. San Francisco: Jossey-Bass Publishers, 1992.

Havighurst, Robert, Jr. *The Public Schools of Chicago: A Survey for the Board of Education of the City of Chicago*. Chicago: Board of Education of the City of Chicago, 1964.

Hayner, Don and Tom McNamee. *Metro Chicago Almanac*. Chicago: Bonus Books and Chicago Sun-Times, 1991.

Herrick, Mary J. *The Chicago Schools: A Social and Political History*. Beverly Hills, Calif.: Sage Publications, 1971.

Hess, G. Alfred, Jr. *School Restructuring, Chicago Style*. Newbury Park, Calif.: Corwin Press, 1991.

Hill, Paul T., and Josephine Bonan. *Decentralization and Accountability in Public Education*. Santa Monica, Calif.: Rand Corp., 1991.

Illinois Bell, Ameritech Foundation, and Chicago Public School Alumni Association. *Local School Councils' Ideas and Successes; Chicago School Reform: Year Three*. Chicago, 1992.

Illinois Criminal Justice Information Authority. *Trends and Issues 91: Education and Criminal Justice in Illinois*. Chicago, 1991.

Kerchner, Charles Taylor, and Julia E. Koppich. *A Union of Professionals, Labor Relations and Educational Reform*. New York: Teachers College Press, 1993.

Kozol, Jonathan. *Savage Inequalities*. New York: Crown Publishers, 1991.

Kyle, Charles L., and Edward R. Kantowicz. *Kids First—Primero Los Niños: Chicago School Reform in the 1980s*. Springfield, Ill.: Illinois Issues, 1992.

Legislative Research Commission. *The Kentucky Education Reform Act of 1990: A Citizens Handbook.* By Mary Helen Miller, Kevin Noland, and John Schaaf. Frankfort, Ky., September 1991.

McDonnell, Lorraine M., and Anthony Pascal. *Teacher Unions and Educational Reform.* Santa Monica, Calif.: Center for Policy Research, the Center for the Study of the Teaching Profession, and the Rand Corp., 1988.

Mathews, Jay. *Escalante: The Best Teacher in America.* New York: Henry Holt and Co., 1988.

National Commission on Excellence in Education. *Nation at Risk: The Imperative for Educational Reform.* Washington, D.C., 1983.

National Education Association, *Rankings of the States,* 1992. Washington, D.C., September 1992.

————. *Status of the American Public School Teacher, 1990–1991.* Washington, D.C., 1992.

O'Connell, Mary. *School Reform, Chicago Style.* Chicago: Center for Neighborhood Technology, 1991.

Peterson, Paul E. *School Politics, Chicago Style.* Chicago: University of Chicago Press, 1976.

Richmond, George H. *The Micro-Society School: A Real World in Miniature.* New York: Harper and Row, 1973.

Smith, Page. *The Shaping of America: A People's History of the Young Republic.* New York: Penguin Books, 1980.

Special Commissioner of Investigation for the New York City School District. *Power, Politics, and Patronage: Education in Community School District 12.* By Lydia G. Segal, Donald F. Schwally, Jr., and Tracy Kramer. New York, April 1993.

————. *A System Like No Other: Fraud and Misconduct by New York City School Custodians.* By Suzan R. Flamm, Regina A. Loughran, and Leah Keith. New York, November 1992.

Texas Education Agency. *Impact of Educational Reform on Students in At-Risk Situations, Phase III, Interim Report, Executive Summary.* Austin, Tex., May 1992.

Waldman, Linda. *My Neighborhood: The Words and Pictures of Inner-City Children.* Chicago: Hyde Park Bank Foundation, 1993.

Washington, Pittman, and McKeever. *Chicago Board of Education Agreed-Upon Procedures.* Chicago, 23 November 1992.

Index

For easy reference, endnote citations are followed by the letter n *and the number of the individual note.*

Accessibility for the disabled at Chicago public schools, 137

Access Living of Metropolitan Chicago, 293

Accountability of schools for student performance, 233

Achievement test scores, causes of low, 73, 136; Chicago's ranking in, 7; improvements in individual schools', 264; initial decline after school reform of, 12, 17, 271; in Kentucky before and after reform, 234, 343n. 7

ACT college entrance exam, results of Chicago public school students on, 3, 88

Adult mentors for graduating eighth graders at Aldridge School, 103

African-American students, growth of enrollment for, 76; mobile classrooms for, 315; school days shortened for, 75; school supply shortages for, 76; teacher shortages for, 76

African Americans, migration from the South to Chicago in 1940s and 1950s of, 75; percentage receiving public assistance in 1962, 303n. 7; resistance to financial overhaul of board's financial accounts by, 331–32n. 26

After-school programs, encouragement of, 283

Aldridge School, 102–3

Alesia, James H., 335n. 49

Alexander, Ellen J., 63–64

Almo, Charles D., 161

Alternative schools,decline in Chicago of, 119–21; effects of, 109; need for highly structured, 282; structure of, 118; for students carrying guns to school, 114–15

American Association of School Administrators, 129

American Health Care Providers, 224

American Institute of Architects study of student achievement levels and new school buildings, 136

Amundsen High School, 8; "behavior disorder" of child carrying gun at, 110; classroom space and enrollment at, 138; expulsion of student for carrying gun at, 108; reform at, impact of, 124; teacherless classes at, 46

Anderson, Beverly, 68

Anderson Community Academy, effects of budget freeze on, 32

Anton, William, 172

Archdiocese of Chicago, nation's largest private school system run by, xxi

Arellano, Jose Luis, 132

Armstrong Elementary School, 29

Arreguin, Eumir, 133

Arrests in Chicago public schools, 1991–92 school year report of, 107; Operation Safe's impact on, 112

Art Resources in Teaching (A.R.T.), 293

AS-2000 computer system, 225–26

Asbestos in Chicago schools, 137

Aspira, Inc. of Illinois, 293

Assessed valuation of property, 247, 330n. 12, 336n. 52

Association of Community Organizations for Reform Now, 146

Audits of school funds, 210, 213, 278

Audy Home, 322n. 39

Austin Community Academy, graduation rate of, 48

Austin High School, monetary discrepancies at, 210

Ayers, William, 82, 271

Bacchus, J. Maxey, 141, 228

Bailey, Adrienne Y., 164, 328n. 26

Bailey, Grady, Jr., 156–57

Balanoff, Clem, 150

Ballis, Stephen R., 157, 170–71, 188, 220

Banks, Floyd M., 19

Barry Elementary School, 29–30

Barshis, Jan, 6

Basic skills programs, employer-sponsored, 7

Bauer, William J., 335n. 50

Beale Elementary School, audit report of, 210

Beasley Magnet School, high achievement of students in, 102

Beethoven Elementary School, 95, 146–47

Behavior disorder as label for dangerous children, 109–10

Bender, Sharon Rae, 52, 133

Bennett, William J., *xix,* Chicago called worst school system in the nation by, 97, 304n. 3; educational meltdown in Chicago schools noted by, 3; self-esteem of students versus achievement described by, 109

Berman, Herbert M., 71

Bidding requirements, tightening, 279

Birts, Warner B., 114

Bishop, Saundra, 158

Blackburn, Darlene, 131

Blackful, Leroy F., Jr., 64–65

Blue Cross-Blue Shield, 223–24

Bond issues, costs of educational, 239–40; used for day-to-day operations, school districts with, 344n. 12

Bond School, 260

Boone Elementary School, 17; Russian bilingual program at, 46

Bossert, Philip J., 227

Bostic, Frank, 120

Bowen High School, asbestos removal at, 137; concession proceeds at, 210

Boysen, Thomas C., 215, 233

Bradshaw, Sylvester, 82–83
Brennemann Elementary School, 39, 264
Bridges, Edwin M., 62
Brighton Park Elementary School, 32
Bristow, Clinton, Jr., 157, 169
Britton, Dennis A., 112
"Brown envelope day," 207–8
Brown, Percy, 54
Brown, Reginald V., 208–9
Brown, Steve, 53, 72, 238–39
Bryk, Anthony, 38
Bryn Mawr Elementary School, student money
  misused at, 210
Budget deadlines, moving back dates for, 279–80
Budget deficit in Chicago school system, 9–10
Building bond program, created by interim Chicago
  school board, 143–44; during 1984, 149; protests
  to begin construction using funds from, 151
Building repairs, lawsuits stemming from need for,
  323n. 14; postponed to fund pay raises, 141–42,
  239; recommendations for, 281–82
Bureaucracy, Chicago's attempt to decentralize,
  29–31; growth of school system, 10–11
Burke Elementary School, staffing problems at, 49
Burks, Darrell, 130
Burley Elementary School, disrepair of, 134
Burnout of teachers, 88–91, 231
Burns Elementary School, 15
Bus transportation system, costs of, 245; kickback
  scheme for, 213; revamping of, 38
Butler, John, 131, 134
Byrd, Manford, Jr., 160–61, 163
Byrne, Jane M., 182, 331n. 24
Byrne, Thomas, 114
Byron community school district compared with Mt.
  Morris, 247–48

Cadavid, Eduardo, 15
Calumet High School, closure of facilities in, 54; Club
  Pre-Med at, 261; discipline at, 121; disrepair of,
  4–5, 131, 134–35; metal detectors used to
  recover weapons at, 114; renovation of, 149–50;
  Saturday Academy at, 261; social promotion of
  students entering, 87; study habits program at,
  261
Cardenas Elementary School, 11
Cardin, Vivian, 132
Career service examinations, 56
Carlson, Karen, 197
Carr, Frances, 151–52
Carson Elementary School, 138
Caruso, Angeline P., 159
Casey, Kirby, 45
Catalyst, Voices of Chicago School Reform, parent
  involvement under reform assessed by, 258;
  survey of union delegates about poorly perform-
  ing teachers by, 70; transformation of "problem"
  student described in, 103–4
Center for Inner City Studies, 294
Center for Neighborhood Technology, 294
Chapter One funds, Aldridge School's use of, 103;
  approval for spending, 29; for computers,
  225–26, 255; diversion of, 282; freeze during
  1993 financial crisis of, 31–32; hiring staff using,

186, 201, 270; hold after 1993 financial crisis on,
  195; impact on class size of, 246; plan for
  spending, 23; transfer to schools of, 333n. 32,
  334n. 37; uses of, 41, 160, 270
Chase, Camille E., 136
Cherkasky-Davis, Lynn, 80
Chicago Area Writing Project, 294
Chicago Black United Communities, 23, 158
Chicago Board of Education, appointment of, 219;
  approval of LSCs' spending by, 29; cafeteria at,
  33, 38; class size negotiations of, 311n. 13;
  contract voting suggested to be placed on the
  record for, 279; cuts under reform at, 38, 221;
  debt of, 181–82; election of president from
  among members of, 278; election recommended
  for members of, 277–78; expulsion policy of,
  125; "game of chicken" regarding budget cuts
  by, 18; lack of understanding of schools' needs
  by, 24–25; limit to not promoting children by,
  91; oversight function of, 220–23; priorities of,
  10; professional library eliminated by, 33;
  prohibition over hiring suggested for members
  of, 278; promotion policy in, 317; revolving
  leadership in 1980s and 1990s at, 155–75;
  scandals at, xx; selection of members of, 340n.
  32; spending inefficiencies at, 33–35; truant
  officers all laid off in 1992 by, 117–18; turnover
  of members on, 155
Chicago Education Initiative, 258
Chicago Panel on Public School Policy and Finance,
  10, 92–93, 294; dropout rate studied by, 111;
  1985 study of cost of retaining students by, 98;
  property tax increases examined by, 248, 334n.
  37
Chicago Parental School, 322n. 39
Chicago Principals Association, 22, endorsement of
  Richard E. Stephenson by, 169
Chicago Public Building Commission, 143, 150–51,
  275
Chicago public school system, average cost of
  education per student in, 243–44; budgetary
  process recommended for, 279; bureaucracy of,
  growth in 1980s of, 10–11; closure during
  summer months of school offices in, 48; financial collapse in 1979 of, xxii, 31, 155, 159,
  182–83, 240; financial crisis of 1993 of, 18–20,
  31–36, 49–50, 157, 184–92, 239–40; foreign-
  speaking students in, 7, 9; hope for, sources of,
  269–85; lack of oversight of, 219–23; leadership
  needed for, xx; mismanagement of, xxi; 1960s as
  turning point in decline of, xxi–xxii; numerical
  breakdown of schools in, 316–17n. 5; poverty
  level of students in, 7, 9; prospective financial
  crisis in 1995 in, 239; questions during 1993
  financial crisis about viability of, 187; repairing,
  legislative will for, 231–51; social conditions in,
  77; student turnover in, 7; transportation costs
  in, 245
Chicago School Finance Authority, budgeting games
  described by, 18; creation of, 183; decentralization analyzed by members of, 12, 30; inspector
  general's office created for, 195, 235–36, 274–75,
  343–44n. 9; Kimbrough's move for decentralizing
  spending presented to, 41; power in school

closing issue for, 327n. 5; role under reform of, 271; waiver during 1993 financial crisis objected to by, 193

Chicago Teachers Union, attitude toward cooperating with Chicago Board of Education of, 41; bargaining rights gained during 1960s by, *xxii*, 181; changes agreed to under reform by, 72–73, 157; early retirement program lobbied for by, 49, 238; evolution of power of, 179–81; grievance against principal by, 69; negotiations during 1993 financial crisis by, 19, 55, 184–92; Quest teacher training center run by, 82, 258; rival organization for members of, 191; teacher training in Quest Center of, 82; truant officers represented by, 118

Chicago Urban League, 295; study of black school funding, 76–77

Chicago Vocational High School, audit of, 210

Child abuse by staff, dismissal cases for, 64–68

Children from broken homes or with illiterate parents, statistics of, 100

Christopher, Gaylaird, 136

Citizens' political movement to inform voters on education issues, need for, 273

Citizens Schools Committee, 197, 295

Civic Federation, 38, 222, 227

Civil service examinations reinstituted under school reform, 56

Civil unrest in 1968, 180–81

Clark, Alfred, 121, 123

Clark, Joe, 329n. 39

Class sizes, 138–39; maximum, under 1993–94 teachers' contract, 191, 311n. 13; recommendations for decreasing, 281

Clay Elementary School, disrepair of, 131–32

Clayborn, Willie, 112

Clayton, Donna L., 12

Clemente High School, dropout rate at, 111; graduation rate at, 100

Clerks, transfers and cuts in numbers of school, 22–23

Coalition for Consumer Rights poll assessing importance of education, 241–42, 345n. 20

Cochrane, Rickie, 69–70

Code, John, 199

Coffey, Raymond R., 37; column about failing students at Beethoven School by, 97; column about waste and misrepresentation of information by, 214; investigation of teacher apathy and student performance by, 88–89, 91

Coleman, James S., 101

Coles Elementary School, 23

Committee for Educational Rights, 247

Community Renewal Society (CRS), 295

Compass Health Care Plans of Chicago, 222

Competency tests for teachers in Georgia, 78

Compton, James W., 24, 161

Computer technology, competitive bids for purchasing, 224–28, 234, 236, 280; cost overruns for, 341n. 36; need for enhanced, 283

Computer vendors, fight for Chicago school system business among, 224–28

Consortium on Chicago School Research, 17; 1992 survey by, 62, 73, 81–82; 1993 report of achievement under reform by, 94–95

Conti, Jenny, 87

Cook County Circuit Court, code violation cases stalled in, 146

Cook County Juvenile Temporary Detention Center, 322n. 39

Cook County Superintendent of Schools, 277

Corcoran, Thomas J., 155–56

Corruption, school systems' offices to investigate, 214–16

Council of Great City Schools, poverty of student population measured by, 305n. 8; study by, 7, 9; tenure of school superintendent studied by, 172

Councils, school. See Local school councils (LSCs)

Courtenay School, 56

Cox, Clifford, 228

Cox, Florence B., 157–58, 161, 168

CPAs for the Public Interest, 295

Crane High School, misappropriation of funds at, 208–9

Creiger Vocational High School, 121–23

Crimes by students, 107–8, 111–13

Cruz, Juan S., 157–58

Cullerton, Timothy M., 148

Culloton, Dennis, 223

Curie High School, 16

Curtis, Charles E., Sr., 157

Cusick, Ralph J., 210

Dade County, Florida, school construction bond issue, 145

Daggett, Illa, 158

Daley, Patricia A., 24, 138, 155–56

Daley, Richard J., death in 1976 of, 331n. 24; electrical inspections at schools ordered by, 147–48; financial gimmicks to settle school strikes by, *xxii*; union ties of, 179–80

Daley, Richard M., anger at school board lack of cuts by, 157; building repair project chaired by, 143–44; changes in state teacher hearing process advocated by, 72; electrical inspections unnecessary according to, 148–49; elimination of state hearings for teachers advocated by, 80; interim board appointed in 1989 by, 156; labor peace during reelection of, 183–84; response to city violence of, 112; stance toward unions during 1993 financial crisis of, 189–90; supporters of, 11; tax proposals of, 186, 346n. 36; tax referendum's impact on, school property, 195

Darwin Elementary School, 261

Davenport, Kevin, 45

Davis, Dantrell, 70, 112

Davis, Joe, 123

Dawson, Grace, 75–77, 81; effects of retaining students with failing performance by, 95–97; expulsion of students carrying guns in Gary, Indiana, described by, 114; Singer board staffing cuts described by, 165

Decentralization of school systems, 5, 30. *See also* School reform movement, Chicago

DeGraff, Warren, 116, 321

Democratic political machine, relationship between school jobs and, *xx–xxii*, 177–81, 201–2

Desegregation decree requiring busing in Chicago schools, 245

Designs for Change reform advocacy group, 17; conflict in schools under reform measured by, 307n. 7; school progress under reform assessed by, 260, 318n. 23; stand against retention of poorly performing students by, 97–98; voter turnout for school board elections tallied by, 304n. 5

Detroit public schools, condition of buildings of, 130; school board members ousted from, 195–96; transfer of power to schools in, 196

Dhanidina, Lutaf, 51

Diaz, Roberto, 15

Discipline in schools, impact of, 103, 107–27

Dismissals of criminal school employees, automatic, 275

Dominguez, Leonard, 189–90

Doyiakos, James, 46

Dranove, David, 223

Drobny, Arnold, 56

Dropout prevention programs, 282

Dropout rate in Chicago public schools, 3, 7, 88; compared with other large urban areas, 304–5n. 7; gangs as cause of, 111; as highest of nation's largest school systems, 111

Drugs, impact on the schools of, *xxiii–xxiv*, 8

Due process hearings, for staff, 70–73; for teachers, 62–70

Dulles Elementary School, 12, 259

Dunbar Vocational High School, 19, 32

Dunson, Joyce, 226

DuSable High School, 77; discipline at, 124–25; effects of violence at Robert Taylor Homes on attendance at, 111; example of social promotion for student entering, 92; experience with LSC at, 12; metal detectors refused by, 113; recruitment program for dropouts to return to, 111; special teacher's reassignment at, 53–54

Dyett Middle School, 261–63

Earle School, 261

Early childhood education, expansion of, 281

Early retirement program for school employees, 49–50, 237–38

Edgar, Jim, 190, 192, 242–43

Edison Comprehensive Gifted Center, 257, 347n. 6

Education organization focused on political lobbying, need for, 273–74

Education tax rate, 1992, 336n. 52

Education Writers Association study of school buildings, 129, 139, 322, 324

Educational funding, 239–43; lawsuits challenging inequitable, 246–47; school district the determining factor in, 246

Educational Management Group, 225–26

Effective Schools Institute, 296

Electrical inspections, 147–49; recommended for Chicago schools, 280

Elementary and Secondary Education Act, 180

Eligibility lists for positions under school reform, 56–57

Emmet Elementary School, 82–98, 259

Engineer-custodians, 196–202, 216, 336–38n. 66, 67

Englewood High School, metal detectors at, 114

Enrollment figures, staffing and, 46–48

Erby, Kathy, 71

Escalante, Jaime, 101–2

Esmond Elementary School, audit of, 210

Espinoza, David, 21

Expelling students forbidden for reason of crime, 107

Facilities study by interim Chicago school board, 130

Fairview Alternative School (Kansas City), 119–20

Families, impact of breakdown of, 77, 138–39

Family Resource Center on Disabilities, 276

Family resource centers, 283

Farragut High School, gang violence at, 166; metal detectors as crime deterrents at, 114

Fatalism of students, 139

Faulk, Carol A., 208, 338n. 4

Fenger High School, 29

Fennerty, Janet, 284

Ferguson, Jason, 255

Fernandez, Joseph A., 172

Fields, Cydney B., 63–64

Financial Research and Advisory Committee (FRAC), 39–40; building repair costs studied by, 142–43

Finney, Leon, 272

Finnigan, Thomas M., 36

Fire alarm disrepair, 146–47

Fitzpatrick, Delores, 198

Flanagan, James D., 157

Floating substitute, 54

Fonseca, Maria, 8

Food purchases and storage by Chicago Board of Education, 34, 224

Foreign-speaking groups of Chicago public school students, statistics of, 305n. 11

Foreman High School, 49, 270

Foundations School, 79–80

Fraley, Barbara, 259

Fullman, Charles, 131

Funding schools, state aid formula, 333n. 32

Funston Elementary School, 35, 267; disrepair of mobile units at, 133; overcrowding at, 140–41

Gage Park High School, teachers given extra money at, 207–8, 338n. 5

Gallagher, Eileen M., 211

Gallagher, Jackie, 53, 188

Garrett, Anthony, 112

Garvey Elementary School, 130–31, 148

Garvey, John J., 49, 270

Garvy Elementary School, 212, 339n. 12

Gary, Indiana, weapons policy for schools, 114

Gay, Mary, 246

Gelsomino, John P., 133, 148, 152, 253

General Assembly approval of 1993 teachers' contract, 192

General Services Administration (GSA) surplus property program, 34–35

Gilliland v. Board of Education of Pleasant View, 313n. 7

Gillispie, Charley, 36, 38, 40, 186, 227, 341n. 36

Gilvary, Paul, 263

Gladstone Elementary School, 116, 263–64

Glascow, Connie, 136

Godfather or *godmother* school board members, 217–19

Golden Apple award, 261

Golden Apple Foundation, 296–97

Golub, Sheila, 65–67
Gonzalez, Faustino, 34
Goodlow Magnet Upper School, 74
Gordon, Barbara L., 134
Graham Elementary School, 132
Grant, D. Sharon, 20, 158, 223, 341n. 41
Grant, McNair, Jr., 228
Grants for special curricula, 82–83
Graves, Ben E., 196
Great Depression, school patronage jobs during, *xxi*
Green, Edwin, assessment of school board by, 156; neglect of Calumet's building noted by, 4–5, 135; reform's promise described by, 12, 151; refusal to readmit returning students at Calumet explained by, 121; renovation program described by, 149; social promotion described by, 87
Griffin, Maxwell, Jr., 18, 30
Guajardo, Raphael, 50

Haley, Richard, 130–31, 148
Hall, Milton W., 25, 56, 209
Hallett, Corinne, 68–69
Hamilton School, 8
Hammond Elementary School, 133
Hannon, Joseph P., 159
Haran, William, 39, 264–65, 348n. 18
Harney, James P., 131
Harold Washington College, 6
Harrigan, Margaret M., 47; assessment of supernumerary teacher status by, 53; Chicago Mastery Learning Skills program assessed by, 160; competency exams for teachers advocated by, 78–79; hiring freeze confirmed by, 311n. 12; inequities in hiring practices under reform described by, 57; promotion policy assembled by, 100; quality of teachers assessed by, 77; retirement of, 51; view of shorter school day of, 94
Hartrich, Toni, 221–22, 227
Harvard University Project on School Desegregation, 75
Harvey, Patricia A., 8, 137–39, 255–56
Hawaiian school system, 227
Hay Group wage survey, 197
Health maintenance organizations (HMOs), 341n. 41
Health-care contract negotiated by the Chicago Board of Education, 35, 183, 222–23, 341n. 41
Health-care premiums for Chicago teachers, 191
Hefferan Elementary School, 137, 255–56
Hehir, Thomas, 36, 38, 109
Heminover, Lillian, 140
Henderson Elementary School, 25, 209
Herbert Elementary School, 20, 57–58
Hess, G. Alfred, Jr., 10, 99–101, 142, 186, 270–71, 334n. 37
High School Re-entry Center, 120–21
High school teachers' education, Chicago versus suburban, 74
Hill, Christopher, 131–32
Hill, Tam B., 114, 121
HMO Illinois, 223
Holt, Barbara, 12
Homelessness rates, city, 7
Homicide rates, city, 7

Honig, Bill, 161
Hoover, Dana, 265
HOPE team, 195–96
Hopkins, Wanda, 71
Hornung, Mary, 259
Hrnciar, Robert J., 131
Hughes, DeCalvin, 48
Hunt, Benny, 231
Hunt, Harold C., 159, 179

Illinois Alliance of Essential Schools, 297
Illinois Bell school funding, 260–61
Illinois Department of Children and Family Services, 66
Illinois Distinguished Educators award, 261
Illinois Education Association, 191
Illinois Federation of Teachers, 191
Illinois Fiesta Educativa, 297
Illinois Goals Assessment Program, 316n. 4
Illinois legislature, 229, 235
Illinois State Board of Education, awards sponsored by, 261; inspection of Schurz High School by, 133; investigatory force needed for, 275; power to remove council members suggested for, 277; summary of dismissal hearings provided by, 312–13n. 5
Illinois Writing Project, 297
Immigration in Chicago, impact on school system of, 7
Incentive pay for principals and teachers, 283
Incompetent teachers, principals' means of handling, 61–62
Institute for Education and Training, 21
Instruction time, study comparing suburban versus Chicago schools', 93; study halls to fulfill, 276
Interim school board, appointed in 1989 by Mayor Daley, 156; building bond program established by, 143–44; engineers' contract signed by, 198; facilities study by, 130; formation in 1989 of, 183; health-care contracts negotiated by, 35, 83, 222–23; raises in teachers' pay by, 77–78, 183–84
Internal accounts, audits of, 213
International Union of Operating Engineers, Local 143 of, 198

Jackson, Jesse, 156, 159
Job guarantees for teachers, 52, 239
John D. and Catherine T. MacArthur Foundation, 258
Johnson, Alexander P., 147
Johnson, Argie K., 20; decision to delay school opening in 1993 announced by, 193; delay in opening schools described by, 309n. 7; hiring freeze denied by, 311n. 12; as superintendent candidate, 169–70; view of "dumbing down" curriculum of, 101
Johnson, Dennie E., 107
Johnson, Eli, 67–68
Johnson, Melvin, 23
Johnson, Robert, 38
Johnson-Vinion, Janet, 211
Jones, Demetrius, 155
Jones, Emil, 190
Jones, Walter, 149
Julian High School, 32, 51–52, 107

Kellogg Foundation, 259–60
Kelly High School, 237; disrepair of, 133, 136, 148;
    effects of budget freeze on, 32; parent volun-
    teers at, 253
Kelvyn Park High School, 65
Kentucky, family resource centers created in, 283;
    income tax revenue increase in, 343; Office of
    Education Accountability in, 232–33; perfor-
    mance test scores in, 234, 343n. 7; school reform
    of 1990, 81, 214–15, 233–34; school system ruled
    unconstitutional in, 232; statewide technology
    plan in, 234
Kentucky Education Reform Act (KERA), 234
"Killing Our Children" (*Chicago Tribune* series), 112
Kilmer Elementary School, 5, 138, 200, 255
Kimbrough, Ted D., 6, 30; accomplishments of,
    167–68; announcement of probe into board's
    computer department by, 222; announcement of
    teachers' pay increases by, 183; budget shortfalls
    under, 184; inadequate teaching and poor
    school management described by, 88; informa-
    tion gaps described by, 37; opinion on pay-raise
    issue during 1993 crisis of, 187; opinion on
    school spending of, 40–41; reform advocates
    angered by, 163–65; school closings by, 165–67;
    selection as superintendent of, 156, 161–62; view
    of social promotion of, 99; view of teacher
    assignment procedures of, 48; view of trade
    prices for union workers of, 201
King High School, 55
Kirst, Michael, 6
Kocoras, Charles P., 192–93
Koldyke, Martin ("Mike"), 271
Konopasek, Katherine A., 32
Kosciuszko Elementary School, 151
Kotsakis, John, 62–63, 72
Kravarik, Fred, 40
Kriz, Donald, 15
Kuranda, John, 5, 253–54
Kuranda, Kathryn, 5, 236–37, 253–54
Kyle, Charles L., 111

Labor rates for school building repairs, excessive,
    143
Lake View High School, teacherless classes at, 45–46,
    52
Lane Technical High School, 19, 210, 245–46
Larney, George Edward, 67
Latino Institute, 298
Laura Ward Elementary School, 67
LaVelle, Avis, 186
Law, Bob, 80–81, 170, 275–76
Lawyers' School Reform Advisory Project, 298
Layng, Joe, 87
Leadership for Quality Education (LQE), 187, 298
Learning disabilities, relation of delinquency and,
    120
LeBreton, Pierre, 19
Legislative summit for dismissal process and improv-
    ing teacher competency, 275–76
Lehman, Lloyd W., 94, 150–51
Levin, Ellis, 150
Levine, Stephen, 207
Libraries, updating and expanding school, 282
Life safety tax, 150

Local school councils (LSCs), authorizations by, 29;
    budget cuts not under control of, 18; burdens
    placed on new, 235; clashes between engineers
    and, 196–98; conflicts of interest of members of,
    236–37; creation of, 5, 11; criminal background
    checks of, lack of, 236; election requirements
    for, 237; inappropriate use of funds by some, 25;
    lack of training for, 23–24; literacy and education
    level of members of, 235, 277; oversight of
    schools by, 220; principals' lawsuit against,
    307–8n. 17; principals selected by, 11, 17, 270;
    punitive damages paid by members of, 16–17;
    removal of, 277; representatives to school board
    nominating commission from, 340n. 32; training
    recommendations for, 281
Los Angeles School Board adoption of weapons
    policy, 114–15
Los Angeles schools, conditions of buildings of, 130;
    costs of special education in, 244
Los Angeles task force on student crimes, 115–16
Lottery, state, 240–41
Love, Ruth B., 159–60
Lowe, Maxine, 65
Lozano, Emma, 151
Lutzow, Charles A., 137

McCord, Jacquelin, 53–54
McCue, Donald J., 199
McCutcheon School, 21
McFerren, Coretta, *xxiii,* 98, 198, 256, 269
McLemore, Ollie, 102
McMillen, Thomas R., 68
McMorrow, Mary Ann G., 35, 222–23
McNeil, Kenneth, *xxi*
McPherson Elementary School, disrepair of, 134, 136
Madigan, Michael, engineers' lines of authority
    protected by, 200; income tax increase at time of
    school reform blocked by, 239; lifetime teaching
    job guarantee protected by, 53; as sponsor of
    legislation to enable principals to expel students
    for offenses with weapons, 110–11; union
    agreement required for state hearing process
    according to, 72; union negotiations during 1993
    financial crisis mediated by, 190
Magnet schools, 3; number of, 317n. 6; reading
    levels at, 88
Mahar, William G., 207–8
Malave, Carlos, 5–6, 200, 254–55
Malcolm X College, 87
Maldonado, Gonzalo, 141
Manojlovic, Mile, 132
Marchiafava, Bruce, 244
Marengo, Paul C., 247
Marquette Elementary School, 40
Marshall High School, 211–12
Martin, Chastity, 29
Martinez, Peter, 258
Masey, Donna J., 46
Mather High School, disrepair of, 136
Mathews, Jay, 101–2
Max McGraw Learning Center, 264–65
Mayer, Kathleen, 138
Melody School, 143
Menacker, Julius, 66
Metal detectors in schools, 113

Micromanagement, 220–21
Microsociety experiment, 116, 263–64
Middle-class families, educational options for Chicago's, *xxi*
Migration of African Americans from the South in 1940s and 1950s, 75
Mijou, Robert, 72
Milken Family Foundation, 261
Mingo, Charles E., attempt to recruit special needs teacher by, 53–55; discipline imposed by, 124–25; discrepancies between suburban and Chicago systems noted by, 238; dismissal hearings for staff described by, 62; inadequate preparation of some students described by, 92; refusal of metal detectors for DuSable High School by, 113
Minor, Yvonne, 261–62
Minority contracting requirements, waiver by Chicago board of, 222
Misappropriate of funds, by local school councils, 25; by principals or other school staff, 208–12
Mitchell, Charles, Jr., 159
Mobile classroom units, 59, 75, 133, 315n. 35. *See also* "Willis wagons"
Moffat, James G., 65
Montefiore School, 118–19, 322n. 39
Morgan Park High School, class sizes at, 32; discipline at, 108; ouster of principal at, 15–17
Moriello, Gary, 264
Morrill Elementary School, injuries after confrontation at, 15; protest after firing of interim principal at, 15
Moseley School, 322n. 39
Motley School, 322n. 39
Mt. Morris community school district compared with Byron, 247–48
Mueller, Warren, 56
Muhammad, Farid, 253
Mulberry, Jay F., 257
Muñoz, George, 165
Muñoz Marin Primary Center, 21
Murphy, Jerome T., 173
Murphy School, 144
Mustafa, Anna, 157

Nathan, Harvey A., 64
Nation at Risk: The Imperative for Educational Reform, 5
Nation of Tomorrow program, 83, 259–60
National Center for Education Information, 91
National Coalition on Television Violence, statistics of, 321n. 28
National Commission on Excellence in Education, 5
National Education Association, 9, 73, 189, 243
National School Safety Center, 113
Near North Career Metropolitan High School, 110
Nelson, Diana L., 187
Netsch, Dawn Clark, 241
New Expressions, 51
New York City schools, building program for, 145–46; condition of buildings of, 130; corruption in, 215–19; costs of special education in, 244; personnel allocations in, 47; special commissioner of investigation for, 275; twelve-month office operations in, 47–48

Newton, Steve, Jr., 114
Niazmand, Marsha, 65
Niles Township District 219, program for behavior and emotional problems at, 120
Noonan, Patrick, 147
North Central Regional Educational Laboratory (NCREL), 264, 298
Northtown Bus Service, 339
Norwood, Shonteal, 15
Noven, Bernie R., 94, 110, 165, 242, 272
Noville, Virginia, 218
Nowlin, Larry A., 93

O'Connor, Patrick J., 190
O'Donnell, Harriet, 124, 138
O'Dowd, Robert, 197, 200
Olds, Edward L., III, 247
"Operation Safe," 112
Orfield, Gary, 74–75
Orr Community Academy, inflated enrollment figures at, 47
Orr, David, 331n. 24
Orr High School, sexual misconduct case at, 64–65
Ortiz-Revollo, Sylvia, 11
O'Toole Elementary School, 259
Our Lady of Angels school fire, 147
Outside resources, school reform most successful with availability of, 260–61
Overcrowding in Chicago public school buildings, 138

Packer, Alvin, 64
Palmer, Lu, 23, 163–64
Pantoja, Jessica, 177
Parent/Community Council (PCC), 299
Parent Homework Training program, 261
Parent volunteers, impact of, 103, 123–24, 253–67
Parents, high expectations of, as integral to student achievement, 100; literacy of, 139; strategies developed by school administrators for poor students', 92
Parents and Community United for Safe, Honest, and Educational Schools (PAC-U), 299
Parents United for Responsible Education (PURE), 24, 94, 299; handling of discipline problems at primary level described by, 110; priorities among LSCs described by, 165; protests during 1987 teachers' strike by, 272
PATCO (Professional Air Traffic Controllers Association) strike, 191
Patronage jobs at schools during the Great Depression, *xxi*
Pazell, George, 103, 200
Peabody Elementary School, disrepair of, 132
Pearce, Calvin L., 108, 171–72, 203, 236, 274
People's Coalition for Educational Reform, 198, 272
Perez Elementary School, 260
Periods, change from forty- to fifty-minute, 19–20, 50, 93, 192
Perot, H. Ross, 273
Pershing Road. *See* Chicago Board of Education
Peterson, Daniel P., 104
Peterson, David T., 49, 55
Philip, James ("Pate"), 235, 243
Phillips High School, 123–24

Piccolo Elementary School, 68–70
Pilditch, Walter E., 15–17
Pinstripe patronage, 202–3, 227
Ploog, Edward A., 21, 271
Poe Classical School, 148
Polan, Julius, 339n. 14
Poltrock, Lawrence A., 54–55, 181
Posner, Richard A., 335n. 50
Prather, Donald I., 83, 260
Precinct defined, 303n. 6
Preferred Meals Systems, 224
Preferred provider organizations (PPOs), 341n. 41
Prescott Elementary School, 196–97
Price, Joyce Combest, 80, 208, 270
Price, Pamela, 69
Principals, appointment of assistant principals and
    head teachers by, 191; engineers placed under
    charge of, 202, 337–38n. 67; expulsion not
    permitted by, 107; expulsion of students for gun
    offenses recommended for use by, 278; four-
    year contracts by councils for, 22; hiring prac-
    tices of, 80; incentive pay for, 283; lawsuit
    against LSCs by, 307–8n. 17; misappropriation of
    funds by, 208–12; opinion of central office
    services of, 37–38; penalties suggested for lack
    of auditing information from, 278; pressures
    placed by reform on, 17–22, 25; probationary
    system for, 276; purchasing by, 38–39; removing
    poor teachers a continuing problem for, 73;
    representation in school board meetings sug-
    gested for, 277; salary and benefits of, 22, 47,
    197, 201; selection by local school councils of,
    11, 17, 270; selection of teachers and staff by,
    52–58, 237; student crime often not reported by,
    113; training for, 280–81; turnover after school
    reform of three quarters of Chicago's, 15;
    vacations of, timing of, 94
Professional services, political purposes in awarding
    contracts for, 202–3, 227
Promotion policy of Chicago public schools, 87–105
Property tax referendum, school, 195, 330n. 12
Property taxes, Chicago, 248; percentage for city and
    county services in, 346n. 36
Proud to Read Aloud program, 256
Pugh, Pernecie, 65–67, 70
Purchasing, changes under reform of, 33–42

Quest Center of Chicago Teachers Union, 82, 258,
    299
Quinlan, William J., 211

Radzilowsky, Michael, 65
Raises in teachers' pay by interim Chicago school
    board, 77–78, 183
Rand Corporation study of decentralization, 31
Randolph Magnet School, computer system at,
    225–26
Rankin, William, 20–21; disadvantages of teacher
    seniority system described by, 57–58; impact of
    social promotion described by, 98; pay for
    engineers during LSC meetings noted by, 198;
    probation system for teachers with poor ratings
    advocated by, 80, 276
Ray Elementary School, 63, 72, 245

Read, Eddie, 158, 168
Reading curriculum, impact of improved, 103
Reading levels, of graduates, 87–88; improved under
    Manford Byrd, 160
Reading programs, recommendations for, 281
Redmond, James F., 159, 329n. 41
Reece, Thomas H., 185
Reform, school. *See* School reform movement,
    Chicago
Repeating a grade, academic achievement of stu-
    dents after, 98; costs of, 98–99; Designs for
    Change's attitude toward, 97–98; Grace
    Dawson's attitude toward, 95–97
Reserve teachers, 52, 191, 336n. 51
Restriction calculation, of school reserves, 332–33n.
    29
Retreats, expensive educator and school council,
    93–94
Reynolds, Patrick T., 144, 149
Richards Vocational High School, 147
Richardson, Gail, 225
Richmond, George, 264
Rivera, Julio A., 133
Rivera, Maria, 107
Rivera, Raul, 100, 207
Riverboat gambling, 241
Robinson, Jacqueline A., 259
Rodriguez v. San Antonio, 247
Rogers, Curtis, 119–20
Rogers, Jerome, 110–11
Royko, Mike, 118–19
Ruiz, Joseph A., 125

St. James, Ethelynn, 253
St. Xavier University, 261, 264
Sampieri, Robert A., 46, 54–55, 225
San Diego, dropout rate decline in, 117
Savage, Joseph, *xx–xxi*
Savary, Katharyn, 51–52
SAVE (Sacrifice Plus Added Value Equals
    Empowerment) plan, 188–90
Sawyer Elementary School, 104, 220
Sawyer, Eugene, 331n. 41
Sayre Language Academy, 54, 211
Schelthoff, John W., 65
Schlaggar, Sheila R., 257–58
Schlessinger, Marcy, 72
Schlichting, David, 19
Schmidt, George, 8, 65, 110, 238
Scholl, Margaret A., 141
Scholtes, Daniel, 150
School board, Chicago. *See* Chicago Board of
    Education
School breakfast subsidies lost by Chicago schools,
    243
School buildings, age of, national statistics about,
    130; disrepair at, 129–53; need for new, 281–82
School day, shortening, 75
School maintenance assistants, 337n. 66
School reform movement, Chicago, areas unad-
    dressed in, 238–39; birth of, 183, 271–72; class
    size reduced under, 246; future concerns of,
    272–85; heroes born of, 5; inception of, *xxiii*, 3;
    percentage of schools that have not improved

under, 94–95; roadblocks to, 10; teacher hiring under, 21; trades and nonteaching unions under, 196–97; transfer of power to parents and educators in, 11; turnover of office and administrative staff under, 36; turnover of teaching staff under, 17; watchdogs introduced by, 270

School year, 1993–94, bond issue to finance, 239; disruption of staffing at beginning of, 49; financial crisis of, 18–20, 31–36; terms of final teachers' contract for, 191–92; training for teachers for, 81–82; union standoff on hiring freeze preceding, 49–50

School-within-a-school philosophy, 263

Schools First, 300

Schools United for Better Education (SUBE), 300

Schubert Elementary School, 29, 39

Schurz High School, 32, 52; concession sales shortages at, 210; disrepair of, 133; graffiti at, 133

Schwartz, Allen D., 65

Segregation of black children in Illinois schools, 75

Self-esteem of students, discipline's effect on, 108–9; repeating a grade's effect on, 98

Sen, Ashish, 224

Seniority rights, in assignments to schools, eliminating, 276–77; of teachers, 52–58

Serapin, Kay, 134

Serrano v. Priest, 247

Sexton, Robert F., 81

Sexual misconduct, dismissal of staff because of, 64–65

Sherman, Leniene, 61

Sick days, teachers' use of, 94

Sienkiewicz, Linda, 68–69

Simeon High School, 131–32

Simon, Paul, 244

Singer, William S., 162, 165, 183, 185, 334n. 37

Site-based management, authority and roles of principals under, 21–22; central headquarters revamping required for, 31; movement in Chicago to, 5–6; teacher tenure rights with impact on, 56

Slay, Joan Jeter, 97–98, 260

Small Schools Workshop, 300

Smith, Marcia, 63–64

Smith, Mary Ann, 130

Smylie, Mark, 83

Social center budget, 198–99

Social promotion of students, 87–105

Solis, Danny, 272

Southeast Asia Center, 300

Special education, classroom needs, 139; expenditures in Chicago public schools for, 244–45; number of children requiring, 345n. 26; state funding for, 282

Stancik, Edward F., 215–19

State life safety code for schools, Chicago exempt from, 147

State support for education, *xxii,* 9, 239–43, 248–49, 333n. 32

States requiring teacher recertification, 78

Steele, John O., 169

Stephenson, Richard E., 37, 169, 228

Steward, Hazel B., 114

Strasburg, Harry, 118–19

Strikes after the 1979 financial collapse of school system, 155, 178; 1983, 175, 332n. 27; 1984, 332n. 27; 1985, 332n. 27; 1987, 160–61, 183, 205, 271–72, 332n. 27

Strikes, listing of teachers', 332

Student disruption and violence, 1991 survey of teachers about, 110; student transfers because of (Los Angeles), 321n. 27

Student mobility, school system contribution to, 48; teacher assignments and, 47

Student monies, lack of accountability measures for and misappropriation of, 207–29, 338n. 1

Study halls, misuse of, 92–93

Substance, 51, 65, 331n. 25

Substitute teachers, Byrd's hiring of, 160; competency of, 76–77; pay for, 76; provision of, 49; rehiring of retirees as, 50; in Teachers for Chicago program, 82

Suburban schools, 238; expenditures per student in Chicago versus, 244, 246; instruction time, study comparing Chicago schools' versus, 93; problems in common with urban schools of, 273; teacher education in Chicago versus, 74

Sullivan, Melody, 114–15

Summer school, cuts to, 164–65; encouragement of, 283; staffing, 57

Summer staffing recommended for district offices and schools, 281

Superintendents, Chicago school, after system's 1979 financial collapse, *xxii,* 155; turnover of, compared with national average, 172

Supernumeraries, 52–55, 190; reclassified as reserve teachers, 191

Supplies, teachers' need for basic, 282

Support staff, supplemental needs of children for, 282

Swift, Stephen K., 234

Tabb, Mark, 74

Tamburrino, Patricia R., 35, 40

Teacher assignment process, 45–59

Teacher demoralization, 88–91

Teacher dismissal process, 61–70, 238, 312–13n. 5 and 7, 344n. 11

Teacher recertification, 78

Teacher selection and tenure, 52–58, 103

Teacher tardiness, 68–70

Teacher training, days paid for under 1993 teachers' contract for, 335n. 4; funds from interim Chicago school board for, 81; recommendations for, 280

Teacher transfers, by the central office, 50–51; midsemester, 160; by principals, 61–62, 312n. 2

Teacher Unions and Educational Reform, 78

Teacherless classes, 45–46, 52, 276

Teachers' contract, class sizes specified in, 139; by interim school board, 183–84; 1990, *xxiii,* 334n. 37; 1991, 333n. 33; 1993, 184–92, 335n. 46

Teachers for Chicago, 82

Teachers, incentive pay for, 283

Teachers' pension fund, 192

Teachers' salary, 77–78; average, 185, 242; beginning, 185–86, 332n. 27; total costs of, 185–86

Teachers' time in classroom, statistics of, 189

The Woodlawn Organization (TWO), 272

Theis, Mary Jane, 66
"39th Street Shuffle," 35
Thomas, Robert, 103
Thompson, James, 239–40
Thompson, Kenneth, 132
Thompson, William Hale, *xx–xxi*
Tilden High School, metal detectors at, 114; student murdered at, 112, 114
Tillman, Dorothy, 168
Tilton Elementary School, sexual misconduct case at, 64
Toliver, Richard, 123
Trade workers, overtime for, 201–2
Truant officers, layoff of all Chicago, 117–18
Truth Elementary School, 65–66, 70
Tucker, Juanita T., 123–24
Turner Construction Company, 255–56
Tyson, Cleveland A., 224

Union of Professionals, Labor Relations and Educational Reform, A, 82
Unions, 177–205; contracts for, 10; opposition to demands during 1993 financial crisis of, 187–89; source of strength of, 177–78. *See also* Chicago Teachers Union and Teachers' contract
United Neighborhood Organization, 272
University of Chicago School Mathematics Project, 301
University of Illinois at Chicago, 259–60
Urban Gateways, 301
Urban Youth High School, 120

Valinote, John F. ("Jack"), 157, 188–89, 220
Van Gorkom, Jerome, 141–42
Van Kast, Carl, 212
Van Vlissingen School, disrepair of, 129, 132, 134, 148; repair of, 152; Van Vlissingen regulars, 151–52
Vaughn, Jacqueline B., 72; death of, 178; negotiations during 1993 financial crisis of, 178, 187, 190–91; opinion of Ted Kimbrough of, 167; school repairs versus raises issue described by, 142; view of poor teachers of, 108
Vesely, Rima, 51
Violence on television, 321n. 28
Vlasto, James, 47
Vocational schools, need for, 282–83
Voices for Illinois Children, 301

Volunteers in Chicago public schools, heroic, 253–67
Voucher system, 171, 191

Walker, Gloria D., 137
Walker, Thomas R., 144–45, 150
Wall, Tony J., 136
Walt Disney Magnet School, teaching positions lost at, 50
Washburne Trade School, 136–37, 282–83
Washington, Harold, 160, 183, 331n. 24
Washington High School, 132
Washington, Theodore, 226
Weapons in Chicago public schools, 107, 113–14
Welfare system, *xxiii*
Wells, William Harvey, *xix–xxi*
Wells Community Academy High School, 49–50; dropout rate at, 111
West Side Consortium Organization, 256, 258
West Side Schools and Communities Organizing for Restructuring and Planning Progress (WSCORP), 301
Westcott Elementary School, 40
White, Johnnie, 116–17
Whitman award, 261
Whitney Young Magnet School, 72, 245
Whitten, Patricia, 143
Wiiams, Smith, 11–12
Williams, Charlie, 3
Willis, Benjamin, 75, 158–59
"Willis wagons," 75, 133, 158
Wilson, Laval Steele, 169–70, 172, 329n. 39
Wilson Occupational High School, 256–57
Wirth Elementary School, 12, 41–42
Withal, Ernest, *xx*
Wnek, Cynthia M., 29, 39–40
Woestehoff, Julie, 24
Woods, Michael M., 40, 226
Worrill, Conrad, 77
Worsham, Vernon, 129

Youth Guidance, 302

Zapata, Ivan, 138
Zavitkovsky, Paul E., 17, 46
Ziemblicki, Steven, 30
Zurer, Erica, 62
Zwick, Morton, 146–47